D0744546

German Literature in a New Century

GERMAN LITERATURE IN A NEW CENTURY

Trends, Traditions, Transitions, Transformations

EDITED BY

Katharina Gerstenberger

AND

Patricia Herminghouse

Berghahn Books
New York • Oxford

First published in 2008 by

Berghahn Books

www.berghahnbooks.com

Library of Congress Cataloging-in-Publication Data
German literature in a new century : trends, traditions, transitions,
transformations / edited by Katharina Gerstenberger & Patricia
Herminghouse. — 1st ed.
    p. cm.
  ISBN 978-1-84545-547-7
  1. German literature—20th century—History and criticism.   2. German
literature—21st century—History and criticism.   3. German literature—
Europe, German-speaking—History and criticism.   4. German literature—
Appreciation—Europe, German-speaking.   5.   Europe, German-speaking—
Intellectual life—20th century.   6. Europe, German-speaking—Intellectual
life—21st century.   7. United States—Intellectual life—20th century.
8. United States—Intellectual life—21st century.   I. Gerstenberger,
Katharina, 1961-   II. Herminghouse, Patricia.

PT401.G455 2008
830.9'0092—dc22

British Library Cataloguing in Publication Data
A catalogue record for this book is available from the British Library
Printed in the United States on acid-free paper.

ISBN: 978–1-84545–547–7 Hardback

❧ Contents

⚘ ACKNOWLEDGEMENTS

The present volume grew out of a 2005 German Fulbright Summer Seminar on the topic of "Current Tendencies in Contemporary German Literature." On-site in Berlin, Leipzig, and Hamburg, a wide range of people involved in the production, distribution, marketing, and reception of German literature today shared their insights and expertise with American seminar participants. On the schedule were readings, lectures, and informal discussions with writers, academics, and those involved in various venues of marketing and distributing literature, such as an independent bookstore, the Hamburg Literaturhaus, and the classrooms of the Literaturinstitut in Leipzig, to give just a few examples. We learned about the organization of large-scale events such as the Leipzig book fair and the challenges of publishing high-quality literature in a media-oriented society. Theater visits and conversations with politicians in charge of cultural affairs rounded out the experience. On behalf of the participants, the editors of this volume would like to thank all those listed below who contributed to the seminar and made it the enriching and stimulating experience that it was. We hope here to offer concrete evidence of the ongoing value of the Fulbright program.

We thank the Fulbright Commission for its generous funding and Director Rolf Hoffmann for his insightful leadership. Our particular gratitude goes to Kerstin Klopp-Koch and Alfred Gehrmann from the Fulbright team in Berlin, whose energy and superb organization allowed us to make the most of this unique opportunity.

A number of writers whose work shapes the literary landscape today gave generously of their time in readings and discussions with us. In Berlin, we met with Emine Sevgi Özdamar and Zafer Şenocak, in Leipzig with Martina Hefter and Armin Petras a.k.a. Fritz Kater, and in Hamburg with the late Walter Kempowski. Traces of these encounters can be found in the essays in this volume. Important insights into the world of publishing and literary reviewing also came from meetings with publishers and editors: Gunnar Cynybulk, Gustav Kiepenheuer Verlag; Ulrich Greiner and Iris Radisch, *Die Zeit*; Volker Hage, *Der Spiegel*; Harald Jähner, *Berliner Zeitung*; Patrick Hutsch, *edit*; and Franz Wille, *Theater heute*.

Beyond journals, magazines, and newspapers, literary life in Germany is increasingly shaped by institutions and events. We were privileged to visit and learn about their goals and operations from the following organizers and managers: Ulrich Schreiber, Director of the Internationales Literaturfestival Berlin and his colleagues Miriam Gabriela Möllers and Jana Thiele; Ulrich Janetzki, Director, Literarisches Colloquium Berlin; Josef Haslinger, Deutsches Literaturinstitut Leipzig; Bénédicte Moncel, Leipzig Book Fair; Birgit Peter, Manager, Haus des Buches, Leipzig; Regina-Maria Vogel, Buchhandlung an der Thomaskirche, Leipzig; Rainer Moritz, Director, Literaturhaus Hamburg.

Academic colleagues also generously spent time with the group, sharing insights both into what sort of literature is being taught in university seminars and lectures today as well as into the promise and problems of the Bologna Process reforms, which mandate comparability in curricula across the European Union. In Berlin, we met with fellow Germanists Birgit Dahlke, Klaus Scherpe, Rüdiger Steinlein, Inge Stephan, and Dean Erhard Schütz of the Humboldt-Universität; Anne-Kathrin Reulecke and Heidi Rösch of the Technische Universität; Rolf-Dieter Janz and Gert Mattenklott from the Freie Universität; and Siegfried Lokatis, Universität Potsdam. At the University of Hamburg we were welcomed by Jürgen Lüthe, President of the University; Dean Knut Hickethier; Jochen Hellmann, Director of the International Center; and by Professor Ortrud Gutjahr and some of her students.

In addition, we want to thank and acknowledge public affairs officers and administrators from both German and American agencies, who made clear their support for the kind of cultural exchange that is being fostered by the Fulbright Commission in Germany. On the American side, Richard Acker and Anne Chermak, US Embassy in Berlin; and Elizabeth Bonkowsky, US Consulate General in Leipzig took time to meet with us, as did the following individuals from German agencies: Birgit Galler, Bundesministerium für Bildung und Forschung; Matthias Kotthaus, Matthias Ohnemüller, and Rolf-Dieter Schnelle, German Foreign Office; Jochen Umlauf, German Academic Exchange Service; and Clemens-Peter Haase, Goethe Institut.

Finally, editors and authors alike wish to express their appreciation for the thoughtful commentaries offered by the anonymous readers of the manuscript.

With this volume, we wish to share some of the insights gained during the seminar and developed in the course of subsequent research. As a first step, most of the essays collected here were presented at the 2006 German Studies Association Conference in Pittsburgh, PA. There our German colleague Birgit Dahlke also presented a version of the paper included in this volume and, with poet Hans-Michael Speier, added further perspectives to the American project from the sphere of German praxis.

Katharina Gerstenberger and Patricia Herminghouse
October 2007

GERMAN LITERATURE IN A NEW CENTURY
Trends, Traditions, Transitions, Transformations: An Introduction

KATHARINA GERSTENBERGER & PATRICIA HERMINGHOUSE

In a "new century" that is still less than a decade old, it may seem presumptuous to try to identify "Trends, Traditions, Transitions, and Transformations" on the German literary scene. However, as observers from another continent, the contributors to this volume keenly sensed that the status of literature in contemporary German society is undergoing significant changes, marked by the emergence of a new generation of writers who not only pursue different topics than their more established predecessors, but who also write differently about traditional topics and often reach their readers in nontraditional ways. The articles contained in this volume are not reports from the 2005 Fulbright summer seminar in which all contributors participated, but research projects subsequently undertaken in order to bring to wider notice some aspects of very contemporary developments. It is, of course, difficult enough to assess the present; it would be even more risky to speculate about future developments in the hope of identifying "the next big thing."

Rather than attempting a "survey" of a literary landscape whose contours are still emerging or even labeling particular texts as "representative," the present volume focuses on some features of this landscape that stand out when viewed by observers who approach it from their own geographic position outside the German cultural scene. Clearly one's perspective on a living culture depends to a certain extent on the location of the observer, and while there will always be some commonalities, French, British, or German observers would be likely to set somewhat different accents than do our American colleagues. With one exception, the location of contributors to this volume in US institutions of higher education inevitably shapes their perceptions of what is interesting and important on the German cultural scene. What is offered here is, by and large, the perception of a younger generation, one that regards cultural diversity in a positive way, is interested in how Germany maintains a higher level of cultural activity than is seen in their own country, and pays deliberate attention to the role of women and minorities on the cultural scene. The internationalization of theory today also leads Germanists to increasingly focus their own scholarship on literary works that respond to particular currents in theoretical discourse, such as constructions of gender and national identity, memory, notions of performativity, and popular culture, to name some of the major ones. They are often on the lookout for texts that will enable them to participate in the larger discourse of the humanities and to produce scholarship that is relevant to the interests of their peers in disciplines less defined by the boundaries of German-language culture, such as Gender Studies, Jewish Studies, Ethnic Studies, and Minority Studies. Last but not least, the authors in this volume are attuned to texts that "work" in an American classroom—not as once was the case, as exemplars of a German national culture, but rather as artists' renditions of a diverse and changing society, some of whose traits are quite familiar to American students, while other aspects remain remarkably different.

In trying to gain a picture of the contemporary literary scene in Germany, one might think to consult the weekly bestseller lists of a popular publication, such as *Der Spiegel*. Similar information about the American literary scene could be gleaned from, for example, the fiction bestseller list of *The New York Times Book Review*. A comparison of the mid-August 2007 lists of these two publications, however, already reveals an important difference: On the *Times* list of sixteen best sellers, one finds only books that were originally written in English, although the leading title is by an Afghan-born American author. Fewer than half of the top sixteen in the German belles lettres market listed by *Der Spiegel*, however, have been written by German-language authors; the top seller, J.K. Rowling's most recent Harry Potter book, was in fact being purchased in the original English edition, since a German translation was not yet available. These proportions are by no means unusual for Germany, where readers have historically consumed enormous amounts of literature in translation. In comparison to the hundreds of literary translations from English published in Germany each year, perhaps two dozen translated German texts appear on the American literary market.[1] Leaving aside the question of why reading tastes in Germany appear so much more cosmopolitan, we should recognize that the sorts of contemporary literature that American Germanists seek out in the German literary marketplace do not correspond directly to what most Germans are actually reading.

Another indicator of the high status of literature in Germany, its international orientation, as well as the significant efforts to sustain and expand the market for books are Germany's two annual book fairs, the Frankfurter Buchmesse in the fall, and the Leipziger Buchmesse in the spring. Together, these events attract more than four hundred thousand visitors every year. Over seven thousand publishers, more than half of them international, from more than one hundred countries exhibit their recent publications. The Frankfurt fair, moreover, focuses on the literature of a particular country each year, underscoring the German reading public's interest in international literature. The Leipzig fair in particular offers a large number of professionally organized public readings and events throughout the entire city, extending the scope of the fair well beyond the exhibition halls. Such live performances of literature and the expectation that authors present themselves to their audiences are indicative of the changing ways in which literature is consumed and marketed in Germany. The Frankfurt fair goes back to the sixteenth century, the Leipzig fair to the seventeenth; today they play a significant role in sustaining as well as changing Germany's literary scene.

We have limited our study to the analysis of literary works and the recent changes within the literary market. This meant that we had to exclude film as well as theater. Film, of growing importance and increasingly international, abides by different mechanisms of marketing and reception than literature. Theater, which continues to enjoy significant support in Germany and has seen the rise of a number of important younger playwrights, has gone through its own process of adapting to changes in funding structures as well as audience expectations. Less transportable into international contexts than literature or film, theater and its performance, we felt, could not be addressed adequately in the context of this volume.

Writing in the Twenty-First Century

The present volume is primarily interested in German literature and literary culture at the beginning of the twenty-first century. In the aftermath of German unification, the cultural scene of the 1990s was one of searching, anticipation, and, sometimes, disappointment. It was, of course, not unreasonable to expect that cultural transformations would follow in the wake of social, political, and economic transformation, but the pace at which new developments seemed to follow upon one another was extraordinary and may explain the ensuing desire for "normalization." Looking back, one can readily identify, for example, the insistent search for and exorbitant expectations of the great *Wenderoman* (novel of unification), a novel that could effectively capture the political, historical, and personal ramifications of the 1989–90 turn of events. The hope for the definitive *Wenderoman* and the search for the ultimate Berlin novel, which occupied the German reading public from the mid- to late 1990s, suggests the continued importance of literature in German culture as an institution that can document and, more importantly, interpret decisive events. Toward the end of the 1990s and into the twenty-first century, however, with the rebuilding of Berlin as united Germany's capital largely completed, the immediate fascination with the post-Wall transformations comes to an end. The search for the *Wenderoman* tapers off, with no clear front-runner established but with over three hundred Berlin texts published. Yet the nonappearance of *the* definitive Berlin novel or *Wenderoman*, and the abandonment of the search in the early twenty-first century, might also be construed as an indication that the German reading public is willing to consider a multiplicity of novels and a plurality of voices on events of national importance. The 1990s saw the emergence of several, often short-lived, phenomena, including an explosion of pop literature and the phenomenon of *Fräuleinwunder* literature. Both of these trends are associated with the advent of a new generation of writers, even though the tradition of pop literature goes back to the 1960s and the label of *literarisches Fräuleinwunder* (literary girl wonder) is the invention of established literary critics rather than a self-definition of the young women writers who were subsumed under the term. Even if the trends of the post-Wall transition period were short-lived, they do confirm the continued interest in literature even as other media gain ground. Their general association with young writers reflects the reading public's desire for new voices and, perhaps, a different cultural function of literature, often connected with the much-cited phenomenon of the so-called *Spassgesellschaft*,[2] which was said to be tired of moralizing and more interested in fun and entertainment. Nonetheless, thoughtful critics also began to advance the argument that serious literature can be both entertaining and of aesthetic quality.[3] The critical calls for a return to storytelling, often invoking what was presumed to be an American model of plot- and character-driven narratives, are at this point well documented, as are the debates about a return to aesthetic standards.[4] Many and diverse voices have weighed in on these issues, but what they have in common is dissatisfaction with the existing state of German literature and a demand for change. Tellingly, a recent volume of essays on literature of the decade since 1995 is titled, rather defensively, *Schwarz auf weiß oder Warum die deutschsprachige Literatur besser ist als ihr Ruf: Eine Werbeschrift* (In Black and White, or Why German-Language Literature is Better than Its Reputation: A Promotional Text, Kraft 2005); or, more assertively, *Deutschsprachige Gegenwartsliteratur wider ihre Verächter* (German-Language Literature against Its Disparagers, Döring 1995).

In the 1990s, the German tradition of looking to writers for political, if not moral, guidance was sharply called into question by a series of highly publicized debates. The dismissal of Christa Wolf[5] as an author of *Gesinnungsästhetik* (aesthetics of conviction) and the rejection of Günter Grass's 1995 Berlin novel *Ein weites Feld*[6] (*Too Far Afield*) as an overbearing master narrative ushered in the end of a period in which writers on both sides of the Wall were revered as the conscience of the German nation and as spokespersons on political issues. Revelations about the Stasi involvement of East German writers[7] seemed to confirm the cooperation between writers and the state that had already been a central issue in the Christa Wolf debate.

An important change in German discourse about the Holocaust can be seen in the exchange between Martin Walser and Ignatz Bubis, president of the Central Council of Jews in Germany, in the wake of Walser's acceptance of the Peace Prize of the German Bookdealers Association in 1998, in which Walser argued that Germany's "shame" must not be instrumentalized and should not be expected to be ever present in the consciousness of the German public.[8] This incident can be seen as one step toward the depiction of Germans as also victims of the Second World War, which has garnered significant attention in recent years. W.G. Sebald's 1999 essay collection *Luftkrieg und Literatur* (*On the Natural History of Destruction*, 2004), Günter Grass's novel *Im Krebsgang* (*Crabwalk*, 2002), as well as Uwe Timm's 2003 autobiographical narrative *Am Beispiel meines Bruders* (*In my Brother's Shadow*, 2005) are examples of such revisionist approaches to German history. Most recently, Günter Grass's revelation of his membership in the Waffen-SS as a seventeen-year-old in his 2006 memoir *Beim Häuten der Zwiebel* (*Peeling the Onion*, 2007) caused an international outcry, not so much about the confession itself but because of its belatedness and, most importantly, because it called into question Grass's credibility as a public figure who shaped the postwar period by insisting that Germany must face up to its Nazi past.[9] Significant differences notwithstanding, these occurrences illustrate that German writers continue to be public figures whose opinions and whose conduct do matter. At the same time, these debates suggest, writers' role as public personae is changing. Since the 1990s, many younger authors have risen to prominence, but their public profiles are quite different from those of their predecessors. Among them are Juli

Zeh, whose critical interventions are discussed in this volume, and Tanja Dückers, who dedicates one section in her recent essay collection *Morgen nach Utopia* (Morning after Utopia, 2007) to the topic of the "Mär von den jungen unpolitischen Autoren" (fairy tale of the young apolitical writers), arguing that young writers, unlike their predecessors, reflect on political issues in their texts but do not offer suggestions for political action.

The most recent works of German literature confirm Dückers's argument about the implicit quality of political commentary in the works of younger writers. In addition, these works tend to introduce broader historical as well as geographical perspectives than do the works of the immediate post-Wall period. The national and international success of Daniel Kehlmann's 2005 historical novel *Die Vermessung der Welt* (*Measuring the World*, 2006), to date one of the most successful works of fiction in the twenty-first century, is illustrative of these developments. The novel, which relates stories about the explorer Alexander von Humboldt and the mathematician Carl Friedrich Gauss, marks a resurgence of the storytelling so many critics demanded, but it is also a sophisticated engagement with the function of the literary work and the role of the artist. Its playful engagement with the Enlightenment and Weimar Classicism invokes the legacies of Germany's most revered literary traditions. The references to colonialism and to the role of science, as well as the ironic allusion to our contemporary period, are in essence political, but they do not seek to convey a message. Most of all, Kehlmann's novel is an emphatic endorsement of the writer's need and right to invent and to tell stories. Similarly, Ilija Trojanow's *Der Weltensammler* (The Collector of Worlds, 2006) is explicit about its use of literary license in rendering the life of the nineteenth-century British explorer Richard Burton. Here, too, the use of a historical subject grounds the narrative in reality while at the same time affirming the task of the writer as artist and storyteller.

Generational change accounts for many of the transformations in contemporary literature, but some of these shifts involve writers of all age groups. The family novel in particular has become an important vehicle for writers across generations to reflect on not only the historical realities of the twentieth and twenty-first centuries, but also on how this history has shaped familial relationships. The collective rejection of the war generation as perpetrators that was so prominent in the *Väterliteratur* (father literature) of the 1970s and 1980s has given way to stories that bring into focus their victimization as well. Tanja Dückers's *Himmelskörper* (Heavenly Bodies, 2003) is an example, but also Uwe Timm's 2003 *Am Beispiel meines Bruders,* a text by a member of the student movement generation. Eva Menasse's *Vienna* (2005) about an Austrian-Jewish family whose members include victims of the Holocaust as well as gentiles and converts explores the implications of family history for contemporary identity formation. In *Gefährliche Verwandtschaft* (Dangerous Affinities, 1998) Zafer Şenocak asks what German history might mean for those who were not born in Germany but have made the country their home. Differences in tone and intention notwithstanding, these recent family novels have in common that they advance the possibility of mixed identities and continuities rather than divisions between generations and historical experience.

Finally, a significant corpus of contemporary writing comes from eastern Germany. The end of the GDR has not meant the demise, at least not immediately, of a literature that is informed and influenced by the experiences of living in the East German state. Some of these works have been accused of *Ostalgie,* the nostalgic longing for the GDR they appear to express. Thomas Brussig's *Am kürzeren Ende der Sonnenallee* (At the Shorter End of Sonnenallee, 1999) has been discussed in those terms, as well as Claudia Rusch's *Meine freie deutsche Jugend* (My Free German Youth, 2003) or Jakob Hein's *Mein erstes T-Shirt* (My First T-Shirt, 2001). Yet there is also a range of aesthetically compelling and politically astute texts about East Germany and its end, an observation that has led some critics to argue that East German literature is more serious than its West German counterpart.[10] Christoph Hein's *Landnahme* (Land Grab, 2004) a novel set in the GDR from the 1950s to the 1990s, is one example, as is Ingo Schulze's 2005 *Neue Leben* (*New Lives,* 2008), a sequel of sorts to Schulze's 1998 *Simple Storys* (*Simple Stories,* 2002), which combines East German experiences after the fall of the Wall with detailed documentation of the conditions during the GDR. *Frau Paula Trousseau* (Mrs. Paula Trousseau, 2007), Christoph Hein's most recent novel, is about the life and death of a painter in East Germany from the 1950s to the 1990s. The artistic quest at the heart of the novel is shown to be influenced by constraints placed on artists in East Germany, but the story's substance goes well beyond the specifics of the GDR. After much of the literature of the 1990s was concerned with the immediate present, by the twenty-first century—if some preliminary speculation is permitted—the need to explain the contemporary period has become less pressing and narratives with broader historical perspectives gain ground. While the marketing of literature is growing ever more professional, writers are stepping back from the role of sociopolitical commentator and presenting works that insist on their status as works of art.

Scholarship

A number of scholarly volumes have already taken stock of the developments of the 1990s. While they highlight different aspects, all emphasize change and transition as defining experiences of the post-Wall decade. Unsurprisingly, with the exception of Stephen Brockmann's pioneering systematic survey, *Literature and German Reunification* (1999), the majority of these are anthologies. Earlier volumes, such as *Wendezeiten, Zeitenwenden: Positionsbestimmungen zur deutschsprachigen Literatur* by Robert Weninger and Brigitte Rossbacher (Times of Change, Changing Times: Where German Literature Is Heading, 1997) offer a range of individual analyses. More recent examples include Gerhard Fischer and David Roberts's *Schreiben nach der Wende* (Writing after Unification, 2001), Stuart Taberner's *Recasting German Identity* (2002) and *German Literature in the Age of Globalisation* (2004), and Ruth Starkman's *Transformations of the New Germany* (2006). These anthologies offer essays on literature and film, often together with articles on Germany's changing political and social culture. Compiled by scholars based outside of Germany, these volumes place united Germany in an international context. Critics and scholars in Germany have taken a somewhat different approach to the topic, emphasizing, in line with Germany's political self-understanding, the Europeanization of German literature.[11]

The concept of normalization has dominated analyses of the developments of the 1990s. (West) Germany, the argument implies, has acknowledged and atoned for the Nazi crimes and can now take its rightful place among advanced Western democracies. The desire for normalization, and even the claim to normalcy, also preceded the fall of the Wall but was sounded more insistently in the unification process. In this context, Stuart Taberner's *German Literature of the 1990s and Beyond: Normalization and the Berlin Republic* (2005) deserves recognition for its comprehensiveness and the wealth of sources it considers. Taberner's study includes chapters on East and West German literature, German-Jewish writing, and changing literary representations of the Nazi past. Normalization, he argues, is but one step, albeit an important one, toward a post-Wall German identity that increasingly defines itself in international, if not postnational, global settings. Taberner's most recent work, an anthology titled *Contemporary German Fiction* (2007), expands on these themes by adding discussions of, for example, German-Turkish writing and German-language literature from Eastern Europe, as well as essays on pop literature and on the generation of 1968. In his introduction, Taberner stresses the centrality of generational change and the shifts this has brought about in the approach to central themes of German national self-understanding, including different ways of integrating memory of the Second World War into the post-Wall era.

German Literature in a New Century builds on the results of studies like Taberner's, but also proposes a somewhat different approach to the topics he and others have identified and analyzed. With its organization around four major themes, the present volume strives for in-depth analysis rather than coverage. Most importantly, many of the essays assembled here take into account changes in the literature industry, including marketing mechanisms, the growing convergence between commercial sponsors and the literary scene, as well as the changed self-understanding of many young writers. Thus, the volume focuses heavily on writers who have emerged since the year 2000 and their contributions to post-Wall literature. This is not to denigrate the recent works of established writers such as Günter Grass, Christa Wolf, Uwe Timm, Peter Schneider, Monika Maron, Martin Walser, or Christoph Hein, to name but a few, but to highlight some of those whose voices have emerged primarily in the post-Wall period. Furthermore, the volume does not revisit phenomena of the 1990s, such as the search for the ultimate Berlin novel or the emergence of German pop literature. Instead, we focus on themes that are indeed the topics of the twenty-first century, such as the shifts in memory discourse or the kinds of literature being written by women after the *Fräuleinwunder* craze. We do briefly revisit some debates of the early 1990s concerning the return to aesthetics, but these questions are examined in the context of changing approaches to identity and identity politics, tracing issues and developments that carry over from the 1990s into the new century. By clustering the essays around specific themes we also hope to show that such trends are always multifaceted and plurivocal. Change, in the end, is perhaps less a question of a writer's date of birth, but rather driven by overall shifting attitudes toward the role of the writer and the function of literature in German culture. At the beginning of the twenty-first century, German literature, highly commercialized and more cosmopolitan than before, has arrived in the age of globalization. This is not to say that it no longer addresses issues pertinent to German culture, but to suggest that the perspectives have become wider, more varied, less rigid, and more inclusive.

Notes

1. See, for example, Rectanus 1990.
2. The term, generally translated as "fun society," is often depicted by its critics as similar to what is termed the "me generation" in English.

3. See, for example, Bogdal 1998.
4. See Köhler 1998 and Harder 2001, for example.
5. See Anz 1991.
6. The debate, including Marcel Reich-Ranicki's polemical rejection of Grass's novel, is documented in Negt 1996.
7. See Böthig 1993.
8. See Schirrmacher 1999.
9. Many international commentators have weighed in on the issue. One of the most insightful discussions is Timothy Garton Ash 2007.
10. Radisch 2000.
11. See, for example, Wehdeking and Corbin 2003 and Wehdeking 2000.

Works Cited

Anz, Thomas, ed. 1991. *"Es geht nicht um Christa Wolf": Der Literaturstreit im vereinten Deutschland.* Munich: Edition Spangenberg.
Bogdal, Klaus-Michael. 1998. "Klimawechsel: Eine kleine Meteorologie der Gegenwartsliteratur." In *Baustelle Gegenwartsliteratur: Die neunziger Jahre,* ed. Andreas Erb. Opladen/Wiesbaden: Westdeutscher Verlag. 9–31.
Böthig, Peter, and Klaus Michael, eds. 1993. *MachtSpiele: Literatur und Staatssicherheit im Fokus Prenzlauer Berg.* Leipzig: Reclam.
Brockmann, Stephen. 1999. *Literature and German Reunification.* Cambridge: Cambridge University Press.
Brussig, Thomas. 1999. *Am kürzeren Ende der Sonnenallee.* Berlin: Volk & Welt.
Döring, Christian, ed. 1995. *Deutschsprachige Gegenwartsliteratur wider ihre Verächter.* Frankfurt am Main: Suhrkamp.
Dückers, Tanja. 2003. *Himmelskörper.* Berlin: Aufbau.
———. 2007. *Morgen nach Utopia: Kritische Beiträge.* Berlin: Aufbau.
Fischer, Gerhard, and David Roberts, eds. 2001. *Schreiben nach der Wende: Ein Jahrzehnt deutscher Literatur 1989–1999.* Tübingen: Stauffenburg.
Garton Ash, Timothy. 2007. "The Road from Danzig." *New York Review of Books.* <http://www.nybooks.com/archives>.
Grass, Günter. 1995. *Ein weites Feld.* Göttingen: Steidl.
———. 2002. *Im Krebsgang.* Göttingen: Steidl.
———. 2006. *Beim Häuten der Zwiebel.* Göttingen: Steidl.
Harder, Matthias, ed. 2001. *Bestandsaufnahmen: Deutschsprachige Literatur der neunziger Jahre aus interkultureller Sicht.* Würzburg: Königshausen & Neumann.
Hein, Christoph. 2004. *Landnahme.* Frankfurt am Main: Suhrkamp.
———. 2007. *Frau Paula Trousseau.* Frankfurt am Main: Suhrkamp.
Hein, Jakob. 2001. *Mein erstes T-Shirt.* Munich: Piper.
Kehlmann, Daniel. 2005. *Die Vermessung der Welt.* Reinbek bei Hamburg: Rowohlt.
Köhler, Andrea, and Rainer Moritz, eds. 1998. *Maulhelden und Königskinder: Zur Debatte über die deutschsprachige Gegenwartsliteratur.* Leipzig: Reclam.

Kraft, Thomas. 2005. *Schwarz auf weiß oder Warum die deutschsprachige Literatur besser ist als ihr Ruf.* Idstein: kookbooks.

Menasse, Eva. 2005. *Vienna.* Cologne: Kiepenheuer & Witsch.

Negt, Oskar, ed. 1996. *Der Fall Fonty: "Ein weites Feld" von Günter Grass im Spiegel der Kritik.* Göttingen: Steidl.

Radisch, Iris. 2000. "Zwei getrennte Literaturgebiete." In *DDR-Literatur der neunziger Jahre,* ed. Heinz Ludwig Arnold. Munich: Edition Text und Kritik. 13–26.

Rectanus, Mark W. 1990. *German Literature in the United States: Licensing Translations in the International Marketplace.* Wiesbaden: Otto Harrassowitz.

Rusch, Claudia. 2003. *Meine freie deutsche Jugend.* Frankfurt am Main: Fischer.

Schirrmacher, Frank, ed. 1999. *Die Walser-Bubis-Debatte: Eine Dokumentation.* Frankfurt am Main: Suhrkamp.

Schulze, Ingo. *Simple Storys.* 1998. Berlin: Berlin Verlag.

———. 2005. *Neue Leben.* Berlin: Berlin Verlag.

Sebald, Winfried Georg. 1999. *Luftkrieg und Literatur.* Munich: Hanser.

Şenocak, Zafer. 1998. *Gefährliche Verwandtschaft.* Munich: Babel.

Starkman, Ruth, ed. 2006. *Transformations of the New Germany.* New York: Palgrave Macmillan.

Taberner, Stuart, ed. 2004. *German Literature in the Age of Globalisation.* Birmingham, UK: University of Birmingham Press.

———. 2005. *German Literature of the 1990s and Beyond: Normalization and the Berlin Republic.* Rochester, NY: Camden House.

———. 2007. *Contemporary German Fiction: Writing in the Berlin Republic.* Cambridge: Cambridge University Press.

Taberner, Stuart, and Frank Finlay, eds. 2002. *Recasting German Identity: Culture, Politics, and Literature in the Berlin Republic.* Rochester, NY: Camden House.

Timm, Uwe. 2003. *Am Beispiel meines Bruders.* Cologne: Kiepenheuer & Witsch.

Trojanow, Ilija. 2006. *Der Weltensammler.* Munich: Hanser.

Wehdeking, Volker, ed., 2000. *Mentalitätswandel in der deutschen Literatur zur Einheit (1990–2000).* Berlin: E. Schmidt.

Wehdeking, Volker, and Anne-Marie Corbin, eds. 2003. *Deutschsprachige Erzählprosa seit 1990 im europäischen Kontext: Interpretationen, Intertextualität, Rezeption.* Trier: Wissenschaftlicher Verlag Trier.

Weninger, Robert, and Brigitte Rossbacher, eds. 1997. *Wendezeiten, Zeitenwenden: Positionsbestimmungen zur deutschsprachigen Literatur, 1945–1995.* Tübingen: Stauffenburg.

TRENDS
Literature in the Public Sphere

PATRICIA HERMINGHOUSE

The much greater role played in Germany by "high culture" and specifically by literature, particularly when compared with the relative isolation of "serious" literature on the American scene, is often a source of considerable fascination to US observers of German cultural life. Germany's high level of public funding for cultural institutions is represented, for admirers and critics alike, by the existence, for example, of three government-subsidized opera houses (plus the independent Neuköllner Opera) in Berlin. By contrast, residents of many major American cities count themselves fortunate if in the course of a year, rather than on one evening alone, they have the opportunity to choose from among three or four operatic offerings. It would be short-sighted, however, to focus on such official backing of the performing arts—a tradition that goes back to the court culture of dukes, princes, kings, and emperors—without paying attention to newer trends that have been emerging in the realm of public participation in the arts, particularly in literature.

The literary public sphere in Germany, as in the US, is confronted with changes in both the distribution and consumption of literature. Independent booksellers—a significantly rarer breed in the US than abroad—are being displaced by powerful chain stores, such as Hugendubel and Thalia in Germany, and Barnes & Noble and Borders in the US, to say nothing of Amazon.com. While such concentration is conducive to mass marketing of popular titles, it tends not to be very effective at what the trained bookseller does best: connecting serious writers with potential readers of their books. In one way or another, all contributors to this section are concerned with ways that are being found in Germany to promote this mediation in a changing economic, technical, and political environment.

In the essay that opens this section, Sean McIntyre explores two aspects of cultural difference that distinguish the literary public sphere in Germany from its American counterpart. At the institutional level, he examines the establishment of the so-called "literature houses," *Literaturhäuser,* in many cities of the German-speaking areas of Europe. While the exact sources of funding of these public institutions may vary, they usually include both the more traditional reliance on government funding (city, state, or federal) as well as more recent recourse to private sponsorship. These literature houses, McIntyre claims, "nourish and expand an artistic-intellectual community" by providing facilities that bring together writers and readers, publishers and journalists in an attractive environment, which often includes office support for the promotion of literary programming, readings and performances, a bookshop specializing in creative literature, and a coffee shop or café. While this particular sort of community venue is generally lacking in the US outside of the occasional author on a book promotion tour reading in bookstores and public libraries, McIntyre does call attention to the unique role played by American colleges and universities in providing a space, albeit somewhat isolated from the broader public, for literary and artistic discourse.

More provocatively, McIntyre also reflects on significant differences in the public presence of and respect accorded to literary intellectuals on opposite sides of the Atlantic. To the often-remarked ubiquity of editorial opinion offered by well-known writers and critics, especially those of older generations, in the feuilleton pages of the German press, he contrasts the near-absence of commentary by serious writers in the American media. Here, again in contrast to the German scene, the role of "public intellectual" has been increasingly occupied by academics, a trend noted somewhat critically in books such as *The Last Intellectuals: American Culture in the Age of Academe* (Jacoby 1987/2000) and *Public Intellectuals: A Study of Decline* (Posner 2001). McIntyre takes as his starting point in this analysis a book written from a German perspective, Ulrich Greiner's 1997 report on his travels across the US, interviewing American writers and seeking their opinions on the role they play—or do not play—in public debate in their own country. Finding them much more politically informed than their absence from the public sphere might suggest, Greiner also discovers that they are much less interested in claiming the sort of role in public discourse that is often played by their German counterparts. This leads McIntyre to push the analysis somewhat further, into an exploration of the differing value systems that define the borders between literature and politics, the private and the public spheres in the US and in Germany.

A somewhat more critical view of the literary public sphere in Germany is offered by Josef Joffe in an interview with Sean McIntyre.

Speaking from his position as a political theorist who has also written on the charged topic of "public intellectuals" (2003), Joffe clearly appreciates the more distinct division of labor between American literary authors and the political pundits. And while American observers of the German political scene speak with considerable admiration of the high quality of writing in the feuilleton sections of the leading newspapers there, Joffe dismisses much of it as "strong on opinion, low on empiricism" and reminds us of the plethora of lively intellectual magazines in the US, to which he compares only one, *Merkur*, in Germany.

Donovan Anderson's case study of the "eventization" of literature in Hamburg introduces a relatively new term to describe contemporary practices of embedding literature in the landscape of popular culture. The creation of "events" around a literary writer has, of course, a long history in Germany. One need think only of the many celebrations, for example, of Friedrich Schiller (1759–1805), especially in anniversary years such as 1859, 1905, and 2005. But such celebrations, often complete with fireworks, marching bands, and prominent speeches, have generally tended to co-opt the (dead) writer in the service of a national or local agenda, be it the glory of the fatherland or the promotion of regional tourism. The new "event culture" that Anderson explores represents a significant shift in emphasis from official glorification of the great writer to the "experience" of the cultural consumer.

Anderson presents three types of literary events that demonstrate how contemporary approaches to marketing and sponsorship are transforming traditional practices of mediation and consumption in the literary public sphere. The first, Macht e.V., is a coalition of writers, small publishers, and literary organizers, who—with sponsorship from the liqueur producer Jägermeister—organized themselves in the late 1990s to take advantage of the lively "club scene" in Hamburg's Reeperbahn district to present unconventional programs of readings, poetry slams, and performances, but have now "moved up" to a venue in the Deutsches Schauspielhaus. Anderson also looks at Hamburg's variation on the literature house phenomenon described by Sean M. McIntyre, emphasizing the fine line such an institution must negotiate between its aesthetic principles and the need to compete for the attention of a public increasingly focused on event culture. As an example of how the Literaturhaus has met this challenge, he singles out its successful staging of a high-visibility initiative to present poetry in public spaces throughout the city, including appropriating advertising spaces normally used for more mundane forms of commercial marketing. Finally, in a striking example of the marriage of commerce and culture, Anderson cites the enormously well-organized annual "Reading

Festival" sponsored by the Swedish energy concern Vattenfall, which maintains an entire department just for the planning and execution of such events. Small wonder, then, that some universities in Germany are developing degree programs in the new field of "event management."

In the concluding essay of this section, Rachel Halverson takes up the attempt to nurture young German creative writing talent at the Deutsches Literaturinstitut Leipzig, now part of the university in that city. In existence in the German Democratic Republic since 1955 as the Literaturinstitut Johannes R. Becher, it was referred to as that state's *"Kaderschmiede"* (training ground) for writers. Despite the impressive careers of many (often dissident) writers who learned their art there, it was targeted for shutdown after German unification, in the belief that such state-funded training was not compatible with the ideals of a democratic society. After considerable protest, the Literaturinstitut was reestablished as part of the University of Leipzig in 1995 and has continued the tradition of graduating students with an impressive record of successes in the world of literature.

In her case study of one such graduate, Tobias Hülswitt, Halverson explores the trajectory of a young writer making his way in a changing literary public sphere. By tracing his experiences as a "writer on the road" of literary tours and his experiments with online journalistic postings about his experiences and impressions, Halverson offers a fascinating account of Hülswitt's creative attempts to maintain contact with his German readers, outside the venues of event culture. At bottom for Hülswitt, as for the literature houses examined by McIntyre and Anderson, it is the printed literary word—the book—that remains central to their engagement with new practices in the literary public sphere.

Works Cited

Greiner, Ulrich. 1997. *Gelobtes Land: Amerikanische Schriftsteller über Amerika.* Hamburg: Rowohlt.

Jacoby, Russell. 2000. *The Last Intellectuals: American Culture in the Age of Academe.* New York: Basic Books.

Joffe, Josef. 2003. "The Decline of the Public Intellectual and the Rise of the Pundit." In *The Public Intellectual: Between Philosophy and Politics,* ed. Arthur M. Melzer, Jerry Weinberger, and M. Richard Zinman. Lanham, MD: Rowman and Littlefield.

Posner, Richard. 2001. *Public Intellectuals: A Study of Decline.* Cambridge: Harvard University Press.

THE LITERARY PUBLIC SPHERE

A Case for German Particularity?

SEAN M. MCINTYRE

From the perspective of a humanities scholar in the United States, the degree of development of the German-language literary public sphere is remarkable. The vibrant cultural debates and long essays by prominent public intellectuals regularly appearing in the feuilleton pages of any one of several excellent newspapers and magazines is enough to register a significant difference from intellectual life this side of the Atlantic. For the bird's-eye establishing shot one need only to open <www.perlentaucher.de>, a Web site that summarizes and links feuilleton articles and book reviews from a large selection of well-regarded newspapers such as the *Frankfurter Allgemeine Zeitung*, the erudite weekly *Die Zeit*, together with a selection of magazines from Germany's *Der Spiegel* to similarly well-established publications from neighboring Poland and France, as well as metropolitan centers from around the globe. There is nothing particularly notable today about being able to link together magazine and newspaper articles from such disparate sources. What does stand out in this context is how extensive and rich such literary communication is within the German-speaking world in particular. A notable feature of this is the role played by literary intellectuals—whether critics or authors of imaginative literature, or both, as is often the case—in public discussion and debate in Central Europe.

For over three decades now the list of the most prominent of these public intellectuals has been surprisingly stable (or rather restricted, as some might see it). Indeed, with few exceptions, such as the philosopher Jürgen Habermas, the most prominent names in German public debate have been authors of prose and poetry. The names are well known to anyone who has followed public discussions in the German-speaking world since the mid-1960s. Even more remarkable than the seeming permanence of this select group of "prominents" is the fact that they comprise two generations, close in years but significantly divided by the effects of World War II. The first is the *Flakhelfer* generation of writers such as Günter Grass, Martin Walser, Hans Magnus Enzensberger, and Alexander Kluge. Born in the late 1920s or 1930s, they were consequently old enough to have joined the Hitler Youth—or even the Waffen-SS as Günter Grass recently admitted—but not old enough to become autonomous actors and therefore perpetrators of the Nazi regime.[1]

The next generation, those born shortly before or after the end of the war, completes the short list of prominent public intellectuals. This generation of "68ers" participated actively in the student revolts of the late 1960s and differs from the *Flakhelfer* generation not only in terms of this experience of political militancy in the student movement, but also in their engagement with the Nazi past. The "68ers" struggled to differentiate between what they perceived as the hypocrisies and shortcomings of the West German constitutional democracy and the moral guilt and failure of their own parents to prevent Nazi genocide and mass destruction.

There is now some question whether these two closely aligned generations of literary public intellectuals continue to possess in the new century the same moral and political authority and effectiveness they undoubtedly held in divided Germany. This may be no more than a question of age; perhaps it is time for the old guard to yield to younger generations of writers—unless, of course, there was something truly particular about the moral and political energy of the *Flakhelfer* and "68ers." Perhaps the burdens and traumas of the Nazi past, although experienced differently by the two generations, indeed shaped a public-spirited consciousness and drive—shared by writers *and* readers alike—hardly to be matched by younger generations of writers, writers more content to concentrate on literature and leave public discussion to others.

Regardless of what answers we offer to these questions, one can say without controversy that there is in the United States little that compares with the public stature of specifically *literary* intellectuals in Germany, not in terms of their prominence in the eyes of the media outlets or the public, and certainly not in terms of the sustained, detailed, and energetic public debate and dialogue in which they participate. Our more prominent writers are rarely involved in public discussions, whereas this is a common occurrence in much of Europe. While controversial topics such as those that have surfaced around immigration controls, ethnic pluralism, and support for Israeli policies or similarly contested foreign policy issues certainly attract public debate among pundits ranging from well-regarded journalists to professional academics, rarely do such debates include the voices of literary intellectuals in the

United States. In a controversy of similar proportions in Germany, by contrast, not infrequently are the terms and frame of the debate determined by the same group of prominent literary intellectuals.

To what might we attribute this difference between the German-speaking lands and the United States? Cultural differences in prestige and public respect for writers surely plays some role in creating this distinction. But perhaps, too, more concretely institutional differences (*institution* understood here in the broadest, sociological sense of the word) between the two countries, such as disparities in the allocation of public resources in support of literary culture and the institutions and facilities available to support writers wishing to engage in public discussion, are equally significant if not determining factors in this distinction.

The German "Literature House"

It might help to approach the question by briefly examining one of the many institutions in the complex web of the German literary public sphere, the so-called literature houses, or *Literaturhäuser*. There are at least twenty-one *Literaturhäuser* in Germany, seven in Austria, and two or more in Switzerland. One can find them in most of the larger cities, in addition to a variety of similar institutions such as "book houses" and small institutes dedicated to the memory of a single author. *Literaturhäuser* are publicly funded institutions dedicated to the mediation of imaginative literature by organizing readings, discussions, and in general serving as meeting points for readers and writers, publishers and booksellers, translators, journalists, and programmers and curators for literary events. These institutions are typically supported through a combination of federal, state, city, and private sponsorship. The Literaturhaus Wien, for instance, is funded in large part by the federal parliament's Arts Division, as well as by a city arts initiative, prominent national corporations, and many national and international book-publishing firms.

The *Literaturhaus* in Berlin, on the other hand, is more typical of German literature houses in its dependence upon city and state funds as opposed to federal grants. Established legally and managed as a club, the Berlin literature house nonetheless receives crucial funds from the city government in combination with private and corporate sponsors. The physical facilities of literature houses often include offices, equipment, and staff. These valuable resources may be used by any number of literature-oriented organizations, such as smaller presses, organizers of literary competitions, prizes, and other literary events.

General support organizations for authors and translators, both novice and established, may also take advantage of these resources. The houses often also offer a comfortable café or restaurant and sometimes a small bookstore. The Literaturhaus-Berlin, for instance, is located in a lovely, historical landmark villa built in 1889 in the affluent Charlottenburg district that includes a café-restaurant, as well as office space, meeting rooms, and exhibition spaces. In addition to providing writers with economic opportunities through their programming, the literature houses often also play a role in the administration and awarding of grants and subsidies for authors and their translators.

A brief example from a series at the *Literaturhaus* in Vienna should give an idea of the kind of programming that is common at these institutions. The autumn 2006 program included presentations and discussions with writers from Ukraine, Egypt, Korea, Turkey, and the Balkans, a recitation and discussion of poetry in Arabic, readings of fiction by Roma authors, and a round-table discussion on contemporary Austrian literature with published authors, critics, scholars, and publishers. From this example it is possible to see how the literature house seeks to bring literature into a publicly discursive environment with an emphasis on discussions, forums, and debates. Through successful mediation between writers, both local and international, and the reading public, press, translators, and publishers, the literature house nourishes and expands an artistic-intellectual community. Moreover, literature houses nourish literary intellectuals in a literal sense by providing opportunities for economic sustenance through their programming. In this manner the literature houses are able to contribute to the formation of a coherent intellectual community, invigorating and renewing the energies of the literary public sphere.

The official language of support for the arts is often straightforwardly pragmatic and does not attempt to justify this support or delimit guiding imperatives or values. Major funding for the *Literaturhaus* in Vienna comes from the Federal Arts Grant. The legislation that created this funding defines its purpose as "support for artistic creativity and its mediation, improving the conditions for sponsoring and the social situation of artists . . . with a declared focus on contemporary art."[2] The current state secretary for the arts and media, Franz Morak, furthermore understands his mandate as one of "enhancing relations with countries of Southeastern Europe, social security for creative artists, and presentation of Austrian artists abroad."[3] In other words, there is no attempt in this legislation or in the language of the current secretary to justify federal support for the arts in the political terms of a public good. There is no language in the arts funding legislation about the quality-of-life of the citizenry or goals that link artistic creativity and its promotion with clear imperatives or definite ends for civic life. Moreover, the target statements leave open what kinds of imperatives may in fact guide this support. For instance, the notion of "enhancing relations" with other nations only suggests a link between arts support and a conventional diplomatic imperative of promoting cross-cultural understanding. Given this open language of support for the arts, bilateral or multilateral cultural and artistic promotions and cooperative projects have as much legitimacy as supporting local artists and creating a climate conducive to artistic creativity. However, because these promotions do operate at times in conjunction with more traditional political imperatives, there is at least an implicit assumption that the arts and artists can serve a definite civic good as well.

From an American perspective, one of the extraordinary qualities of the literature houses is that they do not rely upon the participation of university pedagogues; indeed they appear to be quite distinct from any higher education institutions. By contrast, literary and intellectual discourse detached from the islands of higher education is quite rare in the United States. Although American libraries and bookstores do try to become meeting places for writers and readers by inviting authors for talks and readings, more often than not these events are part of an extensive book promotion tour and afford little opportunity for sustained discussion. Even after taking into consideration the lively artistic and intellectual life of many American college and university campuses, the absence of a similar discursive space for literary and artistic discourse outside of higher education points to a less differentiated literary sphere in the United States. This may also help to explain why Americans do not make the same distinction that Central Europeans do between an academic form of literary criticism and the kind of literary criticism one often encounters in the feuilleton pages. In the United States, contemporary literature typically has a public setting only in the pedagogical, socializing space of the university or in the event and performance spaces of the city. The discursive space for a more civic engagement with literature is the missing center between the academic environment of scholarly or vocational study and private enjoyment. Even the most prominent American fiction writers (Philip Roth, for instance) tend to survive, at least initially, by teaching in university creative writing departments. By contrast, numbers of German writers seem capable of making a livelihood through royalties from their fiction or poetry, supplemented by income from publishing in the feuilletons, giving lectures, and various other engagements within the extensive network of subsidized high culture institutions. These institutions provide the economic as well as the structural and discursive guarantees for a civic mediation between the scholarly-intellectual and merely private, solitary engagement with the literary arts.

Authors in Isolation: A German Perspective on American Writers

Why, despite impressive artistic production in the United States, is there little that is comparable to the European literary public sphere, and certainly not the kinds of institutions that support, promote, and nourish this public discourse? It is not convincing to blame the limited literary public sphere in the United States upon an insufficient government investment in culture and the arts. Other examples of support for the arts show us that where there is public interest, especially on the part of the educated elite, there is generally enough private money and initiative to form and sustain a cultural institution independent of government support. This is as true for Germany, where many of the literature houses (such as Berlin's) began as local initiatives, as it is for the United States. By itself, the evident lack of institutions to support a literary public sphere in the United States does not explain why even the most recognized and successful American writers rarely play the part of public intellectuals.

In the late 1990s Ulrich Greiner, editor and literary critic for the feuilleton pages of the German weekly *Die Zeit*, came to the United States to interview American fiction authors and ask them directly for their opinions on this noticeable difference from their European colleagues. In the book he subsequently produced containing these interviews and his reflections on the writers' responses, Greiner (1997) attempts to understand the social and political isolation of American authors from the type of public discourse that is a common feature of the Central European literary public sphere.[4] Greiner views this remarkable difference as a reflection of American particularity, to be sure, but without reflecting *back* upon the familiar ground upon which he stood, that is, the very presence of a literary public sphere as a feature of European or German particularity. There are nonetheless hints throughout his book of a desire to question the value and meaning of the German feuilleton culture, especially the political voice of literary figures in his own land. However, much of this remains somewhat surreptitious—as if it were his covert agenda to undermine the self-confident authority of the public voice of authors back home in Germany. Here is one such moment where a furtive attempt is made to criticize the European literary intelligentsia, while noting the strikingly different situation of American authors: "American writers do not stand in the center of public debate—they hardly take part, are seldom asked to, especially not when it comes to political matters. Yet they are usually more strongly interested in politics and better informed than many of their European colleagues, who are asked much more frequently for their opinions and are more publicly visible" (14).[5] Every author he interviews confirms this statement regarding the public and political isolation of American writers, often despite a strong personal interest in political matters.

These writers are also well aware that the situation is notably different in Europe where, in addition to frequent publication of interviews with and articles by and about fiction writers in major newspapers such as the *Frankfurter Allgemeine Zeitung* or *Die Zeit*, there are other more exceptional avenues for writers to engage in public discussion. For instance, in addition to the public discussions, lectures, and conferences sponsored by outstanding cultural institutions such as the Goethe Institute, there are established and well-funded radio and television programs, including the television talk show "Literary Quartet," and many reports and interviews created by *Deutsche Welle* that feature fiction authors. Further opportunities for German literary figures to speak publicly and on matters not directly related to literature are the numerous prestigious literary prizes typically involving a "prize speech" by the author being honored. Not only are the speeches themselves newsworthy events supported by the appearance of political and cultural dignitaries in respectful attendance at the acceptance ceremony, moreover many of the speeches are then published in the feuilleton section of major newspapers.

Many American authors experience this difference first-hand on promotional book tours through Europe. Greiner wants to know how *they* explain the relative prominence of writers in Europe compared to the United States. Do they regret their political irrelevance? Do they lament the lack of social prestige that might give them such a public voice? Do they wish for the exercise of public dialogue that their European colleagues enjoy, or regret the absence of an artistic and intellectual discursive community in the United States? The unequivocal response seems to be that they do not miss any of this. All his interviewees convey that they do not long for the public discourse and attention that their European cohorts benefit from. Many even see distinct advantages in their isolation and question whether the European sort of public sphere activity is appropriate for writers as private citizens or for imaginative literature *per se*.

In summing up his investigation into the enigma of America's virtually nonexistent literary public sphere, Greiner at times casts a rather conventional and seemingly un-self-reflected European gaze upon American particularity. The land is too large, diffuse, and diverse to permit or encourage the formation of a literary public sphere, he conjectures. He notes that even the density and attraction of New York City for artists and intellectuals stands as only one cosmopolitan center among many in this vast land. Adding a new twist to an old observation, Greiner also attributes the public irrelevance of American writers to identity politics: the vocation of a writer alone does not often possess a broad enough prestige to rise above the highly segmented, pluralistic politics of the United States. In the absence of the institutionalized centers and networks for literary discourse or promotion and support of authors that one finds in Europe, Greiner remarks that, even with the attention of the relatively insular and dispersed academic communities in the United States, authors will continue to live and speak in relative isolation (Greiner 1997, 270). Acknowledging the autonomy that this irrelevance affords authors, he also recognizes the dark side of this freedom as a marginal existence in a no-man's land.

One of the authors Greiner interviewed, Seattle-based novelist Charles Johnson, suggests a compelling alternative explanation for the lack of a thriving literary public sphere in the United States. Johnson noted the absence of a tradition of political "history of ideas," or *Ideengeschichte*, in the United States and stressed instead the pragmatism of how Americans understand the boundaries of politics and the political sphere. This is a notion worth exploring, as it might help to explain some of the differences between the American and European literary landscapes that in fact have deeper, more culturally and politically rooted foundations than the urban, geographical landscapes Greiner refers to.

Richard Rorty's view of the American pragmatic tradition may be taken as representative of this same tradition, specifically in terms of the relation of politics to literature. Rorty (1989, xv) makes a rather sharp distinction between the private-sphere activity of self-development or what he calls "self-creation," which he associates with the engagement with literature and philosophy, and the public sphere work of the democratic citizen striving to contribute to the constant betterment of the polity and its institutions. For Rorty, what is essentially pragmatic about this distinction between the private pursuits of literature and the public orientation of good citizenship is the affirmative renunciation of the yearning for totality in a political, moral, and practical sense. Stated more positively, Rorty sees this differentiation as operating in a classically liberal manner. Liberalism historically affirms the distinction between individual and citizen in terms of a crucial (yet changing) boundary between the private and the public spheres.

In this context one can understand Johnson's contrasting use of the term *Ideengeschichte* as a reference to the long history of illiberal political and social critical thought in Europe, thought that is aimed at overcoming or transcending the distinction between public and private and furthermore imagines ways to redress the experience of fragmentation and alienation in pluralist modernity. Rorty's "gay science" involves a joyful renunciation of that goal of unity together with an affirmation of the pluralism of values that is inherent in living a life with conflicting or non-overlapping aims and objectives. Put simply, Rorty's pragmatic and liberal notion of the value of imaginative literature is satisfied to recognize that literature is well suited to the aims of Millian (John Stuart) self-development, but not at all to the civic-oriented goals of reducing suffering in the world and contributing to commonwealth institutions.

Thus one could interpret Johnson's answer to Greiner's question as the suggestion that the classical liberal and pragmatic distinction between the private (self) and public (citizen) resonates more with American culture and values than it does in Central Europe. In other words, American authors are simply more ready to accept that their work as authors of imaginative fiction is indeed limited to personal self-development (for themselves *and* their readers, of course) whereas their European colleagues may have a tendency to see their work as authors and public intellectuals in terms of both personal self-development and a legitimate contribution to the betterment of the polity. I do not wish to ignore that there are many individuals on this side of the Atlantic who consistently polemicize against such a distinction between the public and the private spheres, especially for artists and intellectuals. Russell Jacoby is certainly not alone in expressing nostalgia for a putatively "lost" era of American public intellectuals in the early decades of the past century, critics and writers who combined their engagement with imaginative literature with a good citizen's dedication to the health of the commonwealth.[6]

Let us assume for a moment that this pragmatic, liberal view of literature's place in the private sphere more or less captures a conventional American understanding of the distinction of literature from political activity. This would mean that despite the exceptionally well-developed European literary institutions such as the literature houses, the United States maintains a more differentiated understanding of literary activity. However, the European literary public sphere is at the same time clearly more developed than its hardly existent American counterpart.

The evidence for this judgment is overwhelming if we consider the literature houses, the publishers cultivating close relationships with "their" writers (the most prominent example being that of the late Siegfried Unseld of Suhrkamp Verlag), literary critics operating outside the islands of academia, and finally the feuilleton pages imparting innovative literature and erudite, often detailed arguments to the public.

The lines between literature as art, intellectual argument, and political engagement are intentionally less defined in the European context where prominent literary intellectuals frequently engage in all three instances of discourse, sometimes in one essay or speech. In a word, the European literary intellectual indulges in the essay form. Indeed, an older generation of public intellectuals who served as mentors and models for many of today's prominent public voices placed great emphasis on the essay as a form uniquely capable of stimulating free, critical thought. For Theodor Adorno, the essay was the preferred form for revealing particularity per se in intellectual and philosophical thought. It was precisely this exercise of the essay form that he claimed to have missed as an intellectual living and writing in the United States. In a 1965 radio address for Hessische Rundfunk titled "On the Question: What Is German?" (first published in essay form in 1969), Adorno looks back with barely disguised bitterness to the experience of giving a paper at a conference in San Francisco as a way to explain his discomfort and frustration as a German intellectual in America (1999, 210–11). The paper, as one can well imagine, was not well received on account of Adorno's opaque style and doubtless radical departure from the discursive norms of American academic writing.

European Models for the Public Intellectual

But what is the significance of this particular difference? Does it mean that imaginative literature maintains greater autonomy from politics in the United States than in Europe? Does this mean that European literature tends to be more politically engaged than American literature?

In a speech given in East Berlin in 1989, the late sociologist Pierre Bourdieu made an interesting claim for the relation between the autonomy of literature and political engagement. Taking as his paradigm the Dreyfus Affair, Bourdieu (1991, 656) argued that "all the values associated with this autonomy—virtue, disinterestedness, competence, and so on" gave writers credibility and moral authority that enabled them to engage effectively in political life, mobilizing citizens around specific causes and concrete imperatives.[7] In other words, the literary production itself need not be explicitly political for authors to enjoy a certain status and prestige that lends moral weight and prominence to their public voice in matters of specifically political concern. Within Bourdieu's corporatist schema, that is, a schema based upon the closed ranks of a vocational organization, politically engaged literature would not convey the same kind of persuasive power and moral authority in political life as does literary production that is recognized as sufficiently disinterested. Why does a similar arrangement not work in the American context? Within the pragmatic-liberal culture of the United States it is difficult to imagine the "disinterestedness" of apolitical literature producing any kind of social prestige that could easily be translated into an authorial political resonance in the public sphere. In a national context largely favorable to the values expressed in Adam Smith's *Wealth of Nations*, it is far more likely that an individual associated with clear and compelling commercial and political interests would enjoy the sort of authority and legitimacy that Bourdieu sees in the relation between autonomous artist and engaged public intellectual.

Bourdieu's schematic paradigm helps to demystify the notable differences in public prestige and moral authority associated with the literary artists and intellectuals in Europe versus the United States. It also affords a different perspective on the isolation of American authors that Greiner finds so remarkable. For in this difference we see another feature of the pragmatic indifference toward the morally determined political imaginary of European intellectuals, that is, all of their thinking aimed at transcending the perceived alienation of modernity and establishing new forms of authentic community. The relative absence of prominent American writers taking public stands may be as much about popular indifference toward a moral position based upon disinterest as it is about a fundamental affirmation of the benefits of modern life with its concomitant "philistine" and unheroic values of compromise and limitation. In other words, the liberal-pragmatic disposition toward the private pursuit of happiness gives priority to such bourgeois values as material interest, security, and repose over the bold and far-reaching political visions and projects motivated by either conservative or romantic critiques of modernity. In a recent discussion of Günter Grass's role as public intellectual, Ian Buruma sought to explain in cultural terms Grass's penchant for moralizing and scolding political polemics. Buruma (2006) views Grass's abundant energy for public-sphere polemics in part as an expression of a tradition of European intellectual contempt for the kind of "unheroic materialism, . . . lack of a tragic sense" and "indifference to high culture" that rather characterize American pragmatic culture. In this view, then, much of the moral authority—and the drive to use that authority in political life—that Bourdieu viewed as constituting itself through a vocational dedication to autonomy-as-disinterest is also prone to express contempt for the nonautonomous world of commercial or other particular interests.

Given Bourdieu's schema, the corporatist European intellectual engaged in public sphere discussion will be careful to protect his or her special status by maintaining strict standards of autonomy in the literary work. Translating this into artistic terms for novelists or poets, it means that they would want to prevent their art from becoming a political weapon or risk losing the basis for effective engagement and advocacy as mobilizing citizens in the public sphere. Thus, despite the multiple roles of artist, intellectual, and citizen played by the same prominent actors, there are no necessary obstacles to evaluating the literature they produce with artistic standards understood as distinct from the imperatives of politics and the objectives of public sphere discourse.

In Bourdieu's sociological analysis of the hierarchies of prestige involved in French literary production and reception in his book *The Rules of Art*, he noted that artistic prestige often stood in inverse proportion to the actual sales and numbers of readers (1996, 77–89). Moreover, with government-sponsored institutions such as the *Literaturhäuser*, in some cases it is possible for European writers to survive in their vocation without any commercial success, but with only the recognition of critics and administrators within the system of cultural institutions. By contrast such survival is much less likely in the United States. As noted, American writers tend to survive by teaching in college creative writing departments.

The firmer European cultural distinctions between what is considered frivolous, popular fiction and what is held up as "serious" literature makes more sense in light of those factors that can distinguish the career and livelihood possibilities of the European writer. The same holds for Bourdieu's picture of a corporatist intelligentsia confirmed through a recognition of their autonomy: the prestige of the public intellectual is likely to depend in some measure upon a perceived distance from the "interests" of popular and consequently commercial success. In his reflections on the political isolation of American writers, Greiner (1997, 270) suggests that there is a greater emphasis on communication, on accessibility and connecting with readers in the American context than in Europe. Indeed, the politically hermetic life of the American writer rarely translates into hermetic form and style. Although these sorts of general claims are difficult to argue without amassing much more textual evidence, we can at least see that structurally and economically this would make sense given the greater dependence upon readership for public notions of success in the United States. Moreover the general lack of social prestige and status attached to literature recognized by the reading and nonreading public as high culture makes such recognition significantly less desirable for authors as well. In other words, the promise of prestige and status conducive to recognition as a public intellectual in the European mold is less likely to inform the artistic decisions of American authors.

In one of Greiner's interviews, Paul Auster is quoted as saying that "it is not the job of the writer to just talk about politics and comment on the events of the day. His job is to make art, and art responds independently to the world around us. Thus it might be that the American writer is much more political than the European after all" (1997, 55). One could respond to this statement by saying that Auster's European counterparts do not seem to have much trouble doing both: making independent art *and* publishing political commentary. This response would however miss the more challenging suggestion in Auster's conjecture. For it is unlikely that he means for the term "political" to be understood in the conventional sense of persuading, advocating, or mobilizing on behalf of particular positions, actions, or political actors. There is not much to suggest that he means "political" in the sense of the formalist theories of modernist aesthetics, where critical uses of form were thought to have immanent and imminently political significance. Nor is it likely that Auster wishes to intimate a romantic notion of the "political" as the product of a private, antipolitical inward turn in the hope of creating an authentic community. Rather, Auster's enigmatic notion of the "political" American novel might instead be construed as such because of a tacit affirmation of the liberal and pragmatic distinction between public and private spheres, between civic duty and self-creation. This might be a concept of the political similar then to Thomas Mann's protagonist Hans Castorp, "playing king" by sitting alone in the alpine meadows, experimenting with different thoughts and trying out new ideas (1995, 383). Again, this is certainly not "politics" in any conventional sense of the term, but rather a way to emphasize the implicit political valuation in such a positive, self-conscious affirmation of the private sphere of self-development as a constituent of the good life per se, one that carries with it as a logical step an equally strong affirmation of the political underpinnings for this exercise of the self.

Such a one-sidedly private notion of politics as Auster suggests in defense of the isolation of American authors recalls a bitter lesson that one of the staunchest defenders of that romantic privilege of self-creation was forced to learn. Benjamin Constant understood that the Jacobin dictatorship of virtue drove souls like his own into such an extreme instance of civic privatism that they paved the road to Bonapartist neoabsolutism. In his brilliant study of Constant's political thought, Stephen Holmes (1984, 3) writes trenchantly of how Constant came to realize through bitter experience that "private rights are endangered by excessive privatization; individual independence cannot survive without some form of citizen involvement." In other words, with a high estimation of the value of that imaginative space for self-creation there should be an equally acute sense of the civic duty and vigilance entailed in defending it.

This is essentially the middle position that at least one young German writer endeavors to occupy. Born in 1974, the novelist and essayist Juli Zeh (2004) encourages her colleagues to also reject the understanding of politics as "a private matter." Indeed Zeh seems in this regard to be fighting at home against the very same differentiation of literature and politics that Greiner describes in the United States. The fact that Zeh, much like many writers in the United States, has taught what we call "creative writing"[8] at the German Literature Institute in Leipzig (where the writers Hans-Ulrich Treichel, Josef Haslinger, and Michael Lentz all have permanent appointments) may indicate further movement in Germany in the direction of the American self-understanding of literary authors vis-à-vis the public. Zeh's fellow young novelist Andreas Maier, author most recently of the novel *Kirillow* (2005), rejects the notion of "social relevance" as a starting point or even objective for the author of literature and emphatically declares that "as a novelist I do not wish to serve the lofty spheres of society—or society at all" (2005). Zeh's vision for the role of literary intellectuals in the public sphere does affirm a strong differentiation of politics and literature,[9] but she emphasizes that literary authors should *also* develop their capacities as civic-minded political beings with public interventions and positive engagement with organized interests and not leave political discussion only to the "experts" (2005). With this position it may seem that a return to (or preservation of) the privileged status of the writer in German society is invoked. However, Zeh does not promote the political intervention of writers on the corporatist grounds that Bourdieu idealized, nor does she speak from the perspective of the traditional and prestige-oriented culture of German mandarins that Fritz Ringer described so well (1969). Zeh's bid for political intervention grants no more special status to the writer than the fact that she can write and with that skill can contribute to a universally necessary civic dialogue.

What Is the United States Really Missing?

Looking at the literary public sphere in Central Europe and comparing this public dialogue with the lesser public presence of most American authors, one cannot help but ask what the United States is actually missing. In the interview that follows this article I asked Josef Joffe, publisher and former editor-in-chief of *Die Zeit*, this same question. Dr. Joffe notes the somewhat closed-ranks corporatist institutional organization of literary public intellectuals in Europe, and Germany in particular, and has perhaps on that basis good reason to extol the great diversity of public opinion in the United States. Moreover, I would add, the considerable public prestige extended to authors of literature in Germany and other nations of Europe may in fact hinder the development of a democratic public sphere in the more ideal sense that Habermas (1989) first envisioned in 1962 with the publication of his book *Structural Transformation of the Public Sphere*. Habermas's democratic impetus was largely based upon the ideal of an emphatically nonlegislative form of open communication and dialogue, consequently far from the acclamatory public sphere that social prestige and charisma can at times produce. Nonetheless, in addition to this ideal form of public *political* discussion, the United States offers few opportunities for a type of discourse that both combines and transcends the imperatives of the creative artist, the scholarly intellectual, and the citizen. It is a kind of essayistic discourse that allows one to combine all of these modes, strengths, and imperatives into one form. The literary public sphere as form and forum for discussion provides the opportunity or possibility to engage in ways that combine the private sphere pursuits of self-creation with the professional, apolitical vocation of the scholar and the politics of the engaged citizen.

This strikes me as a valuable alternative to discourse dominated by "experts," the concern Juli Zeh raises in her plea for the public political voice of writers (2004). Yet given the significant differences that do exist between Europe and the United States, some of which I have tried to sketch here, what would be an appropriate American alternative to the European model of political discussion led by prominent literary figures? As opposed to having public intellectuals act in a corporatist manner in the United States as well, it might be preferable to develop institutions similar to the literature houses in the United States, but with the mission of sponsoring discussions of literature for the general public on the model of a book club discussion and encouraging the mediation of literature outside of both academic and political contexts. This form of dialogue could serve as an invigorating supplement to the praxis of the political public sphere, while distinguishing itself from this sphere by virtue of its decidedly private, noncivic content.

Notes

1. The term "Flakhelfer generation" refers specifically to this notion of youth or children engaged in military service towards the end of the war, often as "helpers" but sometimes as fully armed "child soldiers" as well. Two significant exceptions to this generational cluster of public intellectuals are of course Heinrich Böll and Marcel Reich-Ranicki. An author of novels and short stories and winner of the 1972 Nobel Prize for Literature, Böll, who was born in 1917, was a leading public and moral voice in postwar Germany until his death in 1985. Born in 1920 to an assimilated German and Jewish family in Poland, Reich-Ranicki until recently had been for nearly forty years perhaps the most influential and best-known literary critic in Germany and Austria.

2. The Federal Art Grants Act (*Bundeskunstförderungsgesetz*) is available in English at <http://www.bundeskanzleramt.at/site/3988/default.aspx> .

3. <http://www.bundeskanzleramt.at/site/3948/default.aspx> .

4. The book is organized as a travelogue of reflections interspersed with interviews with the following authors: Paul Auster, Joan Didion, T.C. Boyle, David Guterson, Richard Ford, Charles Johnson, Louis Begley, Walter Abish, Michael Chabon, and E.L. Doctorow.

5. Unless indicated otherwise, all translations are my own.

6. See, for example, Russell Jacoby's melancholy invocation of the loss of a publicly engaged American (i.e., New York) intelligentsia in *The Last Intellectuals: American Culture in the Age of Academe* (1987, 107–11).

7. Bourdieu extends his argument farther than is necessary for my analysis. In his speech he claims that the authority of the artist turned public intellectual is not only based in the values associated with autonomy, but more importantly with the putative universality of those values. According to his argument, the classic public intellectual trades on that universality to lend greater persuasive power to his or her political interventions.

8. There is a conscious effort being made in Germany today, however, to avoid not only the term *creative writing* for these new programs, such as the prestigious institute in Leipzig, but also to develop a different model for training writers than is commonly practiced in creative writing programs on campuses in the United States.

9. See in particular Zeh's 2004 Ernst-Toller Prize speech "Wir trauen uns nicht."

Works Cited

Adorno, Theodor W. 1999. "On the Question: What is German?" *Critical Models: Interventions and Catchwords*, trans. and ed. Henry W. Pickford. New York: Columbia University Press. 205–14.

Bourdieu, Pierre. 1996. *The Rules of Art: Genesis and Structure of the Literary Field*, trans. Susan Emanuel. Stanford: Stanford University Press.

————. 1991. "Fourth Lecture. Universal Corporatism: The Role of Intellectuals in the Modern World." *Poetics Today* 12, no. 4: 655–69.

Buruma, Ian. 2006. "War and Remembrance." *The New Yorker,* 18 September. <http://www.newyorker.com/printables/critics/060918crat_atlarge>.

Greiner, Ulrich. 1997. *Gelobtes Land: Amerikanische Schriftsteller über Amerika.* Hamburg: Rowohlt.

Habermas, Jürgen. 1989. *The Structural Transformation of the Public Sphere: An Inquiry into a Category of Bourgeois Society,* trans. Thomas Burger with Frederick Lawrence. Cambridge, MA: MIT Press.

Holmes, Stephen. 1984. *Benjamin Constant and the Making of Modern Liberalism.* New Haven, CT: Yale University Press.

Jacoby, Russell. 1987. *The Last Intellectuals: American Culture in the Age of Academe.* New York: Basic Books.

Maier, Andreas. 2005. "Meine Literatur macht, was sie will" *Die Zeit,* 23 June. <http://www.zeit.de/2005/26/Debatte_2>.

Mann, Thomas. 1995. *The Magic Mountain,* trans. John E. Woods. New York: Knopf.

Ringer, Fritz. 1969. *The Decline of the German Mandarins: The German Academic Community, 1890–1933.* Cambridge, MA: Harvard University Press.

Rorty, Richard. 1989. *Contingency, Irony, and Solidarity.* Cambridge: Cambridge University Press.

Zeh, Juli. 2005. "Was soll der Roman? Eine Debatte unter Schriftstellern über die moralischen und ästhetischen Aufgaben der Literatur." *Die Zeit,* 23 June. <http://www.zeit.de/2005/26/Editorial>.

————. 2004. "Wir trauen uns nicht" (Ernst-Toller Prize Speech). <http://www.juli-zeh.de/indexessay.htm>.

⚒ 2

INTELLECTUALS IN THE PUBLIC SPHERE
An Interview with Josef Joffe

SEAN M. MCINTYRE

As the former editor and current publisher of *Die Zeit*, a weekly paper respected in particular for its expansive feuilleton pages and essays with detailed analysis, Josef Joffe is in a unique position to observe and comment upon the phenomenon of German public intellectuals and their discursive habits. Moreover, with a PhD from Harvard University and teaching and research appointments at Stanford University, Dr. Joffe is also much at home in the American intellectual environment. In this interview, conducted by Sean M. McIntyre at Stanford on 29 November 2006, Dr. Joffe offers candid views on the public discourse of Germany's *literati* and tells us why he thinks that American readers are not missing much.

Sean M. McIntyre: In a recent discussion of Günter Grass's role as a public "moralist and a scold," Ian Buruma admits that Grass's voice was often a "necessary moral correction" and even "boosted social democracy" in Germany, while also noting, however, that his public voice could at times be an obstacle "to cogent political analysis." How do you feel about the political and moral voice of artists? Are they "obstacles to cogent political analysis," a serious issue given the moral and political authority of many of these individuals? Or does a healthy public sphere need in equal measure both cogent political analysis and the kind of contributions that artists provide? Which is more necessary in your opinion?

Josef Joffe: Grass is a perfect example of the moralist's trap—or the Biblical homily: "Pride cometh before the fall." In the past fifty years, he has relentlessly denounced the Nazi past of contemporaries. And lo, in the year of 2006, he suddenly divulged his own membership in the Waffen-SS, downplaying it with the argument of youthful ignorance. In the *Frankfurter Allgemeine Zeitung* interview about these memoirs of his, he added a dose of moral myopia, reporting that he was first confronted with racism as an American POW—white on black. You wonder where he had lived since 1933, especially after the Germans took Danzig at the beginning of World War II.

Moralists—and that is the trap—invariably end up as hypocrites and the more strident their voices, the harder the fall. So much for the "necessary moral correction" ex post facto. "Cogent political analysis?" Yes, if you substitute "ideological" for "political." In that respect, he was certainly "cogent," that is, consistent. His analysis was the traditional repertoire of the German Left: anticapitalist, anti-Western, anti-American, antimarket—which is hardly a "corrective," but standard lore of the majority of German intellectuals. To reinforce familiar ideas can hardly be seen as either original or corrective.

To make this more general, one has to ask: What special political wisdom does a writer of novels have to offer? Trained as a political theorist, I would never claim any special authority on literature. Why should a *literatus* claim such authority in political matters? Why would his larger audience assume such an authority on his part? I think that political analysis and a literary sensibility (of which Grass displayed a great deal in *The Tin Drum*) are two very different realms of thinking, beholden to different rules of excellence. I am actually quite glad that Anglo writers respect these boundaries; unless a novelist masters the rules of good political thinking, he should stay with what he can do best. Faulkner brilliantly portrayed the American South in his novels; I don't think there was a Tocqueville in him.

SMM: Your colleague Ulrich Greiner, a critic for the feuilleton section of *Die Zeit*, published a book in 1997 called *Gelobtes Land* (Promised Land) in which he toured the United States, interviewing prominent writers and asking them directly why, unlike their cohorts in Europe, they did not participate in political discussion and public debate. Their answers generally seemed to indicate an acceptance that their role was to create fiction, not give opinions on topics of the day. What would your own response to this question be? How do you explain the relative political isolation of American fiction writers?

JJ: Europeans tend to accord to their *literati* a kind of priesthood status, Americans don't. Maybe this is because in early America, the "doer" was more venerated than the "discourser"—no wonder, when you have to build a country from scratch, and this in a setting that was not very hospitable to those who could not fell trees, fight Britons and Indians, plow the prairies, and tame rivers. This is a culture that praises action and worldly success (possibly because of its Calvinist roots), and hence the saying: "Those who can, do; those who can't, teach." When it became time for the intelligentsia to move toward center-stage, the obvious place was those American universities that became world-renowned from the 1960s onward. Also: with America's rise to world power, the intelligentsia found yet another exalted place—in policy making. European intellectuals and writers, coming out of an absolutist history, were never so inducted into the public sphere; Henry Kissinger, had he remained in Germany, would not have become foreign minister. When your services are not wanted by the mighty, you tend to form your own caste that, like any priesthood, purports to have special knowledge and wisdom.

Add to this, beyond literature, a largely state-financed culture in theater, dance, music, opera, film. . . . In a corporatist culture, which America's is not, artists thus acquired a semipublic stature, with a strong voice in the allocation of funds and status. As co-dispensers of public funds, they naturally acquired a measure of power that Anglo artists never enjoyed. Hence, their partial integration into the governmental process ("Who gets what, when, and where") and the relative isolation of Anglo intellectuals from the public sphere.

SMM: As an individual with significant intellectual experience both in Central Europe and the United States, how do you explain the notable lack of a feuilleton culture comparable to that of Central Europe?

JJ: Once intellectuals see themselves as quasi-political actors (or moralists or secular priests), they will naturally gravitate to a feuilleton that is largely political. It is more exhortation and plea than analysis or critique of literature and the arts. But let's not overdo the difference. If you think about the heyday of America's public intellectuals, like [Andrew] Ross and [Lionel] Trilling, they acted almost like their European colleagues. Critics by profession, they played the role of the public intellectual, discoursing on politics and society, and not just on the arts.

SMM: What is the United States missing by not having our fiction writers engaged in public discussion the way they typically are in Central Europe?

JJ: Not much. In fact the cultural-intellectual debate in the US is a lot livelier, because [it is] a lot more diverse, than in, say, Germany. Look at the plethora of intellectual magazines here: *New York Review of Books, The New Republic, Atlantic Monthly, Harper's, The Claremont Review of*

Books, Weekly Standard, Slate, and *Salon,* the university presses, plus the academic quarterlies. For an aspiring academic in Europe, it is now de rigueur to have published in a refereed American journal—from the *American Political Science Review* to *Science* and *Nature.*

SMM: In your experience as an editor and publisher, have you noticed any significant changes or new trends in the culture of the literary public sphere in Germany? Has the form or the content of feuilleton writing changed noticeably?

JJ: Not in the last twenty years. It is the familiar debate on politics, culture, and economics—strong on opinion, low on empiricism, and sometimes quite repetitive according to the rule: "Everything has already been said, but not yet by me."

SMM: The *Flakhelfer* generation of public intellectuals (Günter Grass, Martin Walser, Jürgen Habermas, Joachim Fest, Alexander Kluge, etc.) has dominated public sphere discussion for some time in Central Europe. Yet the generation of 1968 (Daniel Cohn-Bendit, Joschka Fischer, Peter Schneider, Hans Christoph Buch, etc.) have just as significantly engaged in public sphere discussion. As members of this generation get older, have there been any significant changes in participation in the literary public sphere by newer generations of public intellectuals?

JJ: Not yet, especially for lack of new fora. The feuilletons of *Die Zeit, Frankfurter Allgemeine Zeitung, Süddeutsche Zeitung,* etc. are still dominated by my generation—the sixty-year-olds. I cannot discern any new trends. Perhaps the most interesting intellectual platform in Germany is *Merkur*—a bit conservative, a bit centrist, but mainly eclectic, superbly edited by Karl Heinz Bohrer and Kurt Scheel. It boasts a certain freshness and contrarianism, which is rare in other such magazines.

SMM: What general trends do you see in this shifting of generations of public intellectuals?

JJ: No trend yet. The dominant leftish trend seems exhausted, but there is little to replace it. What is still missing is a liberal *prise de conscience,* liberal not in the modern (that is, leftish) sense, but in the classical sense of the eighteenth century—from Hume to Hayek. "Critical Theory" [*Kritische Theorie*] still has a powerful hold on the German imagination, followed by a strain of postmodernism that seems to be weaker than in either France or the US.

SMM: Do you view the newer generations of literary authors as intensely engaged in the public sphere as the authors of the *Flakhelfer* and 1968 generations?

JJ: I think the newer generations of novelists are too introspective to be political.

3

"Literatur findet . . . nicht nur auf Papier statt"

The Eventization of Literature in Hamburg[1]

DONOVAN ANDERSON

Slam poetry, reading stages, literary jubilees such as the *Heinejahr,* the *Goethejahr,* and the *Schillerjahr* (Heine, Goethe, and Schiller Years), and a multitude of literary festivals throughout Germany paint the picture of a literary industry infused with event character. And, the industry is booming, if the 2006 "lit.Cologne" is any indication, which boasted more than fifty thousand visitors over nine days, or "Leipzig liest" (Leipzig Reads), where tens of thousands of people attended eighteen hundred separate events during the Leipzig Book Fair in March. The "event" has become an integral part of the cultural and marketing landscape in Germany, where advertisers spent three billion German Marks on event marketing in 2000 (Etscheit 2001). Companies like the energy provider Vattenfall Europe have a department, the only focus of which is to plan and to organize the numerous events the company sponsors (Kalnbach 2006b). Private and public universities have seized on this "Trend zum Event" (trend to the event) and established courses of study in *Eventmanagement,* and the emergence of the profession of *Veranstaltungskaufmann* (Event Manager) underscores the ubiquity of the "event."[2] The literary establishment has not been left untouched by these developments. The media success of major literary jubilees and the growth of large literary festivals most clearly attest to this fact. However, the following study of the literary scene in Hamburg will attempt to provide a deeper analysis of the ways in which the literary event has transformed more traditional structures of literary production, mediation, and reception.

A survey of forty-three German cultural foundations established that the event was the dominant form of literary promotion in 2001 (Schütz and Wegmann 2003, 26). However, in essays, commentaries, and articles, critics have bemoaned the literary establishment's turn to "Event Culture" (Greiner 1998; Niemann 1998; Herzinger 1999; Böttiger 1999). In a March 2006 interview with the radio station *Deutschlandradio Kultur*, the literary critic Helmut Böttiger criticized a tendency to equate literary events with literature itself. And, Hortensia Völckers, the artistic director of the federal *Kulturstiftung* (cultural foundation) stated recently that the *Kulturstiftung* intends to resist the trend to the event. In the future, they will support projects that convey cultural fundamentals and leave the financing of events to the private sector ("Kulturnachrichten" 2006). The "event," it would seem, has no role to play in the mediation of "cultural fundamentals" and the "literary event" has little or nothing to do with literature. I would argue, however, that the marriage of literature and event culture is a much more complex phenomenon. From a marketing perspective, "event" is not a monolithic concept. As Stephan Porombka has argued, "The market for literary events is not becoming uniform but, rather, fractal. It is becoming more dynamic as a result of constantly new competition and new trends" (2003, 137). If one looks closely at the hermeneutics of the "event," an infinite number of possibilities for the production of literature as event emerge—each of which conforms to the needs and the goals of organizers (Porombka 2003, 131–33). The establishment of an image concept and a brand name, the identification of a target audience, and analysis of competition are only a few of the considerations involved in event planning. As a result, small collectives of writers and performance artists, city councils, literary houses, and multinational corporations and media conglomerates produce fundamentally different kinds of literary events.

"Der Trend zum Event"

The *Deutscher Kommunikationsverband* (German Communications Association) defines "events" as "staged happenings . . . which present emotional and physical stimuli and trigger a strong process of activation" (2001, 188). Events generate publicity and media attention, and as a result, they are ideal marketing tools. They function particularly well as marketing tools because they manage to link certain experiences and emotions to particular products. These experiences and emotions represent the cult potential of these products and help to distinguish them in an overcrowded marketplace (Porombka 2001, 34).

The effectiveness of this experiential marketing concept has its basis in what the sociologist Gerhard Schulze (1992) has called the

Erlebnisgesellschaft (experience-oriented society). Schulze described the search for happiness and the intensification of experiences that characterized the lifestyle of individuals in Western societies in the 1980s. In terms of consumer demand, the experiential value of products plays a central role in the decisions that consumers make on a daily basis (Kemper 2001, 185–87). As a result, marketers focus on the experiential or cult qualities that products offer, which supplement and even transcend their utilitarian qualities. As experience-oriented happenings, events are uniquely capable of mediating this experiential dimension. Schulze underlines four particular aspects of events that enhance the successful mediation of experiential qualities: "The event's secret of success lies precisely in the fact that the event gives to consumers or demands from them the opportunity to take more responsibility for their experience from the very beginning. At the same time, consumers receive massive support for their undertaking. All four characteristics of events— uniqueness, singularity, community and participation—aim to do just that" (Schulze 1998, 308). Schulze argues that the uniqueness of events makes them attractive to consumers. Participation is mandatory because events are there only for a time and then they are over. The episodic character of events underscores this dynamic as consumers seek to recapture the remembered experience. This experiential quality of events is enhanced by the sense of community they engender among event participants, whose active participation in the event is crucial for its success. Another important element of an event is its attractiveness for the media. Most importantly, event participants become objects of media coverage. Because only relatively few people can actually participate in an event, the construction of a media reality becomes a critical component of the mediation of the experiential dimension associated with a product (Willems 2001).

As Stephan Porombka has argued, the traditional book form was in a relatively unfavorable position to take advantage of these transformations. In contrast to television, movies and the Internet, the book is much more difficult to access. "In a world that is geared toward a continual intensification of experience consumption, the problem for the book consists primarily in the following: in contrast to other media, it offers its users comparatively few experiential qualities and, thus, little cult" (2001, 36). The rise in new media during the 1990s coincided with fears about the end of the book, and some critics evoked the final days of the "Gutenberg Galaxy" and prophesied a dark future for literature and the literary public sphere (Porombka 2001, 32). However, as literary events throughout the country indicate, the literary establishment has survived, and it is flourishing in the first decade of the new millennium. Also, since the crisis year 2003 during which the book industry recorded the third consecutive annual drop in sales, the industry seems to have recovered to some degree (Schulte 2006, 18–21).

In an attempt to capture the complexities of the literary event, I have restricted this study to a single city. An analysis of three groups from across the spectrum of public literary culture in Hamburg will provide insight into the role of the literary event as an integral part of the literary establishment in the twenty-first century: Macht e.V. from the Hamburg club scene, the Literaturhaus (Literature House) as the face of elite literary culture in Hamburg, and the Vattenfall energy company. All of these groups responded in different ways to the changes in the consumption of culture in Germany outlined by Schulze and to the concomitant crisis faced by literature during the 1990s. Since about 1999, all three of these organizations have been actively engaged in the eventization of literature in Hamburg. I intend to go beyond the mere description of the different manifestations of literature as event and to consider the evolution of the literary public sphere in Hamburg and the changed contexts for the presentation, consumption, and reception of literature that resulted.

Hamburg is a particularly interesting case study for three reasons. First, since the mid-1990s, a very active literary club scene has blossomed. Not only has slam poetry flourished in Hamburg since Tina Uebel, co-founder of Macht e.V., and another colleague launched a monthly slam poetry event, "Hamburg ist Slamburg" (Hamburg is the stronghold of slam), in 1997, but other interactive literary projects also abound. Second, the literary establishment in Hamburg has been the beneficiary of generous support from the Hamburg Senate at a time when budgetary pressures have curtailed cultural spending in many places. Finally, a case study of Hamburg is, in effect, a case study from the periphery. The literary critic Fritz J. Raddatz concluded in 1992 that he knew of "no literary scene in Hamburg" and that "the city itself is practically oblivious to art or literature" (Witwentröster 2002). Nevertheless, fifteen years later the city of Hamburg boasts an extraordinarily active literary scene. During these same fifteen years, Berlin has dominated as the literary and cultural center of the new Berlin Republic. In contrast to Berlin, other urban centers found themselves on the margins of cultural life after the fall of the Wall and the subsequent reunification of Germany in 1990. Thus, this study of Hamburg attempts a microstudy of the eventization of literature in a single city space, while simultaneously considering the evolution of that city's position on the larger literary map of Germany.

The Club Scene: Macht e.V.

Faced with a dwindling literary public sphere suffocated by the mechanisms of the neoliberal marketplace and the phenomenon of the one-hit wonder—which gave birth to the expression *"Verheizung junger Autoren"* (burning up of young writers)—the 1997 Bachmann laureate Norbert Niemann reflected in a 1998 essay on the resulting sense of isolation among young writers. He argued that writers will have to ask themselves, "how, if at all, they want to oppose the new laws of the market." Niemann argued that a pluralistic self-organization and consolidation of writers into lobbies was desperately needed in order to reconstruct literature as a *"gesellschaftliches Subjekt"* (social subject). At the same time, a group of writers in Hamburg's *Off-Szene* (club scene) began to reflect on how they might harness their literary energies and undertook the search for an ideal way to present their work. Macht e.V. is a fusion of Hamburg writers, literary organizers, and small-time publishers who were active participants in the local club scene throughout the 1990s.

The collaboration of the *Machtmacher* (Power Makers), as they call themselves, dates back to the late 1990s.[3] In 2000, they organized themselves into an official club—Macht e.V.—and that October they organized the first Machtclub. Since that time, the Machtclub has met on the second Tuesday of each month. When the organizers initially were searching for a space to hold the Machtclub in 2000, they chose the Mojo-Club on the Reeperbahn, the center of Hamburg's nighttime entertainment scene and red-light district. From the very beginning, between 150 and 300 literature enthusiasts found their way to the Tuesday evening events. The Machtclub was often sold out and whoever did not arrive early had to stand in the aisles or sit on the stage. Two different *Machtmacher* organize the Machtclub each month and treat the audience to three performances—usually a young and unknown local poet, an entertaining act that may or may not be related to literature, and, finally, an established writer. Writers such as Alexa Hennig von Lange, Stefan Beuse, Matthias Politycki, Thomas Kapielski, Karen Duve, Juli Zeh, Wladimir Kaminer, Burkhard Spinnen, Thomas Meinecke, and international talents June Melby, Henry Rollins, and Phillipe Dijan have performed at the Machtclub. A highlight of the evening during the first five years was the so-called *Jägermeisterschaften*[4]—a slam intermezzo sponsored by liqueur producer Jägermeister—where audience members presented their own texts on the topic of "hunting, hunters, deer, forest and meadow" against one of the *Machtmacher*. In typical slam fashion, the audience chose the winner.

In addition to the Machtclub, the *Machtmacher* have organized events such as "Macht Imitationen 'Fichte'" in the Haus der Photographie (Power Imitations 'Fichte' in the House of Photography), a "Lovecraft-Nacht" (Lovecraft Night), a poetry slam between Hamburg and Sylt, and "Eine Nacht im Machthotel" (A Night in the Power Hotel). They have also published numerous anthologies, including a collection of the best *Jägermeisterschaften* texts. Macht e.V. has achieved notoriety in Hamburg and beyond. Readers from local publishing houses and Hamburg literary agents regularly attend the Machtclub (Keil 2001). Christina Weiss attended the Machtclub while she was Senator of Culture in Hamburg, and Wolfgang Schömel, who has been the *Literatur-referent* (Literary Consultant) for the *Kulturbehörde* (Office of Culture) in Hamburg since 1992 and is himself a writer, has performed in the Machtclub on two occasions (Keil 2003). Articles in the *Süddeutsche Zeitung, Financial Times Deutschland, Frankfurter Rundschau, Frankfurter Allgemeine Zeitung, Aargauer Zeitung,* and the *Neue Zürcher Zeitung* have featured Macht e.V. and the Machtclub. In addition, two of the original nine organizers have since published novels.

During the 1990s, interactive forms of literary presentation ener-gized the *Off-Szene* and raised the cult potential of literature for a young generation that relished a break with traditional forms of liter-ary presentation. At the same time, as Stephan Porombka has argued, these forms of performative and interactive literature not only attracted a new generation of literary enthusiasts, but also generated extensive media coverage and exposure for literature. As a result, Porombka argues, slam poetry will occupy an important place in the literary his-tory of the 1990s because by drawing on the strategies of event market-ing, slam poetry increased the cult potential of literature in the face of stiff competition from other media (2001, 31–32, 37). Many of the founding members of Macht e.V. were integral members of the local slam poetry scene during the late 1990s. The group's initial success and that of the Machtclub stemmed from their ability to harness the ener-gies of the club scene and to capitalize on the sentiment that traditional forms of literary presentation were no longer considered attractive. As the motto on their Web site read, "Macht does not have any doubt about literature, but Macht does have doubts about the way that literature has traditionally been presented: writer mumbles to glass of water while the public falls into a *Kulturertragungsstarre* (numbness induced by hav-ing to put up with culture) ("Macht-e.V." 2005). The *Machtmacher* drew on the popularity of interactive forms of literary presentation to create a public space for the production, presentation, reception, and promo-tion of literature. As Gordon Roesnik—a founding member of Macht e.V.—argued in the "Machtwort"[5] to their 2002 anthology of texts from the Hamburg club scene, "The writers' drive for the stage did not come first, rather their communication with each other, and only then the search for an appropriate forum for their unconventional texts. Thus, the stage served as a means to establish a public sphere for literature" (275). This new literary space presented an alternative to the traditional literary establishment and created an institutional structure for young writers in Hamburg, which represented potential solutions to the isolation and the sense of loss that Norbert Niemann had described. "The proximity to the public and the non-hierarchical structure of the club scene positively influenced literary production. These two factors made possible a deepening integration of various approaches, an atmosphere of exchange and criticism, which prevented writers from drowning in their own juices" (Roesnik 2002, 275).

Their original home on the Reeperbahn served them well in two respects. The locale enhanced the cult potential of Macht e.V. and emphasized their space as the alternative to the elite literary establishment. The smoke-filled atmosphere, their emphasis on bottled beer, and their claims that the E-U dichotomy[6] was absurd highlighted this distinction ("*Machtinfo*"). Furthermore, they emphasized the interactive nature of the literary performance in the Machtclub. This interactive performativity fundamentally changes the dynamic of the literary experience. For instance, their renunciation of public discussions with writers was paradigmatic for how they sought to distinguish themselves from an elite institution like the Literaturhaus. As Gordon Roesnik remarked in a 2001 interview with the newspaper *Welt am Sonntag*, "As a matter of principle, we do not have [public discussions at literary events] because that can become rigid. We always try to allow people to talk to writers in person. That usually happens informally" (Körnich 2001). This dynamic removes the writer from a privileged position on the podium separated from the audience by a table, a glass of water, and a microphone. The result is that the encounter between writer and event participant becomes private and the author tangible. The audience also participated directly in the event—be it as performers or judges during the *Jägermeisterschaften* or in their noisy response to the performances on stage. As Wolfgang Schömel remarked, "you read in a kind of club atmosphere. People drink beer. They call out in the middle of a performance, and there is loud applause, etc. That is how I envision pre-modern theater to have been" (Schömel 2006).

The successful staging of literature as event in the Machtclub played a critical role in Macht e.V.'s professionalization of literary life within their alternate literary space. Through their locale, their interactive forum for literature, and their anti-establishment rhetoric, they positioned themselves effectively within the urban space. However, they also pursued the construction of a concrete infrastructure that provided an alternative to the literary establishment and aided them in their attempt to gain access to a wider public sphere. Gordon Roesnik's story is paradigmatic. As a young student, he won a sponsorship award from the city of Hamburg for his story "Bei der Großmutter" (At Grandma's Place). However, that prize did not represent a breakthrough for him as a writer because, as he remarked, "Unfortunately, there was no response from the large publishing houses" ("Die Macht der Nacht" 2002). In the "Machtwort" to their 2002 anthology, Roesnik comments further on the evolution of the structures within the Hamburg *Off-Szene*:

> Not only the performances, but also the writing process had become increasingly professional. The founding of Macht and this publication represent the next step: the creation of a receptacle in which the energy from the mature Hamburg scene can be bundled and presented to the public. The establishment of a professional infrastructure at all levels of literary life—writing, presenting, and publishing. (2002, 275–76)

This professionalization that Roesnik describes goes beyond the mere creation of means for writers to publish their work. He describes a comprehensive network of professionalized activities that encompass the entirety of literary existence, beginning with the writing process and extending to the organization of literary events, to publishing and selling, including the promotion of young Hamburg writers. The Writers' Room was established in 1995 as a place for authors to work and to exchange feedback on their work. Other critical elements of this professionalization include well-orchestrated literary events, a series of small Hamburg publishing houses, and a Web site replete with literary texts by unknown Hamburg writers and with reflections on the nature of literature.

The new home of the Machtclub in the Deutsches Schauspielhaus (German Theater), where the group took up residence in October of 2003, the resonance in the press, and the subsequent careers of some of the *Machtmacher* are indicative of the evolution of the Hamburg *Off-Szene*. It is symptomatic of the status achieved by the Macht e.V. that the Literaturhaus Hamburg now provides a link to the Macht e.V. Web site.

High Literature and Elite Culture: The Literaturhaus Hamburg

Since 1989, the Literaturhaus Hamburg has resided in a beautiful villa in an exclusive part of Hamburg and has occupied a central position in the mediation of contemporary literature to the public. In addition to its "Poesie in die Stadt" (Poetry into the City) initiative, the Literaturhaus offers traditional readings, a standing program for children and teenagers, and regular podium discussions on aspects of the literary industry. It also sponsors the biennial "Nordische Literaturtage" (Nordic Literary Festival).

Throughout the decade of the 1990s, the Literaturhaus Hamburg remained a refugium for high literature and elite culture. Comments that Ursula Keller, who was the director of the Literaturhaus from 1992 to 2005, made in a 2001 interview with *Welt am Sonntag* illustrate this attitude. "For a lot of writers, it is a stamp of quality to read here. I always try to offer a variety of presentations with an eye to quality" (Körnich 2001). The subject of this interview, which Hella Körnich conducted with Ursula Keller and two members of the Hamburg *Off-Szene*, was the role of those two spaces in the literary life of Hamburg. Keller's comment certainly intended to imply a qualitative distinction between the Literaturhaus and the *Off-Szene*. In the course of the same interview, Keller also took a strong stand against the perceived transformations in literary culture brought on by the co-opting of literature by the *Erlebnisgesellschaft* and the open entanglement of marketplace and literature that characterized the literary scene in the late 1990s. When the interviewer asked her if she did not have to take care that "literature did not become a part of the lifestyle industry," she replied, "Yes, definitely. This hype surrounding the literature of young writers is changing the literary climate a great deal. For instance, quality and aesthetic criteria are getting watered down and replaced by economic success. I see it as my responsibility to react critically to such phenomena." The director portrays the Literaturhaus as a space where the view of literature as the other to the marketplace is rigorously defended—this, in spite of the reevaluation of this relationship in the literary establishment as a whole. If one follows Schütz and Wegmann's argument, the outsider status of literature and the unique role the literary establishment had ascribed to literature as "the genuine center of fundamental social self-reflection" had become increasingly untenable during the 1990s (2003, 25). The Literaturhaus sought to (re)claim this position of literature as the other to the marketplace and to preserve its reflexive role. "Our public would demand a discussion. I think, they would protest if there were no discussion with the author after a reading," Keller stated. "I don't want literature to be consumed, but tied into the process of self-reflection" (Körnich 2001).

Nonetheless, the Literaturhaus institution found itself in a position not unlike that of the book. Sonja Vandenrath has argued convincingly that *Literaturhäuser* have been forced to pursue new strategies to secure their existence because of their changing position within the urban cultural establishment (2002, 172). The mechanisms of the *Erlebnisgesellschaft* have exerted pressure on the *Literaturhäuser*. The media attention that accompanied the phenomenon of slam poetry, for instance, had the effect of raising the level of competition for attention in the urban literary and cultural public sphere (Porombka 2003, 137).

In spite of the positions Ursula Keller took in her interview, the program of the Literaturhaus Hamburg has evolved since the late 1990s. Although organizers officially maintain the claim on their Web site that they make no concessions to populistic demands, the Literaturhaus has pursued a strategy to open itself to a wider literary public, and the literary event has played an important role.[7] In my view, the Literaturhaus Hamburg has pursued an eventization of literature that is—at least in part—characterized by a double movement that takes advantage of the possibilities of the event, but that simultaneously critiques the mechanisms within which they act and defends the outsider status of literature and its self-reflexive role. The most interesting project in this context has been "Poesie in die Stadt." The Literaturhaus Hamburg initiated "Poesie in die Stadt" in 1999, and since 2000 a cooperation of *Literaturhäuser* has organized this event each July and August.

The organizers of "Poesie in die Stadt" produce a well-orchestrated event. A press conference, readings, radio shows, and a flood of postcards regularly accompany the hanging of poetry in public spaces. Poetry festivals, cross-country literary tours, workshops, and a "Lange Nacht der Poesie" (Long Night of Poetry) have also been included in the program. In recent years, the *Literaturhäuser* have also themed the event. The "Internationales Lyrikforum" in 2003, during which German poets and invited guests from abroad traveled the country and constituted a "Parlament der Poesie" (Parliament of Poetry), "Daheim in der Fremde" (At Home Abroad) in 2004 that profiled Adelbert-von-Chamisso Prize laureates, and, most recently, poetry about soccer in conjunction with the 2006 World Cup in the summer of 2005 served to raise the profile of "Poesie in die Stadt." All of these activities contribute to the "experiential dimension" demanded by consumers in the *Erlebnisgesellschaft*. However, they also help the *Literaturhäuser* to achieve a critical goal for this event: they generate media coverage, garner attention within a crowded urban cultural landscape and, as a result, raise the cult potential not only of poetry, but of the *Literaturhäuser*.

Organizers' comments on the presentation of "Poesie in die Stadt" indicate the goals they pursue and the way they seek to shape their public profile through this event. Above all, they seek to change their image as a static space for the reception of contemporary literature. "From the very beginning, the fundamental idea has been to counter the prose of everyday life with a poetic alternative. In doing this, the Literaturhaus was supposed to be more than a meeting point. The Literaturhaus sought to emanate into its environment and to transform the urban surroundings" ("Poesie in die Stadt"). The *Literaturhäuser* seized this event as an opportunity to revise their image as elite mediators of literature. In essence, they sought to integrate two spheres perceived in opposition: the culture of everyday life and high culture. In doing so, they intended to reach out to those who do not come to them. In spite of their foray into the everyday lives of city dwellers, they maintain a high culture claim for literature. According to Ursula Keller, the short poems should not be "hermetic . . . but they should impart as much meaning and intellectual depth as possible" and "cultivate the urban space" (Pohle 2004).

With "Poesie in die Stadt," the Literaturhaus Hamburg created a literary event in 1999 that illustrates how such an institution can embrace the mechanisms of the event culture and simultaneously assert a self-reflexive role for literature. "With the language of the city, the language of the everyday, of the transitory, of the seemingly exchangeable—in short, with the language of advertising spaces . . . the *Literaturhäuser* brought poetry into the city" ("Poesie in die Stadt"). The *Literaturhäuser* occupied the paradigmatic marketing spaces of the urban landscape and refunctionalized them as spaces for the mediation of high culture. In other words, they appropriated advertising spaces that were representative of the lifestyle industry that was transforming the place of literature in public discourse. They changed the context of literature and refunctionalized not only the advertising spaces but also the poetic texts. In their function as mediators, they participated in the creative process and thereby made a claim for the critical potential of literature.

A cursory look at how the *Literaturhäuser* have organized "Poesie in die Stadt" reveals that they clearly included all of the key elements of a marketing event, yet managed to produce an event that corresponded to their needs and goals as an organization that aims to maintain its reputation as the mediator of serious literature to the public. As a result, "Poesie in die Stadt" is a perfect example of how high culture can appropriate the trend to event to assert itself in a highly competitive public sphere.

The Literary Festival: The Vattenfall *Lesetage*

In the spring of 1999—three months before the debut of "Poesie in die Stadt"—HEW (Hamburg-Elektrizitäts-Werke) initiated the Hamburger

Lesetage (Reading Festival) as a small literary festival for its customer magazine *Metropole*. Since October of 2000, Vattenfall, a Swedish company, has been the majority owner of HEW. From fifty readings and 2000 visitors in 1999, the festival has grown to 150 events and 14,000 visitors. Exhibitions, workshops, movie screenings, concerts, and talk shows on the local television station Hamburg 1 accompany readings in unusual spaces such as the AOL Arena, the Hamburg Dungeon, the Chamber of Commerce, the Institut Français, more than a half dozen museums, a planetarium, a Turkish bath, and the Institute of Forensic Medicine. The highly organized *Lesetage* leave very little to chance. The twelve-month planning cycle covers the gamut from postprocessing of the previous year's festival to the creation of an event concept, the courting of potential sponsors, the establishment of press contacts, Web site conception, and the training of individual assistants who are assigned to each author (Kalnbach 2006a). Collaboration with media partners such as the newspaper *Hamburger Abendblatt* and the radio stations NDR 90.3 and NDR Kultur guarantee media coverage in the run-up to and during the festival. The readings in unusual spaces fulfill the organizers' goal of making literature "experienceable" (Kalnbach 2006b). The concerts, films, talk shows, and writing workshops that round out the program contribute to this experiential dimension. The thousands of visitors who buy tickets and flock to the events not only generate a feeling of community that makes the festival more attractive, but they also become the subject of media attention (Wegmann 2002). However, the wider literary establishment also stands to benefit from the success of literary festivals. A survey conducted by Vattenfall established that the largest group of visitors to the festival consists of well-educated and well-read middle-aged women (Kalnbach 2006a). This is the very same group of readers who make up a large segment of the book-buying public today in Germany ("Buchkäufer" 2005). This fact also further complicates the phenomenon of the event, which, it would seem, does not merely function as a marketing gimmick and an ersatz for actual reading. In this case, the literary event clearly plays a complementary role in the mediation between writers and readers.

As Judith Kalnbach, the director of the festival, remarked, "As organizers and sponsors, we can plan the event optimally so that it fits our concept" (Kalnbach 2006b). The *Lesetage* are completely financed with funds provided by Vattenfall Europe, which gives organizers the freedom to develop a concept and to plan events that fit that concept. In addition to the staging of literary readings in unusual spaces, which has been their modus operandi since the beginning, Vattenfall also structures readings around several rubrics. As a result, the public is not confronted with a random selection of literary texts, public personalities, concerts, and films. Organizers set their thematic points of focus in October, allowing them to cull new releases for books that fit into their conceptual planning. In this way, they create the potential for dialogue among current literary texts on themes that cover the spectrum from *"Krimis"* (Crime Fiction), *"Hamburgensien"* (Stories about Hamburg), and *"Liebe International"* (Love International) to *"Neue Welten"* (New Worlds) and *"Deutschlandbilder"* (Images of Germany). Thus, the *Lesetage* assume a role of literary mediation traditionally occupied within the literary establishment by literary critics, academics and, more recently, *Literaturhäuser*.

Conclusions

When the literary critic Fritz Raddatz claimed in 1992 that he was unaware of any literary scene in Hamburg, he was certainly exaggerating ("Witwentröster" 2002). By 1992, the city's Senate had been presenting sponsorship awards to young writers for ten years, the city-sponsored yearly anthology of Hamburg writers, *Ziegel,* had published its first edition, the Literaturhaus had been established, and the city-sponsored magazine *Literatur in Hamburg* had been reporting on literary events in Hamburg since 1988. Nevertheless, the next fifteen years saw a dramatic increase in the public presence of literature. Recently established literary events such as "Poets on the Beach," *Weblesungen* (Web Readings), "Kaffee.Satz.Lesen,"[8] "Hamburg ist Slamburg," the Hamburger Märchentage (Fairy Tale Festival), and the dozens of public events announced monthly in *Literatur in Hamburg* underscore this trend. As one of the Macht cofounders Dierk Hagedorn remarked, "Fifteen years ago, the booklet 'Literatur in Hamburg' could easily discuss events thoroughly. Today, such discussions are only possible in compact form" (Hagedorn 2006). The eventization of literature played no small part in this transformation. Changes in consumption habits within German society during the 1990s were certainly a driving force behind the popularity of interactive forms of literary presentation, as was the presence of a media-savvy younger generation that embraced the break with traditional and elite forms of literary presentation. The growth of the Hamburg *Lesetage* and the emergence of numerous interactive literary projects in Hamburg since 1999 indicate a literary establishment that has become more communicative.

The "event" is a marketing concept, and the literary event is no exception. Actors within the urban space of Hamburg were able to draw on various mechanisms of event culture, not only to raise the profile of literature in the face of competition from other media, but also to position themselves more visibly within the cultural landscape of the city. However, Hamburg itself has also profited from the higher visibility of the literary scene there. The *Kulturbehörde* of the Senate has invested considerable energy and money into supporting this rejuvenation of literary life in the city. In addition to the numerous sponsorship awards, the city continues to support the Machtclub, the Literaturhaus, the *Ziegel*, and *Literatur in Hamburg*. Political leaders also provide significant moral support for the Vattenfall *Lesetage*. This support has created a literature-friendly environment that has raised Hamburg's profile as a center of German literary life. As Rainer Moritz, who is currently the director of the Literaturhaus Hamburg, remarked, "In recent years, Hamburg, like Munich, has attempted unconsciously to resist the Berlinization of literature. In other words: the opinion, which is still widely held, that one can only write German literature if one lives in Prenzlauer Berg [a hip district of Berlin] is false" (Moritz 2006). All of this literary activity, in which the literary event has played an important role, has allowed Hamburg to emerge as an alternative space to Berlin on the literary landscape in Germany.

The case study of Hamburg also illustrates that the literary event is much more complex than "a singular, spectacular happening," which is how it is often characterized in public discourse in Germany. The popularity of literary events reflects potential transformations in the literary establishment. Most obviously, as Wegmann and Schütz have remarked, the solitary reader no longer represents the sole form of literary reception (2003, 26). More communicative forms of literature embodied by literary events represent an alternative to more established structures. For instance, the *Lesetage* draw on thematic rubrics to initiate dialogue between newly released books, which bypasses the interests of publishing houses and the more elite forms of literary mediation represented by *Literaturhäuser* and professional literary critics. The result is a blending of E and U, high and low culture. Macht e.V. successfully integrated an event strategy into its program to create an alternative public space for literature within Hamburg. Not least of all, the raised level of competition in the literary life of Hamburg has forced the Literaturhaus to become more communicative and to reach out to a public that extends beyond a small and elite group of literary enthusiasts. However, its project "Poesie in die Stadt" illustrates how a literary event can be more than just a mere marketing gimmick. What these literary events have in common is the creation of new contexts for literature that have transformational potential at all levels of literary life.

Notes

1. "Literature doesn't . . . only take place on paper" ("Literatur-Szene" 2001). Unless otherwise indicated, all translations from the German are by the author.

2. *Trend zum Event* is the title of an often-cited collection of essays by Peter Kemper (2001).

3. *Macht* has numerous possible meanings in German. The substantive *Macht* means "power." The verb *machen* contains a plethora of possibilities including "to make," "to do," or even "to act." The form *macht* can either be third person singular (he, she, or it "makes," "does," or "acts") or a second person plural imperative "Make!", "Do!", or "Act!" *Machtmacher* would, thus, signify those who "make" or "create" power. Gordon Roesnik commented that "the name means that we have everything except power" ("Die Macht der Nacht").

4. *Jägermeisterschaften* means "professional hunter championships" and is a play on the name of the corporate sponsor, Jägermeister.

5. *Machtwort* is a play on the term *Nachwort* (Afterword). In German, to say a "Machtwort" means "to put one's foot down."

6. "E" stands for serious and "U" for entertaining literature. The dichotomy of "serious" and "entertaining" literature has been a central component of literary reception in Germany.

7. It is symptomatic of the bad name that the term *event* has received in public discourse in Germany that the director of the Literaturhaus does not consider their projects to be "events" (Moritz 2006). In e-mail exchanges with Judith Kalnbach (Vattenfall), Wolfgang Schömel (City of Hamburg) and Rainer Moritz (Literaturhaus Hamburg), all expressed reservations to varying degrees about the use of the term. A careful distancing from a highly criticized "event culture" is a matter of positioning oneself effectively within the cultural establishment. However, this positioning does not alter the reality of how events function. In addition to the four qualities outlined by Schulze, a defining element of the event is the fact that it is a special form of experience consumption. From a marketing perspective, the event serves the purpose of raising the cult potential of a brand name—be it the Literaturhaus Hamburg, a group of writers from the club scene, an electric company, the city of Hamburg, or literature itself. From this perspective, projects like "Poesie in die Stadt" or even a traditional literary reading are, strictly speaking, events. Moreover, one can reconstruct the success or failure of an event like "Poesie in die Stadt" by using an event hermeneutics as outlined by Porombka (2003, 132–34).

8. "Kaffee.Satz.Lesen" translates literally as "Coffee.Sentence.Read." The compound "Kaffeesatz" translates as "coffee grounds," and "Kaffeesatz lesen" is the German equivalent of "to read tea leaves."

Works Cited

Böttiger, Helmut. 1999. "Die Literatur selbst als Event." *Neue deutsche Literatur* 47.4: 164–71.

————. 2006. "Es gab schon immer den Unterhaltungswert der Literatur." Interview with Liane von Billerbeck. Deutschlandradio Kultur. 14 March.

"Buchkäufer und Leser 2005—Profile, Motive, Wünsche." 2005. Börsenverein des Deutschen Buchhandels (November). <http://www.boersenverein. de/de/69181?rubrik=69174&seite=0&dl_id=98347>.

"Die Macht der Nacht." 2002. *Uni SPIEGEL* (February). Quoted in Macht-Organisierte Literatur, <http://www.macht-ev.de>. Path: Lobby; Presse; Februar 2002.

Etscheit, Georg. 2001. "Porsche im Tiefschnee." *Zeit online* 42. <http://www. zeit.de/archiv/2001/42/200142_z-eventmarketing.xml>.

Greiner, Ulrich. 1998. "Ein paar Beobachtungen zum veränderten Verhältnis von Literatur und Öffentlichkeit: Tanz der Vampire." *Zeit online* 18. <http:// www.zeit.de/archiv/1998/18/literatur.txt.19980423.xml>.

Hagedorn, Dierk. 2006. "Literatur in Hamburg." E-mail to the author. 8 September.

Herzinger, Richard. 1999. "Jung, schick und heiter: Im schönen Schein der Marktwirtschaft: Der Literaturbetrieb entwickelt sich zur neuen Sparte der Lifestyle-Industrie." *Zeit online* 13. <http://www.zeit.de/archiv/1999/13/199913. leipzig_.xml>.

Kalnbach, Judith. 2006a. "Die Vattenfall Lesetage: Fakten, Zahlen und Hintergründe über Norddeutschlands größtes Literaturfestival" (Konzeptpapier).

————. 2006b. "Vattenfall Lesetage." E-mail to the author. 14 August.

Keil, Frank. 2001. "Hamburg, ahoi: Im 'Machtclub' treten sich die Leute auf die Füße, um Literaten zu hören und zu sehen." *Frankfurter Rundschau*, 5 July: 18.

————. 2003. "Sag zum Abschied lauthals: 'Macht nichts!' Die letzte Lesung im Mojo Club vor dessen Abriss war ein voller Erfolg—Jetzt sucht der 'Machtclub' ein neues Domizil." <http://www.welt.de/data/2003/04/10/69153. html>.

Kemper, Peter. 2001. "Nur Kult lässt keinen kalt: Veranstaltungsrituale im Medienzeitalter." In *Der Trend zum Event*, ed. Kemper. Frankfurt am Main: Suhrkamp. 184–200.

Körnich, Hella. 2001. "Die Popliteratur wirkt wie ein Schneepflug. Das gediegene Literaturhaus von Ursula Keller und der popkulturelle Machtclub mit Friederike Moldenhauer und Gordon Roesnik bündeln das literarische Leben in Hamburg." *Welt am Sonntag*, 5 August. <http://www.wams.de/ data/2001/08/05/509135.html>.

"Kulturnachrichten." 2006. Deutschlandradio Kultur. 13 June. <http://www. dradio.de/kulturnachrichten/20060613150000/>.

"Literatur-Szene in Hamburg: Slam Poets, Spoken Word, Underground Literatur." 2001. *u-lit.de Literatur Magazin*. <http://www.u-lit.de/artikel/literaturszene-hamburg.html>.

"Macht e.V. Eine neue literarische Kommunikation." 2005. *Hamburger Abendblatt*, 29 September. <http://www.abendblatt.de/daten/2005/09/29/487538. html>.

"Machtinfo." Macht-Organisierte Literatur. <http://www.macht-ev.de>. Path: Lobby; Machtinfo.

Moritz, Rainer. 2006. "Literatur in Hamburg." E-mail to author. 19 September.

Niemann, Norbert. 1998. "Literatur und Literaturkritik in der Zwickmühle von Medien und Ökonomie: Vom Feind umzingelt." *Zeit online* 22. <http://www.zeit.de/archiv/1998/22/literatur.txt.19980520.xml>.

"Poesie in die Stadt." literaturhaeuser.net. <http://www.literaturhaeuser.net/projekte/poesie/index.htm>.

Pohle, Julika. 2004. "Lyrik im Vorbeifahren." *Welt am Sonntag,* 27 June. <http://www.wams.de/data/2004/06/27/296866.html>.

Porombka, Stephan. 2001. "Slam, Pop und Posse. Literatur in der Eventkultur." In *Bestandsaufnahmen: Deutschsprachige Literatur der 90er Jahre aus interkultureller Sicht,* ed. Matthias Harder, Stephan Porombka, and Thomas Wegmann. Würzburg: Königshausen und Neumann. 27–42.

———. 2003. "Vom Event zum Non-Event-Event und zurück: Über den notwendigen Zusammenhang von Literatur und Marketing." In *Auf kurze Distanz: Die Autorenlesung: O-Töne, Geschichten, Ideen.,* ed. Thomas Böhm. Berlin: Tropen. 125–39.

Roesnik, Gordon. 2002. "Machtwort." *Macht: Organisierte Literatur.* Hamburg: Rotbuch. 274–78.

Schömel, Wolfgang. 2006. "Literatur in Hamburg." E-mail to the author. 14 August.

Schulte, Christina. 2006. "Spürbarer Aufwind." *Börsenblatt. On-line Magazine für den deutschen Buchhandel*: 18–21. <http://www.boersenblatt.net>. Path: Marktforschung; Branchenzahlen/Studien; Verlagsumsätze stiegen 2005 um 2,3 Prozent.

Schulze, Gerhard. 1992. *Die Erlebnisgesellschaft: Kultursoziologie der Gegenwart.* Frankfurt/New York: Campus.

———. 1998. "Die Zukunft der Erlebnisgesellschaft." In *Eventmarketing: Grundlagen und Erfolgsbeispiele,* ed. Oliver Nickel. Munich: Vahlen 1998. Quoted in Porombka (2001), 37.

Schütz, Erhard and Thomas Wegmann. 2003. "Literatur und Marketing." *Humboldt-Spektrum* 1: 24–28.

Vandenrath, Sonja. 2002. "Zwischen LitClubbing und Roundtable. Strategien von Literaturhäusern." In *literatur.com: Tendenzen im Literaturmarketing.* Eds. Erhard Schütz and Thomas Wegmann. Berlin: Weidler. 172–88.

Wegmann, Thomas. 2002. "Lesungen in der Eventkultur." In *literatur.com: Tendenzen im Literaturmarketing,* ed. Erhard Schütz and Thomas Wegmann. Berlin: Weidler. 121–36.

Willems, Herbert. 2001. "Der tägliche Kick: Die Vielzahl neuer Events raubt den traditionellen Festen ihren Glanz, meint der Soziologe Herbert Willems." Interview with Georg Etscheit. *Zeit online* 42. <http://www.zeit.de/archiv/2001/42/200142_z-eventm.-interv.xml>.

"Witwentröster, goldener Reiter, Überseezungen. Literarischer Frühling in Hamburg." 2002. *Literatur in Hamburg.* <http://www.literaturinhamburg.de/>.

4

THE DEUTSCHES LITERATURINSTITUT LEIPZIG AND THE MAKING OF AN AUTHOR
Tobias Hülswitt Hits the Road for Literature
and Ends Up a Writer

RACHEL J. HALVERSON

The Deutsches Literaturinstitut der Universität Leipzig is singular among institutions of higher learning in postunification Germany, building on a tradition of educating young writers established by the Institut für Literatur "Johannes R. Becher" in the former German Democratic Republic between 1955 and 1990.[1] Born in the wake of postunification educational restructuring, the Deutsches Literaturinstitut opened in 1995, seeking to provide its students with "a professional writing competency and the ability to author literary texts, as well as knowledge of literary history and literary theory" (Deutsches Literaturinstitut 2007).[2] With this stated goal, the Deutsches Literaturinstitut does not differ that much from its predecessor, the Institut für Literatur "Johannes R. Becher." In his article "Parteischule oder Dichterschmiede? The Institut für Literatur 'Johannes R. Becher' from Its Founding to Its *Abwicklung*," David Clarke points to the curricular continuity between the two institutes: "Since teaching started in 1995, the new institute has, with the obvious exception of the formerly obligatory courses in Marxism-Leninism, organized the curriculum in a similar way to its predecessor, with lectures on literature and related topics accompanied by practical seminars on poetry, prose, fiction, and drama" (2006, 100). Unlike the Institut für Literatur, which functioned as a separate institution, the Deutsches Literaturinstitut exists under the umbrella of the Saxon Ministry for Science and Culture within the institutional framework of the Universität Leipzig. Similar restructuring was widespread in the new *Bundesländer* immediately following the *Wende* due in large part to the political need to wipe the slate clean of a clearly Marxist-Leninist programmatic agenda and to create an educational system compatible with that of West Germany.[3] One constant, however, has remained. The Deutsches Literaturinstitut is carrying on the tradition of producing publishable authors established by the Institut für Literatur.

The Deutsches Literaturinstitut in Theory and Practice

In the eleven short years of its existence, graduates of the Deutsches Literaturinstitut already have established an impressive publication record—eighty-three books, including among them manuscripts printed by major German publishing houses such as C.H. Beck, S. Fischer Verlag, and Kiepenheuer & Witsch (*Deutsches Literaturinstitut* 2007). This is not surprising considering the institute's highly competitive admission process. Of the six hundred applications they receive yearly, only twenty are accepted (Haslinger and Treichel 2006, 14). Notable young writers who received training at the institute include Tobias Hülswitt, Ricarda Junge, Martina Hefter, and Juli Zeh. The latter two and their literary works will be examined in subsequent essays of this volume by Katharina Gerstenberger and Patricia Herminghouse. These publishing achievements alone quantitatively validate the existence of the program, and entice literary scholars to look behind the numbers and qualitatively define the role study at the Deutsches Literaturinstitut plays in advancing the careers of young German authors.

In his "Ehre, Reichtum, Ruhm und Liebe: Was angehende Autoren in Seminaren lernen" (Honor, Riches, Fame, and Love: What Budding Authors Learn in Seminars), Hans-Ulrich Treichel, Professor for German Literature at the Deutsches Literaturinstitut, addresses just this qualitative dimension of studying to become an author:

> The person who writes is not wise, but rather someone hungry for happiness and recognition, who at times also tends to megalomania. This individual can really only be helped with the development of the technical and mechanical skills of writing. And an institution like the Deutsches Literaturinstitut can be of use in this process. The person must cure themselves of their dreams. It may be that these dreams become a reality. Then the individual still must learn what it means if, given the corresponding demand, a great authorial journey results from the great journey of life. (2003)

Not surprisingly, Treichel's statement on the course of study offered by the institute echoes the mission statement found on the institute's Web site. Although he concedes that the actual writing of literary texts remains a solitary activity, the writer-centered seminar format at the institute, in which students read and critique each other's work, provides an interactive, communal forum for students to develop their skills as authors (Haslinger and Treichel 2006, 9). The unique, insular environment of the institute with its micro-literary community prompts questions about what exactly becomes of writers upon graduation. Surely students who choose to study there aspire to write the next great German novel, play, or volume of poetry. Yet once equipped with the practical, technical knowledge of their trade, these graduates find their dreams of becoming successful authors confronted by the reality of becoming a published author. In other words, they must make their own way in the cold, competitive publishing world upon leaving the academic cocoon. Where once they grappled with their professors and fellow students' feedback, they now must please and appease the publishing house reader, who is concerned not only with the quality of a text but also with its marketability.

Tobias Hülswitt On the Road

The progression of Tobias Hülswitt's career since graduating from the Deutsches Literaturinstitut in 2000 offers a unique lens through which to view the contributions this singular program has made to the career of one young German author, and reveals insights into what this "authorial journey" actually entails. Since the completion of his degree in 2000, Hülswitt has evolved from a traditional print author with his first novel, *Saga: Ein Roman* (Saga: A Novel) in 2000,[4] to a literary road warrior and online writer within the framework of the Goethe-Institut's cultural programs, a multimedia mix of reality and fiction he explores in his second novel *Ich kann dir eine Wunde schminken* (I Can Make You Up with a Fake Wound).[5] His third novel, *Der kleine Herr Mister* (Little Mr. Mister), was released in 2006. My examination of Hülswitt's statements on his experiences as a student at the Deutsches Literaturinstitut and his life as a writer, his publications, and his choice of publication venue will serve as a case study of a contemporary literary career. When viewed with respect to the mission statement of the Deutsches Literaturinstitut, the resulting juxtaposition of Hülswitt's three novels with the accounts he has given of his experiences at the Deutsches Literaturinstitut in newspaper articles, online, and in a personal e-mail exchange demonstrate the influence this degree program has had on one young author's literary career.

Hülswitt was born in 1973 in Hannover and grew up in Bad Berg-zabern. Following his *Abitur*, he completed an apprenticeship in Kaiser-slautern as a stonemason before beginning his studies at the Deutsches Literaturinstitut in Leipzig in 1997. In 1998, he received the Martha-Saalfeld Prize from the State Rhineland-Palatinate—awarded annually since 1994 to four authors who were either born in or live in Rhineland-Palatinate and whose writing is tied culturally to this region in Ger-many—and he became the second winner of the literaturWERKstatt Berlin's Open Mike Competition. In 2002, he was author-in-residence in Cairo. In May 2004, he received the Grant for Literature from the Palatinate District Administration, followed by a stay in Krakau at the Villa Decius as part of the "City People or the Writing Urban Dwellers," a project bringing together young authors from Germany, Poland, and Ukraine.[6] Currently he lives in Berlin.

With his debut on the literary scene, several critics characterized Hülswitt as an author writing in the genre of pop literature,[7] and Hüls-witt's first major publication, *Saga: Roman,* garnered a uniformly posi-tive critical response—which cannot be said for German pop literature in general. Kiepenheuer & Witsch, Hülswitt's publisher, describes *Saga* as "an exquisite novel about departing from one's youth" (Hülswitt 2000b, 2). Reviewers followed the publisher's lead, praising Hülswitt's insights into a provincial puberty in contrast to the hustle and bustle of an urban coming-of-age. Typical of this response to *Saga* is Eberhard Rathgeb's review for the *Frankfurter Allgemeine Zeitung*, in which he points to the book's focus on youth, classifying it as "ein Jugendbuch" (a book for young readers) and singing Hülswitt's praises for his abil-ity to capture the essence of growing up in the country (2000). Other reviewers focus on the book's structure. In his review for the *Mittel-deutsche Zeitung*, Oliver Seifert terms the book a "journal conceived of in nineteen prose miniatures, detailing the search along forest and meadow paths for one's self" (2001). This reviewer clearly singles out the book's subtitle, *Roman* (Novel), as a possible misnomer.

Hülswitt Hits the Road and Rides the Information Superhighway

On the heels of *Saga*'s publication, the Goethe-Institut selected Hülswitt to participate in their North American literary tour "Literatur-Trio on the Road and on the Web: Maike Wetzel, Tobias Hülswitt, and David Wagner" in Fall 2001. Hülswitt chronicled his experiences on this tour through the United States and Canada in an online diary accessible at <http://www.jetzt.de/tagebuch>[8], a Web site sponsored by the *Süddeutsche Zeitung*. Hülswitt's journal-entry style evident in *Saga* had found a perfect outlet for expression in online blogging, and this marks the beginning of Hülswitt's transition from a traditional print author to a literary road warrior and online writer, a transformation that mirrors trends in the contemporary multimedia world. In a personal e-mail exchange with the author, Hülswitt even describes his decision to write in an online forum as "intuitive" (2006b). As Thomas Wegmann points out in his article on literature on the Internet, at the end of the 1990s the Internet had become a public and openly accessible interactive venue, where younger authors especially can publish and communicate with one another—a development that signifies a generational changing of the guard in the publishing world (2001, 56). Clearly Hülswitt is not unique in his cultivation of a parallel cyber presence, but rather part of a generational shift in the literary world.

Two online German literary projects in the late 1990s are symptomatic of the evolution of German literature's presence on the Internet: *Null* and *pool*. *Null*, an electronic anthology project sponsored by Dumont Verlag and edited by Thomas Hettche, presented texts by a number of young German authors, including Marcel Beyer, Judith Hermann, Helmut Krausser, Thomas Meinecke, Terézia Mora, and Andreas Neumeister (Wegmann 2001, 56). Dumont Verlag published *Null: Literatur im Netz* (Zero: Literature Online) in 2000, a print version documenting this project. The online literary collective *pool*, initiated by Sven Lager and Elke Naters, reached a similar terminal point with the publication of *the Buch—Leben am pool* (the Book—Life at the pool) in 2001. Unlike *Null*, the transition from electronic format to print format was not the original goal of *pool* (Wegmann 2001, 57). In an interview with Dirk Knipphals that appeared in *taz*, Lager and Naters extol the unique collective writing process facilitated by the online format that *pool* offered its contributors, a collaborative writing experience that allowed the contributors to move towards the print publication in a highly interactive fashion. In the case of both *Null* and *pool*, the online publication of literary texts has not resulted in the end of the printed word. P. David Marshall, in his *New Media Cultures*, confirms this phenomenon:

> New media often imply a supersession of the older form; but it should be made clear that new media have not historically obliterated their past. Many futurists imagined television spelling the end of radio and this has been replicated with the internet somehow superseding newspapers. The more complicated reality is that media forms change when newer forms appear and there is a different accommodation of a media mix. (4)

As we will see, this melding of forms marks the literary path Hülswitt has chosen to pursue.

Hülswitt's musings on living as a writer illuminate the appeal of an online forum to authors who also publish in traditional print form. Shortly following the publication of *Saga*, an article by Hülswitt entitled "Die Dekonstruktion des Dichters: Krisen als Geschenk des Himmels. Erfahrungen mit dem Schreibstudium" (The Deconstruction of an Author: Crises as a Gift from Heaven. Experiences with Studying Creative Writing, 2000a) appeared in *Die Zeit*. In this article, he chronicles the coincidental nature of the path that led him to study at the Deutsches Literaturinstitut. For Hülswitt, this was a time of intense and exclusive involvement with literature, similar to the experience many have in graduate school. At the conclusion of most intensive periods of study, at least anecdotally, there comes the realization that life continues outside of this insular world, oblivious to the concerns and passions of those who are immersed in it. Hülswitt refers to this phase as "eine Art Aufwachen" (a kind of awakening). This return to the "real world" brought with it a moment of doubt, which he characterizes as "the question whether one actually wants to completely devote oneself to literature, to a very slow and introverted form of expression" (2000a). Going online ultimately solves Hülswitt's postgraduation dilemma by opening another communication bridge between the author and reader and placing the solitary practice of writing into a public electronic forum known not only for its spontaneity and immediacy but also for its interactivity.

Evidence of this link between reader, author, and the author's perceptions of his audience saturates Hülswitt's online diary during his literary tour of the US and Canada. In the short texts posted from various points on his trip (San Francisco, Seattle, St. Louis, Chicago, New York, Ottawa, and Toronto), his comments range from the banal to the insightful, including everything from the disorientation and exhaustion that come with jet lag to the increasing travel security measures post-9/11. One intriguing feature of Hülswitt's online musings is his decision to divide several of his postings into two segments in the following order: "der inoffizielle Text" (the inofficial text) and "der offizielle Text" (the official text). In an interview with Michaela Grom for the online magazine *Papyrus-Magazin,*[9] Hülswitt explains this decision as follows: "I thought to myself: I want to write something that one normally would not write, and therefore I called it the 'unofficial text.' Whoever does not want to read it knows exactly what it is and does not have to read it. Although these types of things tend to make people curious under certain circumstances" (2003). Hülswitt's intent is clear.

The unofficial texts give him creative license, but they also relegate more control to his readers, who may or may not be intrigued by the idea of a text behind the text that he is offering them.

For literary scholars and cultural critics, these unofficial comments expose Hülswitt's insights into his life as an author, writing as a process and profession, and his observations while traveling. In the unofficial text "I haven't really seen anything suspicious" from 6 November 2001, he posits: "writing for newspapers constitutes producing false text. fake text. faked life. writing novels constitutes producing faked life. producing lies, reproducing lies, cementing lies, solidifying lies. if there is something I find strange, then it is aerial photographs" (2001c).[10] With this statement, he essentially glosses over the generally accepted surface distinction between writing journalistic texts and writing fictional texts and in so doing undermines the validity of both. Journalists and authors alike construct worlds that to varying degrees are artificial.

Hülswitt's polemic musings do not go unnoticed. In his posting from 16 November 2001, "das Gesicht ist so radikal offen" (the face is so radically open), he announces that the unofficial text has done damage, which he never intended (2001b). After a several-day hiatus, he returns to submitting postings to his journal, more specifically, official texts. Although the forum of an online journal invites openness, frankness, and unfettered freedom of speech, even here censorship governs the content of Hülswitt's postings. In this case, however, the censor remains undisclosed, and the reader is left to speculate as to its identity and the nature of the problems caused by the unofficial texts. Hülswitt had already commented on circumventing editors in an earlier unofficial posting from 7 November 2001, "inoffizieller text only" (2001d), in which he reveals that he now knows how to make his own postings and thus to avoid the editorial staff and its enforcement of capitalization rules. Thus, the editors at *jetzt.de* and the *Süddeutsche Zeitung* immediately present themselves as likely candidates.

Even with this brief interruption due to Hülswitt's unofficial postings, he consistently utilizes both the official and unofficial sections of his online journal to expound on a wide range of issues, from his nervousness and insecurities before readings in "Eine wildly inappropriate response" (2001e) to the appropriateness of texts containing references to sex, drugs, and women's nipples for a high school audience in the United States in "Daniel of The Old Boots" (2001a). At an Alexander von Humboldt School in Ottawa, the students even supply him with a bottle of beer so that he can demonstrate his description in *Saga* of "Bier glottern" (shotgunning a beer). Since he was traveling shortly after 9/11, Hülswitt also includes observations on security measures at airports as well as condemns Germany's decision to send troops to Afghanistan. Doubtless, reading Hülswitt's online journal is entertaining, similar perhaps to the entertainment reality TV provides its viewers. More important, however, for those who cannot experience Hülswitt reading live, the online diary serves as another access point to the persona behind the novel and adds an immediacy that is not inherent in simply reading the published hardcopy of a literary work. Recalling the comments Hülswitt made in "Die Dekonstruktion des Dichters," this perhaps explains his continued online presence.

Hülswitt's collaboration with the Goethe-Institut continued in 2002, when he was invited to be a *Stadtschreiber* (writer-in-residence) in Cairo. During his stay, he was allowed to choose the venue in which to publish his impressions. He again decided to maintain an online journal:

> I already have had experience with online journaling while traveling in the US last year and I found it quite pleasant. One has so many impressions to digest, and this particular form is very helpful in processing this information. Publishing on the Internet also means that one is writing for an audience, it means that one is constantly communicating to someone, it means that in certain cases one's own emotions are continuously available to everyone. (Grom 2003)

Hülswitt's rationale demonstrates that Internet journals offer authors immediacy, both in terms of processing experiences and in terms of access to their readership. The actuality of what being a *Stadtschreiber* in Cairo entails, however, is less self-evident to Hülswitt. An article about the Goethe-Institut project in *Kulturchronik*, a bimonthly publication by Inter Nationes that is no longer published, includes Hülswitt's frank response to a question regarding this very matter: "Actually, I can't do anything at all with the concept [writer-in-residence]" (Gräfe 2003, 17). Regardless, Hülswitt's six-week stay in Cairo proved to be a life-altering experience, both in terms of defining his role as *Stadtschreiber* and determining his ability to live and write outside of Germany. In an interview with Katja Winkler following his return to Germany, Hülswitt outlines his function in this project more clearly: "I defined my stay as self-experimentation: one takes a foreigner, puts him in a big foreign city, puts the lid on, and observes how the two substances react with each other. I write about Egypt just like I would write about my own home—as something completely normal" (Winkler 2003, 14). It should be noted that Hülswitt's German authorial modus operandi, known for the critical social commentary it offers, did not mesh well with Egyptian culture. At initial readings in Cairo, Hülswitt discovers that

his Egyptian audiences tend to feel attacked by him, since they interpret most of his social commentary about their country to be negative
(Winkler 2003, 14). Although Hülswitt's experiences in Egypt may not
have altered his perception of the relationship between author and subject, they did challenge the relationship between author and audience.

Hülswitt's lack of clarity regarding the title "Stadtschreiber von
Kairo" signals that his visit to Cairo differs from his earlier Goethe-
Insitut-sponsored tour through North America in 2001, where he had
the familiar task of giving literary readings from his latest novel. In
his online journal, Hülswitt shares details about living for six weeks
on a houseboat tethered to the shore of the Nile, his relationship with
the family that owns the houseboat, life in Cairo during Ramadan,
visiting the pyramids, and the culture of taxicabs unique to Cairo.
The latter even includes Hülswitt's "Taxiprojekt," (cab project) for
which he attempts to arrange for an Iranian cab driver, a Cairo cab
driver, and a Berlin cab driver to exchange vehicles and cities for one
day. For the most part, Hülswitt simply writes about his daily life in
Egypt, just as he wrote about daily life on tour in the United States.
Hülswitt reveals the process behind this type of writing in an unofficial text from 11 Nov. 2002: "i have become an observation machine in
the course of years" (2002c). This comment casts his online journal in
a somewhat more negative light and prompts his readers to question
whether Hülswitt's position as author and observer compromises his
engagement with his immediate environment and whether the global
forum of online journals nurtures authors or downgrades them from
insightful social commentators to detached mechanical observers
expected to entertain readers with a daily barrage of insights. Such
comments on the work required to keep his postings vibrant also
mark his growing awareness of the negative aspects of writing in a
forum known for its immediacy and newness, where readers expect
a continuous string of thoughts. The novelty of writing online and
broadcasting his thoughts to anonymous readers had faded and
essentially become work; posting online journal entries for six weeks
as compared to the two weeks of his book tour in North America
clearly is strenuous.

The shift for Hülswitt from author on the reading circuit to a writer-
in-residence also manifests itself in his narrative strategies and to a
certain degree in the content of his postings. He even directly solicits
assistance from his readers with his request that someone send him
the list of the Seven Wonders of the World (2002d). In the closing lines
of several postings, Hülswitt goes so far as to begin to preview the
next installment in order to inspire his readers to return to the site and

continue with him on his journey. Typical of this are the tongue-in-cheek closing lines from his posting on 8 Nov. 2002:

> Tomorrow, there will be something new about the taxi project (whom will the people in Teheran send? What will the Egyptian authorities say? Will we find a Berliner?), about Umm Said [Hülswitt's landlady] (will she have more to do than simply study vocabulary with me?) and—about the frightful, frightful, simply frightful pyramids! (2002b)

Similar to a serial novel published in a newspaper or a soap opera on television, Hülswitt's extended stay in Egypt and his decision to chronicle his adventures in an online journal require him to engage creatively with his readers in order to maintain their interest in his observations on life as a German author abroad. Not only does he have to submit entries to his online journal on a regular basis, they also have to be inspired enough to draw readers back to read the next installment.

Evidence of Hülswitt's effort to connect with his readers is apparent in the content of his postings as well. Similar to the texts from his US tour, his writings from Cairo include genuine insights into cultural practices, the people he meets, the sites he sees, and the physical challenges of travel. New, however, are Hülswitt's ruminations on life as an expatriate. He bemoans his inability to live abroad—something he thought possible when he was in his mid-twenties and full of wanderlust (2002b)—and offers his theory on those who become successful expatriates (2002a). This progression of insights from his own inability to live abroad to the ability or inability of others to thrive outside their homeland brings the intellectual journey Hülswitt has embarked upon in Egypt full circle. His insights into living in and writing about another culture reveal his authorial dilemma. Practicing his craft has honed his observational skills, yet it is this very ability that simultaneously ties him to and externalizes him from the German language and culture both at home and abroad. Ultimately, the tension between the observer and the observed proves to be the common denominator linking Hülswitt's online journals and his next novel.

A Literary Road Warrior Arrives at Destination Literature

Following his experiences in Egypt, Hülswitt tackles the negative aspects of our modern multimedia world in his second book. *Ich kann dir eine Wunde schminken* was published in 2004 and excerpts were performed as a radio play on DeutschlandRadio Berlin.[11] In Hülswitt's novel, life and the media become inextricably entwined as the novel tells the story of Hendrik Nühus, a failed student and struggling comic actor, and his girlfriend, Laura Stern, a theater student, in Leipzig. Laura's signature is her tendency to translate her thoughts because she thinks that everything sounds better in English than in German (Hülswitt 2004, 9). When the comedian Max Dopper hires Hendrik as the "comedy content director" for his new TV show, Hendrik discovers that his life and the show have become one and the same. This is pure "reality TV," essentially a show about the making of a show. When Max makes a move on Laura, it all becomes too much for Hendrik; he loses control and attacks his rival. While recovering in the hospital, he makes a video for Laura to explain the events of the previous days from his perspective, including his secret escapes to a Vietnamese produce store to stack empty crates and his discovery of her indiscretions with Max Dopper. Laura essentially has to watch his show to hear his side of the story. On the surface, *Ich kann dir eine Wunde schminken* appears to be a simple social farce peppered with missed cues and miscommunication. However, consideration of current trends in European television programming discloses the powerful subtext of Hendrik's comic-tragic adventures and reveals the novel's critique of the media and its role in the formation and maintenance of European cultural values. The 1990s have proven to be a time of "transition from a heavily regulated television environment guided by social and cultural objectives to one driven by economic and global imperatives, over which governments have far less influence" (Iosifidis 2005, 2–3). During this time, reality-based television with programs such as *Big Brother* surfaced as the new key players in prime time scheduling (Iosifidis 2005, 150). The cultural implications of reality programming for both viewers and participants underlie the drama that becomes Hendrik's life.

In *Ich kann dir eine Wunde schminken*, alternating narrators relate the story of Hendrik and Laura's odyssey: Hendrik's first-person narrator and the omniscient third-person narrator who focuses on Laura and her experiences. This narrative structure reinforces the novel's movement between life and television, between the viewer and the viewed. In addition, both characters comment on the interplay between life, literature, television, and film. As Max Dopper first approaches Hendrik to write for him, Laura composes an imaginary lecture in her mind:

> [T]elevision, she noted, copied the reality it knew from literature, which for many decades had been drawing its understanding of reality in turn from the movie screen and television screen. The production of reality therefore was caught in a cycle between literature and movie screen.

And normal reality was no longer a matter of discussion, but rather has oriented itself for a long time toward the television screen. (59)

And as Hendrik begins working for Max, a job that entails producing the content for the show's web page and brainstorming on supplementary products like Hendrik's idea for a computer game perversely named "Kosovo Krieg" (Kosovo War), Hendrik notes that he is actually getting paid for what he does for fun (Hülswitt 2004, 100). In other words, his prior life, with evenings spent performing at the cabaret Urst Übelst and days spent stacking crates at the produce stand and watching television, flipping between *The Simpsons* and news reports on the war in Bosnia, is really not that different from living in a reality TV show, except for the addition of an ever-present camera team. For Hendrik, the line between life and the constructed reality of television has been erased, and the two worlds flow into and out of each other. The novel's conclusion drives this point home with Hendrik's videotaped message for Laura. Instead of telling her his version of the story in person, a video film becomes his messenger. Then, just like in the movies, Hülswitt lets the credits roll on the last two pages of his novel. Here he acknowledges contributors to this literary project, ranging from the executive producer—his publisher Kiepenheuer & Witsch—and, for "Eternal Support," Indine and Jule, whose identity and relationship to the author are not disclosed. True to Laura's summary of the matter, Hülswitt has completed the circle between literature and film.

Unlike his main character Hendrik, Hülswitt is very aware of the boundaries of the different venues, in which he lets his voice be heard, and of what crossing these boundaries and combining venues entails. In an e-mail exchange with the author, Hülswitt summarized his position:

> I have to say that the decision to write online was at first purely intuitive, but thinking about it now, you are of course correct—I am a child of the times and I have to deal with the medium of the Internet, and for that matter to do it in a completely natural way, insofar as there is a completely natural way :) What one can't forget with all of this: I enjoy the charms of writing online, the speed, the rawness, the improvisation, the nervousness, the openness—but I believe that it is something completely different from conventional print literature, which I am certain can only be created in silence and concentration, over longer periods of time. (2006b)

Clearly, the Internet offers Hülswitt another venue for creative expression. Yet as evidenced by his postings from Egypt, Hülswitt no longer blindly subscribes to the wonders of online journaling. In fact, his enthusiasm for maintaining an online presence following his US tour and the skepticism towards this medium he expressed while in Egypt demarcate an evolution in his understanding of his métier. Ultimately, his experiences online have confirmed for him the sacredness and uniqueness of the printed literary word, alleviating the doubts he expressed in "Die Dekonstruktion des Dichters" about devoting his life and energies to becoming an author.

The events, honors, publications, and online journal entries examined in this case study of Hülswitt's progression from student at the Deutsches Literaturinstitut to independent author validate his career choice as well. In September 2006, Kiepenheuer & Witsch published his third novel, *Der kleine Herr Mister*. This is the first of his books Kiepenheuer & Witsch has released in a hardbound edition, physically representing the figurative and literal weight Hülswitt is gaining in their stable of writers. *Der kleine Herr Mister* recounts the life of a young artist who refuses to enter a pact with the devil, a plot alluding to Goethe's *Faust*, widely acknowledged as one of the major German-language contributions to world literature. The sheer existence of this novel also answers in part the investigative framework underlying this examination of Hülswitt's writing, specifically the role of the Deutsches Literaturinstitut in the careers of young authors. Hülswitt himself remains unequivocally positive about his choice to study there, but acknowledges that it is not the only avenue one can take to become an author (Hülswitt E-mail from 26 February 2006). Echoing Hans-Ulrich Treichel's sentiments, Hülswitt cautions: "What one doesn't learn while one is studying is what it really means to live as a writer" (Hülswitt E-mail from 26 February 2006). The reception of *Der kleine Herr Mister* will reveal whether Hülswitt has indeed learned that lesson himself. For now, it is clear that Hülswitt has joined the ranks of twenty-first-century literary road warriors, his latest novel in one hand, laptop in the other, and a personal Web site with all his latest professional news: <www.tobiashuelswitt.com>. As he himself noted when asked whether studying at the Deutsches Literaturinstitut was a help or hindrance:

> No one is taught how to write here [at the Deutsches Literaturinstitut], but rather an already-existing natural inclination is stimulated. And that is something that every author has to do with his natural ability—he has to nurture and educate it, and whether he does this at home alone, in writing groups, in workshops, or in a creative writing program, there is essentially no difference. (2006b)

A comparison of these comments Hülswitt made in our e-mail exchange in 2006 with the doubts about a literary career he expressed in his newspaper article "Die Dekonstruktion des Dichters" in 2000 cited earlier in this analysis exemplifies how his experiences with the Internet have defined more concretely for him the unique quality of creating and consuming literature. Hülswitt's "journey" since departing from the Deutsches Literaturinstitut thus speaks for his ability to build on the skills his studies provided him and demonstrates that he has indeed learned to live successfully as a twenty-first-century author. In the case of Tobias Hülswitt, the Deutsches Literaturinstitut in Leipzig clearly has achieved the goals expressed in its mission statement and validated its once-contested existence within the German system of higher education.

Notes

1. Additional avenues to pursue the formal study of creative writing are limited. Aspiring authors can study "Kreatives Schreiben und Kulturjournalismus" at the Universität Hildesheim and at the studio "Literatur und Theater" at the Universität zu Köln. For prose authors, the Bertelsmann publishing company sponsors seminars at the Literaturhaus in Munich, and the Autorenwerkstatt at the Literarisches Colloquium in Berlin provides another possibility to learn the craft (Haslinger 2000).

2. Unless otherwise indicated, all translations from the German are by the author. Similar to its successor, the Institut für Literatur also was considered unique and controversial in its training of authors, with only the Gorki-Institut in Moscow named at that time as a comparable program for aspiring authors (Beyer 1980, 7). For additional statements on the mission of the Institut für Literatur "Johannes R. Becher," see Beyer (1980). For further information on the demise of the Institut für Literatur "Johannes R. Becher," see Clarke (2006) and Finger (2004).

3. For a more detailed account of the events surrounding the establishment of the Deutsches Literaturinstitut, see Clarke (2006, 97–101). Josef Haslinger and Hans-Ulrich Treichel, both professors at the institute, also emphasize the importance of the structure of creative writing programs established by Iowa Writers' Workshop to the reconfiguration of the institute under the auspices of the larger university system (2006, 14). In fact, Haslinger and Treichel emphasize the almost century-long tradition of creative writing programs at American universities, such as the Iowa Writers' Workshop, as models for their work at the Deutsches Literaturinstitut (2005, 8; 2006, 7).

4. *Saga* appeared under the KiWi imprint, a paperback series published by Kiepenheuer & Witsch Verlag that showcases young German authors.

5. Hülswitt also published a volume of poetry (*So ist das Leben* [That's the Way Life Is], 1997, Ventil Verlag) before his debut novel *Saga*.

6. MDR.DE|*via Europa* <http://www.mdr.de/viaeuropa/1436209.html>.
7. The recent phenomena of pop literature and pop culture have intrigued Germanists as well. See Jung (2002) and Mueller (2004).
8. This link is no longer active and Hülswitt's "Tagebuch" from 2001 is no longer accessible online, although jetzt.de continues with an interactive format soliciting and encouraging reader contributions, some of which are labeled "Tagebücher." This supplement to the *Süddeutsche Zeitung* can be accessed at <http://jetzt.sueddeutsche.de/>.
9. According to its Web site, *Papyrus-Magazin* is a German-language publication for those living in Egypt or who are interested in Egypt. It was established in 1980 and appears five times a year. They publish on issues dealing with the history, culture, religions, and traditions of Egypt and include current events and personal accounts as well. Refer to <www.papyrus-magazin.de/start.html> for further details.
10. As is characteristic of informal online postings, Hülswitt often does not follow standard capitalization practices.
11. DeutschlandRadio Berlin—Themen <http://www.dradio.de/php_logic/beitrag_vorschau.php? programm=dlr&sendung=hoerspiel>.

Works Cited

Beyer, Ursula, Eva Maurer, and Gerhard Rothbauer, eds. 1980. *Zwischenbericht: Notate und Bibliographie zum Institut für Literatur "Johannes R. Becher" Leipzig.* Leipzig: VEB Bibliographisches Institut Leipzig.
Clarke, David. 2006. "Parteischule oder Dichterschmiede? The Institut für Literatur 'Johannes R. Becher' from Its Founding to Its *Abwicklung.*" *German Studies Review* 24.1: 87–106.
Deutsches Literaturinstitut Leipzig homepage. 2007. <http://www.deutsches-literaturinstitut.de/>. Accessed 30 January.
Finger, Evelyn. 2004. "Was nützt die Freiheit in Gedanken?" *Die Zeit*, 18 November. <http://zeus.zeit.de/text/2004/48/Literaturinstitut_89>.
Gräfe, Daniel. 2003 "Als Stadtschreiber in Kairo: Ein Projekt des Goethe-Instituts." *Kulturchronik* 2: 17–19.
Grom, Michaela. 2003. "Deckel drauf und schauen, was rauskommt .. . .—Ein Gespräch mit Tobias Hülswitt, dem Stadtschreiber von Kairo." *Papyrus. magazin.* January. <www.papyrus-magazin.de/start.html>.
Haslinger, Josef. 2000. "Die Penne der Poeten. Literarisches Schreiben kann man lernen—im Kleinkrieg mit eigenen und fremden Texten." *Die Zeit*, 19 October. <http://zeus.zeit.de/text/archiv/2000/43/200043_c-haslinger.xml>.
Haslinger, Josef, and Hans-Ulrich Treichel, ed. 2005. *Wie werde ich ein verdammt guter Schriftsteller? Berichte aus der Werkstatt.* Frankfurt am Main: Suhrkamp.
———. 2006. *Schreiben lernen—Schreiben lehren.* Frankfurt am Main: Fischer.

Hülswitt, Tobias. 2000a. "Die Dekonstruktion des Dichters: Krisen als Geschenk des Himmels. Erfahrungen mit dem Schreibstudium." *Die Zeit*, 19 November.
———. 2000b. *Saga*. Cologne: Kiepenheuer & Witsch.
———. 2001a. "Daniel of The Old Boots." *Jetzt.de, Süddeutsche Zeitung*, Chicago, 8 November. <http://jetzt.sueddeutsche.de/texte/anzeigen/25071>.
———. 2001b. "das Gesicht ist so radikal offen." *Jetzt.de, Süddeutsche Zeitung*, Boston, 16 November. <http://jetzt.sueddeutsche.de/texte/anzeigen/25073>.
———. 2001c. "I haven't really seen anything suspicious." *Jetzt.de, Süddeutsche Zeitung*, San Francisco, 6 November. <http://jetzt.sueddeutsche.de/texte/anzeigen/25068>.
———. 2001d. "inoffizieller text only." *Jetzt.de, Süddeutsche Zeitung*, United States, 7 November. <http://jetzt.sueddeutsche.de/texte/anzeigen/25070>.
———. 2001e. "Eine wildly inappropriate response." *Jetzt.de, Süddeutsche Zeitung*, San Francisco, 3 November. <http://jetzt.sueddeutsche.de/texte/anzeigen/25066>.
———. 2002a. "Die berühmte Fähigkeit nichtwestlicher Metropolen." *Jetzt. de, Süddeutsche Zeitung*, Cairo, 9 November. <http://jetzt.sueddeutsche.de/texte/anzeigen/25082>.
———. 2002b. "Die Globalisierung muss halt noch warten." *Jetzt.de, Süddeutsche Zeitung*, Cairo, 8 November. <http://jetzt.sueddeutsche.de/texte/anzeigen/25089>.
———. 2002c. "Die große Gastfreundlichkeit." *Jetzt.de, Süddeutsche Zeitung*, Cairo, 11 November. <http://jetzt.sueddeutsche.de/texte/anzeigen/25085>.
———. 2002d. "Ein rennender Hund." *Jetzt.de, Süddeutsche Zeitung*, Cairo, 25 November. <http://jetzt.sueddeutsche.de/texte/anzeigen/25094>.
———. 2004. *Ich kann dir eine Wunde schminken*. Cologne: Kiepenheuer & Witsch.
———. 2006a. "Re: Your letter." E-mail to Rachel J. Halverson, February 26.
———. 2006b. "Re: Your article." E-mail to Rachel J. Halverson, March 17.
———. 2006c. *Der kleine Herr Mister*. Cologne: Kiepenheuer & Witsch.
Iosifidis, Petros, Jeanette Steemers, and Mark Wheeler. 2005. *European Television Industries*. London: British Film Institute.
Jung, Thomas, ed. 2002. *Alles nur Pop? Anmerkungen zur populären und Pop-Literatur seit 1990*. Osloer Beiträge zur Germanistik 32. Frankfurt am Main: Peter Lang.
Knipphals, Dirk. 2001. "Neue Nachbarschaften schaffen." *taz*, 10 Aug. <http://www.taz.de/index.php?id=archivseite&dig=2001/08/10/a0184>.
Lager, Sven, and Elke Nater. 2001. *the Buch—Leben am pool*. Cologne: Kiepenheuer & Witsch.
Marshall, P. David. 2004. *New Media Cultures*. London: Arnold Publishers.
Mueller, Agnes C., ed. 2004. *German Pop Culture: How "American" Is It?* Ann Arbor: University of Michigan Press.
Rathgeb, Eberhard. 2000. "Kein Pop im Dorf: Tobias Hülswitt gelingt ein Debüt." *Frankfurter Allgemeine Zeitung*, 12 December.

Seifert, Oliver. 2001. "Landleben praktisch portioniert: Der Roman "Saga" wirft den Panoramablick auf eine deutsche Jugend zwischen Neurodermitis und Liebesfrust." *Mitteldeutsche Zeitung*, 24 January.

Treichel, Hans-Ulrich. 2003. "Ehre, Reichtum, Ruhm und Liebe: Was angehende Autoren in Seminaren lernen." *literaturkritik.de*, 10 October. <http://www.literaturkritik.de/public/druckfassung_rez.php?rez_id=6419>.

Wegmann, Thomas. 2001. "Verschaltbar statt haltbar? Eine unvollständige Bestandsaufnahme zur Literatur im Internet." In *Bestandsaufnahmen: Deutschsprachige Literatur der neunziger Jahre aus interkultureller Sicht*, ed. Matthias Harder. Würzburg: Königshausen & Neumann. 43–62.

Winkler, Katja. 2003. "Ein ganz 'netter deutscher Trampel'." *die tageszeitung*, 27 January: 14.

II

TRADITIONS
History, Memory, and Narrative

LAUREL COHEN-PFISTER

Perhaps no greater dichotomy influences cultural memory in the Federal Republic today than the drive to present a "normal," democratic German nation within the context of a European Union concurrent with the need to recognize and validate different German pasts in the last century. While the former trend transcends national borders even as it seeks to transcend history, the latter remains rooted within the country's historical, geographical, and social boundaries (cf. Eigler 2005, 18). Their dialectical interplay in the cultural landscape of the Berlin Republic connects with a literary tradition of questioning German identity in the postwar period just as it expands this tradition with new motives and themes predicated precisely on the realities of German life in the twenty-first century.

The essays in this section explore literary responses to the forces that shape an understanding of self, community, and nation in Germany today. As literature confronts and helps to mold contemporary perceptions of German identity, it questions exactly what "normality" in the Berlin Republic implies. What does it mean today to be German and what are the boundaries of Germanness? What past(s) will be remembered and which voices heard as post-*Wende* Germany creates a new identity narrative both in opposition to and heedful of the history it overtakes?[1] Cultural responses reflect a stark polarity—from "a yearning to escape the fixity of established subject positions, a longing for 'otherness' and the experience of 'difference'" (Plowman 2004, 259) to the "renationalization of German identity" (Monteath and Alter 1997, 12). Within the changed sociopolitical and cultural contexts of unification, globalization, and multiculturalism, ethnocentric cultural understandings of Germanness collide with notions of alterity. The relationship between history, memory of this history, and personal narrative provides striking insight into the plurality of currents informing both private and national self-understanding in the Berlin Republic.

Patricia Anne Simpson begins this inquiry by noting the contradiction between increasingly diverse understandings of self and the constriction of identity positions under normalization. Normalization, she notes, requires a focus on the present—a kind of selective historical amnesia—that further marginalizes or suppresses particularized German stories and histories. Yet, gendered, historical, and ethnically inflected boundaries exist that resist a "normalization" of German identity in the postunification period. Simpson examines a range of works where ethnicity, race, gender, or an unrelenting awareness of Germany's preunification history provides the basis for alternative identities. Using selected works by Feridun Zaimoglu, Jakob Hein, and Hans-Ulrich Treichel, Simpson outlines how contemporary German literature continues to engage the past and, in doing so, calls on a plurality of histories that inform the construct of nation and an understanding of identity. Simultaneously, this literature of resistance reassesses paradigms of masculinity and postwar gender roles, creating with varying degrees of consciousness a gendered ethics in regard to different German histories. Her examination of Zaimoglu's novels *German Amok* (2002) and *Leyla* (2006), Jakob Hein's *Mein erstes T-Shirt* (My First T-Shirt, 2001), and Hans-Ulrich Treichel's *Menschenflug* (Human Flight, 2005) shows how these novels portray subjective identities informed by diverse sociohistorical experiences. Where Zaimoglu contests cultural, ethnic, and gender stereotypes, Hein recuperates the East German experience; Treichel illustrates that the trauma of the German past—here displacement from Eastern territories at the end of World War II—continues to challenge personal identity. Simpson concludes that these works nuance and complicate the idea of a new German normality; they engage a discourse of historical traumas that the premise of normalization would seek to isolate.

Sydney Norton analyzes cultural responses to the Allied bombings of German cities. Her study supports Simpson's claim that history cannot be elided in contemporary constructions of German identity. Norton turns attention to the German ethnocentric experience of suffering from the Allied bombings and its meaning for German national identity. Her examination of textual responses to the air war addresses a revitalized discourse in the Berlin Republic on Germans as victims of National Socialism and World War II. At the same time, it phrases the questions of guilt and complicity that today challenge a one-dimensional interpretation of victimhood. Norton's choice of texts invokes the question to what degree repressed trauma inhabits and informs cultural expression and personal self-understanding of the generations that experienced firsthand the horrors of the bombings. The texts *Hamburg 1943* (2003) and *Zeugen der Zerstörung* (Witnesses of Destruction, 2003), both from Volker Hage, Gerhard Richter's 2005 work "Mustangs," and the 1998 documentary *Little Dieter Needs to Fly* by Werner Herzog all contest rigidified frameworks of national identity. Hage's anthologies contribute to a more differentiated understanding of victim groups, while Herzog's documentary underscores one individual's ability both to suffer trauma and to inflict it in different historical contexts. At a time where war dominates the headlines, Richter's text suggests that the mundaneness of the present overshadows our perceptions of history and that time and space diffuse and deconstruct the historical experience of wartime trauma. All these texts suggest that unresolved trauma from war hides behind the façade of normality. Norton's theses raise questions about the complex relationship between war memories, the art they inspire, and the political positions on war taken by artists with such memories. Norton also draws into question the ethics of aestheticizing memory when the boundaries between fact and fiction are blurred.

Laurel Cohen-Pfister continues with these themes in her study of Tanja Dückers's novel *Himmelskörper* (Heavenly Bodies, 2003). Where Norton's texts focus primarily on the World War II memories of first- and second-generation Germans, Dückers's novel offers a perspective from the third postwar generation of Germans, the generation of the grandchildren. Cohen-Pfister's analysis probes this generational shift in perspective on the legacies of National Socialism, World War II, and the Holocaust and its significance in defining self-understanding in the third generation. Dückers's novel implies that the German past maintains a firm yet unwanted grip on the grandchildren of the perpetrators, who, though thoroughly educated on the atrocities committed under National Socialism, find it difficult to associate these crimes with their grandparents. Understanding history assumes a most private imperative: to comprehend the self within the historical continuity of the family. With its conscious aestheticization of family memory, *Himmelskörper* deconstructs family myth in relation to historical knowledge in order to question the authenticity and transmission of memory. The philosophical underpinnings that Cohen-Pfister deciphers in the novel's aesthetic project parallel in part Norton's reading of Richter's art. By questioning the legitimacy of the artifact, notably the photograph, to relay historical truth, the reader is required to seek this truth, and thus expose the falsehood or hypocrisy of the representation. This process reflects in Dückers's novel the highly private focus of such a pursuit for the generation of grandchildren. Although the legacy of National Socialism continues to influence identity into the third postwar generation of memory, the perspective on this history is more distanced. Historical inquiry represents not the collective social conscience of the nation, but rather the search to understand self and family against the unavoidable backdrop of German history.

The final study in this section, John Pizer's essay on Emine Sevgi Özdamar, returns to themes iterated in Simpson's essay as he explores notions of alterity and diversity in contemporary cultural memory. Pizer sees in Özdamar's oeuvre a persistent effort to recuperate a tolerant, multiculturally inscribed memory from the forces of globalization and ethnic whitewashing. The Turkish-German author's trilogy of *Life is a Caravanserai* (1992), *Die Brücke vom Goldenen Horn* (The Bridge across the Golden Horn, 1998), and *Seltsame Sterne starren zur Erde* (Strange Stars Gaze toward the Earth, 2003) lauds to varying degrees the multicultural vibrancy of now vanished sociopolitical domains in both Turkey and Germany. In this trilogy, the tolerance accorded to ethnically diverse cultures in the Ottoman Republic, long subsumed by forced national homogenization, mirrors the respect for ethnic alterity in former East Berlin, which disappeared, along with the East German city's unique ambience, after unification.

Özdamar's novels, argues Pizer, create a countermemorial to the erasure of these cultural identities. By reclaiming their cultural richness and vibrancy without falling prey to nostalgic whitewashing of their failings, Özdamar resists the official "Westernized" histories of these domains. Her novel *Seltsame Sterne starren zur Erde* most clearly relates the writer's countermemorial project to the memory politics of contemporary Germany. This autobiographical narrative of the author's experiences in divided Berlin in the 1970s posits in the East qualities that the author misses in postunification Germany. Özdamar avoids the *Ostalgie* of some contemporary works from the former East, as she articulates the bureaucracy and chicaneries of the GDR police state. Still, she recuperates the East Berlin experience with this narrative testament to its creative vitality and its tolerance and celebration of ethnic richness. In this manner, concludes Pizer, the author addresses the irony of increased interethnic tensions in the age of globalized identities. Just as Özdamar criticizes the denigration of the East Berlin experience with her positive countermemorial, she also models with her depiction of East Berlin her vision for a more ethnically integrated culture in postunification Germany.

Collectively these essays witness literature's attempt to address the ambiguities of identity invoked or exacerbated by unification. Despite the diversity of texts discussed here, most thematize a consciousness of, and at times a resistance to, the frailty of personal understandings of self—those grounded in individualized historical experience—in the face of greater sociopolitical forces. These narratives illustrate that personal memory remains inextricably tied to different German pasts of the twentieth century, most notably to the histories of National Socialism, migration, and Germany's division and unification. As such, their diverging cultural constructs of Germanness and German "normality" in the twenty-first century offer a cultural contestation to the forces in unification that threaten to overwhelm their individual sociohistorical experience.

Notes

1. For more on the postunification process of "normalization" and its effect on German culture, see Taberner (2005) and Taberner and Cooke, eds. (2006).

Works Cited

Eigler, Friederike. 2005. "Writing in the New Germany: Cultural Memory and Family Narratives." *German Politics and Society*. 76.3: 16–41.

Monteath, Peter, and Reinhard Alter. 1997. Introduction. *Rewriting the German Past: History and Identity in the New Germany*, ed. Reinhard Alter and Peter Monteath. Atlantic Highlands, NJ: Humanities Press.

Plowman, Andrew. 2004. "*Westalgie*? Nostalgia for the 'Old' Federal Republic in Recent German Prose." *seminar* 40.3: 249–61.

Taberner, Stuart. 2005. *German Literature of the 1990s and Beyond: Normalization and the Berlin Republic*. Studies in German Literature, Linguistics, and Culture, ed. James Hardin. Rochester, NY: Camden House.

Taberner, Stuart, and Paul Cooke, eds. 2006. *German Culture, Politics, and Literature into the Twenty-first Century: Beyond Normalization*. Studies in German Literature, Linguistics, and Culture, ed. James Hardin. Rochester, NY: Camden House.

5

DEGREES OF HISTORY IN CONTEMPORARY GERMAN NARRATIVES

PATRICIA ANNE SIMPSON

It is not often that normality makes headlines. Yet in his work on contemporary literature, Stuart Taberner focuses on the processes that have
established a new political "normality" since unification. Normality
informs a discourse beyond the traumas of German history, genocide,
and subsequent division into two nations with their respective opposi-
tional ideologies. Unification provides the historical basis of a national
self-awareness that insists on an ethos of the present. In other words,
some aspects of German normality rely on a kind of forgetting, under-
written by the aesthetics of the moment. While it is unproductive to question the grounding of the Federal Republic in the political, intellectual,
and economic structures of the democratic West, certain trends in contemporary literature reveal a resistance to normalization of the cultural
status quo in Germany. This resistance erupts in the form of a narrative
insertion of ethical remembering, or a conscious choice to forget. These
textual moments reveal a shifting relationship to German history.

In this essay, I foreground several narratives that probe the relationships between their literary present and varying "degrees" of German
history, defined as the respective narrators' position vis-à-vis migration, unification, and World War II. The narratives under consideration
challenge an assumption that specifically German histories can recede
unproblematically into the background. They also reassess postwar
gender roles and paradigms. As they redefine the relationship between
a range of historically specific male identities and the category of the
national, these texts and their authors revise postwar masculinities
in particular. In many ways, the new normality amounts to a revised
palette of masculinities that are "German" in general but inflected by
ethnicity and national genealogies.

In the early 1990s, violence from the right tended to shape the discourse about German national identity. Historical events, including

the wave of violence toward visible minorities, a countermovement informed by the cosmopolitan ideals of multiculturalism, the election of Gerhard Schröder, and the move toward European integration have widened the frame of reference for what a German identity might mean. In political terms "normal," according to Taberner and Paul Cooke, signals that Germany became "an accepted and respected partner, a widely admired champion of co-operation and peaceful coexistence, an esteemed friend to its former enemies, and a country which had learnt from its past and successfully aligned itself with liberal, democratic values" (2006, 1). The consequences of political normality become legible in the prose fiction of several contemporary authors, among them Feridun Zaimoglu, Jakob Hein, and Hans-Ulrich Treichel. Their diverse characters engage the layers of German history that the rubric of political normalization has subsumed into a totalized present. Peter Schneider in his narrative, *The Wall Jumper*, asks the question: "Where does a state end and a self begin?" (1983, 95). I would instead like to ask, where does the relationship to German history in contemporary narrative end and the self begin?

In the context of contemporary literature, the question arises in ways that set in motion a Hegelian dialectic of identity and difference. Issues of personal and national pasts, boundaries, and borders—both of the literal and figural kind—persist. They are accompanied by the problem of understanding the policing of those borders. The boundaries are gendered, generic, historical, generational, and ethnically inflected. The plural histories in Germany define degrees of proximity to a contemporary sense of identity, though still with ambivalence about the relationship between a self and the German nation. The desire for positive national sentiment conflicts with the fear of pathological articulations of any nationalism. This ambivalence infuses the discourse of "New Patriotism" in the Federal Republic. The new "German" feeling does cause concern about political and cultural normalization at the same time. In an excerpt from his book on Germans, Matthias Matussek, cultural editor of *Der Spiegel*, questions the German commitment to national sentiment and quotes the Turkish writer Mely Kiyak: "'How can anyone expect us to identify ourselves with Germany when even the Germans themselves do not?'" (2006).[1] Matussek disparages the inability to develop a new German sensibility, referring to the collective German "we" as the "illiterates of national feeling." Instead, he calls for a transhistorical view of Germany, proclaiming the end of the postwar era. Moreover, he insists: "The construct 'nation' is being reexamined, and everyone is asking the question of identity, even we Germans." Like others who respond to the notion of a contemporary German normalization that includes patriotic intelligence, as opposed to an unreflective national chauvinism, Matussek reverts to a stable sense of self in the face of transnational trends that threaten any naturalized relationship between a self and a state or system of government. "Without a positive identification with our nation, as many prudent people (*Besonnene*) from the Federal President on down have understood," he writes, "our country, in the age of globalization and of jihadist confrontations, will blow up in our faces." He resorts to cultural patriotism: "For a considerable length of time now, a new, carefree generation has been heard and seen, in the movie theaters as well as in literature or pop culture. It is cosmopolitan, it is successful (*unverkracht*), and it is Germany."

Others strike a different note about contemporary patriotism. Thomas Brussig admits to having worn the national colors in response to the soccer fervor that saturated Germany during the World Cup games in summer 2006. With due diligence, he explains the reticence he experienced in the wake of unification: "In 1990, many German flags were being waved, but *not by me*" (2006). In retrospect, the political shouts of euphoria and unity drowned out the more skeptical and suspicious voices in both the East and the West with regard to German unification, but all will recall the reinvigorated use of German national symbols. Brussig proclaims with relief the death of the "old patriotism," to be replaced by the new. However, Brussig does not offer any helpful definitional language: "New patriotism means: not the old one. Another one. We're still trying" (2006). In this piece, Brussig resumes the search for a patriotic feeling appropriate to German history, but remains cautious about preserving the rights of those who are not getting all that excited about Germany.

One of those with a right to count himself among the unexcited would be Feridun Zaimoglu, acclaimed author and assertive commentator. Without pulling the punches of his critiques aimed at the economic realities for immigrants in Germany, Zaimoglu insists on the rights of immigrants to belong as enthused citizens of the nation: "I want to see Turks *waving the German flag* en masse. That would by no means be an overly patriotic gesture. On the contrary, it would be taken here as a welcome sign of commitment. The immigrants, their sons, and their daughters can be bound to honor and conscience by a common oath. They belong there, they are not foreign bodies, and they will not be abandoned to their fate" (2006). Zaimoglu, who is widely known for his role in the Kanaksta movement,[2] his realist fiction, and his critical voice, here advocates flag-waving as a signal of national affiliation from the "migrant kids" (*Migrantenkids*). His literary work averts that type of earnest pledging, however, and his own characters display a fraught relationship to German history, particularly when confronted with those who would use it for aesthetic effect. Zaimoglu eschews moralizing in his writing, and for that reason, the ethical moments involved in recoding any relationship between contemporary German or ethnic masculinity and German history are even more compelling.

In his fiction and nonfiction alike, Zaimoglu charts a possible "patriotic" response from Turkish-Germans to the processes of political and cultural normalization in the Federal Republic. Many are grappling with the range of consequences generated by the new normality. In their work on the politics and culture of twenty-first-century Germany, Taberner and Cooke highlight the potential for re-marginalizing certain social groups based on ethnicity, race, and gender. In their introduction to a volume on Germany's entrance into this century, they write: "And what of Germans from the former East, or of women within a political culture dominated by men of a particular *West* German generation, or of ethnic minorities, for whom the focus on the Nazi past within the currently fashionable conceptualization of German normality may exclude their historical and biographical experience or be incommensurate with it?" (2006, 11). In charting the landscape of contemporary literature, it is crucial to include the texts that offer sites of resistance to normalization.

Many readers, reviewers, and scholars have welcomed the shift in literary discourse. The literary discussion about the aesthetics of moral principle (*Gesinnungsästhetik*), the controversy surrounding Christa Wolf, the objection to historical relativization of genocide, and the charged atmosphere of seemingly incorrigible violence against minorities has begun to accommodate a series of happier headlines that announce the new lightness of German reading. The scholarly reception, too, echoes the reviewers' embrace of novels with plots, realism, and a high degree of readability.[3] An article in *The New York Times* encapsulates the trend in the headline: "The New German Novel: Less Weighty, More Exportable." Carter Dougherty opens the *Times* piece with reference to Sven Regener's *Herr Lehmann* (2001; *Berlin Blues*, 2003), a debut novel that was adapted for the screen, though the novel enjoyed greater acclaim. The element of humor, also present in Daniel Kehlmann's 2005 runaway bestseller *Die Vermessung der Welt* (*Measuring the World*, 2006),[4] adds to sales, and Dougherty devotes much attention to more welcoming markets for German fiction. Critics and reviewers of Kehlmann's novel, which has sold more than one million copies, note that it animates the unlikely nineteenth-century personae of Alexander von Humboldt and Carl Friedrich Gauß. Both figures achieved renown through devotion to the belief in science, instruments, and duty: Humboldt explores the inhospitable, far-flung

realm of South America, while Gauß experiences the limiting episte-
mology of charting the planets by surveying German soil. Gauß exhibits a greater skepticism about the ability to know nature and the world,
and Humboldt exhibits fanatical commitment to his work, accompanied by the unsavory traits of political opportunism. Both characters
ultimately inhabit the attributes of German Enlightenment masculinity that are subject to satire in Kehlmann's bestseller. But his welcoming reception is informed by his singular co-optation of a distanced
German history, effectively eluding the burdened German past.

That past, too, defines contemporary fiction. Dougherty also refers
to the great success of Bernhard Schlink's *The Reader* (1997) after Oprah
Winfrey recommended it to members of her book club. The latter novel
would hardly fall into the "less weighty" category, but sold well nonetheless. The characters, burdened by both the history of National Socialism and the judgmental and occasionally self-righteous anti-German
stance of the 1968 generation, displayed sexualities and subjectivities
informed by national history. It may be time to reconsider or at least
differentiate the "lightness" or "readability" of more recent critical and
commercial success stories. It seems the taking up of specifically German historical burdens in contemporary narrative has become optional.
Forgetting the fraught past or, at the very least, lapses in memory, can
now be forgiven because of normalization, generational succession, and
distance to historical trauma. Much scholarship on contemporary literature rightly locates certain aspects of current prose in the confluence of
economic and historical forces, primarily those driven by globalization
and "glocalization." However, this approach implies that characters in
fiction are little more than allegories of subjectivities shaped by larger
forces. While there is certainly truth to this implication, there are coun-
tertrends as well. In the remainder of this essay, I examine more closely
works of fiction by authors who engage German history from varying
degrees of distance. The moments of resistance to this near casualness
toward history in prose fiction and nonfiction assert themselves, curi-
ously enough, in a pattern that raises questions about the representation of masculinity, normality, and gendered ethics.

The characters inscribed in Zaimoglu's *German Amok* (2002) specifically problematize the impact of unification on their respective
narrative arcs, but with attention to the commodification of ethnic
identity in some social circles. The art world and the culture industry
in general are subjected to the sharpest satire, and encounters with
the new East prove devastating. In Hein's *Mein erstes T-Shirt* (My First
T-Shirt, 2001), the reader gains insight into the coming-of-age story of
a character, not accidentally named Jakob Hein, whose engagement

with politics is contingent upon daily life. In both prose works, possible deviations from the semantic field of the new German normal are inscribed with attention to collective cultural memory. In Treichel's *Menschenflug* (Human Flight, 2005), the author interrogates the meaning of history—and the rejection of history's potential to explain identity—as it can shape or define contemporary subjectivity. This fiction covers a lot of territory, but there is a red thread: in these works, literature circumscribes an imaginative space in which characters respond to and resist historical definition of their identity by analyzing their own responses to issues of gender, nation, and the role these play in constructing a sense of self.

Feridun Zaimoglu and the Ethics of Ethnic Masculinity

Without doubt, the master signifier of *nation* still defines contemporary thinking about prose fiction. The motivation is explicable: languages can be associated with a specific national geography. Homi K. Bhabha has theorized a "third space" and "in-between" to designate the articulation of culture's hybridity, and some have maintained the efficacy of this model for reading Turkish-German literature.[5] Identity is constituted by the "in-between" of the colonial and the postcolonial subject. This model, however, elides, if not erases, certain historical and cultural specifics. Moreover, it is not a good fit for the Turkish-German cultural condition. Leslie A. Adelson challenges the applicability of this "third space" to work by Turkish-German authors. She criticizes the "between-two-worlds" model because "it does more to assuage anxieties about worlds, nations, and cultures in flux than it does to grasp the cultural innovations that migration engenders" (2005, 5). We are caught in an uncomfortable dilemma about the tendency to read the work of Turkish-German authors sociologically, rather than aesthetically, but "realism" must be examined more closely for its intentional indexes to historical relevance. In other words, despite the effort not to read certain types of literature as commentaries on reality, they sometimes are. The social informs the aesthetic. By contrast, Zaimoglu's novel offers a countermodel in which normalization leads to an ethnically inflected, ethical regulation of an aesthetic reading of German history.

German Amok (2002) is a scathing satire of the 1990s Berlin art scene and the brutality of human relationships therein. Taberner has described the narrator of this novel as a Turkish-German artist who occupies an exoticized status due to the commodification of ethnic difference (2006, 216–18). Taberner's reading is insightful, but I claim that gender difference and awareness play a more prominent role in the process of normalization and in Zaimoglu's own resistance to cultural and ethnic profiling. Some reviewers savaged the book.[6] In it, the "Kunstfotze" or "art cunt" (aka Frau Birgit Laarsen) dominates the local art scene and its artists. Her performance pieces and insatiable sexual appetite make great demands on a range of characters from the narrator, his neighbor Clarissa, and some unsuspecting leeches; she embodies the decadence, self-indulgence, and self-importance that insure a successful artistic career in this milieu. Her predatory sexuality and superficial art regulate the scene—no one wants to cross her—that thrives on defining itself in opposition to bourgeois concepts of the normal or conventional.

Zaimoglu's narrator participates grudgingly in this whole enterprise. While some contemporary fiction inhabits the negative spaces of melancholy, embarrassment, and shame, Zaimoglu counters with a sense of shamelessness and disgust in this work. The damaged, self-mutilating "Mongo-Maniac," Clarissa, who becomes the narrator's recalcitrant flatmate, also gets involved with the rapacious art cunt. She animates the suddenly jealous narrator, whose every move redefines any concept of ethnic masculinity against the background of effete German males—betrayed and beguiled boyfriends populate the novel. The putative misogyny, however, morphs into something else. The text itself provides a refuge from the highly mediated stereotype of the "Turk in the arcade" or the woman in a headscarf. Zaimoglu's narrator recognizes innocence in a context that lacks any moral compass in part by subjecting himself to the same critical lens with which he sees the world. In addition, along with innocence comes an ethical imperative to remember German history.

The brushes with history come when a friend hires the narrator to serve as stage designer for a Butoh dance workshop, a type of avant-garde performance dance that originated in postwar Japan. A group of artists plans to stage the performance in an old Russian barracks in the newly opened East. The encounters between the art troupe, which reflects a variety of ethnic origins and sexual preferences, and the locals (provincial yokels) are stereotypical. The "Ostpack" ("Eastern riff-raff") (162) of skinheads attacks them, with the tacit approval of the locals. The art collective itself, there to perform and enact a ritual of self-healing, is fraught with conflict, jealousy, and abuse. OPP TIKK, a dancer whose ethnic difference and dubious experiences in off-theater in Japan credential her, is the creative force behind the endeavor. Her codirector and husband, Daniel, who sought the narrator's help in the first place, insisted, once on site, that women ruled, but there is a mutiny and he himself is deposed. Mauritius Pink takes over the direction of the project and conceptualizes it in three parts, harmony, recuperation (*Erholung*), and "total gas." Upon hearing this plan—while he is attempting to get reimbursed for five hundred Marks' worth of used pornographic magazines he bought for the stage set—the narrator loses his otherwise steely composure: "Pink, you just can't take the extermination of Jews and turn it into kitsch, a cheap metaphor . . . After Auschwitz, gas as metaphor is taboo!" (219).[7]

In the context of this argument between the protagonist and Pink, German history comes to the foreground. Pink responds with the litany of German self-hatred: "Don't piss me off with your boy scout antifascism. I am being consistent. I am opposing German self-hatred, the tendency to rip ourselves apart, with anti-Enlightenment exaggeration. Colonial Beauty is the word. As a foreigner you're not part of the conversation" (219). The "foreign" body of the narrator, excluded from German history, provides a commentary on Pink's abuse of history: "His iron resolve to help himself from history as if it were a theater prop room comes from an intellectual lightness of foot" (220). The narrator connects this mentality with Pink's willingness to offer up his body to OPP TIKK's ministrations, to be penetrated anally with a dildo, and later by the narrator himself. In a moment of angry attraction, the narrator has sex with Pink on his own terms. When it is over, Zaimoglu describes the narrator's reaction to Pink's submission: "When Pink turns around, he searches for a sign of shame or rage, but I smile at him, give him a wink" (237). In this artists' collective, Pink, who aestheticizes history, readily seeks and enjoys being dominated, and the narrator shares no sense of shame or guilt; he is in charge. By denying guilt or shame, his sexual dominance asserts historical superiority as well.

The Turkish-German narrator resets the moral compass of this scene without any attempt to occupy the high ground. He becomes protective of Clarissa, his withdrawn, aggressive neighbor. When he discovers that Clarissa is involved with the art cunt, he becomes jealous. He gains understanding for Songül, the friend who brought him to the art cunt's performance at the novel's early stage. Songül, to whom he is attracted, is the daughter of uneducated Anatolian parents. When the narrator learns that she has the "virus," he exclaims "Songül, a martyr of love!" (20). In an exchange between her and the narrator, he comments on her close observation of the naked men in the art cunt's performance, stating that she had been "staring at the black guys' dicks"; in response she hits him (26). Where she sees art, he sees pornography. The protagonist's art in Zaimoglu's novel is described as unfashionably realistic; it is created with the intent to shock without the ability to do so (196). Contemporary Germany, represented by this cast of characters of sexual predators and charlatans parading as artists, is hard to shock, particularly in light of Pink's glib use of gas as metaphor. Nonetheless, novelist Zaimoglu does succeed in shocking the reader through his insistence on the tragic nature of his material and the ability of his narrator to gain insight into innocence and its loss.

The narrative invokes Songül after the character herself recedes from the story. At one point, the narrator goes shopping and listens to the neighborhood produce seller tell his story:

> I buy tomatoes and feta from the produce guy, he asks as always about a wife and kids. I say, there's time for that, and with the glut of black-friendly Turkish floozies, I'd much prefer a German woman. He is moved and embraces me with heartfelt sympathy, for I have taken the words right out of his heart and mouth, whichever. He is a member of an extreme right-wing male militia against adaptation (*Anpassung*), he sent his grown daughters back to Turkey just in time to prevent a catastrophe—they had begun to wear eye shadow and to flirt with German men. Their hymens were still intact when their father handed them over to upstanding (almost of age) Turks, it is said, they were safe. Poor Songül. (2002, 194)

The sensibility of Zaimoglu's narrator shifts in this moment, away from his worship of Songül as the right woman for him, however infected she may be, to one of sympathy. The portrait of Songül reminds the reader of Sibel, from Fatih Akin's acclaimed film *Head On* (2004), in which the female protagonist pursues multiple sexual partners and suffers from substance abuse to the point of suicide, all in an attempt to redefine herself apart from her loving but conservative and patriarchal family. Here, the novel's narrator acknowledges the limits of Turkish patriarchy and criticizes it. For all the performativity (in Judith Butler's sense) of sex and gender roles in Zaimoglu's fiction, this character takes sides. He refrains from performing as a sexual predator, like the ones, both male and female, who victimize Clarissa. He is indeed the model of a new man whose masculinity is predicated on a culturally and ethnically inflected image of women's role in society.

The content and purpose of Zaimoglu's most recent work, the novel *Leyla* (2006), which is based on his mother's story, align him with many members of his generation who are turning to the history of first-generation migrants in Germany to find their own cultural and political voices.[8] Zaimoglu's novel demonstrates his desire to recover the history of migration as part of a generational identity. In the editorial "My Germany," Zaimoglu cites for his readers the story of women in the first generation in particular as exemplary:

Saying goodbye to a lower class existence and making it into the middle-class world of education and ownership means expending energy
and bracing your nerves—and turning your back on short-term survival
strategies. Here a model is offered by first generation women immigrants. These are the Turkish, Kurdish, and Arab 'rubble women' . . .
who did the impossible and kept their families together in hard times.
And their daughters are now carrying the torch. (2006)

The respect he reveals for the generation of migrant grandmothers calls
for the integration of German history that includes the social history of
ethnic women whose stories go untold.

Jakob Hein's Confessions of a Postsocialist Man

At one point in *German Amok*, OPP TIKK, the directing and driving force
behind Butoh in the new East, accuses the narrator of "normality" that
inhibits his artistic success (2002, 222). Zaimoglu's central figure, who
respects historical ethics and sympathizes with dominated women, represents a new standard of the normal in that work. While the search for
the singular, representative novel (*Wenderoman*) from or about the former GDR continues, the thematization of recent history—focusing on
the former East German states, their demise, and their uniting with the
Federal Republic—continues to find expression in a range of facts and
fictions that attempt to revisit and reconstruct normality in the GDR. The
phenomenon of what I have elsewhere called "retro-nationalism" with
regard to GDR rock music differs distinctly from the nostalgia for things
East German. It is predicated on a represented moment of informed and
critical citizenship, one that evaporated quickly into the atmosphere of
unification (Simpson 2005, 78). The trend observed in music is also manifest in other media, especially those that recast the critical impulses of
popular music. Hein's prose is a retrospective portrayal of a male youth
and his political and personal coming-of-age in relationship to the East
German nation with its questionable internationalist ideology.

Since 1989, a number of novels, films, and works of nonfiction have
appeared that have recuperated the East German experience and made
it available, with varying degrees of success, to an international public:
films such as *Good Bye Lenin!* and *Sonnenallee* are among them, as are collections or novels such as Ingo Schulze's *Simple Storys*. Some works, especially Hein's *Mein erstes T-Shirt*, inscribe a version of GDR normality that
in some cases overlaps with or in others departs from the widespread

representations of life in the West. In the latter, higher levels of consumer culture, multiculturalism and its tensions, harder drugs, and far-flung international travel cut a sharper profile. In the former, retrospective looks intersect more quickly with self-consciousness about personal participation in history, attributable in part to the high saturation of everyday life with the ideological and political practices of socialism.

In *Mein erstes T-Shirt*, Hein, a practicing psychiatrist and reader/performer in Berlin, published a collection of purportedly autobiographical stories (with Jakob Hein as the main character) that trace the arc of his personal and political maturation. Much is typical: he and his friends form a band, girls break them up, they discover punk, suffer from unpopularity at school, tease their teachers, and experiment with alcohol. However, history and historical narrative intertwine more with sexual political contexts than we find in comparable Western experiences. In "Meine private Hölle" (My Private Hell), for example, the second story in the volume, Hein laments the "dishonest" quality of rock in the 1980s; in response, he and his friends lay the groundwork for their own band. For the narrator, recalling this time evokes bad memories, ones that weave the plight of the malcontent adolescent with the larger imperiousness of GDR policies:

> Completely impoverished, I roamed the streets of East Berlin at that time. In search of a net shirt I could wear over a pullover, for a couple of rhinestones for said pullover, for a disco that catered to the sixteen-and-under crowd, for a cure for acne vulgaris. But in the dictatorship of the working class, I did not have a prayer. Don Johnson drove a convertible through the streets of Miami with his three-day beard. I would have to save at least four weeks for such a beard, and probably even longer for the convertible. (2002, 17)

Hein blends the urgent longing of a teenager for better circumstances—some material, some not—with acute awareness of the limited availability of all things retail in the GDR, and some things ephemeral. He does so with humor, in the syllepsis of *sparen*: to save for a beard, a reflection on the state of his hormones, and to save for a convertible, a comment of the state of his impecunious circumstances—but also on the state of production and the general scarcity of cars in the former East.

The element of critique and knowledge of the political stakes of private acts pervade any early memories of the narrator. His personal, physical encounter with a Lenin recording leads to a bloody finger and his becoming an anti-Communist; Western television and comic books threaten not only personal development, but also the future of socialism; and every kid bears and shares responsibility for world peace. Music, particularly punk, became associated with the culture of criticism capable of eliciting serious reprisals from the state.[9] In the story of a private hell, Hein cites the example of his friend and musical accomplice Marco, who produced the beginning: "'Get rid of the State, get rid of the cops, get rid of everything, punk's not dead'. Could have been a classic, but we would have had to make up a couple of filler lines" (2002, 21). Later stories address the issue of punk and criticism more directly and earnestly. In the story "Rinks und lechts" (Reft and Light), the narrator describes his first punk concert in a church as "paradise" (2002, 126), with reference to the "open work" of the Protestant church in the GDR of the 1980s.[10] The specifics of GDR politics, combined with the narrator's personal interpretation of their effect on him, distinguish the recollections and embed them in an alternative normality.

The most prominent examples of GDR-specific normality involve the relationship between sexuality and ideology. In the story "Rinks und lechts," for example, Hein harkens back to the world of the fourteen-year-old in the GDR, and recalls his sorry lot: "At the mercy of teachers narrow-minded unto death, home by midnight, no money of your own, constantly following all sorts of ridiculous fashions and even then not getting close to Jessica Drechsler" (124). A compensatory relationship between the sacrifices of a socialist adolescence and a preoccupation with politics emerges: "In order not to have to think about Jessica so often, I spent my time with ideology" (124). For him, music constitutes ideology; he continues with praise of Nick Cave and the ability of music to create enclaves of critical consciousness. Hein's matter-of-fact delivery is painfully funny—there is innocence in his diction that allows the reader to remain neutral, to cast off any preconceptions about life in the former GDR. Hein describes a past relieved of the West German preoccupation with postwar guilt. The GDR bred other demons, certainly, but Hein revisits them without rancor in this collection, from symptoms of a systematic pedagogic failure to the omniscient presence of the Stasi. Still, sexuality informs politics.

In the story "Die Mauer in meinem Kopf" (The Wall in My Head), the narrator, who has limited luck with both men and women, gets the present of a friend's girlfriend on Nikolaus Day, celebrated on 6 December. Sarah, the "gift," discourages Hein from picking her up at school: this would upset her ex-boyfriend, a Nazi skinhead. The narrator reports his surprise at seeing her photos from the previous summer, in which she appeared to be an authentic skin girl: "I was shocked, but she had learned from her mistakes and now looked like a girl should: backcombed hair, pale face, white shirt, black clothes" (114). She had switched allegiances from one youth cultural extreme to the other, from right to left, in a matter of months. With sex on his mind, they visit her gynecologist, where Sarah gets birth-control pills. When they first have sex, he tries to consider her pleasure: "But then it was over just too unexpectedly, unbelievably, and uncommonly quickly. It was rather embarrassing that I'd just thrown my good sex education overboard for a cheap orgasm" (117). His embarrassment deepens the next morning, when Sarah awakes all cuddly and romantic. Full of self-recrimination, he thinks of her: "Raped without an orgasm or a condom!" (118). Hein takes comfort in the fact that Sarah's parents have officially applied to leave for the West and will take their daughter and all memory of his humiliating sexual exploits with them. Before she leaves, Sarah converts again, this time to a rockabilly boyfriend, but from the narrator's perspective, she cannot leave fast enough. His disappointing experience in this relationship organizes his feelings about the Wall, which he measures by its ability to intervene on his behalf. It plays a part in his personal history: "I didn't hate the Wall any longer, but it hadn't been particularly helpful either in a decisive moment" (118).

The gap between the narrator's belief in sexual equality and his ability to achieve it in personal performance produces the feelings of shame and embarrassment associated with this early sexual encounter. In other words, Hein puts his adolescent GDR masculinity on the line, on the page, and holds it up to close public scrutiny. The most prominent female figure in the story cycle is the narrator's mother, whose humor, progressive thinking, and good sense, combined with a nurturing and unobtrusive presence, perhaps account, at least in part, for the narrator's concern for his girlfriend's satisfaction. His female contemporaries populate the margins of the stories, which focus primarily on male bonds and their relationships to larger political and social structures. There are points of political continuity within the protagonist's development, the most significant of which is the reincarnation of GDR normality as a commitment to the highly theoretical equality of women, both in society and in bed.

Hans-Ulrich Treichel and Flight from the Past

Zaimoglu's narrator knows no shame, remorse, or embarrassment with the exception of his relationship to German history and a growing sense of women as victims in multiple cultural contexts. The quiet sense of personal embarrassment in Hein's work connects with a more light-hearted awareness of German-German history: the Wall's refusal to cooperate in helping him avoid painful recollections regarding his own sexual performance. The leitmotifs of shame, embarrassment, and unease likewise surface in the works of Hans-Ulrich Treichel, whose 1998 novel *Der Verlorene* (*Lost*, 2000) gained critical acclaim for Treichel, who is also professor at the Literaturinstitut in Leipzig. Rhys W. Williams calls attention to the "masterly portrayal of embarrassment, vulnerability, even trauma" in Treichel's work, and concludes: "His apparent retreat into the personal and private does not betoken a refusal to ask fundamental social and political questions, so much as an indirect method of addressing precisely those questions" (2002, 208).

In this final section, I turn to Treichel's 2005 novel *Menschenflug* (Human Flight), for a text that carries my argument to its uncomfortable conclusion. In this novel, which won the 2006 Kritikerpreis (Critics Prize), the author attempts to close the file on a debilitating exploration of family history that intersects with national tragedy, specifically the displacement of Germans from the East. The suffering of Germans during and after the war is a complex emotional and political issue, one that W. G. Sebald's work in some ways reopened. In his work, Treichel explores the legacy of a displaced family, following the main character, Stephan, on a conclusive journey into his past in order to find a lost brother and fulfill his parents' desire for familial wholeness. Stephan's parents were displaced after the war, and in his youth, he learns of an older brother lost during their trek through Poland. The unspoken traumas of the mother's rape and the father's possible execution haunt the narrator. In the narrative present, the knowledge of his father's early death looms large for Stephan, who works as a permanent part-time academic advisor in the field of German as a Foreign Language. Also a writer, he takes a leave of absence from work and his family for a year in search of a self that may or may not exist in such a way that it can be "found."

In many ways, this novel is an extension of the 1998 family romance Treichel explored in *Der Verlorene*. In that work, the narrator is full of guilt and shame, in part due to his resistance to his parents' efforts to find the lost older brother. The burden of guilt permeates the domestic scene, driving the mother into depression and a nervous breakdown, and the father into a distancing and rigid discipline. The child at home, burdened with an array of annoying nervous habits from carsickness to grinning at inappropriate times, is acutely aware that he is a disappointment to his parents. The negative emotions, repressed to preserve some sense of family stability, surface at times of crisis. The narrator's own sense of insignificance is heightened by the competition with a lost brother for parental attention. At one point, when he is old enough, his mother revises the family history, revealing to him that his older brother is not dead, but lost. The bureaucratic pursuit of the lost Arnold begins in earnest.

The younger son is ashamed of his inability to comfort his mother; he feels guilty about everything, from eating to participating in family excursions (1998, 17–18). The family travels to Heidelberg to keep an appointment at an institute for forensic anthropology. The exact measurement of each member's salient features, from the shape of feet to the bones of the head, refutes the parentage of foundling 2307. The disappointed hope triggers the father's crisis. The inability to claim the foundling as his own son and a burglary at home precipitate his heart attack and death. Even for this act he could not have committed, the son feels guilty, imagines himself confessing to the crime, and envisions his fingerprints at the crime scene (129). Eventually the narrator does catch a glimpse of the foundling and assumes the youth is his brother. His mother refuses to look, and the guilt of knowledge carries over into the later novel, with the narrator's devouring past, embodied by the dream mother, at its center.

Nicci Gerrard locates *Der Verlorene* in a context with Bernhard Schlink's *The Reader*, also connecting it to W. G. Sebald's *The Emigrants*: "History as imagination, the novel as a new kind of history. . . ." (2000). I endorse the reviewer's excitement about the potential for fiction to recast history, but ask as well how literature can constitute a new history without being revisionist. What is under revision? The personal reconstruction of both a factual and imagined past seems to be the answer. Further, history enters literary representation in relation to a gendered, ethnic, and national self, however tenuous or arbitrary those affiliations may be. For this reason, it is productive to examine the degrees of historical relationship elected by the characters in contemporary prose. The narrator of *Menschenflug* is conscious of the burdened German past, having written the book about his brother to free himself from metaphorical hereditary illnesses: "arthrosis of the past" and "historical rheumatism" (18) and "phantom pains" (21). Treichel has already explored the territory of a lost sibling (in the earlier work, *Der Verlorene*), and while some reviewers welcome the revisiting of this material, others express impatience. While the latter novel deals with the same thematic, the characters in *Menschenflug* are different incarnations of the same wartime legacy of loss, but they have grown up in context of the "economic miracle." The end of *Menschenflug*, however, takes its characters and the reader past the search for a lost child or sibling, and achieves a closure of sorts. Stephan's own relationships to his family—in this novel there are sisters—are fraught with guilty knowledge of that past, and his relationship to one sister borders on the incestuous. Stephan is married to Helen, a psychoanalyst, and has two stepdaughters from her first marriage. The celebration of Stephan's fifty-second birthday launches a life crisis because his own father died at fifty-four of heart failure. His goal becomes to rid himself of obsessive thoughts. Stephan fulfills a wish to travel to Egypt; has a brief affair and uncomfortable encounters with one reader of his first book, a lost, orphaned brother, Wilhelm, who offers the "du" (informal "you") to the reluctant author. Stephan feels challenged by this precipitous intimacy, and is disturbed by his impatience with the orphaned stranger who behaves as though their historically similar circumstances provide an abiding bond. In other words, Stephan has matured into a character whose emotional lexicon is limited. Family histories, in which war and displacement play a prominent role, are core of his emotional dysfunction.

Gendered familial relationships center Stephan's desire to flee from the oppressive past. In this self-reflexive novel, Helen helps interpret Stephan's disturbing dreams. In this segment, the issue of normality is central. At the breakfast table, she declares his dreams of a devouring mother to be normal. "'Normal?' he asked in return. 'I wake up almost every night, bathed in sweat, in a total panic because my mother is bending over me with the mouth of a shark and either wants to rip me to shreds or even eat me up completely? What's so normal about that?'" (64). Melanie Klein's theories do not carry explanatory weight with Stephan; he avoids therapy even as he tries to recuperate a positive maternal image. He believes that a trip to his father's forcibly abandoned home in Volhynia might release him from his pasts, and he even plans to write a book about the journey, a book against guilt and feelings of guilt (43). In a bookstore, he finds a volume with "his" title by an American author and realizes that his personal explorations have become a literary trend. He is not alone, but that knowledge holds no comfort.

Human flight resonates throughout the text, as intellectual avoidance, as a real monument, as a helicopter lift for a victim of heart failure transported by a "life flight," and as an aesthetic of memory. Treichel's novel recalibrates the relationship between a "self" (Stephan), time, and place. Stephan's ability to remember is not linked to any particular topography: he encounters the pain of memory most acutely in the present, "at locations that did not have the least bit to do with his past" (93). In this sense, *Menschenflug* itself inscribes the act of historical emancipation the main character seeks. Stephan reopens the file on his lost brother, traces his parents' steps in their postwar attempts to locate their firstborn, and comes close to finding him. At that point, one of his sisters resists, for their portion of the parental inheritance is at stake and would have to be shared four ways with the legitimate son. Shocked when confronted by any ambivalence and willing to finance the return of the lost brother to the family fold, Stephan strikes out on his own to visit the middle-aged adopted orphan "Hermann," who may be his brother. Stephan decides to track down his brother alone and travels to his address. But there is no happy reunion. He arrives unannounced at the brother's gate, which remains locked. The lost and now found brother only sees a stranger whose reason for bothering him is unclear. The man threatens Stephan with a crutch. Stephan concludes: "Foundling 2307 was an angry, old, and sick man" (229). Stephan boards the next train, ends up touring a Heimat (folk) celebration, and takes the final leg of his journey back to Berlin in a high-speed intercity train.

This is the final journey to jettison the past and embrace the contingency of one's roots. He has flashes of insight: "Human beings have to have some kind of origin, after all" (225). Treichel loosens and unties any sense of a motivated relationship between the traumatic past and the present. On the train, Stephan experiences his signature embarrassment at cell-phone use on shared transportation, but gets over it: "Now the loud talking did him good . . . All sense of melancholy was gone . . . Ten minutes on the Intercity Hanover–Berlin, and it was as though the whole horrific episode with history and the past (*Geschichts- und Vergangenheitsspuk*) had been obliterated. And the completely normal hatred of the present directed at the telephoning idiots all around him steps right into the place of Stephan's provincial (*weltfern*) Volhynian-melancholy" (229). The hatred he feels for the intrusive talkers around him submerges him in a present, albeit it a noxious one, that frees him from the past. His fury is cleansing: "He felt strong. And a voice inside him kept repeating: No past!" (229). In this moment of immanent presence, he rediscovers a decisive masculinity that is not contingent on national history or even family and sexuality, but on the act of self-emancipation from a genealogical burden.

Treichel's protagonist finds freedom from the burdens of the past in a contentious, even adversarial relationship to the present with all its shortcomings, intrusions, and irritations. It is a completely normal contempt for the present. In each of the prose works discussed in this essay, the characters engage the past and present of one particular layer of specifically German history: Turkish-German (im)migration, the fall of the GDR, and the postwar displaced. Each work opens up a new space for the potential of resistance to totalizing historical moments and movements as completely constitutive of subjective, gendered, ethnic, and national identities. The sense of closure in Treichel's novel comes at a high price: the fate of Stephan, finally flying the "life flight" or *Rettungsflug* of salvation, is ambiguous. Leaving the past may also precipitate death—or not. However, the works I have explored in this essay nuance and complicate any notion of new German normality. They force a reevaluation of "nation" and the narrativization of national history as a category, while cautioning us against any wholesale dismissal of the nation as an organizing structure for the production and consumption of culture. They dwell in the local: an artist's loft, a street corner, a jogging path along a canal, and at the same time they refuse to submit to the vicissitudes of history. The characters in these works select the degree to which a self's relationship to both personal and national pasts are consanguine. Instead, they rely on the postmodern concept of contingency in negotiation with any authentic notion of a self. My focus on male writers and characters in particular foregrounds the issues of contemporary masculinities renegotiating a relationship to the nation and the national past through narrative. My reading of these works by Zaimoglu, Hein, and Treichel challenges a definition of nation as an organic totality, and destabilizes any commitment to German identity as predicated on a naturalized and causal relationship to that nation's plural pasts.

Notes

1. All translations, unless otherwise noted, are my own. All quotations from Matussek originate in this 2006 essay.

2. Many Turkish-Germans of the third generation support the reclamation of the pejorative ethnic slur "Kanak" as a recoded point of pride in identity. Others find the term problematic and avoid it, but Zaimoglu belongs to the former group of advocates.

3. See Finlay and Taberner (2002, 131), who refer to influential reviews by Ulrich Greiner and Frank Schirrmacher.

4. See Harding (2006). Kehlmann's novel first appeared in 2005 and reached its twenty-fourth edition in June 2006.

5. Often quoted from his *The Location of Culture*, 37–38. In order to broach the problem of labels and categories, and taxonomies of authorial belonging, see also Azade Seyhan (2002). She accesses the discourse of borderlands, derived primarily from Chicano/a literature as a "heuristic metaphor," which, she writes, "marks a turning point in contemporary cultural criticism, for it transforms the

notion of a geographical space to include historical sites and passages. It generates a conceptual field where word and act, varying idioms, intellectual legacies, and cultural memories are engaged in confrontation, negotiation, and conversation" (13). The argument weighs in heavily on the side of loss—of memory, of belonging, of cultural collectivity. In addition, Zafer Şenocak's writing deals with the problematic relationship to German history for a migrant community.

6. See Gaschke (2006), who writes: "Insults such as 'cultural mercenary' rained down upon him; repulsive allusions were made to the author's sex life. Zaimoglu knows that he is not entirely innocent in the aggression he attracts; after all, he dishes it out as well—in *German Amok* to the decadent Berlin art world. 'The message of the reviews was perfectly clear, though,' he says. 'Migration-Ali is trying to do artistic. He should forget it.'"

7. For a compelling reading of the "Europeanization" of the Holocaust as a problematic part of Germany's normalization, see Probst (2006).

8. See for example Loh and Güngör (2002, 55–77).

9. The literature on the relationship between punk and criticism in the GDR, and the SED's response to punk as a youth culture, is extensive. For an overview, see Simpson (2001). Further, many original documents have been published regarding the systematic persecution of punks, among others, in the GDR. See, for example, Galenza and Havemeister (1999). A second edition has appeared.

10. In the early 1980s, some Protestant churches in East Germany opened their doors to socially and politically marginalized populations, from punks and gays and lesbians to members of the independent peace movement and alternative performance groups. This "open work" protected a range of activities from support groups to samizdat publications labeled for use "within the church only."

Works Cited

Adelson, Leslie A. 2005. *The Turkish Turn in Contemporary German Literature: Toward A New Critical Grammar of Migration*. New York: Palgrave MacMillan.

Akin, Fatih, dir. 2004. *Head-On*. Bavaria Media GmbH.

Brussig, Thomas. 2006. "Patriots of a New Stripe." *Süddeutsche Zeitung*, 19 June. Trans. Naomi Buck. <http://www.signandsight.com/features/827.html>.

Dougherty, Carter. 2005. "The New German Novel: Less Weighty, More Exportable." *The New York Times*, 20 December. <http://www.nytimes.com/2005/12/20/books/20book.html>.

Finlay, Frank, and Stuart Taberner. (2002). "Emerging Writers: Introduction." *German Life and Letters* 55.2, Special issue (April): 131–36.

Galenza, Ronald and Heinz Havemeister, eds. 1999. *Wir wollen immer artig sein: . . . Punk, New Wave, HipHop, Independent-Szene in der DDR 1980–1990*. Berlin: Schwarzkopf & Schwarzkopf.

Gaschke, Susanne. 2006 . "No More Migration-Ali. At Home Here, Success-
ful Here: Four Portraits of the New Turkish-Origin Middle Class." *Die Zeit*.
Trans. Charlotte Collins (June). Goethe-Institut, *Fikrun wa Fann/Art and
Thought* No 83. <www.goethe.de/ges/rel/prj/ffs/mgr/en1580480.htm>.
Gerrard, Nicci. 2000. "When was the last time you saw my brother? Hans-
Ulrich Treichel never puts a foot wrong in 'Lost'." *Guardian Unlimited*, Sun-
day, 30 January. <www.guardian.co.uk/Archive/Article/0,4273,3956565,00.
html>.
Harding, Luke. 2006. "Unlikely Bestseller Heralds the Return of Lightness and
Humour to German literature." *Guardian*, 19 July. <http://books.guardian.
co.uk/news/articles/0,1823905,00.html>.
Hein, Jakob. 2001; 2nd edition 2002. *Mein erstes T-Shirt*. Foreword by Wladimir
Kaminer. Munich and Zurich: Piper.
Kehlmann, Daniel. 2005; 24th printing 2006. *Die Vermessung der Welt*. Reinbek
bei Hamburg: Rowohlt.
Loh, Hannes and Murat Güngör. 2002. *Fear of a Kanak Planet: HipHop zwischen
Weltkultur und Nazi-Rap*. Höfen: Verlagsgruppe Koch.
Matussek, Matthias. 2006. "Ein neues deutsches Gefühl." *Der Spiegel*, 1 June.
<www.spiegel.de/kultur/gesellschaft/0,1518,419214,00.html>.
Probst, Lothar. 2006. "'Normalization' through Europeanization: The Role of
the Holocaust." In Taberner and Cooke, eds. 2003. 61–74.
Regener, Sven. 2003. *Berlin Blues*, trans. John Brownjohn. London: Vintage.
Schlink, Bernhard. 1997. *The Reader*, trans. Carol Brown Janeway. New York:
Vintage.
Schneider, Peter. 1983. *The Wall Jumper: A Berlin Story*, trans. Leigh Hafrey. New
York: Pantheon.
Seyhan, Azade. 2002. *Writing Outside the Nation*. Princeton, NJ: Princeton Uni-
versity Press.
Simpson, Patricia. 2001. "Soundtracks: GDR Music from 'Revolution' to 'Reuni-
fication'." In *The Power of Intellectuals in Contemporary Germany*, ed. Michael
Geyer. Chicago: University of Chicago Press. 227–48.
———. 2005. "Retro-Nationalism? Rock Music in the Former German Dem-
ocratic Republic (GDR)." In *Rock 'N' Roll and Nationalism: A Multinational
Perspective*, ed. Mark Yoffe and Andrea Collins. Newcastle, UK: Cambridge
Scholars Press. 54–80 and 154–61.
Taberner, Stuart, ed. 2004. *German Literature in the Age of Globalisation*. Birming-
ham, UK: University of Birmingham Press.
Taberner, Stuart. 2006. "From 'Normalization' to Globalization. German Fic-
tion into the New Millennium: Christian Kracht, Ingo Schulze, and Feridun
Zaimoglu." In Taberner and Cooke, eds. 2003. 209–21.
Taberner, Stuart, and Paul Cooke, eds. 2006. *German Culture, Politics, and Lit-
erature into the Twenty-First Century: Beyond Normalization*. Rochester, NY:
Camden House.
Treichel, Hans-Ulrich. 1998. *Der Verlorene*. Frankfurt am Main: Suhrkamp.
———. 2005. *Menschenflug*. Frankfurt am Main: Suhrkamp.

Williams, Rhys W. 2002. "'Mein Unbewusstes kannte . . . den Fall der Mauer und die deutsche Wiedervereinigung nicht': The Writer Hans-Ulrich Treichel." In *German Life and Letters*. Special Issue on *Emerging Writers*, Guest Editors Frank Finlay and Stuart Taberner. 55.2 (April): 208–18.

Zaimoglu, Feridun. 2002. *German Amok*. Cologne: Kiepenheuer & Witsch.

———. 2006. *Leyla*. Cologne: Kiepenheuer & Witsch.

———. 2006. "My Germany." 2006. *Die Zeit*, 12 April. Trans. John Lambert. <http://www.signandsight.com/features/724.html>.

6

Luftkrieg Revisited

Contemporary Responses to the
Allied Bombings of German Cities

SYDNEY NORTON

Literary treatment of World War II subject matter has, as a rule, waned with the passing of time and the coming of age of a younger generation of German-speaking authors. Images of women and children making their way through the rubble, trading valuables on the black market for the fundamental necessities of life, or of the defeated soldier returning spiritually bereft to an annihilated homeland, have receded from the German literary landscape. In their place, the reader encounters varied narratives that reflect the conditions of a transformed and more complex modern Germany. Numerous contemporary plays and novels, for example, depict personal traumas of individuals or families that have resulted from the economic and social shifts caused by reunification.[1] And as contemporary Germany continues to be shaped by the influences of globalism and migration, we read about increasingly differentiated perceptions of the meaning of German national identity.[2]

A notable exception to the general preoccupation with the present is the recent literary and cultural attention dedicated to the Allied bombings of 131 German cities that occurred during the final years of World War II. In 1999, W.G. Sebald published three lectures that deal with this theme. In these essays, titled "Air War and Literature," Sebald describes the circumstances and strategies behind the British and American air attacks on German cities, and recounts enough of the ghastly details of the firestorms to make us aware of the intensity of horror and destruction that German urban civilians experienced at the time. After supplying the reader with sobering statistics—over 600,000 civilians perished during and after the bombings, and over 3 million were left homeless—Sebald offers the provocative thesis that the destruction, "on a scale without historical precedent, seems to have left scarcely a trace of pain behind in the collective consciousness" of the German people (3–4).

Sebald's essays have been the catalyst for a recent wave of books, articles, museum exhibitions, and TV documentaries that attempt to help both Germans and non-Germans come to terms with the unexpressed trauma related to the bombings. In January 2003, Peter Schneider contributed a piece to *The New York Times* called "The Germans Are Breaking an Old Taboo." He opens his article with fragmented childhood recollections of the air raids and cites Sebald's lectures as having brought back the trauma that was embedded deep in his consciousness. In a 2005 exhibition of abstract paintings by Gerhard Richter at the Marian Goodman Gallery in New York, the artist included a mammoth photograph of his painting *Mustang Squadron*, a blurry representation of eight sleek British escort planes flying over German farmland toward Dresden. Richter, thirteen years old at the time of the Dresden bombings, witnessed the glow of the city's inferno from thirty miles away (Schjeldahl 2005, 104).

In 2002 the Berlin historian Jörg Friedrich published *Der Brand: Deutschland im Bombenkrieg 1940–1945* (*The Fire: The Bombing of Germany*, 2006), a controversial history of the British/American air war against Germany, that was printed in conjunction with *Brandstätten: Der Anblick des Bombenkriegs* (Sites of Fire: A View of the Bombing War, 2003), a 240-page volume of images that underscore the massive destruction and death caused by the bombings. His book became a bestseller, partly as a result of a series of excerpts that appeared in *Bild Zeitung*, German's largest and most successful sensationalist tabloid.[3] Translated into ten languages and published in English in 2006 by Columbia University Press, *The Fire* reveals in vivid detail the horrors of what German civilians experienced between 1940 and 1945. During this five-year period, the British, later joined by the Americans, developed and perfected a saturation bombing campaign so exhaustive that bomber pilots often found themselves returning to a city on a mission only to make ruins from ruins.

Friedrich makes clear that the relentless "morale bombing" against German civilians was initiated as a means of halting a seemingly invincible German army by forcing them to turn their attentions back to their homeland. Implicit in the attacks on densely inhabited urban centers was also reprisal against the Nazi aerial attacks on London and Coventry. Yet the author also points out that the attacks substantially intensified during the last months of the war, when it was both clear to everyone involved that Germany would capitulate and that the country's airpower was depleted to the point that it was unable to defend civilians under attack. By this time the aerial attacks served no useful military purpose, but rather had become unhindered acts of vicious revenge that resulted in the massacre of tens of thousands more civilians and the widespread destruction of historic buildings, books, and cultural artifacts. Friedrich comments that the senseless destruction of cathedrals and churches occurred on a daily basis, while plans for bombing the railway tracks to Auschwitz were scrapped because the project was not viewed as a military priority (Friedrich 2003, 110).

While much of the historical information Friedrich presents is not new—he has drawn material from several air war books by distinguished scholars of varying nationalities—the author's approach to the subject matter is atypical in that he indicts as criminal the Allied air campaign without attempting to couch his argument too deeply within the customary context of Nazi Germany as primary aggressor, whose merciless bombing initiatives are what motivated the Allies to alter their more humane bombing policies in the first place. His use of highly charged words such as "incinerators," "ovens," "book burnings," and "mass extermination," while emotionally gripping, is problematic, since these terms, once reserved exclusively for discussions of Nazi war crimes, have been co-opted by the radical right, in order to describe the Allied "Jewish-led" victimization of Germans during and after the war. German, English, and American readers alike have taken serious issue with the above-mentioned aspects of Friedrich's study. Nevertheless, this well-researched and informative history is valuable in its exposure of the air war's barbaric disregard for human life and culture, and will continue to play a significant role in dispelling any remaining myths about the moral integrity of the Allied air campaign.

Literary Representations of *Luftkrieg*

Volker Hage, literary editor of *Der Spiegel*, published two books in 2003 that offer present-day readers insight into the depth of destruction that the German civilian population experienced in the final years of World War II, as well as a wide variety of perspectives about the air war by writers who experienced the attacks firsthand. *Hamburg 1943* is a collection of novel excerpts, police protocols, diary entries, and poems, all of which were written by authors who either experienced the horror of the Hamburg attacks themselves or witnessed the grotesque scenery of the city shortly after the war. Hage, a native of Hamburg, also included texts by exiles Bertolt Brecht and Klaus Mann, who had responded to news of the bombings in journal entries and American newspaper editorials. Not actually having experienced the bombings first hand, exiles were the few who articulated immediate responses to these attacks. Their words comprised a curious mixture of support for the Allied campaign and a sense of helpless despair about the wiping out of the cities they knew so well. In an American newspaper column called "Cities in the News" (9 September 1943), Klaus Mann illustrates his anguished ambivalence about Hamburg's destruction. Rowohlt published the essay in Germany in 1994:

> The news that a vital and individual organism like Hamburg ceases to exist—in any case, for the time being—must inevitably give rise to such an abundance of memories and thoughts for anyone who has known the city for as long as and as thoroughly as I have. It's not that I have compassion for the city and her inhabitants. Did they show regret when Warsaw and Coventry were bombed, London and Rotterdam? Did they ever protest against the terrible crimes that the German government and army committed in Russia, Norway, Poland, and Greece? In France and Holland? If the Germans, including Hamburg's inhabitants, have ever disapproved of these atrocities, they have regrettably been thoroughly unsuccessful at making their outrage heard. (2003a, 14)[4]

More recent accounts of the bombings are written by authors or poets who experienced the bombings as young children. Wolf Biermann, Hans J. Massaquoi, Ingeborg Hecht, and Ralph Giordano agree that the recollections of these few days never once waned from their consciousness, but rather have become more distinct over time. Biermann remarked in a 2000 interview with Hage: "You are familiar with the photograph of the pocket watch from Hiroshima that liquefied and then hardened at the moment of the explosion. When I saw this photograph, I thought suddenly—'that's me'—the tiny life clock inside of me was burnt solid during this night" (2003b, 145). None of the four authors were able to synthesize their trauma into any kind of useful literary form until decades later. Biermann wrote and published his personal account "Die Rettung" (The Rescue) (2003a, 246–52) and his poem "Die Elbe bei Hamburg" (The Elbe near Hamburg) (2003a, 239–40) in the mid-1990s, fifty-two years after the bombings. Afro-German Hans J. Massaquoi, who experienced the attacks at age seventeen, published an autobiographical novel called *Destined to Witness: Growing up Black in Nazi Germany* in 1999. Two chapters dealing with his experiences of the Hamburg *Feuersturm* were featured in Hage's *Hamburg 1943* (2003a, 256–69).[5]

Ingeborg Hecht, born to a gentile mother and Jewish father, tells the poignant story of how her family, with the help of a neighbor, was able to share their final intimate moments in a bunker on the eve of the Hamburg bombings. The next day, her father went his own way, only to be deported and murdered at Auschwitz. The night in the bunker would be the last time she would ever see him. Hecht recorded the details of this night in her journal in 1943, and published a short piece called "Letzte Begegnung" (Last Encounter) in a newspaper during the 1950s. However, she was unable to synthesize the information into book form until 1984, forty years after the trauma (2003a, 196–202). Ralph Giordano, who chronicled one Jewish family's survival of the bombings in his autobiographical novel *Die Bertinis* (1982), wrote in the forward to Hecht's book: "It wasn't until forty years after the liberation that Hecht was able to handle this subject matter, as opposed to the subject matter handling her" (1984, 9–10).

Zeugen der Zerstörung: Die Literaten und der Luftkrieg (Witnesses of Destruction: Writers and the Air War) is the companion text to *Hamburg 1943*. The first part consists of eleven essays by Hage that examine various philosophical and ethical problems related to the literary articulations about the bombings. His essay "Erzähltabu: Die Sebald Debatte" (Narrative Taboo: The Sebald Debate) addresses the question of whether or not there is really a narrative taboo, as Sebald has argued, that has prevented both everyday citizens and writers from articulating their experiences, losses, and emotions in a meaningful way; and if so, how this taboo is connected with the perpetrators' internalized guilt or shame? (2003a, 113–31). Hage, who was responsible for introducing Sebald's thesis to German and European readers through his publication of several interviews and articles in *Der Spiegel*, proves Sebald's fundamental thesis false by featuring multiple literary excerpts and interviews with authors who are able to speak candidly about their experiences. He notes in a recent telephone interview, however, that Sebald's theories about German repression are, nevertheless, valid:

> It wasn't until the 1990s that the distance from the subject matter was great enough that one could speak about this topic. This is connected with my belief that Sebald was nevertheless correct in his repression theory—that Germans had, with good reason, such a bad conscience about what they had caused during the war that they didn't feel they had the right to moan about these bombings. But one must imagine what kind of a worldwide outrage there is about the current bombing of Qana [Southern Lebanon], in which, terribly enough, fifty civilians were killed. In Hamburg, July 1943, fifteen thousand people perished in one night, many of whom were children. Sixty thousand were injured. It would be interesting to imagine what might have happened if the Nazi

propaganda machine had been able to make use of the TV and had not
been so dumb as to conceal the damage caused by the bombings. The
world, then, might certainly have a different opinion about the level of
inhumanity of the bombings. (2006)

Hage addresses other issues related to the air war in these essays, such
as how the use of the atom bomb, the ultimate weapon of the air, has
informed the consciousness of postwar writers; the (im)possibility of
writing productively about these bombings when millions more met a
more drawn out and terrible fate in the concentration camps; and perhaps most relevant for today's reader, the question of how citizens of
contemporary industrialized countries should respond to the fact that
modern war methods continue to move into an ever more abstract and
automated form of killing.

A variety of opinions regarding these concerns are articulated in the
second half of the volume in eleven recent interviews Hage conducted
with authors who have written on the topic. Here he does not limit his
scope to a discussion of Hamburg, but includes interviews with other
Germans authors such as Monika Maron (age four at the time of the
bombings), Alexander Kluge (age thirteen), and Walter Kempowski
(age thirteen), all of whom witnessed and survived the destruction
of their home cities Berlin, Halberstadt, and Rostock, respectively. He
also includes conversations with non-German writers including Kurt
Vonnegut, an American prisoner of war during the Dresden bombings; and Marcel Reich-Ranicki, a Polish Jew who was deported to the
Warsaw ghetto in 1938 and witnessed, while there, the German air
attacks on Warsaw.

These personal accounts and interviews are intriguing and informative on multiple levels. Even now, sixty-three years after the end of the
war, many people respond with reticence to the notion of Germany as
victim. Didn't the Germans ultimately get what they deserved by supporting Hitler's vision of total war? Why should those who did nothing to prevent the destruction of millions of innocent people be pitied
when their own cities are destroyed? Why should we listen to their
story? This attitude, while in some ways understandable, has inhibited
an accurate historical exploration of one of the most all-encompassing
and destructive military campaigns in history. For me, these recently
published accounts have a twofold function: First, they introduce the
reader to a variety of personal perspectives and narratives that provide
us with a more differentiated and deeper understanding of the extent
to which the survivors of these bombings suffered. Better knowledge
of what actually happened helps us situate these bombings within a

broader and more accurate historical context. Second, they help one to reflect more productively on whether or not there is ever justification for a bombing campaign that targets civilian populations.[6]

After reading these accounts, it is difficult to view the victims of these bombings as an abstraction, a homogeneous group of Nazi enthusiasts. Many of the casualties were not even supporters of the Third Reich. In Hamburg on the night of 27 July 1943, for example, the working-class neighborhoods of Hammerbrook, Hasselbrook, and Billbrook were annihilated, and with them tens of thousands citizens, many of whom had never aligned themselves with the Nazi Party.[7] The victims of these bombings were diverse. Most were women, children, and the elderly. While some civilians were pro-Nazi, many were also silent opponents of the regime, inner émigrés, Jews awaiting deportation,[8] and the politically indifferent. Wolf Biermann remarked during an interview conducted by Hage in 2000, "My mother was thrilled about the bombing attacks because she too was a Communist, and also because not only my father, but our entire Jewish family was murdered. The Allies were our friends—if one expresses it in a childish way: our partners, who would liberate us from the Nazis" (2003b, 145).

Whereas some authors identified the bombers as liberators, others questioned the tactics of the English and American bombers. Austrian writer Gerhard Roth points out that the Allies could have saved a tremendous number of lives if their bombers had destroyed the railway tracks that led to the concentration camps instead of churches, concert halls, and apartment buildings (2003b, 257). Walter Kempowski, whose book *Der rote Hahn. Dresden im Februar 1945* (The Conflagration. Dresden, February 1945) appeared in 2001, recalls an afternoon train ride during which Allied bombers rapidly approached the train. From his more or less secure hiding place in a watery ditch, the sixteen-year-old witnessed how numerous women jumped off of the train—most passenger trains were occupied by women and children—and began running desperately across a meadow to find shelter. The low-flying pilots made a game out of shooting them:

> I witnessed how women ran desperately across the meadow, and how they were shot down—an unforgettable impression. One knows this sort of thing from Wild West movies: people are shot and then suddenly collapse as if their legs were knocked off. Women were lying dead everywhere. The Allies, who wanted to drive out totalitarianism and replace it with humanity, should not have been allowed to behave in this manner. Don't you agree? (2003b, 193)

What significance do these varied testimonies of destruction have for us today, sixty-three years later, with German cities fully built up again, their theaters, concert halls, and inner cities restored to pristine condition? Hage offers the following response:

> I believe that many people, including the Americans, are still not aware of what exactly happened over here during the *Feuersturm*. Many don't realize that the attacks in Germany had almost as many victims as the atom bomb on Hiroshima. Of course the conventional bombing did not have the same long-lasting effects as the atom bomb. But the number of casualties was unbelievably high—between five hundred thousand and six hundred thousand dead. Curiously, this fact is not in the consciousness of the average person. (2006)

The Allied bombings over Germany have met with surprisingly little critique over the years. Since 1945, the US government has continued to wage air wars in Vietnam, Afghanistan, and most recently Iraq. There is now talk of a bombing campaign against Iran. These countless bombings, while not specifically targeting innocent civilians, have claimed hundreds of thousands of civilian lives. Increased historical awareness of our government's military strategies, combined with greater exposure to individual accounts by bombing survivors, would help US citizens and citizens of other countries engage more actively in the political process, and in doing so, help prevent unnecessary slaughter and destruction in foreign lands.

Mustangs

The large 35 x 60 inch photograph *Mustangs* shown at Gerhard Richter's New York exhibition of abstract paintings from November 2005 through January 2006 is actually a photograph of a painting of a photograph. Unlike the personal testimonies and literary excerpts by authors featured in Hage's two recent volumes, the work evades direct articulation of trauma, mourning or personal memory. Consequently, the observer is denied an opportunity to empathize with the victims of the massive aerial campaign in which these aircraft were involved.

The photograph reveals a head-on shot of a squadron of eight British Mustangs against a blurry background of nondescript farmland. It is cropped on three sides, and two of the planes have been truncated by the right and left edges of the sheet. A long white strip at the bottom of the photograph lends an air of irregularity and imperfection to the

Figure 6.1 Gerhard Richter, *Mustangs*, 2005
Photograph on laserchrome paper affixed to Antelio Glass with Diasec
34 5/8 x 59 in. (88 x 150 cm)
Reprinted with permission from the Marian Goodman Gallery, New York.

work. In addition, the color appears off: landscape and sky are fused in a washed-out shade of green, and an uneven mass of translucent pink discoloration appears in the left corner of the sky. Without the British Royal Air Force emblems on the side of each plane, it would be difficult to identify the operation or the location of the scene. Indeed, the planes appear suspended in a nameless and timeless mission—somewhere between an unidentified point of departure and an unspecified target. While it is obvious that the aircraft are in midflight, the propellers come across as motionless, a peculiarity that further contributes to an illusion of temporal and geographical stasis.[9]

To make matters even fuzzier, mundane objects located in the same room where the photograph hangs have been incorporated into the work. Visible in the reflective glass of *Mustangs'* frame are what appear to be a doorway with moldings, a white table top, a framed white board, and a glass water cooler. The contours of these commonplace objects interfere with the streamlined synchronicity of the military aircraft, as if to suggest that the very routineness of our daily lives seeps into our perceptions of history, and that the passage of time can render ordinary even icons connected with the most horrific events from the past.

Referred to by President Truman's Senate War Investigating Committee as "the most aerodynamically perfect pursuit plane in existence," the Mustang is considered by military historians to be the most effective aircraft of World War II (Boyne 2006). It was originally used exclusively for photo reconnaissance, but the later version of the plane, the P51B, was fitted with a more powerful engine (the V-1650 Marlin) and fuel drop tanks that provided dramatically increased air mileage, and greater maneuverability and speed. These improvements enabled the Mustangs to function effectively as cover for Allied bombers during the campaign against Nazi Germany. The British Air Purchasing Commission purchased the US-manufactured plane in April 1940, initially as a means to provide sufficient protection for its own bomber squadrons during night attacks over German cities. Once the Americans entered the war after the attack on Pearl Harbor in December 1941, however, the Mustang gave bombers of the US 8th Air Force the fighter cover it desperately needed over occupied Europe.

In addition, the Mustang destroyed 4,950 German fighter planes that remained on the ground due to lack of spare parts and fuel toward the end of the war. Able to carry out an average of "nineteen kills for every Mustang lost," the aircraft's success rate was such that fifty-five countries bought versions of the plane after the war. German civilians were, at the time, unaware of these detailed statistics. Yet they were viscerally conscious of the crucial role these aircraft played in the anni- hilation of their cities and towns. The pervasive presence and drone of these low-flying planes became a fixture of everyday life in Germany both during the raids and in the years of occupation immediately fol- lowing the war.

Mustangs have been a part of Richter's visual repertoire since 1964, when he created an oil painting called *Mustang Squadron*. It was painted in a style that came to be known as Capitalist Realism, a term that Rich- ter and fellow artists Sigmar Polke and Konrad Lueg coined for the title of a 1963 exhibition that featured their works. As implied by the title, Capitalist Realist works are indirect parodies of Socialist Realism, the official art form of the former German Democratic Republic that embraced concrete figuration as a means of celebrating the ideals of the Communist state (Lewis, 1991, lot # 1). As a student at the Dresden Art Academy from 1952 to 1956, Richter mastered the exacting, precision- oriented techniques of the Social Realist style. But in 1961 he defected to West Germany, only to encounter the brash and ubiquitous imagery of Western advertising.

Inspired by Andy Warhol's and Roy Lichtenstein's dynamic repre- sentations of consumer objects and media images, Richter and Polke created works that earned them reputations as German Pop artists. Yet their ambivalence toward any one ideological approach added depth and irony to their images of mass-produced objects. In contrast, works by their American counterparts were celebrations of blankness, articulations of the glittery, yet shallow surfaces that characterize media culture in the United States. Regardless of what Richter painted during the early 1960s—be it rolls of toilet paper, military aircraft, his Uncle Rudi in soldier's uniform, or a nondescript chair—an aura of edginess is always present. There is a feeling that what we see on the surface, despite the image's devotion to realistic detail, fails to capture truth in its entirety. His synthesis of Pop art and Socialist Realism within the same visual field had the effect of canceling out two opposing aesthetic approaches. As a result, a straightforward, matter-of-fact reading of the work becomes impossible.

Just as German writers from the 1960s questioned the validity and usefulness of writing literature and poetry after the Holocaust, so too did visual artists perceive traditional figural painting as an ineffectual method that had been contaminated by the crimes of the immediate past. These deep-seated doubts about conventional modes of representation were closely connected with artists' loathing for the seemingly impermeable façade of normalcy and predictability that characterized every level of German society after the war. According to the art historian Benjamin Buchloh, "not only did the language of the everyday continue to operate in postwar Germany, but its apparently unbreakable stability and false neutrality provided the most reliable medium of repression, safeguarding the speaker from critical reflection as much as from actual experiences of mourning and memory" (2005, 10). Whereas everyday citizens needed to repress their recent memories and traumas in order to move forward during the postwar years, many artists and writers resisted this effort by establishing an "aesthetics of silence and refusal," in which languages and other modes of representation would dissolve and become disjointed, thereby exposing ruptures and inconsistencies in the seemingly stable and steadfast establishment.

It is no coincidence that Richter began collecting photographs in the early sixties—both family snapshots and iconic images from newspapers and magazines—that captured over five thousand slice-of-life scenes from both private and public spheres of German society during the postwar years. The massive collection, later published in a book called *Atlas* (Richter 1997), served as the artist's compendium of visual memories that became the inspirational source for his oil paintings. What Richter appreciated most about these snapshots is that they were devoid of aesthetic pretensions. Whereas the majority of them lacked compositional sophistication, every snapshot expressed raw information in a direct way. By duplicating these photographic scenes in oil paint with tremendous precision, Richter called into question the assumed legitimacy of the photograph as a source of absolute truth. Simultaneously, the traditional notion of the painting as an articulation of creative genius no longer held true. After all, Richter's paintings were mere duplications of the photographic images, a fact that makes it difficult for one to make the claim that these copies were motivated by the artist's aesthetic vision. "Richter's systematic deployment of the grime of the image world," wrote Buchloh, "exposed the hypocrisy and the hubris of the German claim to have simply started a new life" (2005, 11). By questioning the legitimacy of photography and painting, Richter revealed the sites of rupture that existed just below the surface of accepted representational forms.

Mustang Squadron is one of a series of eight paintings of military aircraft that Richter made between 1962 and 1965. The series features realistic, yet hazy representations of military planes taken from newspapers or magazines. Several of the featured airplanes, such as the low-flying Mustangs and the *Luftwaffe* Stukas, are aircraft most commonly associated with bombing campaigns in World War II, while others, such as the Soviet MiGs and American B52s, are icons of the Cold War. The pictures are cropped in such a way that it is nearly impossible to determine their place in space, and all, with the exception of the Mustangs, are entirely removed from the topography over which they are flying. Richter maintains that his choice of warplanes for subject matter was a random and largely insignificant decision. "Pictures like that don't do anything to combat war. They only show one tiny aspect of the subject of the war—maybe only my own childish feelings of fear and fascination with war and with weapons of that kind" (Storr 2003, 41–42). Nevertheless, these paintings appeared at a time when memories of the destruction caused by the Allied bombings were still fresh in peoples' minds, and when a tacit taboo existed regarding showing or discussing any personal opinions related to trauma caused by the bombings. Regardless of the artist's protestations to the contrary, it is difficult to ignore the signification of political and military power that is inextricably linked with these images.

For Germans, the mere glimpse of the artist's depictions of menacing aircraft evoked painful memories and repressed anxieties about their experiences during the bombings and the years immediately following the war. Moreover, the 1960s were a period in which both East and West Germany were trapped within the power plays of the Soviet Union and the United States. NATO was encouraging West Germany to remilitarize, and to produce, once again, fighter planes of its own—two developments that caused fierce debates within and beyond

Germany's borders. Similarly, Richter's 2005 photograph *Mustangs* surfaced in New York at a pivotal time for German and American political relations. Germany's refusal to participate in the US-led coalition in Iraq, a war whose initial invasion strategies featured "shock and awe" aerial missions, resulted in significant strife between the two governments. Gerhard Schröder's resolute stance against involvement served as an indication to leaders around the world that participation in the war was not their only option.

Richter resists offering substantive verbal commentary about the political significance of displaying fighter planes at a time of both intense international controversy regarding the US invasion of Iraq and during a period of increased media attention dedicated to the destruction caused by Allied bombings (Storr 2003, 289). He evades articulation of his personal opinion with circuitous responses like "I never knew what I was doing," or "You could only take it as a joke," or "I am a specialist in airplanes." Yet the political and emotional resonance of the artist's insertion of *Mustangs* into his New York exhibition is striking. This commanding icon of Allied aerial bombardment reemerges at a time when the prolonged American presence in Iraq continues to fuel heated international debates and public demonstrations that challenge the justification of the US-led war in the Middle East.

The Case of Dieter Dengler

Literary and visual portrayals by distinguished authors and artists can function as a kind of all-encompassing testimony of an entire generation of people who have lived through misfortunes of immense proportions. Because these portrayals are also the most publicized, we tend to view them as emblematic of an entire country's collective consciousness. One wonders, however, what everyday citizens, who, for whatever reason, are unable to write or create art about their experiences, or who do not have sufficient access to media or publishers, would tell us about their experiences. It is common knowledge, for example, that the primary victims of the aerial attacks on German cities were women, since most of the men were away fighting. But for reasons that cannot be fully explained by the predominantly male authors in *Zeugen der Zerstörung*, published testimonies by women are few and far between.[10] Surely many of these women, along with underrepresented men from rural or working-class origins, have insightful contributions to make about this topic. While a quest to uncover these unheard voices extends beyond the scope of this essay, such a project would likely reveal testimonies that would substantially enrich scholarship in this area.

Werner Herzog's documentary *Little Dieter Needs to Fly* serves as valuable contrast, both to the discussions by the literati featured in Hage's two volumes, as well as to Richter's nearly impenetrable representation of *Mustangs*. The 1998 film documents, albeit with grand artistic license, the life of Dieter Dengler, a seemingly ordinary man, whose destiny it was to survive the apocalyptic conditions of two wars. Dengler, who was born and raised in Bilburg, a small village in the Black Forest, experienced the destruction of his home and village as a young boy. As was the case for so many other young German children, his father was killed during the war and his family suffered extreme hunger and poverty during the years immediately following it. Between ages fourteen and seventeen Dengler apprenticed in his town as a blacksmith and church clock maker. But immediately upon completion of his apprenticeship, he sailed to the United States in order to fulfill his dream of becoming a pilot. After a period of drifting and working a variety of jobs unrelated to flying, he attended college and joined the US Navy, where he was finally able to learn to fly. But his passion for flying pulled him into active duty in the Vietnam War, and in 1966 Dengler was shot down during his first mission over Laos. He was taken to a prison camp, where he almost starved to death and survived numerous forms of torture, before he managed to escape with a friend.

The film begins with a quote by Herzog, who functions both as omniscient narrator and as a synthesizer of visual narration and Dengler's recollections. His words contextualize Dengler's testimony within the filmmaker's own fascination with single-minded, obsessive figures who suffer psychologically from traumas of massive proportions. "Men are often haunted by things that happen to them in war or other periods of great intensity," Herzog says. "Sometimes you see these men walking on the street or driving in a car. Their lives seem to be normal, but they are not." Herzog's voice makes an almost seamless transition into Dengler's narration, the beginning of which reveals the degree of mental anguish that the retired US Navy lieutenant experiences daily, even many years after his life has gained a semblance of normalcy. Filmed in profile as he drives his vintage convertible towards home along an idyllic road in northern California, Dengler continues where Herzog left off: "When I'm driving my car I often hear the voices of my dead friends. Sometimes my friend Duane Martin calls me and tells me that his feet are cold. Because of this, even on a warm and sunny day, I keep the roof to my convertible top up."

Unlike the authors in *Zeugen der Zerstörung*, who attempt to make some intellectual sense about what they experienced during the air raids, Dengler reflects minimally or not at all about questions such as whether a narrative taboo existed for Germans after the war, or whether the Allied bombings were justifiable acts. He comments briefly that the Allies carried out "senseless attacks" against small villages like his. In general, however, he maintains a nonjudgmental, even fatalistic stance about the acts of aggression that altered his life so radically. Perhaps in a subconscious effort to synthesize the most gruesome events without going mad, Dengler attaches mystical significance to the most distressing episodes in his life, marking these events as magical turning points for him. His near stream-of-consciousness description of his childhood encounter with a bomber who flew at his house in Bilburg captures his perception of the episode as a supernatural phenomenon:

> I had two brothers there, and we were [at] the top window, and we looked out, and we watched all this, and I clearly remember one of the airplanes came diving at our house. And it was so unusual because the cockpit was open. The pilot had black goggles that were sitting on his forehead. He was looking. He actually turned around, and he was looking in at the window, and the machine guns were just firing, because the flashes . . . I keep seeing them coming out. And the left wing tip just missed the house by two or three feet as it whipped by. It was just a fraction of a second. It was like a vision for me. It was like an almighty being. It is just something that is very difficult to describe. But I knew from that point on that I want to be a flier. I wanted to be a pilot.

Mystical beings often come into play at the moment when Dieter finds himself in the most desperate, life-threatening situations. Twenty years after his fateful encounter with the pilot in Bilburg, he is rescued in Vietnam by his father, a man who was killed during World War II when Dieter was still an infant. Barefoot and starving on an escape route he hoped was leading toward the Laos-Thailand border, Dengler had just witnessed the decapitation of his best friend and hears the gunshots and voices of the approaching Viet Cong. Near death, he approaches a fork in the river, where he sees a vision of his father standing in the water pointing in the direction of safety. Throughout the film, Dieter draws on the supernatural to explain the inexplicable, or to help him derive sense out of an utterly senseless situation.

Little Dieter Needs to Fly is problematic as a documentary because it is not always clear whether the narrated events are purely biographical or whether the filmmaker has altered or embellished a scene in order to make a more captivating and visually appealing movie. In a recent article about Herzog in *Harper's Magazine*, Tom Bissel (2006, 74) points out that the filmmaker fabricated a scene in which Dengler acts out "his habit" of compulsively opening and closing the front door to his house. As Dengler demonstrates his impulse, he explains to the viewers that the act of opening and closing a door represents to him the value of freedom, and that most people do not realize what a privilege it is to be able to "open a door" and walk away. We learn from Bissel, however, that while the action performed exemplifies a feeling Dengler has had, he never actually behaved in this manner until Herzog asked him to. Viewers might be inclined to perceive the insertion of a fictional moment like this one into a documentary film as deceptive, but Herzog does not see it this way. By engaging in what the filmmaker refers to as "the ecstatic truth," Dieter articulates the emotional truth, a subjective realm, in which narrative manipulations and embellishments win out over factual accuracy.

More bewildering is the fact that there is not the slightest acknowledgment of the existence of Dieter's wife and two children. Herzog's decision to omit his subject's current relationships alters the way we perceive Dengler's character. If his family and friends had been even marginally included in the film, we would have likely identified Dieter as someone who triumphed over his traumas to a point where he was able to lead a relatively normal life. Instead, we are guided by Herzog's omissions and embellishments into reading Dengler as a tragic loner, a psychically damaged person who has difficulty cultivating intimate relationships and whose life consists mostly of hoarding foodstuffs, collecting model fighter planes, hearing dead friends' voices, and repeatedly opening and closing doors. Thus Herzog presents us with a Dieter Dengler who is, in part, a fictional character invented for the sake of the filmmaker's narrative and aesthetic vision.

Despite this confusing fusion of documentary and fiction, *Little Dieter Needs to Fly* is an intriguing work of art that expresses an altogether distinctive voice within the current discussions regarding the Allied bombings. Dieter's paradoxical status as both bombing victim and bomber, combined with his unlikely identity as both a German and a Vietnam veteran, challenges viewers to transcend the rigid framework of national identity, a vantage point from which it is all too easy to cast blame. Instead, he encourages us to look at bombings from the perspective of a simple man, who like so many other young men and women, enlists in the armed forces for the wrong reasons and unknowingly becomes a cog in the wheel of a vast military operation whose ambitious agendas are unrelated to his personal needs. "I never wanted to go to war," Dieter remarks. "I only got into this because I had one burning desire and that was to fly. But that there were people down there who suffered, who died, really became clear to me much later, when I was their prisoner." Dieter's observation is a troubling reminder of the extent to which bombers become desensitized to the death and destruction they cause from the elevated security of their cockpits. "From the air, Vietnam didn't seem real at all," Herzog adds. "For Dengler it was like a grid on a map. Everything down there seemed to be so alien and so abstract. It all looked strange, like a distant barbaric dream." Dengler's captivating story, enhanced by Herzog's artful blending of historical footage and atmosphere, invites viewers to encounter on a visceral level the massive devastation caused by these aerial campaigns.

Conclusion

Herzog's *Little Dieter Needs to Fly*, Richter's *Mustangs*, and Hage's two volumes on literature and the air war are diverse and compelling articulations of repressed memories, traumas, and opinions that have surfaced over time in response to the Allied bombings of German cities. Both Richter and Herzog employ the documentary medium as a means of allowing the viewer to engage with contrasting aspects of the bombing campaign on a gut visual level. Their integration of documentary forms into their art muddies our perceived boundaries between truth and fiction, a process that can, depending on the artist's intent, effectively enhance or limit the artist's aesthetic freedom. Richter's duplication of "banal" and technically unsophisticated images from magazines and newspapers, for example, helped liberate him from what he refers to as the violence of an imposed aesthetic vision. Herzog's incorporation of documentary film footage into his movies achieves just the opposite: it strengthens the force of his aesthetic and philosophical intentions, thereby intensifying the visual and emotional experience of the viewer. In contrast to Richter's and Herzog's creations, Hage's two volumes function on the most straightforward level as lasting evidence of the degree of annihilation and depth of suffering that German civilians experienced as a result of the bombings. All of these works, despite the contrasting aims and approaches of their creators, are successful in creating a broader arena for productive dialogue and debate about the Allied bombings, their devastating consequences, and their significance for us today.

Notes

1. Ingo Schulze's *Simple Storys: Ein Roman aus der Ostdeutschen Provinz* (*Simple Stories: A Novel from the East German Province*, 2000), Fritz Kater's 2003 drama *Sterne über Mansfeld* (Stars over Mansfeld), and poetry by Barbara Köhler and Lutz Seiler are just a few examples of contemporary literature that responds to the anxieties caused by social and economic shifts that have occurred in Germany since 1989.

2. Emine Sevgi Özdamar's 2003 novel *Seltsame Sterne starren zur Erde* (Strange Stars Gaze toward Earth), Zafer Şenocak's poetry, and his 1998 novel *Gefährliche Verwandtschaft* (Dangerous Affinities) articulate varied perceptions of the meaning of national identity in contemporary Germany. These works, as well as the literature mentioned in footnote 1, are examined at length in other essays included in this volume.

3. See Buruma, 2004.

4. Unless otherwise indicated all translations in this essay are my own. Mann's English-language article originally appeared in a US Army paper called *Camp Crowder Message*.

5. The excerpt "Operation Gomorrha" which appears in the anthology *Hamburg 1943* was taken from *Neger, Neger Schornsteinfeger!* (Bern: Scherz Verlag), the German translation of Massaquoi's 1999 novel.

6. With Amendment I, Protocol I (1977) of the Geneva Conventions, stipulations have been added to ensure that civilians are lawfully protected and that undefended cities and houses of worship are not attacked during war. Employment of weapons, projectiles, and other materials and methods of warfare known to cause unnecessary injury or suffering have been prohibited. Despite these improvements in international law, the amendments are conveniently bypassed when enemy soldiers take shelter in civilian neighborhoods and houses of worship.

7. These once densely inhabited districts located in the southeastern part of Hamburg were leveled to the point that they were never again rebuilt. Today they consist mostly of empty lots, warehouses, and small factories. In his anthology *Hamburg 1943*, Hage includes the short story "Billbrook," written by Wolfgang Borchert in 1946, in which a Canadian pilot named Bill Brook wanders in astonishment through the rubble of the former neighborhood (2003a, 82–101).

8. The firestorms served, ironically, as a saving grace for some Jews who had not yet been deported. The chaos that followed the bombings allowed them to conceal their Jewish identity by removing the yellow stars from their clothing and by claiming to Nazi authorities that their identification papers had been destroyed in the fire (2003b, 103).

9. See Bernhard Schnackenberg's discussion of Gerhard Richter's 1964 oil painting of Mustangs (1982, 69).

10. The phenomenon is briefly discussed in Hage's interview with Walter Kempowski (2003b, 195–96), who mentioned that many women wrote diaries during the war years, but that German publishers, as a rule, consider diaries

an illegitimate literary form, and consequently not worthy of publication. The author also conjectures that women probably did not have the peace and quiet in the years following the war to allow their reflections on their experiences of the bombings to develop.

Works Cited

Biermann, Wolf. 1995. "Die Rettung" and "Die Elbe bei Hamburg." In *Alle Gedichte*. Cologne: Kiepenheuer & Witsch. 179–86, 156–57.

Bissel, Tom. 2006. "The Secret Mainstream: Contemplating the Mirages of Werner Herzog." *Harper's Magazine*, December: 74–77.

Boyne, Walter J. 2006. "P-51 Mustang." *Air Force Magazine*, December: 88.

Buchloh, Benjamin H.D. 2005. "Richter's Abstractions; Silences, Voids, and Evacuations." In *Gerhard Richter: Paintings from 2003–2005*. Cologne: Walther König. 7–27.

Buruma, Ian. 2004. "The Destruction of Germany." *The New York Review of Books* 15.16. October 21.

Friedrich, Jörg. 2003. *Brandstätten: Der Anblick des Bombenkriegs*. Berlin: Propyläen.

———. 2006. *The Fire: The Bombing of Germany, 1940–1945. Books* 15.16. Oct., trans. Allison Brown. New York: Columbia University Press.

Giordano, Ralph. 1982. *Die Bertinis*. Frankfurt am Main: Fischer.

Hage, Volker, ed. 2003a. *Hamburg 1943*. Frankfurt am Main: Fischer.

———. 2003b. *Zeugen der Zerstörung: Die Literaten und der Luftkrieg*. Frankfurt am Main: Fischer.

———. 2006. Unpublished interview with the author. July 31.

Hecht, Ingeborg. 1984. "Letzte Begegnung." In *Als unsichtbare Mauern wuchsen: Eine deutsche Familie unter den Nürnberger Rassengesetzen*. Hamburg: Hoffman und Campe. 123–31.

Herzog, Werner, dir. 1998. *Little Dieter Needs to Fly*. Werner Herzog Film GMBH: Munich.

Kempowski, Walter. 2001. *Der rote Hahn: Dresden im Februar 1945*. Munich: Goldmann.

Lewis, Jim. 1991. "*Mustang-Staffel*." *Contemporary Art from the Kraetz Collection* (auction catalogue). New York: Sotheby's, 13–14 November. Lot #1.

Mann, Klaus. 1994. "Hamburg." In *Auf verlorenem Posten: Aufsätze, Reden, Kritiken 1942–1949*. Reinbeck: Rowohlt. 74–78.

Massaquoi, Hans. 1999. "Operation Gomorrha." In *Destined to Witness: Growing up Black in Nazi Germany*. New York: W. Morrow. 201–16.

Richter, Gerhard. 1997. *Atlas der Fotos, Collagen und Skizzen*. Munich: Lenbachhaus.

Schjeldahl, Peter. 2005. "In the Mood: New Works by Gerhard Richter." *The New Yorker*, 5 December: 104.

Schnackenburg, Bernhard. 1982. "Gerhard Richter." In *Kunst der sechziger Jahre in der Neuen Galerie Kassel.* Kassel: Die Neue Galerie. 69.

Schneider, Peter. 2003. "The Germans Are Breaking an Old Taboo." *The New York Times,* 18 January.

Sebald, W.G., 1999. "Air War and Literature." In *On the Natural History of Destruction.* New York: Random House. 1–104.

Storr, Robert. 2003. *Gerhard Richter: Forty Years of Painting.* New York: Museum of Modern Art. 287–309.

Trueman, Chris. 2000. "The P51 Mustang." <www.historylearningsite.co.uk/051_mustang.htm>.

7

An Aesthetics of Memory for Third-Generation Germans
Tanja Dückers's *Himmelskörper*

Laurel Cohen-Pfister

Pierre Nora has been much quoted in the last decade—no doubt because he recognized a fundamental truth underlying the hunger for recording memories and recollections of the past: "We speak so much of memory, because so little of it remains" (1984, 1, xvii).[1] This observation finds universal application, for there exists in each society at any time a generation that faces extinction. With the passing of this generation pass, too, the first-hand memories of lived history that are both the private history of individual families as well as the shared history of a nation. In the Federal Republic, Nora's thesis deftly circumscribes the state of cultural memory postunification. As the twenty-first century marches forward, witnesses to the catastrophes of the last century become increasingly fewer in number, and younger generations must race to uncover the memories of the World War II generation before none are left to transfer. The proliferation of contemporary German texts that provide literary space for remembering is remarkable. The story—and history—of Wehrmacht soldiers, Nazi perpetrators, expellees from the East, and survivors of Allied bombings alike find expression in texts that recognize, respect, and struggle with the subjective nature of memory.[2] Literature itself becomes a site of memory, a *lieu de mémoire* as Nora phrases it, where representations of the past are consciously reflected upon, contested, and stored.

Third-generation postwar German authors, the so-called generation of grandchildren, figure prominently in this new memory literature. The generational shift in perspective they provide marks a new era in German postwar literature and strongly defines literary production in the postunification era. Whereas the second postwar generation, most readily associated with the 1968 generation, struggled with the silence, guilt, and omissions of its parents—the first generation—its children, the third postwar generation, ask personal questions that demand an unveiled look into familial complicity with National Socialism and/or their family's own wartime suffering. Sigrid Weigel, whose work on generations has helped to define the postwar generational categories, notes that the children of the perpetrators opted for decades to deny or obscure their familial ties to the generation of the guilty. A self-proclaimed "fatherless" generation, the sons and daughters of the perpetrators separated themselves in protest from their parents. In their counting of generations, they omitted what Weigel calls "the concealed first generation" and established themselves as "the *first* authority in questions of politics, truth and morality" (2002, 272; my emphasis). The idea of a second generation only became explicit, Weigel notes, in "later reflections on one's own obvious omissions. It was not until the 1980s that those born before or after 1945 . . . accepted their historical heritage and came to terms with their descent from a collective of perpetrators" (2002, 268).

With the clear emergence of a third generation of memory in German postwar culture, the "tension between the fear of guilt and the desire to recognize the past" (2002, 268) that Weigel sees manifested in the second generation's position on the past is noticeably missing. Instead, texts of this generation examine individual family histories with a new unreservedness, bringing what Weigel calls the "concealed first generation" back into the genealogical/historical record of memory. The need to understand history and one's own place in this history—and if one might put it so magnanimously, the need to search for truth—lie at the heart of third-generation family novels. "As the grandfathers die and the fathers remain silent, the hour for young authors has come," observes the *Stuttgarter Zeitung* (Sander 2004, 30). It is within this framework that Tanja Dückers's novel *Himmelskörper* (Heavenly Bodies) can best be placed.

Intergenerational (Mis)Communication on the Past

The second published novel by the Berlin native born in 1968, *Himmelskörper* portrays the transgenerational battle between memory and amnesia and the quest for truth in both individual and collective memory, as its narrator, or more correctly, narrators, endeavor to disambiguate German history and their familial relationship to this history. The novel questions not only the continuity of history through the generations, but also the boundaries of memory in exploring this history. Dückers constructs an androgynous narrator—a hybrid of male and female, brother (Paul) and sister (Freia), rationality and artistic sensitivity

—to explore the convoluted path of memories hidden in one family's personal history.[3] It is a story of the mixed roles Germans assumed in wartime, being both responsible for atrocities committed throughout Europe, as well as victims of the war they created.

Dückers presents history as an invisible, omnipresent force, one that infiltrates all aspects of the present. In it, personal and collective experiences inextricably intersect. As a voice of the grandchildren's generation, Dückers writes of the need to consciously construct personal historical truth that encompasses the entirety of the German experience, recognizing the existence of German wartime suffering, without exonerating the same sufferers from their culpability. By exploring the processes of memory, Dückers's narrators hope to confront the past in order to enter the future.

The "art of remembering" is central to the novel, particularly since the third generation must complete and even construct its knowledge of the past due to the failure of the preceding generations to address this history with each other and together with the grandchildren. The novel centers on an aesthetic memory project initiated by grandchildren, whose discovery of gaps, or secrets, in the family narrative shatters their belief in their grandparents' innocence. Trusted narratives must be deconstructed—as incomplete or inaccurate representations—and hard-earned constellations of insight must be reframed without constructive or corrective input from the first (deceased) or second (silent) generations. The chance to actively research the "archives" of the grandmother's memory while she is still alive understandably first consumes Freia's memory search: "I wanted [grandmother] Jo to remember—to remember this time that our family talked about so often, yet which contained so many gaps. . . . As long as she was still here" (Dückers 2003b, 212). Yet the grandmother's conscious censorship of politically or morally incorrect opinions and experiences maintains myth, not truth. Only the deterioration of this self-control—wrought by the grandmother's increasing dementia—provides glimpses into that-which-was: the grandparents' belief in and unerring support of Nazi ideology. Jo's death, compounded by mother Renate's suicide from unresolved feelings of guilt, necessitates for Paul and Freia a deliberate, therapeutic search for vestiges of private, family history. Through aesthetic experimentation with the last witnesses to the lives lost—family memorabilia—these grandchildren attempt to transcend temporal, spatial, and generational boundaries, access historical truth, and uncover the mysteries surrounding the lives of lost family.

This essay closely studies this convoluted de- and reconstruction of the hegemonic family narrative, primarily that of the first generation's wartime suffering, as it addresses the intergenerational processes of remembering that influence the grandchildren's perception of family together with the National Socialist past. In detailing the narrators' aestheticization of family memory, with the conscious and artful reinterpretation of family history, the crisis these grandchildren face in understanding self within family and, further, the family in the context of German history, becomes clear. Precisely because the previous generations could not communicate truthfully and comprehensively about their own dark past, Dückers's novel implies that the third generation must find its own way to access and then question this history.

In *Himmelskörper* each generation—grandparents Jo and Mäxchen, parents Renate and Peter, and grandchildren Paul and Freia—has a different way of talking, or respectively, not talking, about the past. For the grandparents, the National Socialist era retains the hint of their "glory days," even though the war brought great personal suffering: flight and expulsion, the grandfather's loss of limb in a cold Soviet winter, loss of possessions, and loss of homeland. Peter, whose early memories stem from Southern Germany, where his family escaped the war fairly untouched, says little—mostly because his in-laws from Königsberg remind him that he has no traumatic war memories to relate. Renate, Jo and Mäxchen's daughter, also remains relatively mute on her young memories. Her silence, one comes to learn, stems from her own feelings of guilt. As a five-year-old child, it was, namely, her right-armed Nazi salute and denunciation of neighbors that won the family a place on the mine ship *Theodor* over one on the *Wilhelm Gustloff*. This expression of the child's unreflected indoctrination into Nazi ideology saved their lives; however, it meant the death of their neighbors, including a like-aged boy, who perished when the *Gustloff* subsequently sank from a torpedo attack. When Renate does speak of the war, her tone is hushed, yet accusatory. Rarely does she allow her parents their stories of suffering without interjecting a touch of "historical reality," so to speak, reminding them it was Nazi Germany that brought its suffering upon itself.

This intergenerational constellation of remembering reflects in part Weigel's paradigm of conflict and silence between the first and second postwar generations: the generation of perpetrators does not speak of its crimes, and its stories of suffering are silenced by its children. For her parents, Renate has become an "authority in questions of politics, truth, and morality"; even her own sense of guilt derives from an unwavering commitment to justice, here to the point of questionable self-condemnation. The grandchildren in the novel—whose personal understanding of the war is informed as much by the grandparents' historically decontextualized, *Märchen*-like stories of flight from the East and the Soviet winter as it is from the dry and routine acquisition of dates and facts in school—provide a more neutral audience for the grandparents' stories of wartime suffering than the generation of their parents. Freia and her brother Paul become the inheritors of the familial myths of wartime, the audience to their narration. Accordingly, the grandchildren, not the parents, are the gatekeepers of family memory and recipients of the uninterrupted transferal of the wartime memories that their parents refused to assume. In their nonadversarial relationship to the generation of perpetrators, the grandchildren are called to evaluate and record the family memories once obscured or suppressed by the second generation.[4]

The Art of Remembering

What do we remember and how? Conversely, why do we forget? In *Himmelskörper*, these essential questions in memory research connect with the intransparency of this family's history—albeit that of a completely normal German family, the narrator asserts. Like the elusive cloud formation *cirrus perlucidus* that Freia, the meteorologist, seeks in vain, so, too, is historical truth difficult to find. What is that intangible quality in this family history that resembles the airy wisps, the smoke, or the mist that reappear as a motif throughout the novel? Memories and secrets, guilt and pain form phantasms whose wispy formations are as ephemeral and yet as present as the smoke of a cigarette or the wisp of a cloud. The sky, "this mysterious stage" (Dückers 2003b, 17), parallels the family stage of secrets. The nebulous description of *cirrus perlucidus* only magnifies the uncertainties and confusion that accompany Freia's professional and, more importantly, private search: "When is something translucent, transparent, invisible? How does the invisible relate to the non-present?" (58).

For Freia and Paul, the answers can be found only beyond the "hegemonic familial ideology" (Hirsch 1997, 8), wherein the first and second generations, while not in political agreement, remained bonded in silence on past transgressions. Paul and Freia's innate tendency to transcend recognized boundaries equips them to overcome conventional perspectives and reflections. Freia explains: "My brother and I, we were fluid. We constantly oscillated between father and mother, between inside and outside, the city and the forest, with and against each other, unsettled, young, formless" (Dückers 2003b, 16). The narrative perspective is theoretically open and unbounded by any socially constructed limitations of gender. The barriers lie in the objects they examine. There, the narrators must confront the obscurity and opaqueness that overlie the family past. Like the onyx beloved by a Polish uncle who commits suicide or the amber necklaces held dear by mother, grandmother, and great-aunt, or even the thick pines lining the Polish/German border, the truth is a dark and unclear place.[5]

Dückers claims the impetus for writing *Himmelskörper* came when clearing out her grandparents' apartment. When confronted with the objects they left behind, she wondered how her grandparents politically and personally experienced the National Socialist era. Unable to question them directly (her grandfather is deceased, and her grandmother suffers from dementia), she employed artistic freedom to create a history for imaginary grandparents—who she insists bear no relation to her own (Dückers 2003a, 54). Accordingly, her fictitious grandchildren Paul and Freia, when confronted with boxes and crates of remnant letters, postcards, and photos, mountains of things "that we had never seen, that had never been mentioned, that were left behind for us as the only trace" (Dückers 2003b, 55–56), must reconstruct the past based solely on the tangible evidence left behind.

Yet, what truth about the past do its relics contain? Objects themselves do not possess the ability to speak the truth. Indeed, they can deceive by unquestioningly transferring the ideological perspectives of the past into the present. Dückers's novel makes clear that for the German past, the answer varies starkly, depending on whether the relics belong to the victims of this past or to their victimizers. While photos and objects of victims can reveal to successive generations the lives and worlds lost to National Socialist brutality, those of the perpetrators can provide the mask of normality, a deceptive portrayal of an era, known to Freia through her grandmother as "the 'happiest time' of our absolutely normal family" (Dückers 2003b, 271). Roland Barthes's position that the photograph is "an emanation of *past reality*" (1981, 88) seems questionable when applied to the photographs of oppressors that inherently represent not loss, but rather the power of the privileged. Paul and Freia's decision to subjectively transform the numerous "Erinnerungsstücke" (memory objects) (Dückers 2003b, 57) into their own narrative text is a conscious attempt to create clarity and transparency and perform one possible "process of self-discovery, a discovery of self-in-relation" (Hirsch 1997, 2).

The narrators' aesthetic deconstruction and recontextualization of material objects left over from past experiences speaks to a fundamental distrust of images—born through realizing the discrepancy between the hideousness of National Socialist ideology and the innocence of family photos and other artifacts. Formed from their disillusionment with their grandparents' lies, this skepticism guides their critical memory project. Freia questions whether the moments a photograph captures are even representative of that-which-was: "You can't trust them, these snapshots that record, make claims, and generalize, when almost all of our gestures, expressions and moments have disappeared into a sea of nothingness and have been forgotten" (Dückers 2003b, 250). For this reason, the image alone is insufficient in mediating truth: it must be transformed in order to unlock the multiple layers of "truth" that it hides. A combination of Freia's —the scholar's—verbal decoding and Paul's—the artist's—aesthetic interpretation of Freia's words, Paul and Freia's "transformation work" (270) infuses lifeless objects with new meaning, recreating a context for the objects that transcends the narrow, subjective perspective of their original owners by including a critical perspective gained through knowledge of National Socialist crimes. By abstracting artifacts from their original context through a twofold process of transformation, Paul and Freia are able to transcend assumed meanings and messages; they work toward the truth hidden beneath the apparent to make visible the invisible: "Paul's pictures, inspired by my [Freia's] stories, would speak another language" (57). With its ability to alter and modify the original image, and hence, original message, the aesthetic transformation process in *Himmelskörper* "reframe[s] the past from various angles and thereby move[s] beyond the tombs of photographic memory" (Koepnick 2004, 101).

A photograph of the pilot Hanna Reitsch, the back signed with "1937" in Jo's handwriting, prompts one such transformation. Freia first simply holds up the picture for Paul to paint. Yet the picture of a smiling Reitsch only confounds Paul's ability to perceive the historical factuality of the image: "That's a hard nut to crack. It's really easier for me to paint when you say something rather than just handing me some object," Paul objects. In response, Freia steps into the role of Hanna Reitsch, reporting energetically for a kamikaze mission for the Führer: "'I understand that this mission ends with death,' I [Freia] barked in a shrill voice and saluted to the three-quarter moon in the window" (Dückers 2003b, 56). In a somewhat pedantic tone, Freia goes on to explain that no fewer than seventy volunteers signed such a declaration, the so-called SO (*Selbstopferung* [self-sacrifice]) Plan, in 1944, and that Reitsch conscientiously trained young volunteers for the mission. "Writing the image," notes Hirsch, "undoes the objectification of the still photograph and thereby takes it out of the realm of stasis, immobility, mortification . . . into fluidity, movement, and thus, finally life" (1997, 3–4). Freia's commentary removes the false objectification implicit in the photograph and injects into the once revered values of honor, *Vaterland*, and patriotic duty the cynicism and criticism gained through historical knowledge of the dark side of these supposedly noble values. While Freia continues educating Paul on Reitsch's unfailing devotion to the Führer and his mission, Paul begins transforming the verbal images into a visual text. His artistic rendering shows Reitsch standing not on a V1 missile, but rather on a colored Easter egg. She is kissing another woman, who is symbolically portrayed with the astronomical sign for Venus. In the background, a line of ants marches to a hot air balloon labeled with the word "SoSo." The color blue—long associated with the intangible and ephemeral—dominates the painting, as it does all of the artist's works (Dückers 2003b, 59).

Paul's paintings and collages, like Freudian dreams, contain the essence of what is real—no trappings of outward falsehoods. The juxtaposition of visual images—here formed through a fusion of the original photograph with a verbal interpretation—decode the original artifact through a process of revisualization and recontextualization. Freia recognizes: "[M]y search for something that was really no longer an object and yet not quite dematerialized, my search for *cirrus perlucidus*, transformed itself in Paul's paintings once more into its original, amorphous state" (Dückers 2003b, 24). Walter Benjamin's concept of dialectical images, in which the "perceptible 'ur-phenomena' of history, heterogeneous moments of truth" break through (Pensky 2004, 193),[6] and Benjamin's idea of montage—"to discover in the analysis of the small individual moment the crystal of the total event" (Benjamin 1999, 461)—seem close to the narrators' conceptual endeavor.

Paul's paintings try to make transparent what is opaque in the original object. The artifact itself has become suspicious, testimony to the lies told by previous generations. Freia and Paul's aesthetic restructuring of family mementos enables them to criticize and correct the hidden stories that have remained unspoken and veiled in the family narrative. Here, photographs do not serve to authenticate history. Instead, they question the authenticity of memory and the veracity of the image. Lutz Koepnick calls such a process a "re-mediation," a "blurring [of] the boundaries between old and new, . . . creative hybridizations and shrewd cross-overs" (2004, 109), words that aptly describe not only the narrative transformation, but also the narrators themselves.

Koepnick's analysis of photographs, which draws heavily from Susan Sontag's work on the subject, notes that "emulsion-based photography isn't as closed, homogenous, and clear cut as many of its commentators, including at times Benjamin and Barthes, often wanted it to be. Meaning and reference,"—here he refers to Sontag—"do not reside in the photograph itself. They emerge from what we do with certain images, from how we invest them with knowledge and desire, from how we allow them to affect us under particular circumstances and position them against the background of competing discourses" (2004, 101–2; cf. Sontag 1978, 21, 23). Koepnick emphasizes the active process of situating an image's formal inventory "against the backdrop of other narratives, discourses, images, and strategies of representation," so that it might "speak in various ways about the past and its bearing on the present" (2004, 102). "[H]ow we engage older myths of reference, objectivity, and truth in order to define the relationships between image-makers, photographic subjects, and viewers as relationships of either asymmetrical authority or mutual recognition," he claims, holds the key to understanding the "meanings and memories . . . constituted behind and beyond their pictorial surface" (2004, 102). Koepnick's—and Sontag's—observations deftly apply to the generational shift in perspective at play in *Himmelskörper*. That the grandchildren generations, born long after the war, carry not only no personal recollection of this period, but also fewer emotional ties to the souvenirs once treasured by grandparents and parents, necessarily influences their engagement with the image. As estranged viewers, distanced both from the period and the myths the images reference, they access the past informed by discourse on German crimes, less readily swayed by photography's visual message of, for example, their mother's childhood innocence or their grandparents' untainted happiness.

The narrators' emotional distance in *Himmelskörper* contradicts the notion that sentiment and emotion influence the interpretation of family artifacts by living generations. Loss and longing only minimally apply to the narrators' memory investigation in *Himmelskörper*. Barthes's understanding of photography, where "the relationship of love and loss, presence and absence, life and death" form its "constitutive core" (Hirsch 1997, 4; cf. Barthes 1981, 73), describe in Dückers's narrative only the relationship of first and second generations to representations of a past experienced either first hand or intimately mediated through first-hand knowledge of the referents. Jo and Renate's obsessive hoarding of the tangible reminders of their lived experiences unsuccessfully defies the immutable passage of time, and with it, the irrefutable loss of loved ones, "homeland," even life itself. For the third generation, however, who were neither witness to the events, people, and places, nor are prisoners of their emotional imprinting, such representations do not *prick* them with the ephemerality of life and the inevitability of death—Barthes's *punctum*. As Freia ponders: "At home my mother had shown me photos, letters, and even crocheted doilies from the prewar period that had survived the flight from the East, and yet Aunt Lila and Uncle Józef, who had died almost twenty-five years before my birth, still eluded me. I fondled the many objects from my mother's trunks and asked myself whether these objects of memory perhaps held meaning only for their owner" (Dückers 2003b, 170).

Whereas the objects hold metonymic power for the mother and grandparents, for the grandchildren, who have had neither a spatial nor a temporal connection with Königsberg, the lost homeland, the flight from the East, or the relatives lost in the war's drama, the objects are void of emotional meaning. The specter haunting artifacts is less the historical subject itself;[7] rather, it is the discrepancy between the subjective, familial interpretation and objectified historical accounts of the National Socialist era. Pictures, or objects, are not signifiers of loss for these third-generation Germans; rather, they signify generations of deception and distorted truths that call for enlightenment. The grandchildren are called to work through them to access family history not only subjectively, but also tempered with objective knowledge gained from outside. The dissolution of the connection between the object and its "spectator-subject" result in "alienation and estrangement." The image has degenerated to a trace—again a Benjaminian concept—and "appearance requires an act of reading the image and an act of interpreting the illusion it projects" (Schlossmann 1997, 85).[8]

Paul and Freia invest their emotion into re-presenting the artifacts in their own language. Their narrative project is an attempt to internalize the referents, to eradicate material ballast, and, in the process, not only understand their family history better, but also to purge their psyche of emotional ballast. Freia's conscious striving to interiorize knowledge about her mother and grandparents even directly opposes these previous generations' unsuccessful attempt to unload emotion and memories into collected objects. The mother and grandparents' inability to break free from the past is impetus enough for the grandchildren to break free from the material. In contrast to her mother and grandmother's obsessive collecting, Freia frees herself of the need to collect anything—the other extreme. She retains only one picture of each family member. Paul's interpretive artistic montages emotionally process the vestiges of lost lives: "Once he had finished his drawing or painting, I threw away the corresponding objects, often with a sense of liberation. But until Paul was finished, these discoveries so occupied me that I could not separate myself from them" (Dückers 2003b, 56). Paul's artistic reinterpretation neutralizes the artifact's ability to act as a countermemory or to distort historical factuality. As a result, family memories, once reframed through an historical recontextualization, must live within the grandchildren.

Private Memory and Historical Consciousness

In an interview, Dückers emphasizes the unavoidability of dealing with the past since almost no German family survived the war without some kind of damage. There is no refuge, she claims, from this "opaque history of violence"—referring to a term coined by Harald Welzer: "I associate a kind of primal historical bang with 8 May 1945, an event that turned the lives of millions of people upside down. The entire postwar order is a product of this date." Even younger Germans, she claims, feel the effect of this explosive, catastrophic event, whose "cosmic background radiation" permeates the present (2005b, 9).

In *Himmelskörper*, this "primal historical bang" informs not only the protagonists' relationship between self and family, it carries through to the relationship between self and society. History, Paul claims—paralleling Dückers's words above—manifests itself as "a kind of cosmic background radiation," as an invisible, omnipresent force (Dückers 2003b, 316–17). Freia knows, too, that she cannot ignore the past: "there was no escape, I had to face it, future and history, which would inseparably blend personal and collective experience" (255). Freia sees herself a part of a chain in a construct she distrusts; yet she knows, too, that she breaks the mold, not only by being the first woman in her family not born in wartime, but also the first to bear a child outside of marriage (26). Her shaven head—a protest against the symbolism of generations of women woven together by their long, golden braids—physically testifies to her attempt to interrupt the continuity of history through the generations. She recognizes in her own face only too well the faces of the women in her family with long hair: her grandmother's braided days in the *BDM* and her mother's braided days as a young child in Nazi Germany. In shedding the weight of the hair, she hopes to shed the weight of their history.

Ultimately, Paul and Freia's artistic transformation of the material cannot offer clearer insight into their family's tangled web of guilt and suffering. Just as the photographic camera might once have been considered to "reveal what could not be seen by the human eye, and thus introduce us to unconscious optics like Freud introduced us to the hidden impulses of the mind" without questioning (Koepnick 2004, 97), so, too, do Paul's paintings first seem like uncensored representations of the unconscious past. Yet, Freia becomes increasingly dissatisfied with their artistic project. In place of transparency, Paul's artwork seems instead to make things more convoluted and mysterious than they were. Paul's paintings are unable to speak truth over the "reality" of the artifacts because they become too coded themselves. Freia laments, "I wanted to gain clarity, not construct another labyrinth" (Dückers 2003b, 271). Paul suffers, too, as he gains no relief from the constant "background radiation" in his head. This force will ease, he fears, only with his death (317–18).

To free himself, he needs to write the story of his family, in a book he wants to call *Himmelskörper*. Freia, too, wants to write everything down so that they will not need anything else "except this book, our private almanac, and your pictures, . . . no cartons, boxes, . . . letters, . . . souvenirs, this collecting mania of our family. Nothing!" (Dückers 2003b, 273). Freia, who has the facts (the logical side), and Paul, who has the words and pictures (the artistic side) will together process the family history "in a memory piece in one 'place': paper" (318). Pierre Nora's thesis finds here its fictional realization: Paul and Freia's personal recounting will itself become a *lieu de mémoire* where the vestiges of family memory rest. Like the description of the elusive *cirrus perlucidus*, the narrators' literary site of memory can be a place where the boundaries between "subjective" and "objective" history/story, between "fact" and "feeling" fuse (307).[9] Writing should provide the alienation necessary to deconstruct the familial myth, allow space to admit their love for mother and grandparents, and offer the final instrument with which they divest themselves of the emotional ballast of family silence. In another parallel to Freia's cloud project, their story, like clouds themselves, can be viewed as a "Geschichtsspeicher," a site where history/stories are stored (307). The analogy is revealing, considering that it comes from Freia's doctoral advisor upon learning that Freia has discovered the *cirrus perlucidus* off of the Polish coast: at a moment when her mother confronts her own history with Poland and the *Gustloff* (303).[10] Whether the narrators succeed with their memory piece in overcoming the weight of German history passed down into the third generation postwar remains unclear. Their story cleverly falls to the reader, who holds the product, the novel itself, in her or his hand.

Conclusion

Dückers's novel shows that the youngest generation of German writers still feels the pull of the past. Daniel Dubiel believes that the passing of the last wartime generation will not "lead to any lessening of the hold of memory on Germany; the next generation—still related by politics, history and familial ties to the 'generation of perpetrators'—will participate fully in the 'civilizing project of acknowledging guilt.'"[11] Dückers clearly assumes this challenge. In an interview, she claims: "My generation is the first that can venture to soberly examine this topic [National Socialism]" (2003d, 42). The young novelist has been called "a prototype" of a new direction of interest in oral history and in subjective memories and private and family memory (Sander 2004, 30). The direction is neither "to preach nor accuse" in reference to a family history intertwined with the history of the Third Reich (Sander 2004, 30). Instead, the move is to *understand* the grandparents' generation, not necessarily *condemn* it. As if seconding Dubiel's comments on history's hold on a younger generation of Germans, Dückers asserts: "I have the impression that among 'my' generation, even as heterogeneous as it is, the atrocities of the NS regime and its fellow travelers are becoming harder, not easier, to understand" (2002b, 16). Yet, she also notes that this intolerance of National Socialist atrocities does not directly transfer to her generation's judgment of its grandparents. Comparing her generation's perspective to that of the second generation, she comments: "You judge your parents perhaps differently than your grandparents" (2003a, 55).

In many ways Dückers counters the image of a young generation that is politically uninterested, one concerned more with its personal pleasures than with social issues. The "grandchildren's generation" remains overshadowed, its new perspectives dwarfed, argues the writer, by the "self-declared Olympians" of the "G[rass] & W[alser]" generation (2002c, 55).[12] Contrary to the political activism of the second generation, the third generation's engagement is more private, more centrally focused on personal, family history and individual stories; it does not presume to represent the collective. Dückers notes: "I am neither the first nor the only author of the younger generation to work extensively with this subject [National Socialism]. We just don't present ourselves as the personified consciousness of a whole nation" (2003a, 54).

Himmelskörper shows that this third-generation writer is invested in understanding and interpreting the meaning of the National Socialist/World War II era. Her novel is a clear indicator that the subject of the German past will not soon fade from cultural memory. Indeed, it continues its hold on the memory of the next postwar generation, who choose to understand it from the most personal of perspectives (through family history) and yet with the emotional distance that time affords. Precisely because younger writers have a historical distance to the events, they can contribute to the discourse in a way not possible for the older generation, Dückers argues. They can provide a new language, less emotional and involved—one that brings with it a fresh viewpoint: a search for "traces" (2002c, 56).

Despite that "primal historical bang" that Dückers claims has left its mark on all Germans of the postwar decades, her ultimate position is one of hope. Good literature, she claims, "transcends reality and briefly conveys the prospect of a better life" (2005a, 16). Her novel *Himmelskörper* reflects that anticipation. In a passage symbolic of the struggle between obscurity and transparency, the past and the future, optimism reigns. Upon emerging through the clouds into a red evening sky, Freia, in flight, sets her sight on overcoming the past: "no history . . .

only future. Destination: my eye" (Dückers 2003b, 60). In its confrontation with a familial legacy of National Socialism and World War II, *Himmelskörper* signals that these third-generation Germans, although conscious of the past, are looking—longingly—toward the future.

Notes

1.   Unless indicated otherwise, all translations are my own.

2.   For examples of recent German memory literature, see my article "The Suffering of the Perpetrators: Unleashing German Postwar Collective Memory in German Literature of the Twenty-First Century" (2005, 123–35).

3.   The novel's unisex narrator is identified throughout the text simply as Freia. Dückers crosses gender barriers in her novel *Spielzone* as well (see Gerstenberger 2003, 262–64).

4.   For more on differences in intergenerational remembering in the novel, see Stüben 2006, 174–77.

5.   For more on Dückers's metaphoric use of objects and colors to convey historical intransparency, see Stüben 2006, 180–85.

6.   Of dialectical images, Benjamin writes: "It's not that what is past casts its light on what is present, or what is present its light on the past; rather, image is that wherein what has been comes together in a flash with the now to form a constellation. In other words, image is dialectics at a standstill. For while the relation of the present to the past is a purely temporal, continuous one, the relation of what-has-been to the now is dialectical: is not progression but image, suddenly emergent" (1999, 462). In his study of Benjamin's concept of dialectical images, Pensky observes that the critic was convinced that the historical truth of the nineteenth century was objectively present in the collected fragments he assembled from that century. Further, this historical truth is only "legible" at certain points, namely, when the dialectical image emerges suddenly, in a flash, and becomes recognizable (2004, 180).

7.   "Like Benjamin's concept of photographic shock, Barthes's notion of photographic reference revolves less around an image's visible content than around how photographs . . . draw our awareness to the many ghosts that populate our own present" (Koepnick 2004, 100).

8.   In her analysis of Benjamin's concepts of trace and aura, Schlossmann observes: "While aura functions on the level of the image, . . . the counter-term of the trace functions on the level of writing as a text-citation and photographic caption, and on the level of appearance as the evidence of a crime, analysed by a subject who is a detective. The end of aura is the end of the connection between viewer and object: like the detective, the viewer observes the evidence of a crime" (85). Significantly, history "for Benjamin, is in the appearance of the image as a trace" (85).

9.   In an interview, Dückers calls her own approach to writing a kind of "sensual historiography" (*sinnliche Geschichtsschreibung*), an approach that

resembles that of the narrators (2002a; see also Schaumann 2005, 264; and Stüben 2006, 179).

10. The search for memory in Poland (at significant places such as the former site of the Warsaw Ghetto or Gydina, where the *Gustloff* sank) plays a significant part in Freia's memory research. Freia's encounters with site-specific memories reveal the same emotional distance she and Paul have toward the artifacts they analyze. For example, the horrors of the Warsaw Ghetto remain abstract for her (Dückers 2003b, 170). While she would like to feel sympathy for the victims, thoughts of her boyfriend are more real and present (172–73). For an analysis of Freia's search for memories in Poland, see Schaumann 2005, 267–69.

11. . Quoted in Moeller 2002, 230. On the other hand, recent sociological studies in the Federal Republic show that younger generations of Germans, while fully knowledgeable of the crimes of the NS period, do not associate their own grandparents with these events: the emotional attachment to family members of the generation of perpetrators, coupled with that generation's silence on its own complicity with National Socialist policies, precludes the belief that these loved ones could possibly have supported a regime known to them as heinous (Welzer et al. 2002).

12. Case in point is the *Gustloff* theme itself. Dückers bridles when asked how her novel compares to Günter Grass's treatment of the *Gustloff* story in *Im Krebsgang (2002)*: "[M]y version is more historically accurate than Grass's" (2003c). The difference in perspective is generational, Dückers maintains. Whereas Grass is understandably more emotionally involved, she has more historical distance and sees the facts. Dückers fears, though, that her age discredits her interpretation of the events: "[O]lder people believe if you yourself didn't stand under the hail of bombs, you don't have a right to write about such things" (2003c).

Works Cited

Barthes, Roland. 1981. *Camera Lucida: Reflections on Photography*. Trans. Richard Howard. New York: Hill and Wang.

Benjamin, Walter. 1999. *The Arcades Project*. Trans. Howard Eiland and Kevin McLaughlin. Cambridge, MA: Belknap Press / Harvard University Press.

Cohen-Pfister, Laurel. 2005. "The Suffering of the Perpetrators: Unleashing German Postwar Collective Memory in German Literature of the Twenty-First Century." *Forum for Modern Language Studies* 41.2: 123–35.

Dückers, Tanja. 2002a. "In Berlin gibt es ein sehr lesungsbegeistertes Publikum." Interview with Sabrina Ortmann. *Berliner Zimmer*. Ed. Sabrina Ortmann and Enno Peter. <http://berlinerzimmer.de/eliteratur/dueckers_interview.htm>.

———. 2002b. "Der Schrecken nimmt nicht ab, er wächst." *Süddeutsche Zeitung*, 27 April: 16.

————. 2002c. "Spuren suchen: 'Fehlt' die NS-Zeit in den Romanen der 'Enkelgeneration'?" *Edit* 29: 53–56.

————. 2003a. "Das Flüchtige und das Doppelbödige." Interview with Uwe-Michael Gutzschhahn. *Neue deutsche Literatur* 51.2: 54–63.

————. 2003b. *Himmelskörper.* 2nd ed. Berlin: Aufbau.

————. 2003c. "'Meine Version ist die richtige.' Tanja Dückers hat ein Buch zum selben Thema geschrieben wie Günter Grass." Interview with Tobias Haberl. *Berliner Zeitung,* 22 March: 69.

————. 2003d. "Der nüchterne Blick der Enkel." Interview with Rebecca Partouche. *Die Zeit,* 30 April: 42.

————. 2005a. "In Reih und Glied." *Süddeutsche Zeitung,* 1 September: 16.

————. 2005b. "Tanja Dückers nähert sich dem Krieg als Schriftstellerin." *Stuttgarter Nachrichten,* 7 May: 9.

Gerstenberger, Katharina. 2003. "Play Zones: The Erotics of the New Berlin." *German Quarterly* 76.3 (Summer): 259–72.

Grass, Günter. 2002. *Im Krebsgang.* Göttingen: Steidl.

Hirsch, Marianne. 1997. *Family Frames.* Cambridge, MA: Harvard University Press.

Koepnick, Lutz. 2004. "Photographs and Memories." *South Central Review* 21.1 (Spring): 94–129.

Moeller, Robert. 2002. "What Has 'Coming to Terms with the Past' Meant in Post-World War II Germany? From History to Memory to the 'History of Memory.'" *Central European History* 35.2: 223–56.

Nora, Pierre. 1984. *Les Lieux de Mémoire.* Vol. 1. Paris: Gallimard.

Pensky, Max. 2004. "Method and Time: Benjamin's Dialectical Images." *The Cambridge Companion to Walter Benjamin.* Ed. David Ferris. Cambridge: Cambridge University Press. 177–98.

Sander, Marcus. 2004. "Aus der deutschen Gruft; Tanja Dückers und Verena Carl diskutieren im Literaturhaus." *Stuttgarter Zeitung,* 24 November: 30.

Schaumann, Caroline. 2005. "A Third-Generation World War II Narrative: Tanja Dückers's *Himmelskörper.*" In *Gegenwartsliteratur* 4/2005. Ed. Paul Michael Lützeler and Stephan Schindler. Tübingen: Stauffenburg. 259–80.

Schlossmann, Beryl. 1997. "Looking Back: Luminous Shadows and the Auras of History." *Nottingham French Studies* 36.1: 76–87.

Sontag, Susan. 1978. *On Photography.* 3rd ed. New York: Farrar, Straus and Giroux.

Stüben, Jens. 2006. "Erfragte Erinnerung—entsorgte Familiengeschichte: Tanja Dückers' 'Wilhelm Gustloff'-Roman 'Himmelskörper.'" In *Wende des Erinnerns? Geschichtskonstruktionen in der deutschen Literatur nach 1989.* Ed. Barbara Beißlich, Katharina Grätz, and Olaf Hildebrand. Berlin: Erich Schmidt. 169–89.

Weigel, Sigrid. 2002. "'Generation' as a Symbolic Form: On the Genealogical Discourse of Memory since 1945." *Germanic Review* 77.4: 264–77.

Welzer, Harald, Sabine Moller, and Karoline Tschuggnall. 2002. *"Opa war kein Nazi": Nationalsozialismus und Holocaust im Familiengedächtnis.* Frankfurt/M: Fischer.

8

The Continuation of Countermemory
Emine Sevgi Özdamar's
Seltsame Sterne starren zur Erde

JOHN PIZER

Early reviews of Emine Sevgi Özdamar's recent novel *Seltsame Sterne starren zur Erde* (Strange Stars Gaze toward Earth, 2003) stress its narrative focus on Germany and its concomitant neglect of the author's Turkish homeland (see, for example, Saalfeld 2004). While this perspective ignores the first-person narrator's repeated flashbacks to Turkey, it is indeed the case that the main focus—as the subtitle *Wedding— Pankow 1976/77* makes clear—is on the years Özdamar spent shuttling between West and East Berlin in the late 1970s. Özdamar's shift in attention is natural, given that *Seltsame Sterne* is the third novel in an autobiographical trilogy. Whereas *Life is a Caravanserai: Has Two Doors I Came in One I Went Out the Other* (*Das Leben ist eine Karawanserei hat zwei Türen aus einer kam ich rein aus der anderen ging ich raus*, 1992) and (to a lesser extent) *Die Brücke vom Goldenen Horn* (The Bridge across the Golden Horn, 1998) tend to reflect Özdamar's life prior to her emigration to Germany, *Seltsame Sterne* narrates her years working at East Berlin's Volksbühne. A more important distinction between the third novel and the first two in the trilogy is its relative lack of performative imagination. Much of *Seltsame Sterne* is composed in diary form. It contains actual sketches Özdamar drew for the Volksbühne, as well as the names of recognizable personalities from East German theatrical life (such as Benno Besson and Heiner Müller) with whom she worked. While *Caravanserai* in particular contains multiple fantastic elements, *Seltsame Sterne* is largely marked by a factual prose style and does not come across as a work of fiction.

Nevertheless, Özdamar's latest novel (as of this writing) shares a common artistic and political telos with the first two novels in the trilogy, as well as with some of her short fiction: the desire to recuperate the tolerant, multiculturally inscribed memory of a now vanished sociopolitical domain without giving in to nostalgia. Particularly *Caravanserai* evokes the vibrancy and plurivocality of the Ottoman Empire, which was dissolved shortly after World War I. These positive elements of the empire, which had been in evidence before its slow demise early in the twentieth century, have been erased from Turkish history books by Kemal Atatürk, the founder of the Republic of Turkey, and by subsequent nationalist regimes in that country. Similarly, *Seltsame Sterne* recalls the solidarity and respect for national as well as ethnic alterity in East Berlin, former capital of the German Democratic Republic. Although this communist country is now scorned by most Western proponents of the contemporary "global" age, the increasing xenophobia and intolerance toward minorities in contemporary Germany, Turkey, and elsewhere is perhaps due in part to the fact that the communist ideal of universal brotherhood has all but disappeared along with the world's "socialist republics."

Neither Özdamar's early work, nor *Seltsame Sterne*, resorts to nostalgia to highlight positive elements in the daily life of vanished geopolitical entities that had been ruled by now vilified regimes. The narrator's maternal grandfather in *Caravanserai* personifies the brutality and misogyny of the Ottoman years. Legalized mistreatment of women at that time was permissible through an interpretation of Islamic law that allowed men to engage in polygamy and to treat their wives as personal property. The grandfather murders one of his wives, the narrator's maternal grandmother, by tying her hair to his horse's tail and having her dragged through Anatolia's stony paths when he returns home from a term in prison and finds her absent. In *Seltsame Sterne*, the GDR's bureaucratic chicanery, obsessive eavesdropping, and the fear the government thereby instilled in its citizens are fully elucidated. Thus, the *Ostalgie*, the nostalgia for the vanished German Democratic Republic, reflected in some works of contemporary popular German culture (see Cooke 2005, esp. 103–75) is absent in Özdamar's third novel. In both her earlier and later writing, as this essay will demonstrate, Özdamar creates a countermemory to officially sanctioned accounts of now vanished domains without whitewashing their blemishes.

Özdamar and Countermemory

Before beginning to explore Özdamar's strategy of sociocultural recuperation in *Seltsame Sterne*, it will be necessary to look at how she enacts this strategy in previous works, and to explain what is meant by the term *countermemory*. I derive this signifier from one of Özdamar's most eloquent and well-known interpreters, Azade Seyhan. In her book *Writing Outside the Nation* (2001), Seyhan argues that "Özdamar attempts to understand a culture that is gradually disappearing into forgetfulness through the medium of the mother tongue and to rewrite the (hi)story of the motherland—as a form of countermemory to official history" (149). Seyhan is referring here to *Caravanserai*, with its consistent allusions to and citations from the language and history of Özdamar's grandparents' generation, who were young people during the waning days of the Ottoman Empire. However, the term *mother tongue* also brings to mind Özdamar's early stories "Mother Tongue" ("Mutter Zunge") and "Grandfather Tongue" ("Großvater Zunge"), originally published in 1990. Seyhan herself borrows the term *countermemory* from a collection of Michel Foucault's essays in English translation, *Language, Counter-Memory, Practice* (1977), which she cites a few pages later (153). The passage to which she refers, in an essay entitled "Nietzsche, Genealogy, History," from the "Counter-memory" section of Foucault's book is worth citing in full:

> The body is the inscribed surface of events (traced by language and dissolved by ideas), the locus of a dissociated Self (adopting the illusion of a substantial unity), and a volume in perpetual disintegration. Genealogy, as an analysis of descent, is thus situated within the articulation of the body and history. Its task is to expose a body totally imprinted by history and the process of history's destruction of the body. (Foucault 1977, 148)

The body registers a countermemory to official historiography, and thus becomes the object of genealogical investigation. Referring to Özdamar's countermemorial articulations of Ottoman language and historical experience in the "tongue" stories and in *Caravanserai*, and of communist East Berlin in *Seltsame Sterne*, as an enactment of Foucaultian genealogy is indeed appropriate, because these articulations are more somatic than discursive in character.[1] They are governed and inscribed by sensual experience rather than ideological reflection. In *Caravanserai*, this sensuality is enacted through the credulous childlike naïveté of the narrative perspective, while in "Grandfather Tongue" and *Seltsame Sterne*, adult sexuality enables this somatic character.

In *Caravanserai*, the directness of the first-person youthful storyteller, unmediated by any value-forming intellectual filter, is evident in both the evocation of Ottoman Turkey's misogynist brutality and its multicultural vitality. In relating the tale of her grandmother's murder at the hands of her grandfather, Özdamar makes no attempt to separate fantastic from prosaic details; both elements are blended into concrete, sensual, matter-of-fact prose: "My Grandfather tied her hair to the tail of his horse September and rode over the stony paths, my grandmother gradually put on the thorny plants and stones as a dress, called for her mother and father who were already long dead, but the dead heard her, came out of their graves and took their daughter with them" (31). While illustrating the extreme violence to which women could be subjected in an age when they had few rights, this passage also evokes the holistic relationship between life and death, the living and the dead, which informed the popular worldview in the Ottoman age and resulted in a comforting sense of connectedness. The cohesive relationship between life and death in Ottoman Turkey is even evident in the novel's title; it takes the common trope of a caravanserai (an inn with a large court-yard to accommodate the caravans traveling back and forth) from that age and extends it into a metaphor for a literally unpunctuated link between the two realms. While Atatürk's Westernizing reforms gave Turkey's women a certain measure of freedom, protection, and equal-ity, David Horrocks correctly notes that the most alienated and lonely women portrayed in the novel are consistently those who lead a highly Westernized lifestyle (36). Although acknowledging the harsh reali-ties of the country's pre-republican past, Özdamar's novel reveals the even greater misery attendant to Atatürk's reforms: economic insecu-rity and dislocation, American cultural and political hegemony, and the emergence of a violent, fascistic nationalism, the development of which is more extensively treated in *Die Brücke vom Goldenen Horn* and, episodically, in *Seltsame Sterne*.

To be sure, growing ethnic discord among various nationalities already began to manifest itself at the close of the Ottoman Empire, when the so-called "Young Turks" of this empire brought about the genocide of its Armenian population during World War I. Özdamar anecdotally alludes to this event in *Seltsame Sterne*. However, through-out most of its existence, Ottoman Turkey was quite tolerant of ethnic and religious minorities and its population was characterized by a high degree of multicultural diversity, even in the Anatolian heartland. As Seyhan asserts in a recent essay, "Özdamar has championed the auton-omy of identities that had once constituted the mosaic of the Ottoman Empire but had been driven underground under the banner of one nation" (2005, 218). As we will see, respect for and interest in such dis-crete identities marks the East Berlin portrayed by Özdamar in *Seltsame Sterne*. In *Caravanserai*, Ottoman multiculturalism comes to expression when the narrator alludes to the genre of the *Karagöz* shadow play, a popular entertainment form during this prenationalist epoch. In these plays, the two main characters are two rivals, the street-wise Karagöz (which means "black eye") and the intellectually effete Hacivat, but secondary roles in the plays were consistently drawn from the empire's diverse minorities, whose accents, dialects, and turns of phrase the puppeteer had to reproduce (Seyhan 2005, 223).

In *Caravanserai*, the narrator visits the grave of the "holy men" Karagöz and Hacivat with her grandmother. These men are described as the real-life precursors to the shadow play's protagonists, two builders executed hundreds of years ago by a sultan furious at their bringing the construction of a mosque to a halt by telling humorous stories to their fellow workers. They become holy men when the sultan, seeking penance for his deed after he hears their stories and is brought to tears by his laughter, has holy gravestones placed at their burial site. The narrator's mother explains the shadow play after hearing about the graveyard visit to the namesakes of the genre's chief protagonists. She explains that "there are Jews, Greeks, Armenians, adolescents, whores in the shadow play, they all talk different dialects, each one is a different musical instrument, talks in his own tongue and doesn't understand the others, goes tın tın tın for themselves [*sic*]." She goes on to equate this colorful assemblage with "our country," poor but rich in people (119). While such ethnically, religiously, and socially diverse figures occasionally populate the pages of *Caravanserai*, the evocation of Karagöz's and Hacivat's burial site, in conjunction with the candles placed there by the child narrator and her grandmother, inevitably suggests that the Turkish multicultural "body" as "the inscribed surface of events"—to again cite the terms of Foucaultian genealogy—has reached the nadir of its "descent," a body so subject to "the process of history's destruction" that it is, on a metonymic level, dead and buried. As the narrative thread throughout the course of Özdamar's three autobiographical novels makes evident, the agent of this destruction is the homogenizing force of Turkish nationalism and its attendant Westernization. Nevertheless, the shadow play is evoked as a countermemory to this homogenization.

The multicultural alterity alluded to in the mother's description of the Turkish shadow play is rooted in the sensuality of language. What distinguishes the genre's Greek, Jewish, Armenian, prostitute, etc., characters is the diversity of their tongues, their function as discrete instruments within a mutually incomprehensible but rich and colorful orchestra. In their analysis of Özdamar's "tongue" stories, Brigid Haines and Margaret Littler point out that Özdamar's "construction of female subjectivity is also emphatically corporeal" (119), but this highly feminine corporeality is entirely rooted in an insistence on the sensuality of language in general and of the Arabic roots of Ottoman Turkish in particular. Indeed, in "Grandfather Tongue," linguistic sensuality and unbound female sexuality are inextricably intertwined. The "grandfather's tongue" of the story's title is, of course, Ottoman Turkish, which used the Arabic alphabet. When the first-person narrator of "Mother Tongue" perceives the loss of her "mother tongue"—modern Turkish—to be the result of both her long residence in Germany[2] and the coarsening of life and language in Turkey through the psycholinguistic effects of the military dictatorship that dominated the country's government throughout much of the later twentieth century, she resolves to learn her "grandfather tongue," which may enable her then to find the path to her mother and her "mother tongue." This decision inspires her to learn Arabic from a "great master of Arabic writing," Ibni Abdullah (1994, 15). While this male teacher views his instruction of Arabic as, first and foremost, a religious tool, the primary step toward enabling a true understanding of the Koran, his female pupil is obsessed with the sensual character of Arabic script; when its letters leave her mouth, they assume the shape of birds, fleeing snakes, pomegranate trees freezing in the rain and the wind, and other images suggested to her by their physical form (1994, 20).[3]

The sheer sensuousness the narrator perceives in the Arabic script not only makes her a poor student in the eyes of Ibni Abdullah, who would have her memorize the Koran, but even plays a large role in her impulse to seduce him, an act that ultimately ends their relationship. Her obsession with the pre-semantic physical properties of Arabic and her single-minded focus on those Arabic words that found their way into Turkish long prior to Kemalist modernity, brings to mind Edward Said's famous articulation of the Orient as a locus of sensual, prelapsarian origin for Western poets, the pure space to which "one always *returned*," a return Said finds particularly exemplified by Goethe in the *West-Eastern Divan* (*West-östlicher Divan*, 1819) (1979, 167, Said's italics). Though Özdamar is herself linked by provenance and background, and not just through literary projection, to the Orient, she is as Westernized as the unhappy women mentioned by Horrocks in his analysis of *Caravanserai*. Özdamar's intense occupation with the plays and dramaturgy of Bertolt Brecht, the most important narrative thread linking the rather disparate episodes of *Seltsame Sterne*, began not in Germany but in Turkey. Nevertheless, her strong bond to her grandparents—her beloved grandmother, still completely linked in custom, spirit, and mentality to Turkey's Ottoman past, is a constantly recurring figure in *Seltsame Sterne* and other works—drives her effort to evoke her nation's pre-Kemalist age with its varied, sensual, plurivocal traditions. This bond helped inspire Özdamar to create a countermemory against the oppressive weight of homogenizing, nationalistic Turkish modernity. Özdamar's evocation of the sensual, pre-Western Arabic roots of the Turkish language, the Turkish of her "grandfather's tongue," is part of this countermemorial project. The rich corporeal character of Ottoman Arabicized Turkish evoked in "Grandfather Tongue"—its sheer physicality—completes in a different generic register the ethnically varied musicality of the language evinced in the mother's discussion of the Turkish shadow play in *Caravanserai*. In *Die Brücke vom Goldenen Horn*, by contrast, the alienating politics of modernity, rather than ethnic diversity or an "exotic" script, are shown to create an incomprehensible language among the various factions and classes in Turkey, an incomprehensibility grounded in spiritual isolation and poverty rather than an alterity-driven richness, as is evident in random city and maritime scenes: "At the newspaper stands the leftist, fascist, and religious newspapers hung next to each other, all were in Turkish, but it was like three foreign tongues. On the ship they all opened their leftist, fascist, or religious newspapers and you couldn't see any more faces" (295–96).[4]

While political misunderstanding, mistrust, and incomprehension mark many interactions narrated in *Die Brücke vom Goldenen Horn*, the inter-national linguistic and cultural fissures between Germans and Turks are constant themes in Özdamar's oeuvre as well. Katrin Sieg in particular has shown how Özdamar's early plays draw on the Turkish shadow play tradition and employ what Sieg terms "ethnic drag" to subtly critique not only German stereotypes about Turks, but also the colonialist traces of multiculturalism in contemporary Germany. These plays indirectly illustrate as well, in Sieg's reading, the hardening of German attitudes toward Turks after reunification without actually referencing this event (Sieg 1994, 118–19; 2002, 221–53). Haines and Littler note that "the very location of 'Großvater Zunge,' set in the divided Berlin, symbolizes the incommensurability of cultures. When the protagonist passes from one Berlin reality to the other, she notes with surprise: 'Ah, hier hat es auch geregnet' ['Ah, it rained here too']. This unexpected sameness within difference underlines the complexity of the East-West divide in Özdamar's writing" (136). In the preunification Berlin that also constitutes the setting for *Seltsame Sterne*, it is the difference within sameness that allows Özdamar to create an implied countermemory to present-day denigrations of the German Democratic Republic's former capital. Özdamar uses countermemory in her most recent novel to recuperate East Berlin's image from the standard treatment it has received since reunification. In *Seltsame Sterne*, East Berlin is shown to be a site informed with the sort of tolerance, openness, artistic energy, and even beauty Özdamar evoked in conjuring Turkey's Ottoman past in *Caravanserai*. This vision of East Berlin is connected to Özdamar's memories of the city from the 1970s, but because her constellation of the former East German capital conflicts with conventional media representations of this locale, one may speak of her strategy as countermemorial. We will see that the novel's somatic character also makes it countermemorial in Foucault's sense of the word. As with the Ottoman past narrated in *Caravanserai*, Özdamar instantiates this countermemory without attempting to whitewash or deny East Berlin's negative aspects.

The sense that psychologically discrete time zones separate East and West Berlin is multiply articulated in Özdamar's work. The line cited by Haines and Littler from "Grandfather Tongue" indicating the narrator's surprise that rain had fallen in both halves of the divided city is repeated in *Seltsame Sterne* in its present-tense variant as the narrator emerges in West Berlin from her tram car: "It rains here just like in the East"(40). Indeed, in a footnote containing the English translation for the passage from "Grandfather Tongue," Haines and Littler remark that *Seltsame Sterne* contains "beautiful evocations of the time lag between East and West Berlin, which would explain the protagonist's surprise at this simultaneity." They cite the work of Homi Bhabha in employing the term *time lag*, a temporal perception, they note, that Bhabha associates with a specifically "minority or diasporic consciousness" (136 and 136, n. 55). Turkish political suppression, as well as the pain the narrator feels at her recent divorce in Istanbul, seem consciously highlighted in the novel in order to imbue her voice with the authority of a diasporic outsider who stands removed from the antagonisms in preunification Germany between the governments based in Bonn and East Berlin. Her apparent surprise, however, at the subjection of both East and West Berlin to the same rainy weather is born of a perception that anyone who had experienced both halves of the divided city, including Germans, would have had; the Western half was loud, vibrant, and not a little chaotic and anarchic, while East Berlin was quiet, peaceful, and orderly. One could of course legitimately argue that this distinction manifested Western European freedom vs. Eastern European subjugation during the Cold War, but coming to Berlin from a Turkey depicted in the novel as both subjugated *and* chaotic, the narrator finds the serenity of the GDR's capital a welcome respite from the noisy, disorderly communal life she leads in the Western neighborhood of Wedding.

Özdamar's East Berlin: Regeneration and Repression

East Berlin's calming effect on the narrator is a constant trope in the novel. The opening line of *Seltsame Sterne* describes a ceaselessly barking dog that deprives the narrator of her sleep. Her recitation, even screaming, of the lines from the poem of Else Lasker-Schüler from which the novel's title is derived has no effect (9). In order to escape the dog's noise, the narrator literally flees to the East, where she feels like she has rescued herself from the barking in a manner reminiscent of a fairy tale, in which a thrown comb turns into a sea and saves one from a pursuing giant (18). The few consumer goods in East Berlin shop windows enhance her sense of tranquility with what she perceives as their childlike packaging (19). This paucity contrasts with the clutter of her West Berlin commune, which seems literally to "explode" with household objects and detritus. Looking for something among this material surfeit is so fatiguing that she must constantly sit down. Therefore, she always finds it comforting to travel to East Berlin. Its contrasting image of just a few stores with just a few objects causes her to think, as she often does, of Brecht and Besson. She reflects on Besson's working notes to Brecht's drama *The Good Woman of Sezuan* (*Der gute Mensch von Sezuan*, 1938–40), with its portrayal of the oscillation between socioeconomic ups and downs in capitalist systems (67–68). In the second half of the novel, written in diary form, and after she has obtained a visa allowing her to live in the East (so that she does not have to repeat on a daily basis the crossing of the divided city's border), she remarks in the second diary entry: "The night is so quiet here" (87). It even comforts (*beruhigt*) the narrator that, on New Year's Eve, the border crossing is unmarked by any holiday spirit and work goes on as usual (185).

The contrast between the hectic West and the tranquil East extends even to the narrator's respective sexual relationships on both sides of the border, although this polarity does not apply to the various nationalities of her lovers. In her essay "Play Zones: The Erotics of the New Berlin," which discusses eroticism in novels by women writers set in the late 1990s in this now unified city, Katharina Gerstenberger argues that, in these works, "the female body is the surface on which the contradictions and tensions of the New Berlin become visible" (260). Conversely, in *Seltsame Sterne*, the narrator's erotic episodes become a means by which the discrete urban atmospheres of the still-divided city's two halves in the late 1970s are rendered genealogically transparent (that is, in Foucault's sense, grounded in bodily history). In her West Berlin commune, occupied by seven men and women for whom privacy is rarely a desideratum, pairing-up—*Zweierbeziehungen*—is (officially) not allowed among the members (54), but sex is quickly established at the outset of the narrator's residence in the crowded apartment as an activity no less communal than any other. On her first day there, she pairs with Peter; as they run to his room to consummate their relationship, they hear typewriter noises from another room, and, as they make love on his mattress, they can clearly hear conversations from the bordello located in the building's ground floor (56–57). By contrast, after she begins an affair with an American professor of German and English named Steve, who normally resides and works in Copenhagen (the city where they first make love, and which is portrayed to be as peaceful and tranquil as East Berlin), her colleague Gabi, at whose home the narrator resides in Pankow throughout much of the second half of the novel, ensures their security and privacy: "Steve is in East Berlin for three days. Gabi applied for a visa for him and gave us her bed. She also left us alone during the day" (226). Ironically, communist East Berlin is portrayed as a *non*communal site affording its inhabitants peace and tranquility, in contrast to its crowded, noisy Western counterpart.

Despite this contrast that consistently paints East Berlin in a more positive light than the capitalist Western sector, Özdamar does not engage in unbridled *Ostalgie*; the GDR capital in *Seltsame Sterne* is marked neither by genuine privacy nor by authentic freedom. The novel recounts the bureaucratic chicanery, pervasive eavesdropping, and repressive measures endured by private citizens and visitors to East Germany, as well as historically well-known episodes such as the forced expatriation of poet and singer Wolf Biermann, an event the narrator's Volksbühne colleagues find worthy of protest (178–79). The automobile of her friend Barbara is completely disassembled when the border police find a scrap of paper with dates and times listed on it. She had made these entries as a log of her cigarette consumption, part of her campaign to quit smoking. Because the border police suspect the list is connected to some sort of conspiracy, they question Barbara for many hours. In connection with this event, her boyfriend Manfred, himself a refugee from the GDR who ultimately loses his sanity because of past and present pressures that may stem from either or both sides of the border, ridicules the East German guards by describing a successful escape reflective of their obtuseness (76–77). The narrator herself is a victim of the GDR's absurd repressive measures: an Italian book she had purchased in the West is confiscated because it supposedly glorifies fascism, even though she argues that precisely the opposite is the case. When she relates this event to Gabi, this East German friend responds: "You can't teach the blind what the color white is" (191–92).

Clearly, these particular delineations of East Germany's totalitarian measures are mixed with humor, but this is not always the case in the novel. Because a native Turk who has fallen in love with an East German woman travels to East Berlin one day before his visa takes effect, he becomes permanently barred from the GDR (197, 199). The arrest of the prominent GDR intellectual Rudolf Bahro is refracted through the lens of the personal crisis this causes among the narrator's friends and colleagues in Pankow, because Bahro's ex-wife Gundula is part of this circle. Bahro's claim in his 1977 book *Die Alternative: Zur Kritik des real existierenden Sozialismus* (*The Alternative in Eastern Europe*, 1978)—the publication of which in the West helped trigger his arrest, and which is cited in *Seltsame Sterne*—that "'the world socialist system' and the world communist movement are torn apart by fundamental internal contradictions" (8) is concretely illustrated in Özdamar's third novel through anecdotes such as those cited above. The GDR's flaws are also revealed through discussions of the narrator's East German acquaintances, who sometimes contradict the narrator's positive perception of the socialist state. This occurs most directly when Gabi responds to the narrator's comment that she has found happiness at the East German theater: "You normalize the Wall. For you being here means the expansion of your possibilities in life and work. Others, however, see their possibilities limited" (182). Clearly, *Seltsame Sterne* is no exercise in *Ostalgie*.

Nevertheless, the novel's positive countermemorial vision of the East German capital has a stronger valence than its numerous evocations of the GDR's dark side, and not primarily because it constitutes for the narrator a locus of peace, repose, and fulfilling work. More significantly, Özdamar portrays East Berlin as a place where her Turkish ethnicity finds an overwhelmingly positive reception. This is the case not only with her friends and colleagues, but also with ordinary citizens and even some border police. The first person she meets in East Berlin, an obese young woman with an affectionate black dog, inspires the narrator with a vision of intoxicating solidarity; she imagines, as in an opium intoxication, that this young woman's land will become her land, and that she, the young woman, and the dog will hold hands, fly from one riverbank to another, and smoke together. Her next acquaintance there gives her his matchbox when she tells him how attractive she finds it. She ends up spending the night with this gay man, whose appearance is identical to that of Albrecht Dürer, and she finds herself in love with the East German people, loving them like she adored her grandmother as a child, which is to say without comprehending them (34–37). Indeed, she later meets her converse, an

East German child who knows nothing of Turkey but treats her with courtesy and respect (102). Elderly GDR women are also interested in her country and appreciate the care she shows them during a visit to their nursing home, kissing her as she leaves (217). Heiner Müller tells her: "You are a phenomenon here in the East, you have the warmest eyes in the city" (215). The narrator's acquaintance Murat, the Turk who later becomes the victim of the visa confusion that tragically separates him from his East German lover, proclaims that Turks are regarded as Westerners in the GDR capital (69). The narrator does confront an East German racist, but he mistakes her for a Slav, and he is mainly interested in seducing her (137). She is also treated with respect in West Berlin, but that city's atmosphere at the height of RAF activity[5] reminds her of the paranoia she had so recently experienced in Istanbul. Her sense of solidarity with the GDR is enhanced by her constant communion with the spirit of Brecht, the towering, ghostly force still driving theater life in that country some twenty years after his death. He inspires her even when she is writing to her siblings in Turkey and admonishing them to care for her elderly grandmother although she talks too much, for "Brecht says the old people talk so much because they no longer have much more time" (222).[6] Of course, for Özdamar, Brecht was, in large measure, the embodiment of German cultural life before she had even visited that divided country, so the narrator's obsession with Brecht, particularly evident in his ability to inspire in her feelings of transnational unity, is unsurprising. In sum, East Berlin's negative aspects, which stem from the oppressive government of the German Democratic Republic, are clearly elucidated in Özdamar's third novel. However, this aspect of life in East Germany is well known. Thus, the countermemorial focus in *Seltsame Sterne* is the embrace of ethnic alterity in the former GDR capital.

Özdamar on Germany after the "*Wende*"

In considering *Seltsame Sterne*'s depiction of the respect and tolerance Özdamar apparently experienced in preunification Berlin in the late 1970s, the question naturally arises as to whether she consciously intended the novel to be read in juxtaposition to Germany after the "*Wende*," when incidents of racism and xenophobia directed against people of color in general and Turks in particular escalated dramatically. An avenue toward answering this question may be opened by considering an essay originally published by Özdamar in February 1992 in *Die Zeit* (reprinted and translated in Horrocks and Kolinsky 1996, 55–63).

When this Hamburg newspaper asked her to discuss the relationship between Germans and non-Germans at that time, just a few years after reunification, she agreed to accept the invitation, but forewarned that her response would be something quite at variance with what the paper and its readers might anticipate. What she presumably expected them to expect was a detached, objective, third-person account of the obviously increasing tensions between native "ethnic" Germans and dark-skinned minorities, tensions that soon were to culminate in murderous attacks against Turks in Mölln and Solingen. What she wrote instead was a highly personal, indeed first-person account of her experiences as a writer and theater director in Germany during the 1980s. The title of her essay is "Black Eye and His Donkey" ("Schwarzauge und sein Esel"), as it is centered on the inspiration for, and initial production of, her first play, *Karagöz in Alamania* (1982). Özdamar's choice to focus her essay on this play anticipates her countermemorial strategy. For, as indicated earlier in discussion of the novel *Caravanserai*, Karagöz was always the chief protagonist in the highly multicultural, dialect-rich Turkish shadow plays of the Ottoman Age. Thus, rather than simply writing a critique condemning increasingly violent right-wing campaigns for ethnic and religious homogeneity in Germany in the aftermath of unification, Özdamar's strategy of resistance is to look back at a personal work linked by theme and title to a profoundly plurivocal theatrical tradition in her native land's pre-republican past.

Subsequent to the brief recounting of the inspiration for *Karagöz in Alamania*, the *Zeit* essay is entirely taken up with an account of two richly multinational, multiethnic tableaux: a train ride Özdamar took from Germany to Turkey in order to invite a former *Gastarbeiter* (guest worker), who inspired the play, back to Germany so he could attend its premiere, and the rehearsals for this event. The train contains Greeks, Turks, and Yugoslavs who sit together and communicate in their "common language," broken German, about their trials and tribulations. Their conversation practically becomes an oratorio, and their language mistakes unite them, making them a "we" ("*wir*") (1996b, 58). When Özdamar discusses her experiences in directing *Karagöz in Alamania* at the Frankfurt Schauspielhaus in 1986, she emphasizes the multinational character of her troupe, consisting of Turkish, German, and Spanish performers. During the rehearsals, ethnic and national insults and jealousies surfaced, but the narrator makes these outbreaks seem rather comical (1996b, 55–63). As Horrocks notes in his reading of *Caravanserai*, "graphic representation" seems more significant to Özdamar "than any ideas or messages" (1996, 39–40). In "Black Eye and his Donkey," such powerful iconic anecdotes, rather than detached discursive critiques, serve to illustrate both the comforting cohesion of transnational solidarity (the train ride) and the ludicrousness of interethnic squabbling (the rehearsals). A recourse to her personal past, rather than third-person ideological analysis, informs Özdamar's response to the newspaper's request that she comment on the present (early 1990s) nature of the relationship between Germans and non-ethnic Germans in her adopted land. Precisely such an autobiographically informed countermemory drives the narrative in *Seltsame Sterne*, which can therefore be read, at least in part, as an imaginative rejoinder to racist, xenophobic trends in postunification Germany.

A similarly indirect response to problems of racial hatred characterizes Özdamar's handling of interview questions on this subject. Asked in the course of a 1994 conversation with David Horrocks and Eva Kolinsky about the recent wave of antiforeigner violence in Germany in places like Mölln and Solingen, she first reacts by noting that incidents such as the fall of the Berlin Wall "can change things dramatically." This dramatic event even inspired West Germans to speak to each other on the train: "It was as if all at once they found themselves on an open stage and began talking" (51). This train/play juxtaposition naturally brings to mind the tableaux of the essay "Black Eye and His Donkey," stripped in the interview of their multiethnic cast of characters and populated purely by Germans. This resetting of the juxtaposition perhaps subconsciously reveals a hurt at being excluded from the new dialogue taking pace in the country,[7] a sentiment widespread among Turkish intellectuals in Germany after reunification.[8] Özdamar claims in the 1994 interview that "xenophobia" may be an inappropriate term, since even children can be "targets of aggression." She seems most disturbed by the circumstance that seeing a foreigner instinctively inspires in Germans the need to show they are "*not* xenophobic,"[9] whereas they had lived side-by-side with non-Germans unselfconsciously, "especially in big cities," prior to reunification, as is evident in *Seltsame Sterne*. When Özdamar is "confronted" with such a spectacle, her recourse is simply "staring into space" (1996a, 51, 52, italics in the original). In her response to a question posed to her at the conclusion of her reading for the participants in the summer 2005 Fulbright German Studies Seminar on how she experienced reunification, Özdamar responded laconically that she approved, finding reunified Berlin more beautiful and less provincial, that it depended on the weather (perhaps making this latter incongruous remark because she could no longer delight in realizing, as the narrator in "Grandfather Tongue" and *Seltsame Sterne* had, that it rained on both sides of the Wall), that it had been difficult to live with a Wall, and that Besson and other directors she knew in her GDR days were highly critical of that nation[10] (a circumstance also reflected in *Seltsame Sterne*). Clearly, Özdamar is uncomfortable with xenophobic tendencies in postunification Berlin, but chooses storytelling and poetic allusion over direct political discourse in responding to them, for she prefers to create images and tropes resistant to these tendencies. These are the imaginative techniques rooted in personal experience upon which she draws in order to create a countermemory that challenges contemporary characterizations of Germany's multicultural, multiethnic alterity as a negative and unfortunate circumstance. In *Seltsame Sterne*, countermemory is constituted by Özdamar's recollection of East Berlin's positive response to *her* ethnic alterity, and her reminiscence of the city's artistic vitality.

This approach is evident even in the concluding scene of Özdamar's third novel, another train ride, this time in Paris, where she stands in a full Métro car with Besson: "Black Faces. White Faces. Vietnamese. Algerians. I closed my eyes and heard the voices. Besson said: 'You are tired from the trip, lay your head on my shoulder and sleep a little'" (247). At a certain level, the narrator seems to have found, as the novel comes to an end, a fulfillment to the intensely yearned-for love evoked in the Lasker-Schüler poem from which the novel derives its title, a poem the novel repeatedly cites (9, 168, 243). The transnational Parisian Métro car harkens back to the previously mentioned tableau of "Black Eye and his Donkey," also constellated as both a personally experienced yet utopian projection, redolent of solidarity and plenitude, in response to contemporary interethnic tensions in the newly reunified Germany. Both train rides draw upon the personal past in a metonymical projection of the kind of postunification Germany in which Özdamar would like to live.[11]

Notes

1. While not indebted to Foucault, Aleida Assmann's seminal exploration of countermemory also construes this paradigm as an antidote to discursive, pragmatic, majoritarian approaches to articulating history. Drawing on the writing of George Orwell, Christa Wolf, Peter Sloterdijk, and Jean-François Lyotard, she defines countermemory "as the capacity to keep up the sense of another reality which undercuts the standards of the common world of experience" (1994, 223).

2. On the subtle chronicling of this loss of the "mother tongue" in Özdamar's story, a chronicling seen as grounded in her perception of linguistic interculturalism as the immediately retrievable treasury of a "fully nuanced vocabulary," see Brügmann (2000, 339–41).

3. Ghaussy's linguistically focused reading of *Caravanserai* (1999) views that novel as another example of Özdamar's enactment of a feminine language corporeality resistant to patriarchal semantic instrumentalization of the Koran. See esp. 11.

4. Unless otherwise indicated, all translations from the German are my own.

5. The "Rote Armee Fraktion" (Red Army Faction) was a leftist German terrorist organization particularly active in the 1970s.

6. Because the narrator treats Copenhagen, which she visits with her American lover Steve, as a site (like East Berlin) of great tolerance, and writes the letter with the Brecht quote on the loquacious elderly in the Danish capital, it is interesting to note some of Brecht's core ideas concerning old age were inspired by the Danish writer Karin Michaëlis. (See Eddy 1994).

7. The rather negative, seemingly alienating reminiscence is consistent with Özdamar's association of train rides with deracination (Entwurzelung) in *Caravanserai* and *Die Brücke vom Goldenen Horn*. (See Konuk 1999, 64).

8. In *Ethnic Drag*, Sieg notes how Turks and those generally involved with migrant politics were disturbed at the German Left's apparent lack of interest in these politics in the immediate aftermath of reunification, when Leftists became preoccupied with "'things German.'" She notes that Özdamar's 1991 play *Keloglan in Alamania* "seems to downplay" reunification "as a factor in German-foreigner relations," although Sieg finds that the play alludes to the far friendlier treatment afforded former GDR residents (as opposed to Turks) as "new arrivals" at that time (2002, 234).

9. Özdamar's observation here is reminiscent of the conclusion to her brief tale "Franz" in the collection *Der Hof im Spiegel*. As a streetcar rolls by, the narrator believes all its passengers are looking at her, and their (in her perception) absurd solicitousness instills her with fear: "'Now they think that they have to protect me, now they are afraid.' Then I was afraid that they were afraid" (116).

10. Özdamar's presentation took place on 10 June 2005 at the Fulbright Center in Berlin. She read from *Die Brücke vom Goldenen Horn* and *Seltsame Sterne*. Her reading and her answers to questions from the seminar participants provided the inspiration for this essay.

11. My thanks to Jill Twark and Azade Seyhan for their helpful comments on earlier drafts of this essay.

Works Cited

Assmann, Aleida. 1994. "The Sun at Midnight: The Concept of Counter-Memory and Its Changes." In *Commitment in Reflection: Essays in Literature and Moral Philosophy*, ed. Leona Toker. New York: Garland. 223–44.

Bahro, Rudolf. 1978. *The Alternative in Eastern Europe*, trans. David Fernbach. Oxford: NLB.

Brügmann, Margret. 2000. "Jeder Text hat weiße Ränder: Interkulturalität als literarische Herausforderung." In *Postmoderne Literatur in deutscher Sprache: Eine Ästhetik des Widerstands?*, ed. Henk Harbers. Amsterdam: Rodopi. 335–51.

Cooke, Paul. 2005. *Representing East Germany since Unification: From Colonization to Nostalgia.* Oxford: Berg.

Eddy, Beverly Driver. 1994. "Bertolt Brecht's and Karin Michaëlis's 'Streitigkeiten': Reflections on Old Age and Literature." *Germanic Review* 69: 2–6.

Foucault, Michel. 1977. *Language, Counter-Memory, Practice: Selected Essays and Interviews*, ed. Donald F. Bouchard, trans. Donald F. Bouchard and Sherry Simon. Ithaca, NY: Cornell University Press.

Gerstenberger, Katharina. 2003. "Play Zones: The Erotics of the New Berlin." *German Quarterly* 76: 259–72.

Ghaussy, Sohelia. 1999. "'Das Vaterland verlassen': Nomadic Language and 'Feminine Writing' in Emine Sevgi Özdamar's *Das Leben ist eine Karawanserei*." *German Quarterly* 72: 1–16.

Haines, Brigid, and Margaret Littler. 2004. *Contemporary Women's Writing in German: Changing the Subject.* Oxford: Oxford University Press.

Horrocks, David. 1996. "In Search of a Lost Past: A Reading of Emine Sevgi Özdamar's Novel *Das Leben ist eine Karawanserei, hat zwei Türen, aus einer kam ich rein aus der anderen ging ich raus.*" In Horrocks and Kolinsky 1996. 23–43.

Horrocks, David, and Eva Kolinsky, eds. 1996. *Turkish Culture in German Society Today.* Providence, RI: Berghahn.

Konuk, Kader. 1999. "'Identitätssuche ist ein [sic] private archäologische Graberei': Emine Sevgi Özdamars inszeniertes Sprechen." In *AufBrüche: Kulturelle Produktionen von Migrantinnen, Schwarzen und jüdischen Frauen in Deutschland*, ed. Cathy S. Gelbin, Kader Konuk, and Peggy Piesche. Königstein/Taunus: Ulrike Helmer. 60–74.

Özdamar, Emine Sevgi. 1994. *Mother Tongue*, trans. Craig Thomas. Toronto: Coach House Press.

———. 1996a. "Living and Writing in Germany: Emine Sevgi Özdamar in Conversation with David Horrocks and Eva Kolinsky." In Horrocks and Kolinsky 1996. 45–54.

———. 1996b "Schwarzauge und sein Esel/Black Eye and his Donkey: A Multi-Cultural Experience." In Horrocks and Kolinsky 1996. 55–63.

———. 2000. *Life is a Caravenserai Has Two Doors I Came in One I Went Out the Other*, trans. Luise von Flotow. London: Middlesex University Press.

———. 2001. *Der Hof im Spiegel.* Cologne: Kiepenheuer & Witsch.

———. 2002a. *Die Brücke vom Goldenen Horn.* 1998. Cologne: Kiepenheuer & Witsch.

———. 2002b. *Mutterzunge.* 1990. Cologne: Kiepenheuer & Witsch.

———. 2003a. *Das Leben ist eine Karawanserei hat zwei Türen aus einer kam ich rein aus der anderen ging ich raus.* 1992. Cologne: Kiepenheuer & Witsch.

———. 2003b. *Seltsame Sterne starren zur Erde: Wedding—Pankow 1976/77.* Cologne: Kiepenheuer & Witsch.

Saalfeld, Lerke von. 17 February 2004. "Emine Sevgi Özdamar: Seltsame Sterne starren zur Erde." <http://www.radiobremen.de/online/service/buchtipp/seltsame_sterne.html>.

Said, Edward W. 1979. *Orientalism*. New York: Vintage Books.

Seyhan, Azade. 2001. *Writing Outside the Nation*. Princeton, NJ: Princeton University Press.

———. 2005. "Is Orientalism in Retreat or in for a New Treat? Halide Edip Adivar and Emine Sevgi Özdamar Write Back." *Seminar* 41: 209–25.

Sieg, Katrin.1994. *Exiles, Eccentrics, Activists: Women in Contemporary German Theater*. Ann Arbor: University of Michigan Press.

———. 2002. *Ethnic Drag: Performing Race, Nation, Sexuality in West Germany*. Ann Arbor: University of Michigan Press.

III

TRANSITIONS
Form and Performance after 1989

KATHARINA GERSTENBERGER

One of the most significant features of literature after 1989 is the emergence of forms and plots that not only reflect the sociocultural changes brought about by the Wall's fall but also challenge some of the political assumptions and narrative patterns that dominated postwar German literature. As we approach the twentieth anniversary of the fall of the Wall, the transition period from divided to united Germany has come to an end. But the experience of unification continues to reverberate in literature. Importantly, these echoes are felt in literary form as well as in content and, as the essays in this section show so clearly, it is the interplay of aesthetics and plot where some of these shifts come to the fore.

The changing role of identity illustrates some of the significant differences between pre- and post-Wall literature. Not only have the political circumstances that frame the identity debate changed, but the modes of thinking about the issues are different today than they were twenty years ago. In the (West German) literature of the 1970s and 1980s, identity politics served to assert the voices of those who had not been heard before: women's writing and migrant literature are the most pertinent examples, but the works of sexual or ethnic minorities come to mind as well. Much of this literature was autobiographical or documentary. In the East German context, the emphasis on the collective brought forth different models, but here, too, female identity was a prevalent topic, as was as the tension between individual and community.

After 1989, the search for a post-Wall or united German identity ensued, with literature playing a remarkably prominent role in the process. Quickly, however, it became clear that multiple issues were at stake. East Germans asserted their history and experience against West German assumptions; young West German writers challenged their parents' narratives about the significance of Nazi history for German identity. At the same time, some members of the student movement offered critical reflections on their role in postwar culture; second-generation writers of Turkish or other non-German backgrounds began to write stories that were markedly different from those of their first-generation predecessors. Women writers continue to incorporate feminist positions into their texts but, more often than not, the assertion of a specifically female voice is no longer the prime focus. Sexuality, too, becomes part of larger narrative frameworks. As German identity after 1989 must define itself in a global context, literary texts probe the specificity as well as commonalities of subject positions, allowing individual, social, ethnic, gender, and national identities to rub against one another. Identity becomes textual rather than solely biographical or biological.

Form and performance are two key concepts that run through the essays assembled in this section, and both tie in with questions of identity and literary identity politics. Form is an aesthetic category that lost some of its critical appeal in the 1970s and 1980s with the shift toward a literature (and scholarship) in which social issues and struggles occupied considerable ground (Beutin 2001, 608ff). The renewed emphasis on form in the 1990s, however, as the essays here show, is as much a political move as it is about aesthetics. While the literary debates of the late 1980s and early 1990s were to a significant degree about the return of aesthetics at the expense of political engagement (Schirrmacher 1990; Bohrer 1995), the contributions in this section revisit and challenge this division. Literary form, i.e., aesthetics, these essays show, becomes increasingly important to express political concerns as well. Form, importantly, has a long tradition in delimiting the corpus of German literature. The writers discussed in this section appropriate this tradition for the aesthetic and political purposes of contemporary German literature.

Performance, similarly, entails the representation of identity, including gender and ethnicity, and the political implications of such categories. The term, which gained currency among literary critics in the early 1990s, implies that gender, sexuality, or race are socially constructed and can, therefore, be appropriated by individuals and groups for purposes of pleasure, subversion, or outright resistance against social constraints or oppression. Drawing on Judith Butler's ground-shifting work on femininity (1990), critics used the concept in conjunction with ethnicity and race and began to analyze these categories as examples of performance (Sieg 1998). In the literary text, performance functions to expand and to rewrite constructs such as Germanness or gender. The importance of form and performance for the transformations following the fall of the Wall suggest that identity in the twenty-first century is more fluid, more aware of its constructed nature, and more contextualized than before 1989.

All the essays in this section reflect on questions of form. Two pieces focus on poetry as the genre traditionally most closely tied to formal issues; one looks to the novel as the genre that is often considered most flexible in terms of structure and language. All three link issues of form to questions of identity and performance, making the case for more complex relationships between writing and the subject positions it creates. In different ways, all three address questions of Germanness after 1989 and its changing meanings. All of them argue, again from different perspectives and vantage points, that literary tradition, which historically has always been closely linked to definitions of Germanness, today is a powerful tool to challenge, expand, and rewrite notions of Germanness. Two of the essays engage with the works of German-Turkish writers, the third deals with East German poets after the Wall. This selection is no coincidence. More than with other writers, such authors' backgrounds and biographies raise certain reader expectations about the authentic nature of their texts. As the following essays show, these writers' postunification texts engage with specific circumstances and histories, but at the same time strive to move out of literary and social niches that have become restrictive.

Erika M. Nelson's essay "A Path of Poetic Potentials: Coordinates of German Lyric Identity in the Poetry of Zafer Şenocak" argues that Şenocak uses the German as well the Turkish literary tradition to complicate notions of home and belonging. Through his lyric poetry in particular, Şenocak, a leading intellectual and one of Germany's most renowned writers of Turkish descent, challenges preconceived notions of ethnic identities and national distinctions. Şenocak's blurring of linguistic and ethnic boundaries works toward multicultural communication. Highly conscious of form, Nelson argues, Şenocak's poetry expands the boundaries of German literature. The writer's background fades into the lines of his poetry, focusing our attention away from biographical facts to the intricacies of form. Through form, he communicates individuality as well as the complexities of difference.

In her essay on East German poetry, titled "Performing GDR in Poetry?: The Literary Significance of 'East German' Poetry in Unified Germany," Birgit Dahlke arrives at similar conclusions as Erika Nelson about the significance of form. Dahlke argues for a "GDR literature after the GDR" even in the case of writers who began their publishing careers after 1989, because the GDR, with its emphasis on community, encouraged a different aesthetics than West German individualism. Through her careful close readings, Dahlke highlights the importance of poetic form and rhetorical strategies as these poets engage with their

East German upbringing and socialization, closely intertwining political and aesthetic concerns. The result is a critical engagement with the GDR and the self-understanding of its writers. At the same time, these texts insist on their difference from West German traditions and West German assumptions about the GDR. The question mark in the essay's title suggests that there is no authentic East Germany. Instead, Dahlke argues, we have aesthetic products that engage with the GDR's past realties and their resonances in the present.

In "Feridun Zaimoglu's Performance of Gender and Authorship," Gary Schmidt reflects on the connection between form and performance in the work of German-Turkish writer Feridun Zaimoglu. Like Nelson, Schmidt begins his essay by challenging existing categories of migrant literature. In particular in the depictions of young Turkish men in Germany of his earlier writings, Zaimoglu, Schmidt shows, draws on the concept of performance. His use of an aggressive and hypermasculine language served to challenge the subservient position of the Turkish guest worker in society as well as literature. In his later works, however, Zaimoglu returns to a more traditional language and genre, a move Schmidt describes as the writer's performance of German authorship. Critics like Zafer Şenocak have attacked Zaimoglu's use of a Turkish female narrative voice in his latest novel as a reinstatement of essentialism. For Schmidt, Zaimoglu's narrative strategy is an indication that performance, once an expression of protest, can also be used to enter the literary mainstream.

In concert, the three essays in this section argue the case for the importance of literature to express shifting identity constructions and to explore new subject positions. Performance, both as a social practice and as a literary strategy, makes productive the tension between the desire for authenticity and the possibilities afforded by forms that are open and connective rather than exclusive and dividing. Identity politics have lost some of their urgency in post-Wall literature, but that does not mean that the issue no longer causes controversy. The writers discussed here draw on German literary traditions to broaden the scope of what is considered German history and culture. The intense focus on language and form makes their texts specific to the German context and at the same time gives them an aesthetic appeal that transcends the boundaries of national literature.

Works Cited

Beutin, Wolfgang, et. al. 2001. *Deutsche Literaturgeschichte. Von den Anfängen bis zur Gegenwart.* 6th edition. Stuttgart: Metzler.

Bohrer, Karl Heinz. 1995. "Erinnerung an Kriterien: Vom Warten auf den deutschen Zeitroman." *Merkur* 49: 1055–61.

Schirrmacher, Frank. 1990. "'Dem Druck des härteren, strengeren Lebens standhalten'." *Frankfurter Allgemeine Zeitung*, 2 June. Reprinted in *"Es geht nicht um Christa Wolf": Der Literaturstreit im vereinten Deutschland*. Ed. Thomas Anz. Munich: Edition Spangenberg. 77–89.

Sieg, Katrin. 1998. *Ethnic Drag and National Identity: Multicultural Crises, Crossings, and Interventions*. Ann Arbor: University of Michigan Press.

9

A Path of Poetic Potentials
Coordinates of German Lyric Identity in the Poetry of Zafer Şenocak

ERIKA M. NELSON

People are curious to know where I come from.
Few are interested in the path that I have taken.
                    –Zafer Şenocak, "Territories"[1]

Biographical introductions are commonplace in the presentation of an author's work and have, at least historically, played a role in the reception and understanding of the author's work and its canonization. Usually it is through a writer's biography that critics and readers seek to understand the context of a writer's literary achievement, searching perhaps for some clue that points to life circumstances, situations, and conflicts that served as inspiration and motivation for the literary work. This search is not always misguided, as authors often do draw upon their own life experiences and acknowledge these experiences as part of the creative material from which they draw inspiration. Nonetheless, as is so often pointed out in basic introductions to the field of literary criticism, an author's country of origin and biography do not equal, determine, or in any way fully account for the production or outcome of his or her work. In the case of transnational authors, attention to their background, nationality, and heritage often complicates or even overshadows the literary works and has repercussions on their reception. The authors' transnational identity often becomes the center of attention, and their work is relegated to a position of secondary importance or even placed in a special category of "minority writing" outside of serious literary discussions or of the canon itself. Transnational literary identity thus has both liberating and confining connotations.

The term *transnationalism* suggests that both an author's persona and his or her work encompass experiences of two or more cultures and national contexts, and that the writer is able to draw upon both literary and linguistic traditions. The transnational author thus transcends national boundaries and creates an experience of being "in-between," able to move freely and mediate between the cultural landscapes. Nonetheless, for many authors, this space of "in-between" also easily becomes a no-man's land that exiles them to the space of the "other," shutting them out of the mainstream discussions, or at least relegating them to the margins of culture. Increasingly, transnational authors understand the complexities of their experiences and embrace a wider transnational perspective that places them centrally in the context of the "adopted" culture, while their language and place of origin retain significance in their work, not only for them, but for their audience as well.

Such is the case of Zafer Şenocak, a prize-winning poet, translator, editor, and political and philosophical essayist who is considered to be one of the most innovative literary figures in contemporary Germany, yet who is consistently asked to comment on his ethnic and linguistic background. Şenocak's hard-hitting essays and complex novels have placed him at the center of current cultural debates on national identity, multiculturalism, and memory (Cheesman and Yeşilada 2003; Adelson 2002, 326–38; Gerstenberger 2002, 235–50). Yet critics and journalists continue to place him and his work, particularly his poetry, either decisively outside of German culture or in a limited space and capacity somewhere between German and Turkish culture, where it functions to elucidate either side to or for the other.

This study investigates the role and place of Şenocak's poetry within his oeuvre and within German literary culture. In particular, it explores the way Zafer Şenocak's poetic identity is imagined, produced, and received. It also addresses how this poetic identity simultaneously conforms to and resists attempts to commodify his ethnicity and background in the reception of his work. Şenocak uses certain assumptions that arise in the reception of his work and the work of other authors to address and challenge both the obvious and subtle ways in which stereotypical notions of nationality and citizenship reveal themselves in society and culture. His work itself, as well as his active questioning of its reception, also seeks to clarify the function of the somewhat elusive boundary between the national and the transnational German-language literary canon.[2] As Şenocak affirms: "Every border separates and joins at the same time. It can be a fence but also a crossing" (2005a). As Leslie Adelson has pointed out, intercultural encounters take place within German culture, not between German culture and something outside it. In her article entitled "Against Between: A Manifesto," Adelson argues that the "trope of 'betweenness' often functions literally like a reservation designed to contain, restrain, and impede new knowledge, not enable it." She further maintains that "cultural contact today is not an 'intercultural encounter' that takes place between German culture and something outside it, but something happening within German culture between the German past and the German present" (2003, 41).

It is indeed within German culture that Şenocak is best understood. He has been described by Sargut Şolçün (2000, 151) as an "agitated lyricist" and an "angry essayist."[3] Şenocak's stylish and provocative essays[4] explore taboo and repressed aspects in the "Occidental" understanding of the "Orient," as well as the role of Islam within Europe, definitions of national and cultural identity, and Turkish-German culture. His contribution to postunification literature and to the changing landscape of German cultural memory is well acknowledged; his essays, novels, and poetry have won him international acclaim in France, Turkey, the United States, and the United Kingdom. As a result, Şenocak's has become one of the most important critical literary voices concerning Turkish-German as well as post-*Wende* multicultural affairs.

Although Şenocak is generally recognized as a "public intellectual," it becomes clear that his reception in Germany, particularly as a poet, lags behind his international acclaim, even though—according to his own self-portrayals in interviews—it is his identity as a poet with which he most closely identifies and which he privileges.[5] This lack of recognition of him as a "German poet" calls for a reconsideration of his poetic work beyond the transnational label within the German-language literary canon. In its harking back to both modern and traditional German poetic models, his poetry embodies the individual, visionary voice of the German lyric tradition, which ponders, questions, and probes, while formulating, articulating, and offering up its findings to its readers and listeners.

Şenocak's identity as a poet—expressed in his self-presentation, as well as in the nontraditional subject positions created within his work—moves within German culture and the German literary canon and, transnationally, beyond the boundaries of this single national literary tradition. The poetry initially appears sparse and highly symbolic, without many direct references to identifiable national or geographic markers. Upon closer examination, however, it emerges as highly layered and multivalent with poetic images and symbols that refer back to both well-known and lesser-known German, Turkish, and international models. Şenocak's self-understanding as a poet and the lyric identities created within his poetry undermine the essentialist equation of the author's biography to the author's work.

Şenocak emerges as a writer who resists simple classification in terms of nationality, heritage, and language. In this refusal to be enclosed in narrow definitions, he is happily "homeless," geographically-speaking, and simultaneously "at home" in literature and in language. Şenocak's poetry pays particular attention to the power of words, often isolating individual words in his usage and renegotiating critical terms, definitions, and key themes and concepts central to transnational authors and their identities, such as "home," "language," and "crossing." Şenocak revises stereotypical patterns of perception, not only to challenge fidelity to certain assumptions, but also to recover the power of the word in order to articulate his own subjectivity and sense of "home" on his terms: He opposes the geographically determined categories of home and language that critics seem to want to impose upon him, and instead reinscribes within language, literature, and metaphor a linguistic or literary home, which allows him to validate his own position as a poet in the German literary canon, and not simply within the smaller, peripheral subcategory of a transnational or migrant literature.

The Biographical Challenge: Overcoming Transnational Origins

Against homogenizing models, Şenocak's insistence on being recognized as a poet echoes throughout many interviews he has given in which he also emphatically rejects being seen as a spokesman for all Turkish-Germans: "I always speak for myself. I write about my topics and there are people who can identify with these things. But I am not a group poet. I am far too critical socially. How I'm seen is another matter" (2006).

Understanding that the transnational identity of a writer has value as an aesthetic cultural product, which is both realized and threatened through its unavoidable participation in consumer culture, Şenocak resists the commodification of the transnational aspect of his identity as a poet. In line with what Katharina Gerstenberger has suggested, Şenocak's lyric identity signifies "agency, resistance, and a generally more nuanced assessment of the immigrant experience" (2004, 210–11). He argues emphatically against stereotypical ethnic appropriation of his works within the context of commodity culture, refusing to appease the German audience's desire for him to act as a spokesperson for improved Turkish-German relations. Instead Şenocak stresses the imaginative and poetic aspects of his innovative writing.

Şenocak's work is a hybrid cultural product born out of migration, yet decisively shaped by German influences. He does not easily fit into any existing category: as a Turkish-German, he does not correspond to the image of Turkish labor immigrants in Germany, as he was born in Ankara in 1961 and moved with his middle-class parents from Istanbul to Munich when he was nine years old. Furthermore, he is well versed in multiple literary, cultural, and historical traditions and genres, often transgressing familiar aesthetic parameters by introducing competing narrative voices, multiple narrative perspectives, and numerous imbedded and interwoven examples of intertexuality. Şenocak describes his poetry as moving between defined spaces, in "a third place, where perhaps a broken, fleeting mother tongue hides, where the placelessness [*Ortlosigkeit*] of my inner world and the positioning [*Verortung*] of my outer world are cancelled out, where inner and outer touch and filter each other" (1992c, 99). It is in this third space that his work imaginatively pushes one to think and perceive beyond national and transnational boundaries.

To the issue of whether he sees himself as a Turkish-German author, Şenocak states that this is "always a special discussion" in Germany (2006). He sees descriptions and labels as burdensome. They might initially aid in introducing, publishing, and marketing a new minority author, but in the long term they can limit the potential scope of the author's reception. Furthermore, as Katharina Gerstenberger indicates regarding such labeling:

> The classification of an author in terms of ethnic background presumes that literary output stands in a causal relationship to biography and, moreover, that the writer's non-Germanness makes her or him interesting to a presumably German audience. The minority writer's rejection of the label "ethnic writer" in favor of "German author" lays claim to German culture as a realm in which ethnic difference is neutralized by a common language and literature. (2004, 209)

Şenocak repeatedly reminds his audience and critics that his "transnational" situation is by no means unique: "Germany has also a tradition of authors who come from other countries and write in German" (2006). In an interview with Tom Cheesman, he called attention to the transnationalism of the German literary tradition, which was lost when German began to be thought of as a "national" language rather than a "Kultursprache":

> Because the German language knew something like this before the war, before National Socialism, but after that only as fragmentary, broken—actually about the situation of exile. It was an unbelievable

homogenization machine, the extinguishing of all types of difference, of variations in stylistic situations, of languages within the German language space, in all of Europe. (Cheesman 2003, 19)

Typically, this question of how to assess the place of minority or transnational literature in relation to national literature functions, as Gerstenberger has asserted, as a challenge to "two categories through which Germans traditionally imagine themselves as distinct from others: ethnicity as a marker of difference and German literature as a nationalistic tradition" (2004, 210).[6]

Şenocak, however, asks a somewhat different question: "It may be that the poet is part of his poem, yet where does the poem belong?" His 1994 essay "Germany is More a Language Than a Land" clarifies that for Şenocak, language is his home. Asked by Halil Gökhan in a 1994 interview where he would situate himself and his poetry against the background of home and belonging (*Heimat und Zugehörigkeit*), he responded:

If you approach the poem as a scholar, then you can assume that the poem belongs to the language in which it was written. A sociologist or a literary scholar interprets the poet in the context of the society, the country, the environment in which he lives. Generally the poet is regarded as a being that has provisionally settled into society. . . . Perhaps the point of departure for a poem is the moment in which a human being does not feel that he belongs to the world in the midst of which he sees himself; the poem is the echo of a dissonance. In the poem I am not looking for the answer to the question "Where do I belong?" For the poem gives no answers. To a certain extent it is a question, a structure unto itself, woven out of questions that have not been asked. (2000c, 49)

Şenocak understands his poems to be "echoes of these questions" (49), which form a sort of inner "map" of one's childhood that one carries inside oneself. It is the "path" that one has chosen, the inner map that one follows, which most interests Şenocak. Thus, for him, the "nation" or "country" of Germany is seen not in terms of an externally drawn, geographically defined space of cultural norms, but rather in terms of the inner language of one's own life, as captured in literature. Reflecting back to the inner map of his own childhood, Şenocak recalls: "I first perceived Germany as a book. An alphabet that smells good and delights in colors. The book that taught me German. Later I read Kafka, Bachmann, Rilke, and Trakl in high school. At the time, Germany appeared to me more as a language than as a land. To date, nothing about that has changed" (2000c, 50). In his work, Şenocak reveals the porosity of boundaries (national, geographic, ethnic, cultural, mental, and institutional) that are all too often selectively drawn between what are considered mainstream and minority writing. As Matthias Konzett asserts, this is what makes Şenocak's work particularly compelling within the debate on national/transnational writing: "In Bakhtin's sense of carnivalization, Şenocak explodes the genre of minority writing and restores its openness and potential as a genre yet to be discovered" (2003, 52).

Şenocak's poetry, as opposed to his critical essays and prose works, does not directly dramatize cultural hybridity in overt terms; it functions, according to Konzett, as a "performative" rather than a pedagogical facet of culture (43). With what Konzett points to as its deceptively simplistic poetic style, subversive humor, and "ironic distance from all forms of sentimental identity politics" (50), Şenocak's lyric work transgresses the boundaries that characteristically confine and limit the genre of minority writing. As Konzett demonstrates in his article, Şenocak takes on the "role of public intellectual" who is "both an outsider and insider to society," appealing to as wide an audience as possible yet deliberately choosing the path of "dissent against the status quo" (43).

These descriptions of Şenocak as public intellectual carry over in many ways to Şenocak as a poet. Critics, it appears, have marginalized the significance of his contribution to the field of German-language poetry, perhaps unsure of how to approach what Hans-Jürgen Heise (1997) has described as Şenocak's ability to write "with a calculated look of innocence" (14). Alternative frameworks for thinking about the cultural reorientation of Şenocak's poetry, not in terms of geographic but rather of linguistic dislocation, are needed, which in turn challenge the models of identity and subjectivity that underpin much of the discussion of German-language transnational literature. Within his poetry, Şenocak creates a nexus for interaction between multiple discourses that reevaluate cultural values, yet he resists thematizing ethnically identifiable experiences in overt poetic terms. In this very act of resistance to normative categorizations of his work, Şenocak carves out a place for his own authentic poetic voice.

The Poetic Challenge: Redefining Şenocak's Way Home in Lyric Terms

Şenocak's use of language to draw out new perspectives lies at the heart of his work, particularly his poetry. The title of his most recent publication, *Übergang* (Crossing, 2005), suggestively alludes to a central theme of transnational literature, an indication perhaps that his work nonetheless participates in the ever-widening debate on ethnic, migrant, and transnational literature, which includes a growing body of literature dealing with "crossing borders" between cultures and the identities associated with these experiences. This anthology is a compilation of new and hitherto unpublished poems, as well as poems selected from prior collections that date back to 1980 and to the beginning of his career as a writer and poet, including *Flammentropfen* (Drops of Flame, 1985), *Ritual der Jugend* (Ritual of Youth, 1987), *Das senkrechte Meer* (The Vertical Sea, 1991), and *Fernwehanstalten* (Institutes of Wanderlust, 1994). In *Übergang*, poems are numbered and grouped together in cycles, comprised of both new and previously published poems from different collections, many of which are now no longer available. This selection allows the reader a better sense of Şenocak's poetic style and of how he has developed specific themes and his laconic tone over time. The lyric voice often remains private and aloof, a keen, somewhat quiet, yet observant commentator of the peculiarities of often mundane events and musings, mirroring in many ways Şenocak's own stance: "I consciously take a marginal position, in order to taunt society from its margins" (2006).

Rather than offering information about Turkish-German identity in his poetry, Şenocak's poems interrogate key concepts and terms well known in the German lyric tradition, such as, for instance, Rilkean evocations of *Haus, Heim,* and *Land* (house, home, country) in modern terms. Metaphors become wordplays that alienate, contradict, and subvert conventional ways of understanding these key phrases. As Şenocak explained in "Zwischen Herz und Haut" (Between Heart and Skin), a speech delivered when he received the Adelbert-von-Chamisso Prize[7] in 1988, metaphors are the backbone or—as he prefers to call them—"*das Muttermal*" or "birthmark" of his poetry. Here he describes the metaphor as "an indispensable expression of poetic perception, in which the boundaries between the abstract sphere of thinking, the porous world of feeling, and concrete sensuous perception dissolve" (1992c, 100). As he explained in the interview with Halil Gökhan, metaphors for him are "junctures that the subject creates in language," "the subject's points of linkage [*Verknüpfungspunkte*] in language" (2000c, 51). Şenocak's highlighting of these points of linkage often reveals a new underlying meaning of words, as for instance in his use of "*Wort Schatz*" in the title of one of his poetry collections entitled "Wort Schatz Insel". This is a play on the word *Wortschatz*, which means "vocabulary" or a "treasury of words." The splitting of the two words is understood as "Word Treasure," which implies that each word is in itself a treasure or has a treasure inside it. The isolation and emphasis of each word is further underscored by the addition of the concept of *Insel* (island).

In his poetry, thinking and feeling come together and are resolved in concrete sensual perception of such commonplace terms as *home*, *house*, *door*, and *tree*. In his use of them, they take on new signification as they expose ruptures, contradictions, and duplicitous, even illogical meanings. For instance, in Poem VII of the cycle "Vor der Festung" (In Front of the Fortress), a meditation on whether an exit can exist without human beings coming and going through it leads into an existential discussion of how language—here the label *Ausgang* (exit) usually hung above doors—both conditions and limits perception. Then the English word *exit* is introduced as another word for *exile*, leading to the statement that one only believes in the possibility of the exit in certain circumstances: either one does not know the language, which defines and limits the exit's function by naming it, or one is an optimist. The latter is envisioned here as an old man who tucks away visitors into the pages of a book:

> nennt man einen Ausgang Notausgang
> wenn keiner gesehen worden ist der kam oder ging
> dahinter das Zimmer das niemals betreten wird
> ein stickiges Zimmer
> dunkel
> es gibt keinen Durchgang
> Exit ist nur ein anderes Wort für Exil
> man glaubt an den Ausgang
> wenn man die Sprache nicht kann
> oder ein Optimist ist
> so nennen sie den dessen Knochen in diesem Haus
> alt und brüchig geworden sind
> einen Optimisten
> wenn Besuch kommt
> öffnet er sein Buch
> und die darin Platz finden
> werden seine Vertrauten (2005b, 68)[8]*

It is clear from the poem that the book offers people refuge from this confusion, as well as a home that is more appealing than the stuffy dark room of potential exile. The optimistic old man is able to offer

---

* *translation on page 174; German passage used with permission.*

visitors who are entered into his book this refuge, and it is in the book and in language that the visitor becomes a confidant and privy to his hope. Here, the power of writing presents an alternative to the traditional understanding of "exit" and "exile."

Şenocak's poetry muses, experiments, and ponders, often traversing long stretches of imaginative possibilities to reach a presumed destination, which nonetheless often remains ambiguous and elusive. The poetic voice is highly subjective, at times a deeply internalized investigator of the self. As Heise (1997) has described, in Şenocak's poetry the subject who expresses himself appears often as "a stranger to himself" and approaches himself as a scientific object of investigation. The poetry is also noticeably tamer in tone than his essays and prose. Nonetheless, it still maintains its keen wit, as for instance in "Poem X," also from the cycle "Wort Schatz Insel":

> du lernst sprechen
> Wort für Wort
> nicht aber das Warten
> in diesem Land
> ist die Sprache
> ein so grosser Wartesaal
> selbst für Lautsprecher (2005b, 54)[9]*

Exhibiting Şenocak's simple yet undeniably clever linguistic invention and inversion, this poem equates the language one learns to speak with a waiting room that is considered to be large, even for loudspeakers. The process of learning a language does not prepare one for the process of waiting. Given the beginning of the poem, it is virtually impossible to understand loudspeakers as audio equipment at the end of this poem. Instead, these loud speakers are seen in conjunction with the one who learns to speak, but not to wait, and finds him/herself waiting, stuck in the language waiting room, even though he/she can speak out loudly. The poem undermines the power and agency typically associated with linguistic ability, i.e., the belief one can effect change by learning to speak a language, to speak up for oneself, or to voice one's opinions. Here, the lack of a determined goal or an anticipated response is highlighted: language becomes the place where one waits, unsure of any change. It is also in the lines of the poem itself that this uncertainty and waiting appears. As there is no punctuation, a reader must pause after

---

* translation on page 174; German passage used with permission.

the word "Warten" in order to make sense of the whole poem, as the line "in diesem Land" belongs with the line "ist die Sprache" and not with the line "nicht aber das Warten."

This poem portrays tensions readily identifiable with situations non-native speakers of a language confront when dealing with a foreign bureaucracy, for instance. In this context, the poem can be interpreted within the national/transnational context. At the same time, the poem speaks as easily to anyone who has struggled to articulate a vision and finds oneself stuck in a place of uncertainty. This multivalence of possible readings is a key feature of Şenocak's poetry and highlights that there is no one way of interpreting the poetic images and experiences created by the linguistic oppositions and contradictions commonly found in his work. In a 1996 essay, "Which Myth Writes Me?" Şenocak locates the source of his writing in what he calls the "ambivalence between a rational and a mystical (or in more modern terms, a mysterious) experience of the world, between physics and metaphysics" (2000g, 79). Şenocak articulates these imaginative potentials and poetic spaces of possibility:

> oft sitzt man Rücken an Rücken
> und denkt über den Weg nach
> der sich in Blickrichtung auftut
> den man gehen könnte
> ein Leben lang zu Fuss
> bis man sich wiedertrifft (2005b, 45)[10*]

His writing, Şenocak asserts, "arises in a field of tension between personal experience and linguistic imagination" (2000g, 77). The way in which the world of experience intersects with the imaginative power of language yields the style and form of his literary production. This tension creates the experience of what Şenocak has termed *Doppel-züngigkeit*,[11] an image that recurs in his work, whereby this double-tonguedness expresses itself in Şenocak's poetry as small aesthetic subversions (Beil 2003, 34). In this poem, for instance, the contrast of meeting oneself again is conceived as a face-to-face encounter, yet is imagined in the sense of meeting with an unknown self as other while seated back-to-back. Thus, imaginatively, one must conceive of both happening simultaneously and successively, transversing both time and space.

---

* *translation on page 175; German passage used with permission.*

Şenocak never allows for a simple mapping of one cultural convention or stereotype onto one's expected experience of it: these expectations are constantly challenged and undermined by his exploration of potentials. Again and again, key issues, including *Heimat*, ethnicity, nationality, and geography, are presented as unreliable and even unimportant markers of difference in his poetry, thus defying readers' expectations, classifications, and definitions. As the poem suggests, one can travel the world a life long in one's imagination, never leaving the place where one is to ultimately come to a sense of meeting up with oneself. This reunion suggests a homecoming to one's potential, seen here as a long lost, or even an unknown, sense of self, which although imagined outside of oneself, is ultimately found within oneself.

The poem chosen for the back cover of the collection *Übergang* is an example of how his poetry often presents unexpected turns on stereotypical cultural iconography:

gehst du zum Wald
vergiß nicht
das Märchen
das wird dich verstecken
wenn du kein Haus
mehr findest.[12]*

Here one is presented with the world and metaphor of the *Märchen* (fairy tale), and perhaps the forest and house of the German *Märchen*. One might also think of other *Märchen*, including those of the Orient, such as the *The Arabian Nights*.[13] However, in this poem, it is not the Oriental fairy tale, but rather the genre of the German fairy tale—not the geography or the house itself—that promises to provide refuge and shelter, in case one cannot find a home. It is in literature, here in the form of the fairy tale genre, central to both the "Oriental" and "Occidental" (i.e., German-language) canons, where the poetic voice, perhaps by extension even Şenocak himself, has hope of finding a home. Şenocak's poetry also highlights the tendency to see the *Märchen* in nationalistic terms as belonging to a canon that is defined through nationhood and national ideas rather than language. Here Şenocak reclaims it in literary terms as a place of refuge within language.

There are also echoes in the verse "Gehst du zum Wald" to a significant passage in Nietzsche's *Also sprach Zarathustra* (*Thus Spake*

---

* translation on page 175; German passage used with permission.

Zarathustra, 1883–1885), when Zarathustra goes into the forest and meets the holy man who describes his frustration with people and has chosen to live in the forest, singing and praising God, unaware that God is dead, thereby introducing the modernist crisis of the Western tradition.[14] Furthermore, this *Märchen* evokes discussions in which Şenocak and other writers have addressed Western fascinations and preoccupations with "the Orient" including early, often misguided attempts at understanding and categorizing minority literature in the 1980s, when this body of work was termed *Ausländerliteratur* (foreigner literature) and *Gastarbeiterliteratur* (guest-worker literature). In his essay, "Ein Türke geht nicht in die Oper" (A Turk Doesn't Go to the Opera), Şenocak sums up this persistent stereotypical view by saying: "From this perspective, the literature of the Orient to this day still consists of fairy tales. An Arabic author is always only a fairy tale teller [*Märchenerzähler*]" (1992b, 25).

In this vein, Şenocak's *Märchen* also evokes Kemal Kurt's essay "Not an Oriental (Fairy) Tale," in which Kurt emphatically rejects any tendency toward exoticism of Turkish-German affairs as far-off Oriental fairy tales by addressing the harsh reality of escalating racism in Germany and listing the locations and the details of countless hate crime incidents against foreigners in Germany. In his sober evaluation of current realities, Kurt evokes the words of the poet Paul Celan, to assess the situation and voice his criticism:

> "Death is a master from Germany," Paul Celan wrote. The master has worked overtime in the past few years: In Eberswalde, a man from Angola is beaten to death by skinheads. In a Mecklenburg hall, youths kill the eighteen-year-old Romanian Dragomir Christenel. The Vietnamese Nguyen Van Tu is stabbed to death by right-wing extremists in Berlin-Marzahn. . . . To be continued. (1998, 265)

Kurt's inclusion of the verse "Death is a master from Germany" from Celan's poem "Todesfuge" ("Death Fugue") is both a reminder of the past and an imminent warning for the present. It should not be surprising that Şenocak also considers Celan to be one of his most important influences as a poet. For Şenocak (2000d, 69), Celan's poetry "is borne by remembrance . . . Celan's entire oeuvre serves as a legacy of linguistic (im) possibilities," and as Şenocak further describes: "The poet, who resides within the word, leaves the land. Rarely was Celan at the place where his words were born. His words were far away from their roots. German is a language, but what is Germany? A land without its language? For Celan, German is a language, his language without land" (2000d, 70). Here, the discussion within which both Kurt and Şenocak situate their work is one that is decidedly German, decidedly within Germany's past and present, connecting the atrocities of the Holocaust to recent racial and xenophobic attacks. It continues a much larger debate within German literary criticism surrounding German postwar poetry, launched with Theodor Adorno's questioning the writing of poetry after Auschwitz.[15] This question of poetry's role in the face of violence seems particularly pertinent to post-*Wende* poetry, given recent racial attacks within the same language and literary culture that has been so implicated in the past, and which, as Kurt implies in his essay, has not yet fully overcome its past.

In Poem VII of the cycle "Wort Schatz Insel," the awkwardness of coming to terms with a complex predicament finds expression in the image of dealing with the three-armed orphan child:

> wen wundert's
> das Kind drüben hat drei Arme
> beim Aufheben ist es verschwenderisch
> und zum Umarmen fehlt noch ein Arm
> wen wundert's
> einem solchen Kind genügt keine Mutter
> den Vater hat es nie gesehen
> es brachte sich selbst auf die Welt
> und hat sich selbst aus der Welt geschafft (2005b, 51)[16]*

Şenocak's provocative image of this child evokes a circumstance that is in many ways unnatural and precarious to deal with. Metaphorically, it seems to address an issue that is difficult to grasp and take hold of; it appears to be addressing a myriad of situations, including, for instance, the struggle Germany faces in coming to terms with its past and present, its national and transnational identity, and the unexpected third "appendage" this child has. The additional arm emerges as Germany's historical appendage, a visible challenge, not to be overlooked, which requires special attention and care. One mother is not enough. The father is not known. This difficult predicament brought itself into the world as a child and must find some way to come to terms with himself in the world and take himself out of it.

The allusions in Şenocak's work to both cultural and historical issues echo those found in the writers he credits with having helped shape his

---

* *translation on page 175; German passage used with permission.*

own poetic voice, particularly poets of the 1950s, including Günter Eich, Ingeborg Bachmann, and Nicolas Born. Şenocak's work continues in the vein of these writers' attempts to articulate modern subjectivity and in their discussions within the postwar German-language lyric canon, which once was, as Şenocak points out transnational (Cheesman, 19). His work is thus part of these writers' project of restoring language and literature to a multifaceted multiculturalism. Şenocak's work, as Leslie Adelson argues, is central to contemporary German literature. It signals cultural transformation beyond the mere themes of unification and *Vergangenheitsbewältigung* and envisions a broader, more inclusive understanding of historical and current social, cultural, and linguistic realities.

Much of Şenocak's poetry is fragmentary in nature, reminiscent perhaps of Eich's poetry. Ulrich Beil has interpreted this characteristic of Şenocak's poetry as an "elliptical gesture," which is nomadic in nature and, as Beil describes, gives the impression that the poems are verses quoted from a dream sequence, whose beginning and end have been forgotten (2003, 34). They thus resemble the remains of a preconscious, nomadic language. These nomadic structures that characterize Şenocak's often sparse poetry again underscore this search for a home or shelter (*Obdach*). Furthermore, they represent the spaces in between, which Şenocak sees as places of joining, where pain but also poetic potential lie:

> We have long lived in a world in which pain arises not from what separates but from what joins. The aesthetic agenda of the present is to find a language to describe the pain felt today by the many people who are exposed to the most diverse cultural influences. . . . The collision of contradictory worlds necessitates a translating power whose aim is not the levelling of differences but the transfer of different interpretations. (2005a)

Thus, in his poetry, Şenocak depends on the permeability of these borders of meaning and understanding—on the crossing or "*Übergang*" as he has called it, a term key to transnational discussions of flows and linkages. He finds these crossings in language and in the mind. Poetry for Şenocak takes one into one's inner world. It is here where dialog starts. Şenocak's solution "would be the attempt to understand ourselves better. To pose the questions we usually ask others, also to ourselves. To have a dialog within before we address another" (2005a). In his poetry, the poetic voice dares to ask itself these questions and to wonder what linguistic patterns and what poetic conventions can be revised so as to suggest a new way of thinking, imagining, and speaking a new common language of the self, what Şenocak calls "liveable language," (*bewohnbare Sprache*):

Maybe we Germans and Turks should learn a third, common language that nobody understands but us. Which makes us accomplices . . . A third language in which our children could talk to one another about the beauties of their common father- and motherland, and lament the lack of love and sympathy the others show, in which coldness and warmth are united, without being neutralised. A third language from the alphabet of the deaf and dumb, of broken sounds, a bastard language which turns misunderstandings into comedy and fear into understanding. (2000b, 35)

Conclusion

Şenocak's poetic work might best be described as an exploration of the labyrinth of contradictions, a field between imaginative worlds of potentials, with the poetic self as the instrument of investigation, functioning as a sort of "linguistic bridge" between worlds. Leslie Adelson describes his texts as "places of rethinking," "imaginative sites where cultural orientation is being radically rethought" within poetic language itself (2003, 134). Şenocak's lyric work restores the power of the poetic word to expand one's imagination by isolating words, ideas, and concepts from their typical meanings, thereby revealing new ways of understanding.

Perhaps it is in his role as poet in a secularized sense of "prophet" or mediator for the public that Şenocak offers a real vision of a possible "homecoming" within a shared language. This is the role with which he himself so closely identifies and which German critics seem more reluctant to embrace, preferring instead his persona as cultural critic and essayist. Şenocak's blurring of linguistic boundaries forms an important step toward intercultural communication and reclaims a wider, now forgotten, transnational perspective in the German-language lyric tradition—namely within poetic language itself. Above all, Şenocak's poetry defies narrowly defined categories of migrant and transnational literature and emphasizes again the need to undertake further investigations of the potential of nonterritorial literary and linguistic paradigms in the age of globalization.

Notes

1. Şenocak 2000f, 75. Some of the essays in Adelson's collection *Atlas of a Tropical Germany* are also found in Şenocak's 1992 *Atlas des tropischen Deutschland*. For those essays which are not in Adelson's edition I refer to the German edition.

2. The commodification of an author often reveals itself both in the marketing and positioning of the author and his or her work in the literary marketplace and in the academy. In Şenocak's case, his work has often been relegated (on bookstore shelves and in course catalogs at universities) to a specialized category of Migrantenliteratur or foreign literature, which is often misunderstood as somehow being outside the boundaries of the narrowly defined German canon comprised of works written in German by "native" Germans, i.e., by those authors who, for a variety of sometimes arbitrary reasons, such as their ethnic background, nationality, heritage, or mother tongue, are identified as German.

3. Unless otherwise noted, all translations by the author.

4. The essays are included in such volumes as *Zungenentfernung* (2001, Tongue Removal), *Atlas of a Tropical Germany* (1992) and *Was Hitler an Arab?* (1994), and his prose works, which include *Der Mann im Unterhemd* (1995, The Man in the Undershirt), *Die Prärie* (1997, The Prairie), *Gefährliche Verwandtschaften* (Dangerous Affinities, 1998) and *Der Erottomane* (1999, The Erotomaniac).

5. Others have also asserted Şenocak's poetic identity as his "real" identity, including Yüksel Özoğuz, a Turkish translator of Şenocak's poetry, who states that this "real identity expresses itself" in his poems and in the poetic mode of his fiction (see Şenocak 2000c, 50) and Yeşilada (2003) in her essay "Poetry on its Way: Aktuelle Zwischenstationen im lyrischen Werk Zafer Şenocaks," in which she asserts: "Zafer Şenocak is a poet. This might have gotten a little obscured from the field of view, as most of the contributions in this collection deal with the comprehensive prose work of an author, who for the last decade has also been more readily viewed as a public intellectual than as a poet" (112). Karin E. Yeşilada's 2005 Marburg dissertation, "Poesie der dritten Sprache. Die deutsch-türkische Migrationslyrik der zweiten Generation," deals extensively with Şenocak's poetry and will soon be published.

6. For further discussions on definitions of citizenship based on ethnicity and place, see Antje Harnisch et al. 1998; Kosta and Kraft 2003; and Friedrichsmeyer et al. 1998.

7. The Adelbert-von-Chamisso Prize is an award given to non-native authors of literary works written in German in recognition of their contribution to German literature.

8. does one call an exit an emergency exit / if no one was seen who came in or went out / behind it the room that has never been entered / a stuffy room / dark / there is no passage / Exit is only another word for exile / one believes in the exit / when one doesn't know the language / or is an optimist / this is what they call the old man whose bones in this house / have become old and fragile / an optimist / when visitors come / he opens his book/ and those who find a place within / become his confidants

9. you learn to speak / word for word / not however to wait / in this land / the language is / such a large waiting room / even for loud speakers.

10. often one sits back to back / and thinks about the path / that appears in the line of vision / which one could follow / a life long on foot / until one meets oneself again.

11. Şenocak expressed this early in his work in a poem entitled "Gedicht XIV" published in 1983: "ich trage zwei Welten in mir // . . . die Grenze verläuft / mitten durch meine Zunge" (1983, 4).

12. if you go to the forest / don't forget / the fairy tale / it will hide you / if you no longer find a house. This poem can also be read as a play on the popular misquotation of Nietzsche's "Du gehst zu den Frauen? Vergiß die Peitsche nicht" as "Gehst du zum Weibe, vergiß die Peitsche nicht."

13. Şenocak references *The Arabian Nights* in his 1992 essay, "The Poet and the Deserters," in which he discusses Salman Rushdie's work against the background of both "Occidental" and "Oriental" culture and what he describes as Rushdie's "talent for storytelling and his penchant for the fabulous, which everyone loves to compare with *The Arabian Nights*" (Şenocak 2000e, 41).

14. This section refers to Part 1, Number 2 in Friedrich Wilhelm Nietzsche's *Also sprach Zarathustra: Ein Buch für Alle und Keinen.*

15. Theodor Adorno's 1951 statement "To write poetry after Auschwitz is barbaric" is seen as a critical moment for postwar German literature and its subsequent orientation of coming to terms with the legacy of the Third Reich (Adorno 1981, 34).

16. Who would be surprised / the child over there has three arms / for picking things up it is wasteful / and for hugging an arm is missing / who would be surprised / that for such a child one mother isn't enough / he has never seen his father / he brought himself into this world / and has managed to take himself out of the world.

Works Cited

Adelson, Leslie A. 2003. "Against Between: A Manifesto." In Cheesman and Yeşilada 2003. 130–43.

———. 2002. "The Turkish Turn in Contemporary German Literature and Memory Work." *Germanic Review* 77.4: 326–38.

Adorno, Theodor. 1981. "Cultural Criticism and Society." In *Prisms*, trans. Samuel Weber and Shierry Weber. Cambridge, MA: MIT Press. 17–34.

Beil, Ulrich Johannes. 2003. "Wider den Exotismus: Zafer Şenocaks west-östliche Moderne." In Cheesman and Yeşilada 2003. 31–42.

Cheesman, Tom. 2003. "Einfach eine neue Form: Gespräch mit Zafer Şenocak." In Cheesman and Yeşilada 2003. 19–30.

Cheesman, Tom, and Karin E. Yeşilada, eds. 2003. *Zafer Şenocak*. Cardiff: University of Wales Press.

Clifford, James. 1997. *Routes: Travel and Translation in the Late Twentieth Century.* Cambridge, MA: Harvard University Press.

Friedrichsmeyer, Sara, Sara Lennox, and Susanne Zantop, eds. 1998. *The Imperialist Imagination: German Colonialism and Its Legacy.* Ann Arbor: University of Michigan Press.

Gerstenberger, Katharina. 2002. "Difficult Stories: Generation, Genealogy, Gender in Zafer Şenocak's *Gefährliche Verwandtschaft* and Monika Maron's *Pawels Briefe.*" In *Recasting German Identity: Culture, Politics, and Literature in the Berlin Republic,* ed. Stuart Taberner and Frank Finlay. 2002. Rochester, NY: Camden House. 235–50.

——. 2004. "Writing By Ethnic Minorities in the Age of Globalization." In *German Literature in the Age of Globalisation,* ed. Stuart Taberner. 2004. Birmingham, UK: University of Birmingham Press. 209–28.

Harnisch, Antje, Anne Marie Stokes, and Friedemann Weidauer, eds. and trans., 1998. *Fringe Voices: An Anthology of Minority Writers in the Federal Republic of Germany.* Oxford and New York: Berg.

Heise, Hans-Jürgen. 1997. "Mit kalkuliertem Unschuldsblick: Prosa und Werke von Zafer Şenocak." *Süddeutsche Zeitung,* 23 October: 14.

Konzett Matthias. 2003. "Writing Against the Grain: Zafer Şenocak as Public Intellectual and Writer." In Cheesman and Yeşilada 2003. 43–60.

Kosta, Barbara, and Helga Kraft. 2003. *Writing Against Boundaries: Nationality, Ethnicity and Gender in the German-Speaking Context.* New York: Rodopi.

Kurt, Kemal. 1998. "Not an Oriental (Fairy) Tale." In Harnisch et al. 1998. 264–71.

Nietzsche, Friedrich Wilhelm. 2000. *Also sprach Zarathustra. Ein Buch für Alle und Keinen.* Frankfurt am Main: Insel.

Şenocak, Zafer. 1983. *Verkauf der Morgenstimmungen am Markt.* [Haidhauser Werkstat(t)texte 4]. Munich, Edition Literazette.

——. 1992a. *Atlas des tropischen Deutschland: Essays.* Berlin: Babel.

——. 1992b. "Ein Türke geht nicht in die Oper." In *Atlas* 1992a. 20–30.

——. 1992c. "Zwischen Herz und Haut." In *Atlas* 1992a. 97–101.

——. 2000a. *Atlas of a Tropical Germany: Essays on Politics and Culture, 1990–1998,* ed. and trans. Leslie A. Adelson. Lincoln: University of Nebraska Press.

——. 2000b. "Dialogue about the Third Language: German, Turks, and Their Future." In *Atlas* 2000a. 32–36.

——. 2000c. "Germany is More Than a Language." In *Atlas* 2000a. 49–52.

——. 2000d. "Paul Celan." In *Atlas* 2000a. 69–71.

——. 2000e. "The Poet and the Deserters: Salman Rushdie Between the Fronts." In *Atlas* 2000a. 37–42.

——. 2000f. "Territories." In *Atlas* 2000a. 74–76.

——. 2000g. "Which Myth Writes Me." In *Atlas* 2000a. 77–82.

——. 2005a. "Between the Sex Pistols and the Koran," trans. Lucy Powell. Originally as "Die Hilflosigkeit des religiösen Dialogs." In *Die Welt* 20 July. <www.signandsight.com/features/281.html>.

——. 2005b. *Übergang: Ausgewählte Gedichte 1980–2005.* Berlin: Babel.

————. 2006. "Ich bin kein Gruppendichter." <www.foreigner.de/in_zafer_senocak.html>.

Şolçün, Sargut. 2000. "Literatur der türkischen Migration." In *Interkulturelle Literatur in Deutschland. Ein Handbuch*, ed. Carmine Chiellino. Stuttgart: Metzler.

Yeşilada, Karin E. 2003. "Poetry on its Way: Aktuelle Zwischenstationen im lyrischen Werk Zafer Şenocaks." In Cheesman and Yeşilada 2003. 112–29.

10

Performing GDR in Poetry?

The Literary Significance of "East German" Poetry in Unified Germany

BIRGIT DAHLKE

TRANSLATED BY AINE ZIMMERMAN

Seventeen years after 1989, the debates about the aesthetic value of GDR literature have come to a close, and the politically motivated re-evaluations of individual texts and authors have entered into the revised literary histories of the 1990s. The majority of texts that have become a part of the literary canon in German schools are those that either refer directly to political events or whose authors have a known history of persecution or censorship. In the US as well as in Germany, this diminishing of an extensive literary legacy, of generally high aesthetic quality, has been accompanied by a decrease in university course offerings on the history of the GDR and its literature. Discussions about the significance of this part of German literary history will resume once an integrated history of German literature has actually been written. As a result of generational change and a change in the elite guard, however, important voices will be missing in such a debate.

Many were surprised at how long the GDR lived on in post-Wall literature, for instead of the expected critical reckoning, the so-called *Wendeliteratur* (reunification literature) produced melancholy childhood memoirs and *Ostalgie* (nostalgia for the GDR), i.e., defiant re-creations of the lost ways of everyday culture. For a decade, this prose about childhood satisfied both the West German need for information and exoticism and the East German desire for identity. While contemporary West German authors were being accused of having nothing to say, eastern Germany's *Zonenkinder*-prose was received with great enthusiasm both in Germany and abroad.[1] Its function was a product of the times and has now run its course. The only texts and films that have a chance at having a longer shelf-life beyond the times in which they were created are those that do not decontextualize the everyday reality of the GDR—as Leander Haußmann and Thomas Brussig did in their successful film *Sonnenallee* (1999)—but rather place them in the proper historical context, as does Annett Gröschner in her essays (1999).

As late as the year 2000, one could still appropriately speak of a "GDR literature of the 1990s" (Arnold 2000). This not only referred to the fact that authors from the GDR such as Volker Braun, Christoph Hein, and Christa Wolf of course continued to write, but also acknowledged that the conception of literature, themes, perspectives, and narrative styles of East German writers differed from those of their West German colleagues. East German texts did not merge into the postunification literary market nearly as quickly as expected. Even among the younger generation of authors, it is easier to come to conclusions about the authors' background and socialization from the kinds of poetological details in their poetry or prose than from their works' content. The linguistically, historically, and socially critical texts by writers such as Wolfgang Hilbig, Andreas Koziol, Reinhard Jirgl, Johannes Jansen, Kurt Drawert, Jan Faktor, Annett Gröschner, Ulrich Zieger, Bert Papenfuß, Angela Krauß, and Kerstin Hensel simply cannot be put in the same category as the cultlike descriptions of superficial consumer and youth culture or role-playing as dandies, *Fräuleinwunder* (literary girl wonders), or pop literati. Clearly, growing up as a matter of course in a democratic and economically powerful social state creates a different aesthetic than the abrupt "vault over the Wall" does. More than a few authors who did not begin publishing until after the end of the GDR contributed to a "GDR literature after the GDR."

What is discernable in prose also crops up in surprising ways in poetry, whose generic conventions might cause one to expect a greater distance to upheavals outside of the literary sphere. Poetry by poets of East German background plays an astonishingly important role in the literary landscape of unified Germany. Volumes of poetry by Kathrin Schmidt, Barbara Köhler, Durs Grünbein, Kerstin Hensel, or Lutz Seiler caused a sensation because of their originality, but they were not alone: many of the much-discussed debuts put out by kookbooks, a small, successful publishing house, were by authors of GDR origin, such as Steffen Popp's *Wie Alpen* (Like Alps, 2005) and Uljana Wolf's *kochanie ich habe brot gekauft* (darling I bought bread, 2005).[2] It should come as no surprise that poems written fifteen years after the end of the GDR have content that refers back to the recent past. Rather, it is more important to emphasize the ways in which the poetic voices of East German lyricists differ from those of their West German counterparts of the same generation. Small wonder that Kathrin Schmidt (1995, 14) self-deprecatingly comments: "anders zu sprechen gewohnt sein ist eine süße bestimmung" (to be used to a different way of speaking is a sweet lot in life). Yet this means neither that there is aesthetic homogeneity nor that writers should be classified together in a group; the majority of the poets named here who started publishing after 1989 would not want to be reduced to the status of a "GDR author after the GDR." Rather, I am referring to conspicuous poetical traits, and to the fact that GDR socialization, as well as the experience of a social and political rupture, are all factors that apparently contribute to poetic production of a high aesthetic quality. It is striking that the texts by the previously mentioned poets are, despite all of their differences, united by their interest in social questions that go beyond the individual.

The "Bum" Has the Last Word

Kerstin Hensel, born the same year that the Wall was built, in 1961, gives alcoholics, bums, and the unemployed a central place in her poems. With their sociolect (for instance 1995, 57), a corrective to the frequently thematized arrival in the affluent society makes its way into poetry:

> Siebenschläfer
> Ich habe sieben Tüten aus den sieben Himmeln
> Aus dem KaDeWeh habe ich sieben volle
> Bunte Tüten voller himmlischer
> Siebensachen, die trage ich auf
> Händen die bunten vollen Tüten, daß ich
> Müde werde davon. Draußen
> Liegt schon einer auf einer
> Bank sieben und siebzig Jahre alt oder lang.
> Ach, könnt ich auch meinen Rausch
> Schlafen, ich wäre im siebten Himmel.
> Gib schon her, sagt der Alte, nimmt eine Tüte, kippt
> Auf die Straße Austern von Benetton,
> Mieder frisch aus dem Mittelmeer.
> Ich wiege nur noch, sagt er, sieben Kilo–
> Steckt in die Tüte hinein was er hat, seine ganze
> Person. Irgendwas, denke ich,
> Ist zuviel. Irgendwer
> Wird sich schon drüber freun. (1995, 27)[3]*

---

* translation on page 192; German passage used with permission.

A lyrical "I" leaves the "Kaufhaus des Westens" (KDW—here ironically referred to as "KaDeWeh" in pseudonaïve phonetic transcription), the department store that is the incarnation of West Berlin consumer culture. Visibly weighed down by "seven bags," the speaker staggers under the supposed fulfillment of all desire, invoked here by a combination of symbolic numbers and the topos of fairy-tale wish fulfillment. However, the fairy-tale-like feeling of happiness is quite short lived, as the bags full of the "heavenly odds and ends" soon grow heavy; that which is carried (literally: cared for) instead of a loved one grows profane. As soon as the speaker steps "outside" the consumer paradise, the exaltation is destroyed by an old man; he does not beg, but rather demands matter-of-factly and proceeds to scrutinize the contents of the bags with a homeless person's standards. In this light, the brand-name products appear as grotesque and worthless treasures, because the homeless man cannot live on "oysters from Benetton" or "corsets fresh from the Mediterranean." Instead, the empty bag becomes the useful object into which he can pack everything that he owns. Is "his entire person" determined by what he (or the lyrical "I") possesses? Lofty philosophical debates about needs, individuality, and self-realization are sarcastically brought down to earth. While the old man has (and is?) nothing, "something" is still "too much." What began as a fairy-tale-like wish fulfillment ends with a sense of vague irritation. Hensel's laconic and derisive way of seeing the paradoxical prevents any moralizing. As in the poetry of her older colleagues, such as Uwe Greßmann (1933–1969) and Karl Mickel (1935–2000), here folk wisdom is given the authority to pass judgment on the new reality; it is the bums and the alcoholics who see and point out that the emperor has no clothes. Similarly, Hensel's satire "Hofstaat" (court society) passes over the castle's ghost, the court poet (!), the chambermaid, and the court doctor, to give the outcast figure of the "last bum" the final word. The author rejects the position of admonisher, and it is the bum, not the corrupt poet-cum-court jester, who has the last word:

Es ist was faul im Staate, sagt der letzte Penner
Und zeigt mit schwarzen Fingern unter jeden Rock
Er lüpft die Kronen und versenkt den Becher
Und drückt dem Narrn die Schellen ins Gesicht.
Das ist das Ende. In den leeren Schlössern
Tanzt Wind mit Wirklichkeit und läßt die Zukunft fallen
Wer aufsteht geht ins Nichts. Er geht mit Allen. (2001, 50–52)[4*]

---

* translation on page 192; German passage used with permission.

Heimat as a Way of Walking, Also in Poetry

Lutz Seiler, born in 1963, once said that a speech therapist told him his diction would always be socially and locally marked, and that his vowels were *"angeknarrt"* ("creaked") and could never be fixed. I would like to pick up on this amusing remark about dialect in order to describe a characteristic of Seiler's poetry: even the most beautiful and poetic landscapes that he creates are marked by traces of the speaker's conflict-ridden background. His pictographic and phonic portrayal of the Thuringian landscape does not create an idyllic backdrop for childhood memories, but is rather an expression of a highly problematic conflation of the sociopolitical with nature: this countryside is contaminated by uranium mining waste. Seiler's birthplace, the town of Culmitzsch near Selingstädt, ceased to exist in 1968:

pech & blende
was uns anblies aus grossen, bevölkerten bäumen
war von haus aus vertieft
in die zeit der gespräche, baumsprache
war baumkuchen und lag
schwer zu haus, wie ausgeruhter knochen, der
wie wir kinder oft riefen *vor deiner zeit*
unterwegs gewesen war, der die felder durchschritten

und beatmet hatte, den wir nun
lang und gern zu loben wussten und sahen
dass auch vater ihm gut war, ihn
eine *stütze der erinnerung*, ein stellwerk
seines herzens nannte und saatgut
kaum noch geläufiger schritte, der ketten-
fahrzeuge, der erze und öle, heraus gebrochen

aus dem quartier seines gehens, weit hinter
den dämmen von culmitzsch, weit heraus
gerissen aus einer seltenen arbeit bei selingstädt
mit russischen erzen und ölen. und obwohl
wir selbst längst hätten schlafen müssen
drängten wir zu mutter hinunter, wenn vater
nachts umherging und schrie
den knochen das weiss das waren die knochen
mit russischen ölen und erzen
so sagten wir uns, er wittert das erz, es ist der knochen, ja

er hatte die halden bestiegen
die bergwelt gekannt, die raupenfahrt, das wasser, den
                                      schnaps
so rutschte er heimwärts, erfinder des abraums
wir hören es ticken, es ist die uhr, es ist
    sein geiger zähler herz (2000, 36–37)[5*]

This enigmatic text, which may refer to the misfortune of Pechma-
rie ("Pitch Mary," a character from the fairy tale "Frau Holle"),[6] or to
something else that cannot be easily discerned from the title "pech &
blende" at first glance, was included in Lutz Seiler's 1995 debut, but
it, along with the rest of the volume, published by the obscure Chemnitz Oberbaum publishing house, was virtually overlooked. Within
the small German-language poetry community, however, people took
notice immediately, and Seiler's sovereign unique new style received
prestigious poetry awards such as the Kranichsteiner Literaturpreis
(Kranichstein Literary Prize) and the Lyrikpreis Meran (Meran Poetry
Prize). Public interest grew overnight when it became apparent that
Seiler's poetry dealt with his childhood in Thuringia and his father's
perilous work in the hazardous Wismut uranium mining operation.
"pech & blende" then became the title poem of his second volume of
poetry from 2000, published this time by Suhrkamp. As was the case
with Wolfgang Hilbig, a reason for Seiler's canonization is the political-
geographic localization of text and author as belonging to one of the
"darkest industrial regions of the GDR." One reviewer commented:
"The GDR perished more than ten years ago. In Seiler's poems its catastrophic landscapes resurface; for example, there is the "ticking rubble"
of the poem "Grasland" (Grass Land) which begins: "sonntags wird
der himmel geschleift. / und, an den verträumten / todestagen ihrer
dörfer, wiederholen / sie das spiel: aus / der schonung kommt wind"
(Müller 2000, v).[7*]

    Clearly, the title of the Suhrkamp volume *pech & blende* intentionally
refers to the radioactive, contaminated ground of Seiler's hometown.
Additionally, the title also adds another connotation: the word *Blende*
also connotes a (camera) shutter, that is, a glittering brightness. The
words *Verblendung* (blindness, infatuation) and *Ausblendung* (fade-out,
suppression) can also be associated with the term. Thus a poetology is
mined from autobiographical facts. Yet the majority of reviews make
no mention of this, as they only discuss the content. As soon as GDR

---

[*] *translation on page 192; German passage used with permission.*

history can be identified in any way in a text, outdated literary criticism approaches seem to resurface, and a sociological, ideology-critical point of view displaces the aesthetic point of view. And yet Seiler's poems are so carefully composed and cryptic that without a careful consideration of their form, they are almost incomprehensible. Certainly there are leitmotifs that refer to a childhood in the GDR, and words specific to a childhood and youth spent in the GDR: *Milchdienst* (handing out milk at recess), *Fahnenappell* (flag-raising ceremony), Gagarin (Russian cosmonaut), *Grenzlandhunde* (border area patrol dogs). However, just pointing to such sociological keywords does not engage with the suggestive power of the surreal and magical landscapes and linguistic sculptures that the poet creates. The metaphors that Seiler coins are as unpredictable as some of the keywords he employs are seemingly familiar. His images of dreams and memories are marked by a deceptive calm, his cool gaze exposes wounds, and the musicality of his language does not cover up coarseness but rather reveals it. In his sequences of bold, quick images, one recognizes both a sharp mental acuity in his analysis of social conditioning and historical layering as well as great poetic intuition. These poems do not aim to please, but rather contain a poetic surplus of condensed, compressed experience whose meaning far exceeds any attempts to interpret them by rationalizing their reality content.

It is the poetic images themselves that reveal analytic powers. They "tell" both *more* and *less* about the GDR than the sociological perspective can discern. The poems unsettle rather than accuse. They trace "the one song" of their "singer"—a pattern that becomes visible only in the totality of rhythms, tones, images, and syntax, defying all attempts at categorization, even the category of GDR literature after the GDR. The volume *pech & blende* forces us to look at an unpoetic object: the darkness and the dirt of mining is not thematically and partially relegated to the father's world of work, but rather is the structural basis for the whole of childhood and the texts. *Pechblende* (pitchblende) is the technical term for the radioactive uranium ore that was mined in the GDR as part of reparations owed to the Soviet Union: the "Soviet-German Corporation Wismut" was the sole communist stock company on German soil that mined fissionable material for Russian atom bombs from 1946 on. In a 2001 lecture about poetics, Lutz Seiler provided some insight into his literary work and in that context also talked about the "tired villages" of his childhood:

> Die Leute dort, hieß es, wirkten phlegmatisch, schlaff und sie selbst klagten über anhaltende Müdigkeit. . . . Eine Schwere lag auf den Dingen. . . . Die Uranhalden, ihr aschgrauer Auswurf, die dünne Birkenbehaarung am Fuß dieser Berge gehörten zum Horizont meiner Kindheit wie

für andere vielleicht das nahe Alpenmassiv oder die Trauflinie der gegenüberliegenden Häuserreihe. Wenn ich pendelnd über dem Gatter lag, das sich nach hinten hinaus zu den Feldern öffnete, stieg ihr Horizont in meine Träume.... Abwesenheit, Müdigkeit und Schwere prägten diese Zeit. Wahrnehmungszustände der Kindheit, die später wie affine Medien wirken, in denen man die Welt am unmittelbarsten zu spüren vermeint. Deshalb werden daraus Textqualitäten, präpoetologische Axiome, wenn man so will, von Kindsbeinen an. Die Heimat als Gangart, auch im Vers... (2004, 34, 36, 37)[8]*

Separating the words *"Pech"* and *"Blende"* enriches the terminology of mining with the dimension of camera technology but also of psychological memory, and thus poetics.

We encounter here a specific quality of poetry: its ability to compress and store a surplus of historical experience that can only be conveyed metaphorically. The tragic connection to a "radiant" landscape can be made accessible through a wealth of individual sensual impressions, rhythmic parataxis, splinters of memory, and magical words of longing, without falling prey to rational explanations and stereotypical judgments. In the final line, "his geiger counter heart," more than biography or GDR history, shines through: the metaphorical crossing of a Geiger counter and the topos of the grim reaper who plays the violin (*Geige*) suggest the price that people of the twentieth century must pay for their violent abuse of nature (see Geist 2001, 163–80). Seiler's poetic creativity succeeds in taking biographical facts and molding them into atmospheric sculptures, and, through mimetic recreation of the thus-created perspective, in opening up a vast imaginative space for the reader. Some are able to find an element of their own experiences in his work, while others sense the foundations of a mentality that is foreign to them. The sum of melancholy associations has no need to pass judgment and nonetheless disrupts the oversimplified narrative about GDR history.

The Vertiginous Self

One of the most interesting phenomena in poetry by post-1989 East German poets is their work with the first person narrator. The poets' GDR socialization thus adds additional motivation to the poetic task. The question of separating or even saving the self is quite different within the context of a society whose norms are oriented toward the community; it takes on a different insistence than in a society geared toward individualization.

---

* *translation on page 193; German passage used with permission.*

The socialization of the empirical self finds expression and form in the work on the lyric or poetic self, but the lyric self cannot be subsumed under the empirical self by any means (Susman 1910, 15–28). One cannot reject vehemently enough interpretations that disregard this fact even today. The poems on which I draw here are not autobiographical sources, but rather the results of poetic construction. Only through mediation, namely, through the analysis of their form, can connections be made to the social psychology of the self in a thoroughly controlled society (Kocka 1994).

Seiler's poem entitled "vertigo" is dominated by a *Gruppen-Wir* (group self) for three stanzas. The self that finally emerges in the last line of the third stanza is an element of the standard oath formula "I solemnly promise," which was common to the Young Pioneer organization as well as the National People's Army. Paramilitary structures are habitual for the members of a group collective when remembering their childhood. Normal ways of orienting oneself and perceiving the surroundings have shifted: instead of eyes, they have their ears in the light; their gaze is outward (not inward) and most importantly it is a "gaze as sharp as cuts." In an atmosphere of multiple negations and paradoxical standstill while in motion, the narrative "I" emerges only behind the symbol for "and" (&), which is to say that it is of minor importance.

vertigo

gabs eine zeit da sassen wir drinnen am tisch mit
den ohren im licht & nach draussen
ein blick wie aus scharten gewetzt. dazwischen

    insekten, in gaze erstickt. wer
hinten ging, der hatte seine eigne welt, ein
warmes ohr zur sonne hin, der schaufelte
das laub wie lob vor seinen füssen auf
& sägte abends

    noch am krümmer
seiner kopf-und-kragen-spedition. frisch
    gekappt stolzierte auch
das glück vorbei auf seinen stümpfen, schon
mit overall, mit mokassins, zugleich
indianisch & amerikanisch . . . so
beginnt das wispern an den nüstern
der legenden *ich gelobe* doch

wer immer einmal diese bleichen
linkshocker der vorzeit waren, gebenedeite
girlanden unter der decke
begraben mit schüttelndem kopfe
zum tore hinaus—egal. nichts
geschah. nicht

der leiseste anflug: nur
ein klapprad, ein klappbett, dementis, nur
ein leben voller gegen-beispiele, voller
flaschen&gläser für angela davis, das

lachen im leergut & ich
war der spätling, der nachflog, der
den handwagen zog, der noch roch
nach dem blut seiner zahn—

durchbrüche: die
dinge hielten still in ihrer form, so dass
vergessen auf erinnern kam und all
die archivare tränen lachten. (2003, 12–13)[9]*

The "I" stands apart, and yet it is constituted in part through the collective experience of the group. It is formed in the space between collective conditioning, a longing for connectedness, and desire for autonomy. The title "vertigo" (a medical term derived from the Latin for dizziness or the feeling of imminent fainting) can be read as a metaphor for the insecurity of this "I." With the historical distance of a later time, when "the archivists laugh tears," the point of origin that prepared the ground for the self's insecurity is sought. Archivists can find things that "were preserved in their form"—they alone are immune to a dizzy spell. However, gazes "sharp as cuts" and ears (not eyes) in the light, traces of a prehistory that have become second nature—this childhood legacy can neither be archived nor remembered without dizziness (or lies?). Seiler uses facts that are stored in one's memory about actual events as rhetorical sculptures, as catalysts for reconstructing perspectives, moods, fears, and worldviews (which still influence one's current actions). This image of a group of children reconstructs the daily diminishing of a self and makes it available for reflection. And yet it also defends this provenance:

---

* *translation on page 193; German passage used with permission.*

"gelobtes land" (promised land) is the title of the cycle to which the poem belongs. The sacralization of the childhood world, however, is immediately contradicted by the repetition of the oath "this I solemnly promise." The poem's title "vertigo" can also be understood as a poetological reference. Alfred Hitchcock, after all, had used a new camera technique in his 1958 film of the same name, which made cinematic history as the "Vertigo effect": the camera pulls back from an object while simultaneously zooming in on the same object (or vice versa). To the viewers it appears as if the middle of the picture is moving away from them more quickly than its perimeters. This creates a vertiginous effect to which the poet mimetically subjects the reader through his use of memory images.

The Vagaries of the Subject

"Aber uns ist kein Schnabel gewachsen: / wir reden, wie uns der Mund gestopft wurde" (Köhler 1995, 38) (But we have not grown a beak: / we talk, the way our mouths have been stuffed). This is a two-line poem called "Vogelbild" (Bird Image) by the poet Barbara Köhler, who was born in 1959. The amusing cross between two common figures of speech ("reden, wie einem der Schnabel gewachsen ist" = "to speak one's mind," and "jemandem das Maul stopfen" = "to shut someone up") can be linked to the difficult position of a woman speaking and writing in a patriarchal society, but can also refer to the position of the individual in a collective society. That the "I" in this poem cannot be taken for granted is apparent in the fact that it is repeatedly the object of the poetic address: the "possibilities" for practicing "the first person singular" is the "Aufgabe" (task) of the poem's title.

AUFGABE
Die Ordnung der Sätze
Hat Zukunft: sie wird
Gewesen sein Üben Sie
Die Möglichkeiten der
Ersten Person Einzahl
Als wäre das nur eine
Frage der Grammatik &
Würde ein Konjunktiv. (1995, 42)[10]*

---

translation on page 193; German passage used with permission.

In "DIE TÜCKE DES SUBJEKTS," the question "wer spricht mich?" (who speaks me) lends a self-reflexive tone that can be found in most of Köhler's texts and, in my view, refers to the power of ideologies experienced by the individual. A part of the answer is already included in the question's formulation, as it not only calls into question the sovereignty of one's own voice, but is also an inquiry into the existence of a partner. In order for subject formation to take place, there must be dialogue. This concept also generates the text's structure, which is invested in communication from the first line on. Before "ich" (I) is said once, "wer" (who) appears seven times, and the first person singular is an object five times before the nominative is used. Even when "I" is said formally, its subject character is called into question semantically: "wem denke ich nach" (after whom am I thinking/ whose thoughts am I emulating):

DIE TÜCKE DES SUBJEKTS
Wer spricht mich wer will mich
sprechen wer redet ein wer ent
zweit wer vergleicht verwertet
mich rechnet mit mir wer zählt
auf mich & macht sich ein bild
stellt sich vor wer geht davon
aus was bleibt wer fordert ein
sicht hat eine perspektive hat
zukunft & keine zeit wem denke
ich nach wer sagt ich wer weiß (1995, 52)[11]*

Both Barbara Köhler and Lutz Seiler assure themselves of a lyric subjectivity aimed at unity in an entirely "premodern" fashion. Their poetics insist on a unified subject as authority of poetic address. When a self cannot be taken for granted, its creation is the aim of the writing process. In doing so, both Seiler and Köhler differentiate themselves from other contemporary poets who accept and exhibit fragmentation and hybridity as a given. The struggle for a sovereign self is the result of an early experience of the danger of being silenced, or what Seiler (2004, 47) refers to as the fear of the "tote Stimme" (dead voice).[12]

---

* *translation on page 193; German passage used with permission.*

Metamorphoses

When searching for traces of the historical caesura of 1989 in literature, one should not only look to entertaining novels that deal with reunification (*Wenderomane*), but also especially consider the transformed poetic spaces and rhetorical models in the lyrics of those East German poets who published before the end of the GDR in both East Germany and abroad. If one compares the volume *Der Stoff zum Leben 1–3* (The Stuff of Life, 1990) to *Auf die schönen Possen* (To the Beautiful Antics, 2005) by Volker Braun (b. 1939) or the poems in *zwischen den paradiesen* (between paradises, 1992) to *Bilder vom Erzählen* (Images from Storytelling, 2001) by Wolfgang Hilbig (1941–2007), one discovers a plethora of aesthetic differences that cannot simply be explained by the fact that the writers are getting older (see Geist 2007, 579–93; Geisel 2007, 613–22). Political disillusionment can also push poets to the zenith of their aesthetic talent. It can allow scientific concepts to permeate historical-philosophical reflections, charge landscape topoi with symbolism, or initiate changes in perspective, as in Volker Braun's recent poetry. It can make a playwright return to the potency of Homer or Shakespeare's orderly meter or to the sonnet form, as Heiner Müller (1929–1995) did in his later texts. However, it can also demonstrate the supertemporality of a poetic concept, as in the case of the poetry of Elke Erb (b. 1938).

Additional insight is gained by comparing how the topographical descriptions of places differ before and after 1989. The landscape of the Elbe River around Dresden, as well as the city itself, are both vanishing points in earlier and more recent texts by poets as varied as Heinz Czechowski (b. 1937), Volker Braun, Thomas Rosenlöcher (b. 1947) and Durs Grünbein (b. 1962) (see Deckert 2005; Braun 1999, 25–27; Braun 2005, 27–29; Grünbein 2005). How a hometown is invoked, and which historical stratum is uncovered in the process, reveal a great deal about the position of the speaker.

Addendum about Poetry and Dogs

If I previously noted that an author like Kerstin Hensel self-deprecatingly mistrusts the "song of the court poet," then perhaps it can be noted now that the collapse of the GDR also put an end to its intellectuals' and artists' overestimation of their capabilities. Heiner Müller's late poetry is so interesting because of its reflections on the "Ende der Handschrift" (End of Handwriting/End of the Script/End of Personal Style) (1998, 322). And with a light tone, rare in his poetry, Volker Braun bid "farewell to the magnificent antics of yore" (den glänzenden Possen von einst Lebewohl, 2005, 96), alluding mockingly to Philip Sidney's 1585 defense of poetry. The texts of Uljana Wolf, born in 1979, however, presuppose an awareness of poetry's limited social influence and thus can ironically play with the relationship between poetry and the world:

nachtrag an die kreisauer hunde

wer sagt gedichte sind wie diese hunde
im dorfkern vom eigenen echo umstellt

vom warten und scharren bei halbmond
vom sturen markieren im sprachrevier

der kennt euch nicht ihr rasenden kläffer
kassandren im lautrausch der walachei

denn ihr fügt was wort ist und was wade
hinterrücks in tollkühnen biss

zusammen als wär ein bein nur ein blatt
und die ordnung der dinge ein tausch:

in meinem stiefel noch der abdruck
eurer zähne—vom tacker vier zwacken

so lohnt ihr dem vers der euch nachlief
folgt welt wohl der dichtung bei fuß. (2006, 61)[13]*

The verse or poet who tries to run after yelping dogs (politicians, philosophers, authorities of daily life) is in turn painfully punished by them. Thus the discourse of disillusioned ex-communists: "The revolution devours its children." While the young poet does not rationalize ambiguities, there at least resonates, in my ears, a poetic knowledge of the painful life lesson of a Marxist like Volker Braun, who was pummeled by the GDR authorities. The younger generation of authors enters society differently from its predecessors—more playfully, easier. But Uljana Wolf is clearly not content with surrounding herself by the

---

translation on page 194; German passage used with permission.

echo of the poems, with the complacency of *l'art pour l'art*. Derisively, she accepts the scars.

Notes

1. The expression refers to Jana Hensel's memoir *Zonenkinder*, whose title is a play on the terms "Ostzone" (Eastern Zone) and "Sowjetische Besatzungszone" (Soviet Occupied Zone) for the GDR.

2. "kochanie" is Polish for "darling" but it also sounds like "(I) never cook." The poem is about someone who invites her lover to dinner, but spends the evening with him in bed.

3. Seven Sleepers // I have seven bags from the seven heavens / From KaDeWeh ["Department Store of the West," famous department store in Berlin] I have seven full / Colorful bags full of heavenly / Odds and ends, I am carefully carrying / The full colorful bags, so that I / Grow tired. Outside / Someone is already lying on a / Bench seven and seventy years old or long. / Oh, if only I, too, could sleep / my intoxication, I would be in seventh heaven. / Give it to me already, the old man says, takes a bag, dumps / Onto the street oysters from Benetton, / Corsets fresh from the Mediterranean. / I only weigh, he says, seven kilos– / Stuffs into the bags what he has, his entire / Person. Something, I think, / Is too much. Someone / Will be happy about this. (The title refers to the German folk belief that rain on June 27 will last for seven weeks.)

4. There is something rotten in the state, says the last bum / And points with black fingers under every skirt / He lifts the crowns and lowers the chalice / And throws the bells in the jester's face. / This is the end. In the empty castles / Wind dances with reality and lets the future fall / Whoever arises, disappears into nothing. He goes with all.

5. *pitch & blende* // what blew on us from big, populated trees / was always immersed / in the time of conversations. tree-language / was layered cake and sat / heavy at home, like rested bone which, / as we children often yelled / had been on the move / *before your time* / which strode across the fields // and respired them, which we now / knew to praise gladly and long and saw / that father also treated it well, that he called it / *a support for memories*, a signal box / of his heart and seeds / of scarcely still-familiar footsteps, of track / vehicles, of ores and oils, quarried out // of the quarters of his goings, far behind / the dams of culmitzsch, far / torn out of strange work near selingstädt / with russian ores and oils. and although / we should have already been asleep / we scrambled down to mother, when father / walked around at night and screamed / *to the bones the white those were the bones* / *with russian oils and ores* / then we said to ourselves, he can smell the ore, it is the bone, yes // he had climbed the slag heaps / had known the mountain-world, the bulldozers, the water, the / schnapps // so he skidded homeward, the creator of mine

waste tailings / we hear it ticking, it is the clock, it is / his geiger counter heart / (Formatting and italics in the original.)

6. The German word "Pech" refers to both "pitch" and "bad luck."

7. on sundays the heavens are razed. / and, on the dreamy / death days of their villages, they repeat / the game: from / the newly planted trees comes wind

8. The people there, it was said, seemed phlegmatic, lackadaisical, and they themselves complained of continual tiredness. . . . A heaviness lay over things. . . . The uranium waste dumps, their ash-gray emissions, the hair-like stand of birch trees at the foothills of these mountains all belong to the horizon of my childhood, the way the towering Alps or the line of eaves of the houses across the way might for other people. When I lay swinging on the gate that opened out onto the fields in the back, it was this horizon that rose into my dreams. . . . Absence, tiredness, and heaviness were characteristic of this time. Perceptive states of childhood that later seem like related media, through which one thinks to sense the world most directly. This is why they transform themselves into textual qualities, prepoetic axioms, if you will, from childhood on. *Heimat* as a way of walking, also in poetry.

9. vertigo // *there was a time* when we sat inside at the table with / our ears in the light & to the outside / a gaze as sharp as cuts. In between // insects, suffocated in netting. whoever / was walking behind had his own world, a / warm ear toward the sun, he shoveled / the leaves like praise in front of his feet / & evenings was sawing // still on the instrument / of his life-and-limb-risking shipping company. freshly / chopped, happiness strutted / by too on its stumps, already / in overalls, with moccasins, at once / both indian & american . . . so / begins the whisper on the nostrils / of legends *I solemnly promise* still // whoever these pale / squatters on the left of the distant past were, blessed / garlands buried under the covers / with shaking head / out of the gate—no matter. nothing // happened. not / the merest trace: only / a folding bicycle, a folding bed, denials, only / a life full of counter-examples, full of / bottles&glasses for angela davis, the / laughter among empty bottles & I / was the latecomer, who flew behind, who / pulled the hand wagon, who still smelled / of the blood of his teeth—// newly erupted: the / things preserved in their form, so that / forgetting came to remembering and all / the archivists were laughing tears.

10. TASK // The order of the sentences / Has a future: it will / Have been. Practice / The possibilities of the / First person singular / As if it were only a / Question of grammar & / became a subjunctive.

11. THE VAGARIES OF THE SUBJECT // Who speaks me who wants to / Speak me who talks at who di / vides who compares exploits / me counts on me who reckons with me & forms an image / imagines who takes for / granted what remains who demands in / sight has a perspective has / a future & no time whom am / I thinking after who says I who knows. (The title of the poem is a play on the expression "die Tücke des Objekts"—the perversity/ vagaries of things.)

12. Seiler (2004, 47) also talks about "Deformationen durch sprachliche Notzucht" (deformation by linguistic rape).

13. addendum for the dogs of kreisau / whoever says poems are like these dogs / surrounded in the center of the village by their own echo / by waiting and scrabbling at half-moon / by stubborn marking in their language territory / he does not know you, you raving yelpers / cassandras in the sound-intoxication of Walachia / for you unite what is word and what is calf / from behind into foolhardy bite / together as if a leg were only a page / and the order of things an exchange: / on my boot still the impression / of your teeth—from the stapler, four incisions / thus you reward the verse that ran after you / follows world after poetry at its heels. (Ironically, this addendum is indeed preceded by a poem "an die kreisauer hunde," 2006, 60)

Works Cited

Arnold, Heinz Ludwig, ed. 2000. *DDR-Literatur der neunziger Jahre*. Sonderband *Text und Kritik*. Munich: Edition Text und Kritik.
Braun, Volker. 2005. "Die sächsische Flut 2002." In *Auf die schönen Possen. Gedichte*. Frankfurt am Main: Suhrkamp. 27–29.
———. 1999. "6.5.1996." In *Tumulus*. Frankfurt am Main: Suhrkamp. 25–27.
———. 1990. *Der Stoff zum Leben 1–3*. Frankfurt am Main: Suhrkamp.
Deckert, Renatus, ed. 2005. *Die wüste Stadt: Sieben Dichter über Dresden*. Frankfurt am Main and Leipzig: Insel.
Geisel, Sieglinde. 2007. "Wolfgang Hilbig." In *Deutschsprachige Lyriker des 20. Jahrhunderts*, ed. Ursula Heukenkamp and Peter Geist. Berlin: Erich Schmidt. 613–22.
Geist, Peter. 2001. "Überdunkeltes Atmen durch die Umzäunung: Über die Lyrik Lutz Seilers." *die horen* 203.3: 163–80.
———. 2007. "Volker Braun." In: *Deutschsprachige Lyriker des 20. Jahrhunderts*, ed. Ursula Heukenkamp and Peter Geist. Berlin: Erich Schmidt. 579–93.
Gröschner, Annett. 1999. *ybbotapra: ausgewählte essays, fließ- & endnotentexte 1989–98*. Berlin: Kontext.
Grünbein, Durs. 2005. *Porzellan: Poem vom Untergang meiner Stadt*. Frankfurt am Main: Suhrkamp.
Hensel, Jana. 2003. *Zonenkinder*. Reinbek bei Hamburg: Rowohlt.
Hensel, Kerstin. 2001. *Bahnhof verstehen: Gedichte 1995–2000*. Munich: Luchterhand.
———. 1995. "Trinker fährt U-Bahn." In *Freistoss: Gedichte*. Leipzig: Connewitzer Verlag. 57.
Hilbig, Wolfgang. 2001. *Bilder vom Erzählen*. Frankfurt am Main: Fischer.
———. 1992. *zwischen den paradiesen*. Leipzig: Reclam.
Kocka, Jürgen. 1994. *Historische DDR-Forschung. Aufsätze und Studien*. Berlin: Akademieverlag.

Köhler, Barbara. 1995. "Vogelbild." In *Blue Box: Gedichte*. Frankfurt am Main: Suhrkamp. 38.

Müller, Heiner. 1998. *Die Gedichte. Werke*, Vol. 1, ed. Frank Hörnigk. Frankfurt am Main: Suhrkamp.

Müller, Lothar. 2000. "Sonntags wird der Himmel geschleift: Wie die Bilder den Menschen in die Knochen fahren. Lutz Seiler, der Dichter der ostdeutschen Landschaft." *Frankfurter Allgemeine Zeitung* Literaturbeilage, 2 September: v.

Schmidt, Kathrin. 1995. "kein wunder." In *Flußbild mit Engel: Gedichte*. Frankfurt am Main: Suhrkamp. 14.

Popp, Steffen. 2004. *Wie Alpen: Gedichte*. Idstein: kookbooks.

Seiler, Lutz. 1995. "pech & blende." In *berührt / geführt: Gedichte*. Chemnitz: Oberbaum. 44–45.

———. 2000. *pech & blende: Gedichte*. Frankfurt am Main: Suhrkamp.

———. 2003. "gelobtes land II." In *vierzig kilometer nacht: Gedichte*. Frankfurt am Main: Suhrkamp. 12f.

———. 2004. "Heimaten." In *Sonntags dachte ich an Gott: Aufsätze*. Frankfurt am Main: Suhrkamp. 34–39

Susman, Margarete. 1910. "Ichform und Symbol." In *Das Wesen der modernen deutschen Lyrik*. Stuttgart: Strecker und Schröder. 15–28.

Wolf, Uljana. 2006. *kochanie ich habe brot gekauft: Gedichte*. Idstein: kookbooks.

11

Feridun Zaimoglu's Performance of Gender and Authorship

GARY SCHMIDT

German literature in the twenty-first century reflects the reevaluation and contestation of German national identity that has followed not only in the wake of reunification, but also as part of the ever-increasing discussion of the meaning of immigration for Germany's cultural identity. In spite of the literary successes of authors of immigrant backgrounds, neither Germany nor the German literary public sphere has become a multicultural paradise: just as such authors continue to be received differently than their counterparts without an immigrant background, their writing continues to thematize inequalities and persistent cultural essentialism in German aesthetic and political discourse.[1] The texts of Feridun Zaimoglu, who was born in Turkey in 1967 but has lived most of his childhood and adult life in Germany, have often been described by scholars as subversive interventions against hegemonic representations of Turks and Turkish-Germans, whether these be the recognized literary narratives of migration, the recurrent cinematic images of ghettoization and criminality, or the political discussion of Islam and gender, for example in the omnipresent headscarf debate. Yet, Zaimoglu's literary responses to the rubrics under which issues of German-Turkish identity and German-Turkish relations have been all too easily compartmentalized often appropriate these very categories and, in particular, recirculate images of gender inequality that are often defining markers of Turkish or Turkish-German identity in contemporary public discourse in Germany. In particular, Zaimoglu's use of culturally coded stereotypes of masculinity in the creation of first-person narrators seems to pursue a strategy of authorial legitimation based on a recuperation of misogynist and homophobic masculinities. At the same time, these hypermasculine narrators are often ironically undermined, making it difficult for readers to unambivalently embrace or reject them.

The present analysis looks at two of Zaimoglu's novelistic creations, *Liebesmale, scharlach rot* (Love Marks, Scarlet Red, 2000), and *Leyla* (2006) within the larger context in which Zaimoglu has pursued legitimacy as a German author by deploying a variety of strategies that sometimes appear subversive and sometimes seem to reinforce the existing structures of meaning in which Turkish-German stories have been inscribed. Zaimoglu's early texts, for example *Kanak Sprak*[2] (1995) and *Abschaum* (Scum, 1997), appeared to have little to do with the earlier guest-worker literature or the *Literatur der Betroffenheit* (literature of the affected)[3], which often aimed at evoking the sympathy of readers for the plight of immigrants but, like Günter Walraff's *Ganz unten* (Rock Bottom), "denie[d] voice and agency to the Turkish subjects it feature[d]" (Cheesman 2002, 183). Yet, as Tom Cheesman convincingly explicates, texts like *Kanak Sprak* can be seen as a "creative reworking" of the documentary guest-worker genre: Zaimoglu claims the twenty-four short pieces are based on actual interviews with highly marginalized Turkish-German men; but rather than simply recording their words in a protocol, Zaimoglu used the material to fashion a new language that has not only become the author's trademark but also, in popularized forms, the argot of various Kanaksta personae and pop culture movements (Cheesman 2002, 2004). The stylized street language developed by Zaimoglu irritated conservatives and liberals alike by violating taboos against racist and sexist speech and recirculating stereotypes of Turkish-German masculinity.

North American and British scholars of German studies have responded with enthusiasm to Zaimoglu's early texts. Their research, however, has focused overwhelmingly on *Kanak Sprak*, and, from various theoretical perspectives, has emphasized the author's subversive performance of an ethnic identity: as a recuperation of a negatively charged stereotype, i.e., a reversal analogous to the reclamation of "queer" (Yildiz 2004, 332); as an ironic affirmation of exaggerated stereotypes held by Germans about Turks (Fachinger 2001, 102; Cheesman 2004, 84); as a deliberate and carefully constructed literary "anarchistic hybridization" of registers and dialects (Yildiz 2004, 326); as a conscious violation of the official German culture of memory that provocatively challenges Germans to juxtapose fantasmatic German-Jewish and German-Turkish relations in order to reevaluate them (Adelson 2005, 96ff.); as a making visible of the marginalized or abject using the very stereotypes that create such abjection (Günter 1999).[4]

Such critics seem to view Zaimoglu's literary accomplishments as an example of the kind of cultural labor called for by Turkish-German poet, novelist, and essayist Zafer Şenocak, who has repeatedly stressed the need for a new language that is neither German nor Turkish, a language in which the rules of signification are created through equal participation by all interlocutors and whose ideas resonate with the theorization and celebration of hybridity in postcolonial theory.[5] A careful reading of Şenocak, however, reveals his healthy skepticism about ostensibly hybrid literary interventions in an environment of socioeconomic and political inequality in which cultural and semiotic capital is largely controlled by one group that clings to a self-definition that is exclusive and ahistorical. His observations suggest the need to theorize hybrid cultural productions within the contexts in which they are created, performed, and received. If we apply Şenocak's considerations to Zaimoglu, we are forced to note that the latter has moved increasingly toward the mainstream of the literary community by switching publishers, writing in more traditional literary genres such as the novel and story (*Erzählung*), and obtaining increasing recognition as a producer of "literature" by critics. These developments have been accompanied by a more intense focus on issues of authorship and recognition in Zaimoglu's work: in his first two books to be called novels, *Liebesmale, scharlach rot* and *German Amok* (2002)[6], first-person protagonists who function as thinly-veiled author imagos express resentment towards the established literary and artistic community and explore ways in which they might gain recognition and legitimacy in German cultural circles.[7] In the epistolary novel *Liebesmale, scharlach rot*, this author imago is split into two first-person male voices that mutually ironize one another. Zaimoglu's recent novel *Leyla* (2006), which narrates the experiences of a young woman growing up in a patriarchal family in Anatolia in a first-person female voice, maintains a consistent narrative style throughout, in which Kanak language has completely disappeared. *Leyla* appears to be a breakthrough for Zaimoglu in two respects; it represents his success in finding a coherent narrative voice to master an accepted genre—the novel of migration—that has in turn brought him the recognition as an author that he thematized in his earlier attempts at novel-writing. Yet *Leyla*'s accessibility to critics appears to stem in part from its reception as the portrait of the first generation of female guest workers, i.e. the possibility of it being read sociologically—as a key to understanding current intercultural conflicts in Germany—conforming to the expectations of the earlier literature of the affected. The novel represents a significant shift for the author who previously had "disrupt[ed] the state sanctioned dialogue between 'Germans' and 'Turks'" (Cheesman 2004, 83). All of this suggests a need for an analysis of Zaimoglu's writing that moves beyond celebration of subversive potentials to critically reevaluate the author's instrumentalization of gender as a strategy of authorial legitimation.

Masculinity, Performance, and Authorship

Gender and sexuality have been central to Zaimoglu's writing from the beginning, although sometimes overlooked in scholarship in favor of issues of ethnicity. These themes in no way distinguish Zaimoglu from other Turkish-German authors; different cultural expectations of gender and sexual identity repeatedly surface in the discourse of multiculturalism and immigration and were already central themes to the early guest worker literature.[8] Yet, just as with ethnicity and culture, discussions of gender in the literature, scholarship, and political discourse of multiculturalism have often essentialized male/female identities within the Turkish-German community; different cultural expectations of men and women have in turn been invoked to posit unbridgeable differences between Turkey and Germany, in which gender inequality is often believed to be obsolete.[9] While Zaimoglu's assertion of Kanaksta identity through the language of *Kanak Sprak* can be said to challenge essentialized representations of ethnicity and gender via hyperbolic exaggeration of stereotypes and recontextualization of hate speech, until *Leyla* Zaimoglu's interest has been overwhelmingly in masculinity. In spite of exceptions, most notably *Koppstoff* (Head Stuff, 1998), the Kanaksta personae that he has created are in the majority performances of an assertive ethnic masculinity. This suggests that the relationship between ethnicity and gender in Zaimoglu's texts is more complicated than what can be described by simply invoking terms such as "subversive," "anarchic," and "hybrid."

One angle from which to approach the intersection between gender and ethnicity can be found in the concepts of performance and performativity, which have provided the analytical framework for much scholarship in gender studies and queer theory, although there is by no means consensus about the political effects of the performative, as has been seen in various intellectual controversies surrounding the function of drag and other forms of mimicry and masquerade.[10] Judith Butler's approach to gender performativity outlined in *Bodies That Matter* (1993) (in part an elaboration of the earlier *Gender Trouble*, 1990) claims that performances that clearly foreground the construction of gendered "identity" as the citation of previous performances that can always only be approximated, but never perfectly copied, are subversive because they demonstrate the impossibility of locating an origin to

gender in biology or anywhere else. Theorists critical of Butler emphasize the context in which performances occur and the material conditions, including arrangement of space and relations of capital, which
circumscribe the sphere of effectivity of such performances and hence
limit their subversive potential.[11] Still others emphasize the difference
in how gender performances are read in different communities.[12]

Performance manifests itself in various ways in Feridun Zaimoglu's
prose texts. Not only do his writings themselves self-consciously perform particular subject positions that are both gendered and ethnicized,
such subject positions are intricately linked with particular genres,
both high and low, for example the epistolary novel, the *Künstlerro-
man*, the detective novel,[13] the story,[14] and most recently, the so-called
novel of migration. We are challenged to rethink queer interpretations
of performativity in light of Zaimoglu's appropriation of performance
in the literary context. Zaimoglu shows that it is possible to use performances such as drag or camp to recuperate hegemonic masculinities, not by grounding them in nature, but rather in performance itself,
which connotes not only the calling into being of gender through its
citational representation (i.e., re-presentation), but also performance
in the German sense of *Leistung*—achievement in a particular field of
activity (often gendered), such as an impressive athletic or economic
performance, or in the case of Zaimoglu himself, the performance of
an author who constructs his own legitimacy through the voice of a
gendered narrator.

Texts such as Zaimoglu's reconstruct masculinity by appropriating
the very concept of performance, a theoretical tool of feminism and
queer theory, as well as aesthetic strategies traditionally associated
with the gay male community, such as camp and drag, in the service
of an ethnicized straight male masculinity, and by ironically rewriting
literary genres at the heart of the German literary canon: *Liebesmale,
scharlach rot*, for example, can be read as a parodistic "Turkification" of
Goethe's *The Sorrows of Young Werther*. I suggest the use of the term *ethnic straight male drag* to describe Zaimoglu's aesthetic: a self-conscious
parody of high and low culture that demonstrates the writer's ability to
perform both hegemonic and marginalized subject positions in order
to assert his authorial voice.[15] Zaimoglu fashions a new male authorial
subjectivity through writing that, paradoxically, seems to both confirm
and challenge queer theory's critique of identity.

Drag is a term of relevance to Zaimoglu's writing to the extent that
he repeatedly narrates, analyzes, even mocks the ways in which Turkish-German men construct their masculinity and ethnicity through
clothing, speech, gesture, and so on. Yet the performance of identity

works in two directions: while aggressive heterosexual masculinity is perhaps made less harmless as it is revealed to be a construction, the very space of performance is expanded to include all areas of speech, such that the narrators created by the author can appropriate what in other contexts would be called hate speech as part of their performance. In this context, such language is completely under the control of the male narrators, as for example in the following passage from *Liebesmale, scharlach rot*, in which Serdar describes a hypothetical masquerade as a gay man on a Turkish beach, which, ironically, he performs in pursuit of heterosexual conquest:

> Ass-devouring pants are the gays' trademark: the strikingly strong-chested variety—I've caught sight of a few specimens here—get bewitched by young things like you wouldn't believe, because they hope somehow to take these beautiful homos by surprise. Damn! I'm thinking, of course, maybe when I traipse the half mile to the hip swimming pier I should stop suddenly, shape my hands into a trumpet and announce my coming out at the top of my voice so a barely legal girl will take me under her wing. For form's sake I would first bitch and moan and, as far as I'm concerned, gripe about her semi-extravagant nail polish and then after, let's say, three days of chattery flirting return home to heterosexual headquarters. But never all the way, so the girl doesn't lose interest in her summertime mission after the work is done. "I'm bi now," I'd announce in a falsetto, "but I don't really know: you know, what I like about us gays is that we don't embellish our hankering, we stand behind it. It really is different with you heteros, you have to get to know each other, you have to get drunk and always somehow have baby-making on the horizon. You shove the anti-sex locks back and forth and that is SOOOOOO childish. (2000, 54–55)[16]

In an essay on *Kanak Sprak*, Manuela Günter cites Judith Butler's assertion that any reproduction of hate speech is both citational and performative (Günter 1997, 19). According to Butler, hate speech is invested with the potential not only to reinstate prejudice but also to reduce its own negative effects: by demonstrating its performative functionality, hate speech can undermine the assumption that there is a predetermined direction of cause and effect from which there is no escape (Butler 1997, 36–38). The speaker who recontextualizes hate speech (for example, Zaimoglu's use of stereotype in his construction of Kanaksta personae, or his misogynist and homophobic diatribes in *Liebesmale, scharlach rot* and *German Amok*) breaks the alleged bond between a speech act and the injurious effects believed to follow automatically from it.[17] Yet, I would caution against an overly optimistic application of Butler's provocative claims about hate speech to Zaimoglu's writing. As an author, Zaimoglu uses what might elsewhere be construed as hate speech to stake a claim to an area of representation and play with dangerous signifiers in which their dangerousness is ostensibly suspended: the literary space of the performance. Alternatively, it is an area in which the author can utilize politically incorrect speech by creating a fictional world in which such speech is directed at characters rather than real people. For Zaimoglu, the struggle for control of such speech has been central to the negotiation of his authorial identity, as will be seen below in the discussion of *Liebesmale, scharlach rot*.

Liebesmale, scharlach rot: "Re-masculating" the Author

Significantly, the Kanaksta persona and voice is all but absent from *Leyla*; this is by no means a sudden disappearance, but can be seen rather as part of a trajectory along which Kanak language has gradually become problematized in Zaimoglu's oeuvre. It is precisely the problem of authorial legitimacy, staying true to the subversive potential of *Kanak Sprak* while gaining recognition as an author, that Zaimoglu negotiates most explicitly in *Liebesmale, scharlach rot*. Serdar functions as an author-imago, Hakan as his alter ego. The letters exchanged between the two are less interesting as narration of a plot than as the two characters' struggle to define themselves culturally, sexually, and professionally.

Serdar, who has fled the northern German city of Kiel ostensibly to get away from various women, vacations at his parents' home at a resort on the Aegean coast of Turkey. His return to his "homeland" is riddled with ambivalence: while he notices his back straightening after passing through passport control, he quickly begins to suffer erectile dysfunction: "I can't feel my penis any more, what should I say? It has parted from the rest of my body" (Zaimoglu 2000, 11). The first letter written by Serdar to Hakan foregrounds the concerns of the novel: the author's search for legitimacy and recognition, a quest inseparable from his masculinity crisis. Zaimoglu alludes to the idea that writing itself is an effeminizing occupation: it is referred to as a "womanly craft" by one of the local men, Baba[18] (2000, 157); further, Serdar's decision to become a writer followed his dropping out of medical school, causing his father to be concerned that he would never become a "real guy" (2000, 167). Serdar's occupation is, apparently, particularly effeminizing for him in the eyes of Turkish men. Although he is known as the "Lion of Istanbul" north of the Elbe, his male dysfunction upon crossing the border points to his loss in status as a "Deutschländer" in Turkey and to his difficulty in negotiating the requirements of sexuality and art. Serdar clearly wishes to move beyond his popular success to gain recognition as an author of literature, which, comically, pushes him to pursue all sorts of absurd strategies for doing so, including writing haiku; in this manner he incurs the wrath of his pen-pal Hakan, who rejects his attempts at literary assimilation.

Serdar's voice is one that still contains many elements of *Kanak Sprak*, including ironic references to hegemonic discourse[19] and use of exaggerated insult, yet it is one that is striving to move beyond it. Serdar expresses a need to construct meaning in ideas and metaphors, as opposed to the raw unreflected expression of physicality he associates with Hakan (and hence *Kanak Sprak*). The rhetorical contrasts between Serdar and Hakan recall the distinction made by Friedrich Schiller between sentimental and naïve poetry. Hakan, who is militantly antiassimilationist, has no patience for Serdar's brooding about identity: "I don't give a shit for your meta-level," he writes (Zaimoglu 2000, 21). Hakan's thoughts center on food and sex, not ideas—even in the very process of reprimanding Serdar for his pondering of esoteric questions he is distracted again by his libido. Significantly, Hakan's ridicule of Serdar reiterates Zaimoglu's own denunciation in the 1990s of the received representatives of the older guest-worker literature (Cheesman 2002, 190). Serdar, on the other hand, mocks Hakan for his lack of education and his crude physicality, although he at times seems envious of his "naïveté" (Zaimoglu 2000, 78). The opposition between Hakan's "poetry of life" (Zaimoglu 2000, 41) and Serdar's poetry of ideas positions Serdar as the weak and ineffectual—hence effeminized—Werther, who cannot accept that adults wander through life without meaning, motivated by "biscuits, cake, and birch twigs [*Birkenreiser*]" (Goethe 1774, 13).[20]

Hakan's language is closer to that of *Kanak Sprak* than Serdar's; its orality is foregrounded by Zaimoglu in abbreviated articles and pronouns and elided verb and case endings; it also makes no attempt to euphemize bodily functions or sexual body parts, using street terms as direct expressions of feeling. Calling Serdar's poems the highly pompous (Zaimoglu 2000, 20) work of an "enormously sensitive" author (Zaimoglu 2000, 19), Hakan gives Serdar an explicit lesson in how to talk about sex and his body:

> First of all, old man, the piece of meat between your loins is not called penis or organ but dick, all shame is wasted with me, so quit pulling some sort of superfine worms out of your nose and smearing them on the paper. . . . Your problem is that you look from top to bottom instead

of it peeping up, and that, you ass, is a problem with you assimilationist Alis. You all are so fucking refined that you've forgotten how to fuck at full speed or, so you get my meaning: make love. You all are Webster windbags [*Dudenschwätzer*], so you go by definitions, but cock and pussy are just there waiting for the juices to whirl. (Zaimoglu 2000, 24)

For Hakan, Serdar's problem is physical; he takes the penis literally, refusing to read it as a symbol for anything else (as is demonstrated when he begins to talk about the birth mark on his own penis). As a naïve writer, he is concerned with direct expression of experience, not its interpretation. Yet, when Hakan gets an erection at a nude beach (a stereotypically German facility), Serdar reprimands him for his stereotypically Turkish inability to control his sexuality.[21] While an erection at a nude beach may be the most direct expression of heterosexual male desire, it is also one that, according to Serdar, excludes the aroused Turk from his civilized German surroundings. Ironically, in his aspiration to admittance to *German* literary culture, Serdar has lost control of his body in precisely the opposite fashion.

The epistolary form of the novel makes it possible for Zaimoglu to foreground how performances of masculinity are directed at specific audiences and how these performances vary according to their addressee. The male protagonists perform masculinity for other males, including for each other. In one of Hakan's letters to Serdar, he describes a contest that he engaged in with his buddies to see who could describe his state of sexual frustration in the most extreme manner possible, the climax being reached when Hakan conjures up two pork cutlets to service his libido. The underlying homoeroticism might be read as a cue for reading such hypermasculine performances as camp[22], yet it also functions in a far less subversive way. At the end of *German Amok*, for example, which in many ways can be read as a continuation of *Liebesmale, scharlach rot*—since it once again treats the concerns of an artist who bitterly mocks the contemporary German art scene and speaks in a masculinist Kanak voice—the Turkish-German narrator plays the active role in a homosexual encounter with a German artist named Pink (2002, 235–241).[23] The subversiveness of revealing a homoerotic component to the narrator's aggressive masculinity is overshadowed by the narrator's affirmation of his own subject status when he reduces Pink to an object.[24]

Zaimoglu repeatedly resorts to the strategy of creating a masculine authorial persona by writing against effeminized others. Hakan's aggressive heterosexual masculinity is asserted against a German cultural and literary tradition that is often coded as feminine. Hakan, for example, further displays his Kanak poetry of life to Serdar in his narration of "Operation Asia," an unsuccessful nocturnal hunt for a swan that he and his friends pursue in order to still their hunger pangs. Hakan and the other young immigrant men's quest for the swan might be interpreted as a spoof on the romantic idealism of Richard Wagner's opera *Lohengrin*, for example, or poet Rainer Maria Rilke's modernist aestheticism ("Der Schwan" 1907, 38) Indeed, Hakan explicitly remarks on the discrepancy between the men's need of the swan for food and its status as a protected animal in a Germany dominated by environmentalists. Hakan's manifesto of a "poetry of life" exemplified in his invocation of two pork cutlets is also reminiscent of Thomas Brussig's narrator-protagonist Klaus Uhltzscht's diatribe against the abstract, metaphysical language of Christa Wolf in the highly successful novel *Heroes Like Us* (1996), which culminates with Klaus exposing his swollen penis to East German border guards in order to open up the Berlin Wall. Just as the characters Klaus and Hakan resist control of their penises, their respective authors seek to gain legitimacy for an aesthetic that allows for sexual street talk, in which raw expressions of male physicality are set against a dominant literary tradition, which in *Heroes Like Us* is explicitly associated with the mother. Seen from this perspective, Klaus, Hakan, and Serdar are all equally misogynist characters; all three spew vitriol against female figures who threaten their masculinity. For example, in what seems at times a gratuitous use of obscenity, such that certain passages can be read as pornography, Serdar's letters to his former girlfriend Anke describe in detail the sexual acts they had supposedly engaged in. The addressee clearly plays an important role in these; the sexual descriptions in these letters directed at women differ from the missives addressed by Serdar and Hakan to one another. The performance of masculinity through obscenity and pornography not only plays upon German stereotypes of the oversexualized, aggressive Turkish male (as has been duly noted in the secondary literature on *Kanak Sprak*) but also participates in the same kind of reassertion of male heterosexuality performed in Brussig's novel, in which specific speech acts are directed at maternal figures, as in the narrator's strategic citation and subversion of Christa Wolf's *Der geteilte Himmel* (Divided Heaven) in the form of *der geheilte Pimmel* (the healed pecker), not to mention Klaus's act of genital exposure, which has been described as exhibitionism directed against the mother (Gabler 1997, 150).[25]

While Brussig directly links maternal figures to restrictive literary traditions, Serdar's mother in *Liebesmale, scharlach rot* is associated with familial storytelling and nostalgia, in contrast to his father, who reiterates the kind of physical insults that are central to the Kanaksta persona (Zaimoglu 2000, 16). Hakan explicitly warns Serdar to avoid the influence of his mother: "And maybe your mommy cast an impotence spell on you, as often as you write about her she probably has a big, fat influence [*Einfluss*] on your discharges [*Ausflüsse*]. So listen to your buddy and hands off your mother, even in your head!" (Zaimoglu 2000, 63). Zaimoglu plays upon the possibility of reading "discharge" not only literally, as bodily excretions, but also as the flow of the pen. That there is a difference between male and female discharge is further seen when Hakan, in spite of his desire to impress a beautiful neighbor, cannot suppress a spontaneous visceral aversion to feminine corporeality when he gags upon being confronted with her bloody tampons.

Female epistolary discharge flows in the missives of Anke and Dina, two of Serdar's former girlfriends whom he left behind in Germany, whose letters attest to very different styles and elicit quite divergent responses from Serdar. Dina, who is Jewish, and possibly the child of Holocaust survivors[26], alludes repeatedly to Jewish folklore and mysticism. Her mentioning of the "Messiah" causes Serdar to imagine himself as a bloated corpse drifting down a river until he is fished out by a hippopotamus and left to rot: "Maybe Dina doesn't mean it that way, but a story that begins with the Messiah and ends with a water monster is not a good starting point for hanky panky," writes Serdar to Hakan (Zaimoglu 2000, 78). Dina, who fashions herself as the bearer of stories, clearly unsettles Serdar's masculinity, but she also prompts him to remember and narrate events of his own childhood and adolescence, when his masculinity first became marked as an ethnic one by his German classmates as they began to take notice of his black body hair in the locker room. Dina also responds positively to Serdar's haiku and claims to recognize much that is familiar from her own "tribe," which she sees reincarnated in the Turks who inhabit Germany's cities. Not only does she explicitly juxtapose Jewishness and Turkishness, she also aligns them with femininity—that of her mother, whose suffering and sorrow lay at the core of her own early reading of literature. Dina is hence less a living woman than a personification of a literary path for Serdar (and Zaimoglu?)—at one point he refers to his affair with her as a "plot strand" (Zaimoglu 2000, 156)—and a call to turn away from masculinist *Kanak Sprak* to memory and the narration of the familial past.

Anke, who by all appearances is a German woman without immigrant or ethnic background, expresses quite different desires than Dina in her letters to Serdar; exploring the reasons for their breakup, she regrets the fact that he did not treat her more roughly. Serdar obliges her by performing in writing what he had failed to do in real life: he recounts a sexual act in which he roughly penetrated her "without being considerate" (Zaimoglu 2000, 138). Anke responds with enthusiasm to Serdar's new epistolary style, characterized by a "new self-confidence and honest tone" that arouses her (Zaimoglu 2000, 274–75).

While Serdar eventually rejects Dina's appeal to the narration of memory and suffering, returning to sexually explicit language and insulting the odor of her feet, the author Zaimoglu has returned to Dina's position to narrate his recent novel *Leyla*, which begins with the following lines: "This is a story from the old time. Yet it is not an old story" (2006, 7). The opening prologue of *Leyla* narrates in the present tense how a pack of wolves hunts a human being. Of the wolves, the narrator reminds us, "They are not sly, they are not stupid: they are animals, that's enough. Their attack, their desire, their snapping teeth: how can one call the hunters evil?" (Zaimoglu 2006, 7). The anaphora creates a sense of urgency in a pseudomythic context just as throughout the novel, the present tense narration without any alienating or distancing devices creates an immediacy that leaves little room for irony: the temporal and spatial distances between the act of telling and what is told are suspended. A feminine-coded style that is satirized in *Liebesmale, scharlach rot* is celebrated in *Leyla*.

Leyla: Writing as a Turkish Woman

In *Leyla*, the issue of masculine performance and authorship all but disappears. The narrative style described above dominates not only the first-person passages, but the entire novel—even scenes that Leyla seems unlikely to have witnessed, although Zaimoglu offers a plausible explanation for Leyla's omniscience in the conceit of eavesdropping (*lauschen*), for example when she listens from behind a door to a conversation regarding her proposed marriage with Metin. In spite of the novel's traditional narrative style, it is far from painting a monolithic portrait of Turkish society; indeed, we encounter a wide variety of female characters ranging from Leyla's mother (a typical victim), to "free-living" women such as Ipek Hanim and Manyola (who already as a Kurd is an outsider, but also is a strong female figure refusing to accept that her role is to become a faithful wife and mother just because she has been told this is "the Law.") In the middle of these is Leyla herself, who is subject to the competing influences of American cinema, Marxist ideology, Islam, and Kemalism. Familiar themes of Turkish-German literature of the affected reappear: for example, violence against women and male sexual hypocrisy. Language is thematized, although its performance is not foregrounded; Halid Bey, for example, does not understand the sophisticated language of the school director; "stylish" women insist on using French expressions. While one can identify differences in the language of female and male characters—the men, for example, are again masters of the insult—the role of the author in creating and manipulating this language is no longer foregrounded, neither is its context and addressee; everything is integrated into a realistic pseudoautobiographical narrative through Leyla's voice.

While critical readers can recognize Zaimoglu's female voice as a performance, which, based on the author's own admission, actively mimics the speech of the immigrant women of his mother's generation, the structure and rhetoric of the novel itself tends to promote the kind of readings that Zafer Şenocak finds regrettable for their essentializing, sociological approach to literature. Such readings recognize the female narrative voice as one that the male author has successfully identified and faithfully reproduced (e.g., Weidermann 2006). The controversy surrounding the intimations of plagiarism brought against Zaimoglu in the summer of 2006 are revealing in regard to how questions of authenticity and authorial legitimacy are negotiated when authors of immigrant background are involved, and when the sex of the author does not align with the gender of his narrator. Before public attention was drawn to similarities in plot and style between *Leyla* and Emine Sevgi Özdamar's 1992 novel *Life is a Caravanserai, Leyla* had received high praises from a number of critics, who congratulated the author for giving a face to an immigrant woman of the first generation, and for writing a highly poetic, yet realistic story. Zaimoglu also reportedly required one and a half years to find the right tone for his narrator and, when questioned about his method in writing from a woman's perspective, he responded, "Women talk differently. I visited my Turkish friends and listened to the women" (quoted in Schlosser 2006). Zaimoglu was also reported as saying that before he found the right tone for the novel he had felt like a man in drag when trying to write the story (quoted by Schröder 2006). Zaimoglu's having "found the right tone" for his female narrator-protagonist seems to have lent the text a great deal of its perceived authenticity. In this manner, Zaimoglu has established his legitimacy as an author and found recognition for his writing as having high literary value.[27]

Citing a telephone call that literary critic Volker Weidermann made to Zaimoglu's mother, Zafer Şenocak notes that the response of Weidermann and others to the plagiarism controversy underscores the fact that Turkish-German authors tend to be read sociologically. He is justifiably annoyed by the certainty expressed by many critics "who believed they knew all about the Turkish woman from provincial Anatolia after reading novels by Turkish authors" (Şenocak 2006). One might indeed argue that *Leyla* encourages sociological readings through its pseudoautobiographical form; further, the integrative narrative style of the novel might be seen as an about-face, bringing Zaimoglu back into the realm of guest-worker literature, a move that has implications for the representations of both ethnicity and gender. If Zaimoglu did not wish to "feel like a man in drag" when writing the novel, this can only mean that he desired to find a voice in which the gender of the narrator appeared natural. In his efforts to find such a voice, it is not surprising that other aspects of the novel would become naturalized as well. Precisely when he tells the story of a woman, his mother no less, he returns to a narrative tradition that he previously denounced as assimilationist and was coded in his earlier texts as both feminine and effeminizing to the male narrators.

Notes

1. Zafer Şenocak is the most consistent and cogent critic of essentialism in German discourses on multiculturalism, most specifically things Turkish and Islamic. To date, the only English translation of his essays is the volume *Atlas of a Tropical Germany* (2000), translated by Leslie Adelson, although several more recent collections have appeared in German.

2. One might translate the title as "Wop Speak" or "Dago Speak," since "Kanake" is a derogatory racial epithet that, although now most commonly used against Turks, has also been directed at other guest workers such as Italians, Spaniards, Greeks, etc. Yet, since the ethnic slurs mentioned above usually do not connote Turks for English-speakers, it might be more appropriate to translate the title as "Ali Speak," since this name is commonly applied pejoratively to men of Turkish heritage in Germany and is frequently used by Zaimoglu himself.

3. I am using the translation by Rob Burns, who outlines the origin of the German term (1999, 744).

4. A far more detailed overview of the scholarship on *Kanak Sprak* than is possible here can be found in Adelson (2005, 95ff.).

5. See for example *Atlas of a Tropical Germany*: "We must confess our own speechlessness" (2000, 46–47).

6. This title is particularly difficult to translate, since it contains the English word "German" and the noun "Amok," which is usually used in the verbal phrase "Amok laufen" (to run amok, run riot). If one reads the German title as if it were English, one might think that it refers to a German running amok, but it more appropriately should be read as a condition of "Amok" (disorder, craziness) that is German.

7. Cheesman sees this move to the mainstream as being accompanied by a decline in quality as the pure language of Kanak Sprak becomes diluted or tamed (2002, 192), but I would suggest that *Liebesmale, scharlach rot* offers a level

of complexity and sophistication based in allusion, irony, and self-reflexive structure.

8. See McGowan (2001) for a detailed and insightful summary of literary treatments of masculinity in Turkish-German writing up to and including Zaimoglu's early work. For an overview of the representation of Turkish-German women's issues in literature and film of the 1980s and early 1990s, see Burns (1999).

9. Author Emine Sevgi Özdamar pokes fun at such essentializations in her witty short story "Die neuen Friedhöfe in Deutschland" in *Der Hof im Spiegel* (2001, 121–23).

10. I found Carol-Anne Tyler's article "Boys Will Be Girls" (1991) to be particularly helpful in thinking about these issues. Tyler summarizes and evaluates queer and feminist approaches to gender impersonation and convincingly insists on the necessity of bringing race, ethnicity, and class into discussions of gender performance and its reception.

11. Ki Namaste offers a scathing rebuke of queer theory's erasure of the material conditions under which cultural performances celebrated by academics for their subversiveness are actually produced (1996).

12. Tyler illustrates the problem of interpretation effectively when she writes, "It is only from a middle-class point of view that Dolly Parton looks like a female impersonator; from a working-class point of view she could be the epitome of genuine womanliness" (1991, 57). For our purposes, this demonstrates that we need to be cautious when imposing a particular interpretation on the textual performances of gender in Zaimoglu's writing, since such interpretations may well be informed by very different viewpoints than those held by many of Zaimoglu's readers.

13. *Leinwand* (2003).

14. *Zwölf Gramm Glück* (2005).

15. I owe my use of the term ethnic drag to Katrin Sieg. "Ethnic drag," writes Sieg, "includes not only cross-racial casting on the stage, but more generally, the performance of 'race' as a masquerade" (2002, 2). While Sieg is interested primarily in Germans' appropriation of racialized identities (e.g., Jewish and Native American) to "disavow" and "contest" their own Germanness, I suggest that Zaimoglu's masquerade of Turkish-German masculine identity is no less a form of drag because it is being performed by a Turkish-German male author, in the sense that it is the deliberate masquerading of a stereotypical identity.

16. Unless otherwise indicated, all translations from the German are by the author.

17. As Cheesman notes, criticism of Zaimoglu from the political center fails to comprehend the deconstructive aspect of his performances, viewing his citation of "hate speech" as the mere repetition of a fixed meaning (2004, 93ff.).

18. Baba is Turkish for "father."

19. This includes the official discourse of memory. For example, Serdar refers to his "Gnade der späten Bildung" (grace of late education), a play upon Helmut Kohl's phrase "Gnade der späten Geburt" (grace of late birth), which

expressed the former German chancellor's gratefulness for not being born into a time period when he could have become complicit in Nazi crimes.

20. It seems more than a coincidence that Serdar, who, like Werther, distances himself from the common people around him, mentions the women's discussion of "Besenreiser" (spider veins) that they have had removed through laser surgery. This is only one of several parodistic allusions to the language of Werther, which, unfortunately, cannot be explored in the context of this essay.

21. Hakan explicitly states that "dick matters" (Pint-Angelegenheiten) are the mark of distinction between German and Turkish culture.

22. According to Tyler, "gay sensibility" has been invoked repeatedly to identify camp and to distinguish it from a nonsubversive heterosexual gender mimicry (1991, 54).

23. For a discussion of *German Amok* as a critique of the Berlin Republic, see Taberner (2005, 96–99).

24. This scene can actually be described as a rape. McGowan's discussion of Hermann Tertitl's study of the Frankfurt Turkish Power Boys is extremely relevant (2001, 294–295): Zaimoglu transforms the street insult of "Ich ficke dich" (I'll fuck you) into a literary act demonstrating the superiority of the author over his efffeminized German rivals. In *Liebesmale, scharlach rot*, Zaimoglu plays repeatedly with jokes about homosexuality: in one of Anke's letters to Serdar, she says she took him to be gay at first because he was too courteous and well bred; Serdar, in describing his fight with Baba over a woman, Rena, says he will probably have to give him a blow job to make amends; when he opens a dildo that Hakan has sent him as a prank, his father thinks he is using it to penetrate himself; finally, in his final letter to Hakan, he describes how he is going to move in with a gay student from Bielefeld.

25. The question then becomes, to what degree can we or should we interpret such writing as an aggressive speech act that performs the subjugation of women and homosexuals, the most radical expression of this position being Catharine McKinnon's interpretation of pornography (Butler 1997, 17–18), or as a subversive act that reveals itself as performance by drawing attention to its positioning, its function, and its citationality.

26. She writes, "My father torments me in the hospital with stories of that time" (121, emphasis added).

27. Eva Maria Schlosser wrote in the Stuttgarter Nachrichten that *Leyla* distinguished itself clearly from Zaimoglu's earlier work, particularly in terms of linguistic style (2006).

Works Cited

Adelson, Leslie. 2005. *The Turkish Turn in Contemporary German Literature*. New York: Palgrave Macmillan.

Brussig, Thomas. 1996. *Heroes Like Us*. Trans. John Brownjohn. New York: Farrar, Strauss and Giroux.

Burns, Rob. 1999. "Images of Alterity: Second-Generation Turks in the Federal Republic." *Modern Language Review* 94: 744–57.

Butler, Judith. 1990. *Gender Trouble: Feminism and the Subversion of Identity.* New York: Routledge.

———. 1993. *Bodies That Matter: On the Discursive Limits of Sex.* New York: Routledge.

———. 1997. *Excitable Speech.* New York and London: Routledge.

Cheesman, Tom. 2002. "'Akcam—Zaimoglu—Kanak Attak': Turkish Lives and Letters in German." *German Life and Letters* 55: 180–95.

———. 2004. "Talking 'Kanak': Zaimoglu contra Leitkultur." *New German Critique* 92: 82–99.

Fachinger, Petra. 2001. *Rewriting Germany from the Margins.* Montreal: McGill-Queen's University Press.

Gabler, Wolfgang. 1997. "Die Wende als Witz: Komische Darstellungen eines historischen Umbruchs." *Literator* 18.3: 141–54.

Goethe, Johann Wolfgang. 1774. *Die Leiden des jungen Werthers.* Stuttgart: Reclam, 1990.

Günter, Manuela. 1999. "'Wir sind bastarde, freunde . . . ' Feridun Zaimoglus *Kanak Sprak* und die performative Struktur von Identität." *Sprache und Literatur in Wissenschaft und Unterricht* 83: 15–28.

McGowan, Moray. 2001. "Multiple Masculinities in Turkish-German Men's Writing." In *Conceptions of Postwar German Masculinity,* ed. Roy Jerome. Albany: State University of New York Press. 289–312.

Namaste, Ki. 1996. "'Tragic Misreadings': Queer Theory's Erasure of Transgender Subjectivity." In *Queer Studies: A Lesbian, Gay, Bisexual and Transgender Anthology,* ed. Brett Beemyn and Mickey Eliason. New York and London: New York University Press. 117–24.

Özdamar, Emine Sevgi. 2001. *Der Hof im Spiegel.* Cologne: Kiepenheuer & Witsch.

Rilke, Rainer Maria. 1907. *Neue Gedichte.* Frankfurt am Main: Insel, 1974.

Schlosser, Eva Maria. 2006. "Ein Strickkurs für die große Kunst: Eine Begegnung mit Feridun Zaimoglu, seiner Heldin und seinen Bildern im Literaturhaus." *Stuttgarter Nachrichten* 17 Februar, Kulturmagazin: 17. LexisNexis: <http://web.lexis-nexis.com/universe/document?_m=6b9cae4f130fcf0579 32afa71e2993e9&_docnum=1&wchp=dGLbVzb-zSkVA&_md5=85b3d07173 b5e4fa059dd5851abb42d8>.

Schröder, Christoph. 2006. "Unbedingt weiterschreiben: Feridun Zaimoglu stellt sein neues Buch *Leyla* in der Frankfurter Romanfabrik vor." *Frankfurter Rundschau* 10 April, 14. LexisNexis: <http://web.lexis-nexis.com/ universe/document?_m=242a2df64efeafbbb275193d62525135&_doc num=1&wchp=dGLbVzb-zSkVA&_md5=af7320051509eb9e0acf9ff0901b c1f2>.

Şenocak, Zafer. 2000. *Atlas of a Tropical Germany: Essays on Politics and Culture 1990–1998,* ed. and trans. Leslie A. Adelson. Lincoln: University of Nebraska Press.

———. 2006. "Authentische Türkinnen." *taz,* ed. and trans. Leslie A. Adelson. 10 June, Kultur 13. LexisNexis: <http://web.lexis-nexis.com/universe/

document?_m=cbbdffcfe34e0b137f90072e6992ee59&_docnum=1&wchp
=dGLbVzb-zSkVA&_md5=313a12760178c1eb380dd8fca8c483f0>.

Sieg, Katrin. 2002. *Ethnic Drag: Performing Race, Nation, and Sexuality in West Germany*. Ann Arbor: University of Michigan Press.

Taberner, Stuart. 2005. *German Literature of the 1990s and Beyond: Normalization and the Berlin Republic*. Rochester, NY: Camden House.

Tyler, Carol-Anne. 1991. "Boys Will Be Girls: The Politics of Gay Drag." In *inside/out: Lesbian Theories, Gay Theories*, ed. Diana Fuss. New York and London: Routledge. 71–92.

Weidermann, Volker. 2006. "Der fremde Bräutigam; Unsere Vorgeschichte spielt in der Türkei: Feridun Zaimoglu erhellt die dunklen Seiten des Islams." *Frankfurter Allgemeine Zeitung*, 12 February: 23. LexisNexis: <http://web. lexis-nexis.com/universe/document?_m=75569f345b8a19a3e65fce2cc67582 d6&_docnum=1&wchp=dGLbVzb-zSkVA&_md5=351bfadc2dff0ab1bc7985 d5bb98a1db>.

Yildiz, Yasemin. 2004. "Critically 'Kanak': A Reimagination of German Culture." In *Globalization and the Future of German*, ed. Andreas Gardt and Bernd Hüppauf. Berlin and New York: Mouton de Gruyter. 319–39.

Zaimoglu, Feridun. 1995. *Kanak Sprak*. Hamburg: Rotbuch.

———. 1998. *Koppstoff*. Hamburg: Rotbuch.

———. 2000. *Liebesmale, scharlach rot*. Cologne: Kiepenheuer & Witsch.

———. 2002. *German Amok*. Cologne: Kiepenheuer & Witsch.

———. 2004. *Zwölf Gramm Glück*. Cologne: Kiepenheuer & Witsch.

———. 2006. *Leyla*. Cologne: Kiepenheuer & Witsch.

IV

TRANSFORMATIONS
Women Writing in the New Century

PATRICIA HERMINGHOUSE

Readers of this section may initially be surprised to note how minor a role terms such as "feminism," "*Frauenliteratur*" (women's literature), or the recently popular "*literarisches Fräuleinwunder*" (literary girl wonder) play in the individual chapters. On the one hand, the present-day absence of a widespread women's movement in Germany, characterized by the proliferation of women's groups, women's bookstores, and women's book series in the 1970s and 1980s, may be taken as prima facie evidence that the feminism of that era is now considered passé. On the other hand, the years since the turn of the new century have witnessed increased attention to a new generation of women writers, who have earned recognition as serious literary artists and whose texts have been honored with dozens of major literary prizes. Unlike the *Frauenliteratur* of their mothers' generation, which focused on issues that were thought to be primarily of concern to women, the texts of these writers probe the broader questions of identity, culture, and politics in Germany today. Nonetheless, questions of gender, while perhaps not foregrounded, clearly matter in their texts.

Julia Franck, Martina Hefter, and Juli Zeh, who are treated in this section, as well as Tanja Dückers in Section II, are included in the present volume as representatives of the diversity that characterizes writing by younger women today, a diversity that was not anticipated at the end of the twentieth century when the unfortunate label *literarisches Fräuleinwunder*, a sort of German counterpart to the Anglo-American "chick lit," began to circulate.

With the apparent loss of relevance of many of the political and pragmatic features of what has been called "second-stage" feminism (Friedan 1981) came also the end of much of what might be termed the feminist literary public sphere, replaced by what Julia Karolle-Berg and Katya Skow here term the *Frauenliteraturbetrieb*, the cultural industry that markets books "by women about women to women." In examining the way in which publishing houses target women as the primary consumers of literature today, Karolle-Berg and Skow focus on the role that influential media outlets, such as the popular women's magazine *Brigitte* and a television program by the well-known moderator Elke Heidenreich (who also writes for *Brigitte*), play in "presenting" books to potential readers. Books promoted on Heidenreich's show "Lesen!" (Let's Read), like those chosen by US talk-show moderator Oprah Winfrey for her televised "Book Club," are often quickly propelled onto the nation's bestseller lists because the profile of her viewers is generally similar to that of the average German book buyer: female, in her forties, educated middle-class. Such media "presentations" of literary texts generally do not engage in highbrow literary criticism and, to a certain extent, play into the commodification of literature as part of a lifestyle that is being promoted to women. Karolle-Berg and Skow conclude, however, that the great variety of literature publicized in this way—books written by non-Germans as well as Germans, fiction and nonfiction, by male and female writers of both serious and light literature—conveys what Evelyn Finger (2005) described as the "inexhaustibility of human creation" and thus does offer emancipatory potential.

The three women whose work is represented in this section cannot be contained in easy categories beyond the fact that they are generally *under* forty years of age, educated, female, and successful. Two, Martina Hefter and Juli Zeh, are products of the Deutsches Literaturinstitut Leipzig, discussed by Rachel J. Halverson in the first part of this volume, and only marginally have any of them been named in connection with the *literarisches Fräuleinwunder* phenomenon. With the exception of Juli Zeh, who has had much greater presence in the media than Julia Franck or Martina Hefter, they are generally not recognized as "political" writers of the sort of "engaged literature" that was produced by politically committed authors in previous decades. Instead, one finds in their carefully crafted texts nuanced reflections on the social and moral ambiguities of post-*Wende* Germany.

As Beret Norman and Katharina Gerstenberger make clear in their approaches to Julia Franck and Martina Hefter, respectively, important themes lie just below the surface of their polished narrations. Norman introduces Berlin author Julia Franck, who employs a highly developed narrative technique in order to depict a contemporary gendered enactment of the ubiquitous surveillance practices of the Cold War era. In Franck's first three works, Norman demonstrates how women's experiences of the "very full emptiness" of life in contemporary society lead them to engage in petty surveillance as a means to fill up their otherwise empty days and, they hope, to improve their own social position by gaining some power over those they so assiduously observe. Self-absorbed and lacking meaningful human relationships, they are further alienated by their outsider status in the "event society" of postunification Germany, a development addressed by Donovan Anderson in the first part of this volume. What can be traced between the lines in these three works emerges more openly in Franck's recent novel, *Lagerfeuer* (Campfire, 2003), set in the West Berlin relocation camp that received refugees from East Germany during the Cold War. Beyond the numbing of moral scruples that surveillance practices inevitably entail, Norman points to another form of numbing in the way in which memories of the Holocaust are desensitized—except for its victims.

History likewise plays a role in Katharina Gerstenberger's attention to the effects of changing political borders and systems in two novels by Martina Hefter. In the first, *Junge Hunde* (Young Dogs, 2001) characters also lead lives marked by lack of purpose and meaningful relationships, neither focused on the GDR past nor able to envision a different and better future in the new "normal" of contemporary Germany a decade after unification. The fragmented narrative perspective of the novel, Gerstenberger points out, corresponds to the characters' own aimless and fragmented lives. Hefter's most recent novel, *Zurück auf Los* (Back to the Beginning, 2005), continues her exploration of the tenuousness of relationships, to people and to places, set this time in a Bavarian hotel owned by the narrator's mother. But rather than observing the hotel guests as did Julia Franck's narrator in *Der neue Koch* (The New Cook, 1997), discussed in the essay by Beret Norman, Hefter's narrator contemplates her own tangled network of relationships to her lover, to her family, and to its experience of the vicissitudes of German history. The concern here with memory and how it is passed on from generation to generation recalls in some ways Laurel Cohen-Pfister's analysis of family memory from the perspective of the grandchildren's generation in Tanja Dückers's *Himmelskörper* (Heavenly Bodies, 2005) in the second section of this volume.

In the final essay of the section, Patricia Herminghouse comes back to the public role of writers, discussed in the articles in Section I, in her examination of the combination of literary achievement and political engagement that has given Juli Zeh a level of visibility in the public sphere that generally has been reserved for the prominent male writers of an earlier generation. In her numerous public appearances and opinion pieces in the major German newspapers and magazines, Zeh has addressed a range of sociopolitical topics, including the 2005 German election campaign, the heated debate about capitalism and investment, and her own generation's attitudes towards consumption and politics. The two novels she has published to date, *Adler und Engel* (*Eagles and Angels*, 2001) and *Spieltrieb* (Game/Play Instinct, 2004) take on the big problems of contemporary society, namely, international drug dealing and asocial behavior in the schools. The narrative style for which she is admired, however, is far more brutal than that of her peers treated in this volume, involving charged depictions of the degraded underside of life and of adolescent cruelty in a society that seems to have lost its moral bearings.

In her literary texts, Zeh pays less attention to issues of gender than do Julia Franck or Martina Hefter. In fact, she dismisses engagement with feminist questions as "fighting empty battles." The observer of the contemporary German scene, however, may well wonder about the apparent irrelevance of feminist concerns for German women writers of this generation. The implementation of legal equality (*Gleichstellung*) and the much greater representation of women in elected and appointed political office as compared with the American scene do, of course, suggest progress. But not only do women continue to be seriously underrepresented on the boards and in the executive suites of major corporations, in the world of finance, and on university faculties; most recently those women who have succeed in careers as well as the many who labor in low-paying service jobs are being blamed for the social, economic, and demographic challenges facing the country today. The debate became particularly heated in summer and fall of 2006 when the former news and talk-show moderator Eva Herman, herself a "career woman," published an article entitled "Die Emanzipation—ein Irrtum?" (Emancipation—a Mistake? 2006a) blaming working women for the precipitous decline in births in Germany, for developmental problems of those children who are born, and for their own burn-out.[1] The ensuing intensity with which her thesis was debated in the public sphere[2] no doubt served as advance publicity for the subsequent book-length version of Herman's reactionary plea for a return to traditional gender roles in *Das Eva-Prinzip* (The Eve Principle, 2006b), which was an immediate bestseller upon its appearance that fall. While Julia Franck (2006) was one of the first of the new generation of writers to publish a response, it remains to be seen whether or how the attention focused on this issue in the public sphere will be thematized in any of their future texts.

NOTES

1. In September 2007, Herman was dismissed from her job by public television broadcaster ARD after she made remarks on air praising Nazi policies re-

garding the family and children, although she did disavow the horrors of the regime. Her dismissal set off a heated public debate on freedom of speech regarding aspects of the Third Reich.

2. There was, for example, a series of articles in *Die Zeit*, including one that turned the question "Brauchen wir einen neuen Feminismus?" (Do we need a new feminism?) into an assertion ("Wir brauchen einen neuen Feminismus"), in which fifteen women, including writers Karen Duve and Alexa Hennig von Lange, responded. Feminist Alice Schwarzer also responded with outrage in *Der Spiegel* (2006).

Works Cited

Finger, Evelyn. 2005. "Weiblich kann fast alles heißen: Warum das Gerede von Frauenliteratur aus der Mode gekommen ist." *Die Zeit*, 31 March. <http://zeit.de/2005/14/Frauen_2fSchriftstellerinnen>.

Franck, Julia. 2006. "Lust am Leben." *Kölner Stadt-Anzeiger*, 29 April. *<http://www.ksta.de/html/artikel/1144673394004.shtml>*.

Friedan, Betty. 1981. *The Second Stage*. New York: Summit Books.

Herman, Eva. 2006a. "Die Emanzipation—ein Irrtum?" *Cicero: Magazin für politische Kultur*. May. <http://www.cicero.de/97.php?ress_id=7&item=1111>.

———. 2006b. *Das Eva-Prinzip: Für eine neue Weiblichkeit*. Starnberg: Pendo.

Schwarzer, Alice. 2006. "Panik im Patriarchat." [Interview]. *Der Spiegel*, 29 May.

"Wir brauchen einen neuen Feminismus." 2006. *Die Zeit*, 24 August. <http://www.zeit.de/2006/35/Feminismus-Editorial>.

12

FROM *FRAUENLITERATUR* TO *FRAUENLITERATURBETRIEB*
Marketing Literature to German Women in the Twenty-First Century

JULIA KAROLLE-BERG & KATYA SKOW

In summer 2004, the Zweites Deutsches Fernsehen conducted a survey to determine Germans' favorite books. The results were aired on *Unsere Besten—Das große Lesen* (Our Best—The Big Read), on 1 October of the same year. Of those who responded, 66.4 percent were women ("Wie haben die Zuschauer" 2004), suggesting that women make up the majority of Germany's reading public. In a related study, the opinion polling institute *forsa* found that Germans in their forties read the most books, with women more likely than men to read "amusing novels [*heitere Romane*], cookbooks, fairy tales/legends, women's literature [*Frauenliteratur*], as well as children's and youth literature" ("Mehr Lust" 2004).[1] Gunnar Cynybulk, editor and program director of the Kiepenheuer publishing house, has described this trend in the literary market succinctly: today's average book buyer is female, in her mid-forties, university-educated, and purchases fifteen books a year (2005). Consequently, German-language publishing houses today deliberately and persistently court women readers, and magazines and television shows market literature to the female reader-consumer.

In analyzing this strategic marketing of books to women in Germany today, we trace these trends to the popularization of women's literature (hereafter: *Frauenliteratur*) in the 1970s through the women's movement and subsequent large-scale book series marketed to women. However, while proponents of *Frauenliteratur* in the 1970s sought to educate a predominantly female readership by disseminating critical texts, the concept of *Frauenliteratur* lost its relevance for the mainstream female readership in the wake of German unification, and today is used only in limited contexts. The literary establishment, in turn, has responded to this shift in sentiment by the largest share of the literary market, and has changed its marketing strategy to a model we term the *Frauenlite-raturbetrieb*, the aggressive marketing of literature to the woman reader-consumer based on the editorial principle of the *Frauenliteratur* book series of the 1970s, but without an explicitly political agenda. This style is promoted by media forces such as the women's magazine *Brigitte*, Elke Heidenreich's television show "Lesen!" (Let's Read!), and related (audio-) book series.

Mainstreaming *Frauenliteratur*: Women's Book Series in the 1970s

The strategic marketing of books to women has its roots in the politicized literary culture of the women's movement of the 1970s. While the term *Frauenroman* (women's novel) had already been in currency since the nineteenth century (Soltau 1984, II), *Frauenliteratur* became current in the 1970s in an attempt to signify a literature independent of trivial romance novels, written by women, about women, and for women, and as such an integral component of the politicization of gender (Bammer 2000, 216).

Despite its antiestablishment intentions in the 1970s, *Frauenliteratur* did not long remain the exclusive domain of the small, feminist publishing house (Bammer 2000, 223–25). By the late 1970s, large-scale publishers responded to the changing demands of the marketplace by creating new book series specifically targeted at women (Jurgensen 1983, 31; Vorspel 1990, 3–4). The attempt to mainstream *Frauenliteratur* as literature written by, for, and about women is mirrored in the rise and fall of these series. Although several publishing houses launched series targeted at women, only a few were commercially significant. The two longest-lived and most successful were Rowohlt's *neue frau* (new woman), which concentrated on fiction, and Fischer's *Die Frau in der Gesellschaft* (Woman in Society), which published nonfiction only.[2]

In a 1997 article on the history of Rowohlt's *neue frau* (1977–1997) written shortly before the series ended, editor Angela Praesent reflected on her early involvement in *neue frau*, observing that she "planned to edit a series that would work like a magazine in many respects" (43). She explained that readers would buy the newest volume based on their positive experience with previous volumes, regardless of whether or not they were familiar with the author (43). The books were published on a monthly basis, and the cost of each volume was relatively low, especially when compared to other literary series (Vorspel 1990, 168). The series mainly published works of fiction that were, with very few exceptions, written by women. Rowohlt chose the cheaper paperback format, because as Praesent pointed out, women buy and read more books than men, but have less money at their disposal (42). Praesent's "editorial concept," as she called it, was also quite simple. She assumed that if a book held her interest it would also interest others (45). Praesent's personal "radar system" for selecting books for the series *neue frau* proved effective, as did Rowohlt's marketing of a literature series for women. In 1996 approximately half of the books published in the series since its inception in 1977 were still in print (Praesent, 45).

When Fischer launched its series *Die Frau in der Gesellschaft* in 1978, a year after the start of the Rowohlt series, it deliberately sought to complement Rowohlt's *neue frau* by concentrating on nonfiction (Mues 1998, 10). Ingeborg Mues, founder and editor of the Fischer series, explained that her series arose from the desire to make available "books . . . that took issue with its [the women's movement's] history, with the search for roots, with women who influenced the early women's movement" (1998, 10). Indeed, some of the earlier publications in the series include books by early feminists like Hedwig Dohm and others. In the mid-1980s, the series began publishing fiction as well. From 1986 until its end, the series published some very successful novels, such as Hera Lind's *Das Superweib* (The Super Broad, 1994) and Eva Heller's *Beim nächsten Mann wird alles anders* (1987; *With the Next Man Everything Will Be Different*, 1992). Mues credited the success of the series to its flexibility and its mix of genres (1998, 11). When the female reader changed, the series began publishing a new style of literature. Today's woman is more self-aware and better versed in equal rights, Mues explained, which made a new style of literature popular: "Complaining, whining, and sighing is passé . . . and a kind of jolly feminism is on the way in" (1998, 14). The humorous and self-ironical novels by Hera Lind and Eva Heller proved to be a winning formula and the books became phenomenal bestsellers (1998, 14). It is probable that the inclusion of bestselling authors like Lind and Heller kept the series alive until 2003—well after the demise of *neue frau* in 1997. In his book *Generation Golf*, which became a cult classic, essayist Florian Illies even went so far as to attribute the rising popularity of works by Lind to the final demise of feminism: "Praise God we have gotten over feminism. But what has stepped into its place is really not that simple. Strong women with soft hearts. They get the necessary jolts to their self-confidence from appropriate women's magazines, the new German Katja Riemann films, or the books of Gaby Hauptmann and Hera Lind" (2001, 171–72). Despite these attempts to adapt to changing times, by the late 1990s, both *neue frau* (in 1997) and *Die Frau in der Gesellschaft* (in 2003) had fallen out of fashion. Even as early as the early 1990s, editor Angela Praesent noticed a change, "as though for reading women, everything that smacked of feminism, feminine exclaves, or feminine special ways" was embarrassing (50). She further notes that at some point bookstores stopped displaying books in the context of series and began shelving them alphabetically. This diminished the impact of individual book series (9). Tanja Seelbach, an editor for the Fischer series, lists several reasons for the decision to end *Die Frau in der Gesellschaft*. When Ingeborg Mues, the creator and long-time editor of the series retired, the series "that was heavily shaped by her character" no longer fit the concept of the publishing house. In addition, Seelbach notes the absence of a widespread women's movement in Germany such as there was in the 1970s. She also points to parallel developments in the popularity of women's groups and feminist or women's bookstores, both of which have suffered (Seelbach 2006).

From the Academic to the Trivial: The Lessening Impact of *Frauenliteratur* in the Literary Market

As the fates of *Frauenliteratur* book series reflect, neither the women's movement nor the publishing establishment was able to rehabilitate the term *Frauenliteratur* into a positive and enduring designation or even a broadly based genre. While Manfred Jurgensen could observe in 1983 that the "$64,000 question" (*Gretchenfrage*) of contemporary literature was "what's your position on women's literature?" ("wie hältst du es mit der Frauenliteratur?", 13), later uses of the term *Frauenliteratur* in scholarly and popular print forms suggest that the battle to reappropriate the designation in an affirmative sense has since been conceded. In most academic contexts, *Frauenliteratur* is not understood as a productive category, but as a designation applied to an ossified genre. In an essay on *Frauenliteratur*, for example, Angelika Bammer employs the term to represent women's writing between 1968 and 1989 (2000, 217). Notably, in the same literary history, Anna Kuhn contributes an essay titled "Women's Writing in Germany since 1989" without mentioning *Frauenliteratur* (2000). Similarly, when Sigrid Lange elsewhere titles a piece "Topographical Irritations: Women's Literature after the End of the GDR" ("Topographische Irritationen. Frauenliteratur nach dem Ende der DDR"), she qualifies her understanding of *Frauenliteratur* significantly, pointing out that the category of women's literature "as a thematically determined definition" is a disappearing phenomenon, although it remains present as a "fragmented tradition of ways of writing that are individually very different" (1994, 258).

Even in the late twentieth and early twenty-first century, after the *Frauenliteratur* designation had already been judged unfavorable and obsolete, it is occasionally invoked to emphasize what should succeed this limited and outdated form. When Beatrice von Matt, for example, released *Frauen schreiben die Schweiz Aus der Literaturgeschichte der Gegenwart* (1998), a review in the *Neue Zürcher Zeitung* found it necessary to emphasize that this new anthology of women's writing should not be taken for *Frauenliteratur*, for the author "is not concerned here with women's literature in the disparaging sense," and "the gender question is not the primary issue" (Kedves 1999). Rather, the anthology features texts that reflect Switzerland (Kedves 1999). Similarly, Evelyn Finger, staff writer for the arts section of *Die Zeit*, declared in 2005 that the "chatter about women's literature" as a feminist or academic designation had fallen out of fashion with good reason (2005).

The domain in which *Frauenliteratur* remains a productive term today is in its conflation with formulaic romance novels. Indeed, it seems to be one of the few truths that journalists of all stripes accept. In an article appearing in *Der Spiegel*, Harald Martenstein establishes the distinction between "literature" and *Frauenliteratur* thus: "There are a lot of books that are written by women. Then there are books that women write especially for other women, or that are mainly bought by women. The former is considered 'literature' by the experts, the latter 'women's literature' (2004). And although Evelyn Finger wryly observes that *Frauenliteratur* today denotes something along the lines of "prosecco-Tupperware-party-lovesickness novels" (2005), she argues that the same elements are at work in both the attempt to infuse *Frauenliteratur* with a feminist agenda as well as the effort to dismiss it as fluffy romance. Both categorizations reduce works to some kind of biological-biographical essence, resulting in the trivialization of content and author. Finger sees the ongoing danger of the *Frauenliteratur* label latent in the recent coining of the "Literary Girl Wonder" (*Fräuleinwunder*) which, according to Finger, certain influential figures in the literary world have used to describe indiscriminately the works of young women authors in Germany and reduce them to a catchy, magazine-friendly label (2005). Finger's proposal for what should succeed *Frauenliteratur* in the twenty-first century is unambiguous: an all-inclusive literature that derives its emancipatory potential from "the inexhaustibility of human creation." As we argue below, it is, in fact, a similar vision of literature that Elke Heidenreich promotes.

From *Frauenliteratur* to *Frauenliteraturbetrieb*

Even if works are not termed *Frauenliteratur* or associated with the *Fräuleinwunder*, even if they have not been classified under the "prosecco-Tupperware-party-lovesickness" genre, the strategy of marketing novels by women about women to women continues in the *Frauenliteraturbetrieb*. Intent on holding sway among women reader-consumers, publishing houses design book covers with women in mind (Moritz 2005a), and zealously reproduce combinations that prove particularly successful. Rainer Moritz has recorded one recent phenomenon among publishing houses to "incessantly throw novels onto the market whose titles reflect exotic women's professions" (2005b), a trend he traces back to the enormous success in Germany of Dona Cross's 1996 *Pope Joan* (translated into German in 1997 as *Die Päpstin*, or the female pope).

A survey of Germany's literary market reveals that more has changed in the past thirty years than just *Frauenliteratur* book series. Affecting the literary landscape in general has been the declining influence of book reviews in leading newspapers such as the *Frankfurter Allgemeine Zeitung* and the *Süddeutsche Zeitung*. Germans have apparently become less loyal to individual media sources, now drawing their information from several sources, including television shows, magazines, and the Internet (Moritz 2005a). The financial constraints under which publishing houses operate today translate into reduced spending on advertising new books; publishers instead pursue "free advertisement" through reviews in influential media sources (Moritz 2005b). Two such influential sources are the women's magazine *Brigitte*, and Elke Heidenreich's television show "Lesen!"[3]

The marketing strategies of today's *Frauenliteraturbetrieb*—in which *Brigitte* and Heidenreich play significant parts—reflect fundamental continuities with the editorial concept of the *Frauenliteratur* book series of the 1970s. Both employ a marketing strategy akin to selling magazines, in which readers are encouraged to return to the series based on previous positive experiences with selections regardless of their familiarity with the author, and both emphasize that the editors hand-select works with the hope of achieving concurrence between their tastes and the tastes of their readers. Departing from the editorial strategies of the 1970s, however, neither *Brigitte* nor Heidenreich promotes works based on a political agenda, the gender of the author, or a women-centered focus, appealing instead, it seems, to perceptions about readers' lifestyles and literary aesthetics. Building on the reputation they establish with their readership, *Brigitte* and Heidenreich have also recently released series of print and audio books, which more closely reflect the other editorial principles of earlier book series, in that the works appear regularly, are priced affordably, and primarily feature women authors.

Brigitte

The most popular women's magazine in Germany, the biweekly, high-gloss *Brigitte* has become a very desirable venue for presenting new literature. In a recent interview with *Der Spiegel*, Andreas Lebert, the editor-in-chief of *Brigitte*, recognized the significance of women readers to both his magazine and to literature in general: "Women are more curious and have more varied interests than men. Without them there would be no market for books and also no market for magazines" (Lebert 2004). Because of its wide access to women and its longevity, *Brigitte* has been very successful in marketing literature to women through book recommendations, author interviews, prize sponsorships, and even their own literature series.

Unlike *Die Zeit* and *Der Spiegel*, which review literature critically in their publications, *Brigitte* systematically markets reading and literature in its pages (Greiner 2005). For example, *Brigitte* dedicates a section of its culture rubric to "presenting" (*vorstellen*) literary works. "Presenting" literature is entirely different from reviewing it critically, and this method of showcasing literature signals a clear break from the manner typical in publications such as *Die Zeit*, *Der Spiegel*, *Frankfurter Allgemeine Zeitung*, and the *Süddeutsche Zeitung*.

Brigitte presents a wide variety of books on its book page. Often, contemporary fiction is presented next to a nineteenth-century classic with no clear connection, or a biography is described next to a fantasy novel. The common denominator in these cases is that each book has been hand-picked by *Brigitte* for presentation in the issue. The page is called "Die fünf *Brigitte*-Favoriten" (Five *Brigitte* Favorites), and as the caption suggests, there are no negative reviews. In ten to thirty lines (plus a picture of the book cover), the reviewer describes the basic plot, locates the book within a genre, and provides an endorsement. While each book receives a positive review, or presentation, as mentioned above, the five books that are reviewed are generally quite varied.[4] And while many of the books selected for *Brigitte* are clearly destined to become bestsellers (or already are bestsellers), the magazine can and does rely on its established position as a venue for presenting literature, including new authors and reintroducing classics from earlier years.

In addition to the biweekly "Fünf *Brigitte*-Favoriten," *Brigitte* expands its book page several times a year and publishes thick special sections devoted to different types of literature. It also publishes interviews and profiles of notable authors with some regularity. In 2005, there appeared interviews with or profiles on Nick Hornsby (Gerstenberger 2005), Ildikó von Kürthy and Svende Merian (Kürthy 2005), Edward P. Jones (Schnitzler 2005), and Orhan Pamuk (Küchemann 2005), as well as profiles of the "strong voices" in its audio book series, and elaborate introductions to the books in the Brigitte-Buch-Edition (both discussed below). Since 1992, *Brigitte* also sponsors its own literature prize, the "Bettina-von-Arnim Prize," and since 2004, its own novel contest. The 2005 winner, Markus Lüngen's novel *18*, was subsequently "presented" in *Brigitte* (Wittmann 2005b, 86) and the author was profiled in the following issue ("Markus Lüngen" 2005).

Perhaps to underscore once and for all the extent of its influence, *Brigitte* affixed a free Reclam edition of Heinrich von Kleist's classic novella *Die Marquise von O. . .* to its front cover shortly before Christmas in 2005.[5] That people read a novella from the first part of the nineteenth century because *Brigitte* suggested it is truly testament to the magazine's sway. Letters from readers to *Brigitte* in the ensuing months attest to the success of the ploy, although it bears mention that the ones printed in the magazine do not reflect any intellectual involvement with the text. One reader writes for example, "Good move, *Brigitte*! I hope this niveau will be honored and revered" ("Stark, stark!" 2005, 201), and a high school pupil complains that his German teacher had been so inspired that she required her entire class to read the work. Yet another reader notes that although she does not like that particular Kleist work, she does like "the idea with the Reclam volume." *Brigitte* editor-in-chief Andreas Lebert denied that the move was purely a marketing strategy, emphasizing that "one can do something other than inserting lipstick and makeup samples in the contested market of women's titles" ("Bildung mit 'Brigitte'" 2004). Lebert's good intentions notwithstanding, this gesture reveals that like lipstick and makeup samples, literature is a product that *Brigitte* markets and its readers consume in pursuit of a certain lifestyle.

With a circulation of over 800,000 issues, *Brigitte* is Germany's biggest biweekly magazine for women (Lebert 2004), and as one might expect, it influences the market for many of the commodities featured in its pages. Often, books that *Brigitte* presents appear soon after on *Der Spiegel*'s bestseller lists. Those that do appear frequently remain bestsellers for many weeks, a testament to *Brigitte*'s taste, or at least to the magazine's ability to predict what will sell. Although other factors influence which books make *Der Spiegel*'s list, the frequent coincidence between a mention in *Brigitte* and an appearance on the bestseller lists suggests a connection.[6] Despite an almost certain connection between being reviewed in *Brigitte* and appearing on *Der Spiegel*'s best-seller list, there seems little else in common among the recent works by Anna Gavalda, T.C. Boyle, and Cecilia Ahern.[7] Anna Gavalda is a young French author who is taken seriously by the critics, and *Brigitte* describes Gavalda's novel as a "stately novel, light-footed and of French grace" (Wittmann 2005c, 100). On the other hand, T.C. Boyle's *The Inner Circle* is a fictional biography of Alfred Kinsey, which *Brigitte* calls "the story of a revolution" (Wittmann 2005e, 72). About the latest novel by Cecelia Ahern, who is known for her light romances, *Brigitte* reports that the new work "serves up love again" and mentions that her last book sold over 250,000 copies (Wittmann 2005d, 71).

Brigitte's offering of a wide range of literature reflects Andreas Lebert's overall concept of his magazine in the twenty-first century. While women of the 1950s defined themselves according to a limited range of life issues, today's women seek fulfillment in a number of different areas, are better educated, and are more likely to work outside the home (2004). According to Lebert, this formula seems to be successful. *Brigitte* prides itself on having a close relationship to its readers (it receives over five hundred communications from readers per day), and so the magazine knows when it has not represented the interests of German women well (2004). *Brigitte*'s successful formula of presenting old works and new ones, hand-picked by a thoughtful editor, is similarly a distinguishing feature of Elke Heidenreich's editorial principle on her television show "Lesen!"

Elke Heidenreich's "Lesen!"

Although she has been a long-time contributor to *Brigitte* and has written several fictional works,[8] Elke Heidenreich has risen to popular prominence since 2003 primarily through the success of her television show "Lesen!" (Let's Read!). Since the disbanding of the *Literarisches Quartett* in 2001 and the conclusion of Marcel Reich-Ranicki's solo career in 2002 ("Sein letztes Solo" 2002), no one has been able to vie for the title of Germany's "Literature Pope" ("Literaturpapst" or "Literaturpäpstin") like Elke Heidenreich. As Joachim Lottmann observed in *Der Spiegel*, "Lesen!" has become "almost the only, the last program for books" (2005, 168). The half-hour program currently airs seven times a year at 10:15 PM on ZDF, is re-broadcast twice, and is available after the original broadcast via the ZDF Web site.[9] And though Heidenreich never states it explicitly—and there are always men present in the studio audience—it seems to be understood that Heidenreich's show primarily attracts women (cf. Lottmann 2005, 166).

Like *Brigitte*, Heidenreich's "Lesen!" is not concerned with "taking notice" of literature in the high-brow style of the weekly *Die Zeit*. Together with her guests, Heidenreich "presents" literature, including new works as well as classics from around the world, children's literature, and selected nonfiction. Heidenreich opens the show with a presentation of a few new works, followed by the appearance of a guest—ranging from Marcel Reich-Ranicki to Doris Dörrie—who presents a favorite book and reads a selection; other features include video clip summaries of recommended books and audio books. Fiercely maintaining her autonomy, Heidenreich declines recommendations from other authors and readers alike ("Noch Fragen?" 2006), selecting the works to feature on "Lesen!" according to deceptively simple criteria: they must be "good stories, told well" (Vetter 2006a). Heidenreich measures her success at meeting these criteria by seeing if featured works subsequently appear on the bestseller list (Vetter 2006a).

Heidenreich's approach to presenting literature appears, in the main, to reflect the editorial principles of the 1970s book series. Indeed, it would seem at first blush that the *Literaturpäpstin* shared Florian Illies's relief that Germans have finally "gotten over" feminism when she observed that *Brigitte*'s audio book series "Starke Stimmen" appealed to her because it tapped into women's primal connection to literature "without coming out of the women's lib corner with a swinging sword" (Heidenreich 2005b). Joachim Lottmann also suggests that in trying to draw in a large audience, Heidenreich has come to focus more on the books and less on feminism. "After seventeen episodes, she's naturally become a bit mainstream. 'Hey girls, this is something for you!' doesn't cross her lips anymore, and she hardly hugs sisters-in-arms in front of the rolling camera anymore, in general: that whole display of feminism appears today like a misunderstanding" (2005, 169). However, despite the claim to have distanced herself from women's libbers, Heidenreich suggests elsewhere that she still believes in the emancipatory potential of literature, albeit without references to politics or feminism. In the foreword to Stefan Bollmann's *Frauen, die lesen, sind gefährlich* (Women Who Read Are Dangerous), for example, Heidenreich offers a brief history of women's reading, establishing early in her introduction that "women who could read and write knew something, and the books where this knowledge could be found were dangerous" (2005b, 13), and Heidenreich describes herself as the "last committed 68-er" (Lottmann, 169). What distinguishes Heidenreich's message from the *Frauenliteratur* book series of the 1970s and 1980s is that Germany's strong women can draw their strength from any number of sources. All novels can make it onto Heidenreich's show, as long as they meet her criteria of being "good stories, told well," because women are capable of identifying with any protagonist, male or female: "'Women read differently,' is one interesting observation on this theme made by Ruth Klüger. They also read more. And reading, they are both, man and woman, genderless, they suffer with the hero and the heroine, with the male author, the female author" (Heidenreich 2005b, 16).

Like Reich-Ranicki before her—whose praising or panning of a book markedly influenced book sales (cf. Moritz 2005)—Heidenreich has faced the criticism over and over again that she unduly influences the German-language literature market (Lottmann 2005, 168). Indeed, a comparison of the works recommended on "Lesen!" and their appearance on *Der Spiegel*'s bestseller list suggests a correlation, though not all recommended books become bestsellers. Heidenreich's response to this critique has been to review several books during each episode (Lottmann 2005, 169), and to recommend a wide range of German literature and works in translation by both men and women. Of the over sixty works presented in 2005 (including nonfiction and children's books), ten subsequently appeared on the fiction bestseller list within a few weeks of broadcast. Among them were two German-language novels, the others translations from British and American English, French, Dutch, Swedish, and Hungarian.[10]

Book Series

Linked to *Brigitte*'s contributions to the literary landscape through book recommendations are book series that expand *Brigitte*'s product line. Using its firmly established reader base to market the product, *Brigitte* has to date launched three book series: "Starke Stimmen für starke Frauen" (Strong Voices for Strong Women) in 2005, "*Brigitte*-Buch-Edition" in 2005, and a second "Starke Stimmen" in 2006. Reflecting a predominantly female readership, the book series seem to favor books that will appeal to women, although male authors and books that might appeal to men are by no means excluded.[11]

The strategy of drawing on an already important readership base is hardly unique to *Brigitte*; in 2004, the *Süddeutsche Zeitung* featured a collection of the fifty great novels of the twentieth century such as Umberto Eco's *Name of the Rose* and F. Scott Fitzgerald's *The Great Gatsby*, and in the same year *Bild* introduced a series under the motto "great novels, great feeling" (große Romane, großes Gefühl), which includes works such as Mario Puzzo's *The Godfather* and Stephen King's *The Shining*.[12]

Inspired perhaps by the book series put out by the *Süddeutsche Zeitung* and *Bild*, *Brigitte* launched "Starke Stimmen für starke Frauen" as an audio book series. It follows the same principles as the *Süddeutsche Zeitung* and *Bild* in that volumes (in CD-format) are released regularly (in this case bi-weekly), are affordable (just under €10.00), and offer selections that appeal to a wide segment of the (female) population. The audio book series debuted on 2 February 2005 and ran twenty-four weeks for a total of twelve audio book releases. The books themselves were read by celebrities (hence the "strong voices") starting with Heidenreich herself reading a collection of Dorothy Parker's *New Yorker* stories. As Heidenreich explains in a 2005 interview with *Brigitte*, "I think that women have a much more primal access to literature. And therefore the idea of having women read for women is not so bad" (2005c). The series proved wildly successful, and a second edition of twelve "strong voices" was launched in 2006.

In addition to its audio book series, *Brigitte* also launched a printed literature series in August 2005, the "*Brigitte*-Buch-Edition." Heidenreich, the editor of the series, explains the rational behind the selection of the twenty-six books that comprise the series. "It isn't about a canon, about books that one should have read, [. . . .] It is about books that until now haven't had the success that they actually deserved. Wonderful stories that weren't noticed enough and that are waiting to be discovered" (2005a, 8).

The editions are released every two weeks, and in a pattern that has become familiar, are hard-bound "and because Elke Heidenreich loves the color red, the linen spines glow in all shades from poppy to burgundy" ("Neu! Die *Brigitte*-Buch-Edition" 2005, 13).

Brigitte's three book series have been successful. Reader letters attest to the popularity of the first audio book series "Starke Stimmen," calling the series a "super idea" and "inspired" ("Gigantisch" 2005, 123), and the launching of a second audio book series in 2006 surely reflects success rather than failure. The "*Brigitte*-Buch-Edition," the printed book series also launched in 2005, has also been well received.[13]

Conclusion

In this treatment of the marketing of literature to women in Germany today, two main points emerge: first, women carry the market in sales of fiction and thus are a force to be reckoned with; second, using gender as a marketing tool in the style of *Frauenliteratur* was reductive, trivializing, and, in many circumstances, very profitable. Yet while many media critics embraced the decline of the term "*Frauenliteratur*" as a productive category, few have opined on what has—or should have—succeeded it. This essay offers one response by drawing an arc between the *Frauenliteratur* of the 1970s and the marketing strategies used today to attract women readers. Our coining of the term "*Frauenliteraturbetrieb*" points to the origins of today's mass-marketing of literature to women in the 1970s, while it also emphasizes that this designation is not another typecasting of the literature women read, but rather a description of how media present a wide range of literature to women.

The *Frauenliteratur* of the 1970s and 1980s and the *Frauenliteraturbetrieb* of the twenty-first century both promised a product much larger than a paperback book, although there are notable distinctions between what the two claimed to deliver. In lieu of an explicit feminist message, media sources like *Brigitte* tap into literature as a commodity essential in the fulfillment of a certain lifestyle, and the phenomenally influential Elke Heidenreich makes the plea today for the more general potential of literature to liberate.

We have suggested here that there is strong circumstantial evidence that *Brigitte* and "Lesen!" influence what German women read. And while Florian Illies suggests that the "strong women" of the twenty-first century are flocking to *Frauenliteratur* of the species that Finger calls "prosecco-Tupperware-party-lovesickness novels," *Der Spiegel's* bestseller list suggests that women readers in Germany today have much broader reading interests. To be sure, the latest book by Cecelia Ahern is guaranteed a place on the list. However, without the help of Elke Heidenreich, recent German translations of works by Truman Capote, János Székely, and Marcelle Sauvageot might not have been. This is a clear strength of the *Frauenliteraturbetrieb*: a wide range of works are presented to women readers. While some may nevertheless mourn the loss of feminism and regret the increasingly explicit commodification of literature, the *Frauenliteraturbetrieb* realizes—however imperfectly—Evelyn Finger's wish for an all-inclusive literature that can derive its emancipatory potential from "the inexhaustibility of human creation" (2005).

Notes

1. This and all subsequent translations in the text are the work of the authors.
2. For a list of other literary series targeting women see Vorspel 1990, 3–4.

3. Regina-Maria Vogel, manager of the Buchhandlung an der Thomaskirche bookstore in Leipzig, noted the influence of Heidenreich's show on sales in her store (2005), and Rainer Moritz identified *Brigitte* and "Lesen!" as two influences on the market (2005a).

4. The week of 20 July 2005, *Brigitte*'s "five favorites" are Goliarda Sapienza's *In den Himmel stürzen* (2005; orig.: *L'arte della gioia*, 1994); Kirsty Gunn's *Der Junge und das Meer* (2005; orig.: The Boy and the Sea, 2006), Petra Hammersfahr's *Schatten der Vergangenheit* (2005), Christa Wolf's *Mit anderem Blick* (2005), and an audio book of Flaubert's 1856 *Madame Bovary* (Wittmann 2005a, 58). Again, these books have little in common. Although Gunn and Wolf are prominent contemporary authors of New Zealand and Germany, respectively, their topics and style are vastly divergent. Hammersfahr writes psychological thrillers, and Flaubert, of course, comes from a different age entirely.

5. Reclam editions are inexpensive reprints of the German classics that have long been associated with school and university reading.

6. In 2005 alone, twenty-one novels appeared on the bestseller list of *Der Spiegel* after having been reviewed or discussed in *Brigitte*. Listed here with original titles is a sample of works. Michael Crichton, *Welt in Angst* (2005; *State of Fear*, 2004); Hennig Mankell, *Tiefe* (2005; orig.: *Djup*, 2004) Isabel Allende, *Zorro* (2005); and Orhan Pamuk, *Schnee* (2005) (*Kar*, 2002).

7. Anna Gavalda's *Zusammen ist man weniger allein* (2005; orig.: *Ensemble, c'est tout*, 2004) was reviewed in *Brigitte* on 2 February 2005 (Wittmann 2005c, 100) and appeared for the first time on the bestseller list 14 February 2005. T.C. Boyle's *Dr. Sex* (2005; orig.: *The Inner Circle*, 2004) also made a quick transition, reviewed in *Brigitte* on 2 March 2005 (Wittmann 2005e, 72) and appearing in *Der Spiegel* on 14 March 2005. Cecilia Ahern's *Für immer vielleicht* (2005; orig.: *Where Rainbows End*, 2004) was even quicker: the *Brigitte* review also appeared 2 March 2005 (Wittmann 2005d, 71) and appeared on *Der Spiegel*'s list 7 March 2005.

8. Heidenreich's oeuvre includes youth literature, such as *Nero Corleone: Eine Katzengeschichte* (2003) and several collections of short stories, among them *Der Welt den Rücken* (2003).

9. In the show on 21 Nov. 2006, Heidenreich announced that "Lesen!" would return in 2007 with more shows, and would switch from Tuesday to Friday night (Vetter 2006b).

10. The ten works with original titles are: Sven Regener, *Neue Vahr Süd* (2004); Daniel Kehlmann, *Die Vermessung der Welt* (2005); Steve Tesich, *Ein letzter Sommer* (2005; orig.: *Summer Crossing* 1982); Jeanette Walls, *Schloss aus Glas* (2005; orig.: *The Glass Castle* 2005); Julian Barnes, *Der Zitronentisch* (2005; orig.; *The Lemon Table* 2004); Philippe Claudel, *Die grauen Seelen* (2005; orig.: *Les Ames grises* 2003); Marcelle Sauvageot, *Fast ganz die Deine* (2005; orig: *Commentaire*, 1936); Diane Broeckhoven, *Ein Tag mit Herrn Jules* (2005; orig.: *De buitenkant van Meneer Jules*: 2001); Per Olov Enquist, *Das Buch von Blanche und Marie*, (2004; orig.: *Boken om Blanche och Marie*, 2004); János (John) Székely, *Verlockung* (SchirmerGraf edition, 2005; orig.: *Kisértés*, 1948). Noteworthy is that Regener's *Neue Vahr Süd* had already appeared on the bestseller list in January and February 2005 before Heidenreich's discussion of the work.

When Heidenreich featured the work on 7 June 2005, the novel returned to the bestseller list for another three weeks.

11. Heidenreich herself notes that women, by reading books and then handing them off to their husbands, are ultimately responsible for which novels men read (Heidenreich [2005c]).

12. In a press release entitled *"Bild* Bestseller-Bibliothek: 'Große Romane, großes Gefühl'"* from 7 October 2004, the publishers of the series (*Bild* and the publishing group "Weltbild") state as their goal the wish to "bring people near to books, to inspire them to read."

13. Reich-Ranicki himself gives his approval, listing his favorites in the series: Ruth Klüger's *Weiter leben* (1994; *Still Alive: A Holocaust Girlhood Remembered*, 2001), Haruki Muramaki's *Gefährliche Geliebte* (2000; orig.: *kokkyō no minami, taiyō no nishi*, 1992), John Updike's *Gertrude und Claudius* (2001; orig.: *Gertrude and Claudius*, 2000) and Antonio Tabucchi's *Erklärt Pereira* (1995; orig.: *Sostiene Pereira*, 1994) (*See* Schnitzler 2006).

Works Cited

Bammer, Angelika. 2000. "Feminism, *Frauenliteratur*, and Women's Writing of the 1970s and 1980s." In *A History of Women's Writing in Germany, Austria and Switzerland*, ed. Jo Catling. Cambridge: Cambridge University Press. 216–32.

"Bild Bestseller-Bibliothek: 'Große Romane, großes Gefühl.' Jeden Donnerstag ein Bestseller." 2004. Press release from 7 October. <http://www.axel-springer.de/inhalte/presse/inhalte/presse/zeitungen/994.html>.

"Bildung mit 'Brigitte'." 2004. *Spiegel Online*, 13 December. <http://www.spiegel.de/Spiegel/0,1518,332421,00.html>.

Cynybulk, Gunnar. 2005. "Wie verlegt man junge Autoren?" *Fulbright German Studies Seminar* Berlin. 24 June.

Finger, Evelyn. 2005. "'Weiblich' kann fast alles heißen: Warum das Gerede von Frauenliteratur zurecht aus der Mode gekommen ist." *ZEIT Online*, 31 March. <http://www.zeit.de/2005/14/Frauen_2fSchriftstellerinnen>.

Gerstenberger, Beatrix. 2005. "Weinen oder Lachen." *Brigitte*, 25 May: 76–80.

"Gigantisch." 2005. Briefe an *Brigitte*. *Brigitte*, 15 March: 123.

Greiner, Ulrich, and Iris Radisch. 2005. „Literaturkritik in den Medien." *Fulbright German Studies Seminar*. Hamburg. 21 June.

Heidenreich, Elke. 2005a. "Liebe Lese-Menschen." *Brigitte*, 17 August: 8.

———. 2005b. "Kleine Fliegen!" Introduction. *Frauen, die lesen, sind gefährlich*. By Stefan Bollmann. Munich: Elisabeth Sandmann.

———. 2005c. "Starke Stimme: Elke Heidenreich." Interview with Stephan Bartels for *Brigitte*. <http://www.brigitte.de/hoerbuch_2005/elke_heidenreich/index.html>.

Illies, Florian. 2001. *Generation Golf: Eine Inspektion*. Frankfurt am Main: Fischer.

Jurgensen, Manfred. 1983. *Frauenliteratur: Autorinnen-Perspektiven-Konzepte.* Berne: Peter Lang.

Kedves, A. 1999. "Spiegelbilder/ 'Frauen schreiben die Schweiz.'" Rev. of Beatrice von Matt, *Frauen schreiben die Schweiz. Aus der Literaturgeschichte der Gegenwart. Neue Zürcher Zeitung* 55. 23 February. <http://nzz.gbi.de/web cgi?START=A20&T_FORMAT=5&DOKM=370287_NZZ_0&WID=26482–0380806–03664_3>.

Küchemann, Fridtjof. 2005. "Großer Bahnhof." *Brigitte,* 29 September: 82.

Kuhn, Anna. 2000. "Women's Writing in Germany since 1989." In *A History of Women's Writing in Germany, Austria and Switzerland,* ed. Jo Catling. Cambridge: Cambridge University Press. 233–53.

Kürthy, Ildikó von and Svende Merian. 2005. "Brauchen wir heute überhaupt noch emanzipierte Frauen?" Interview. By Till Raether and Sina Teigelkötter. *Brigitte* 22 June: 80–84.

Lange, Sigrid. 1994. "Topographische Irritationen: Frauenliteratur nach dem Ende der DDR." *Colloquia Germanica* 3.27: 255–74.

Lebert, Andreas. 2004. Interview. "Der Refrain des Lebens." By Claudia Voigt and Marianne Wellershoff. *Der Spiegel,* 3 May. <http://www.spiegel.de/spiegel/0,1518,297980,00.html>.

Lottmann, Joachim. 2005. "Ihr Lieben!" *Der Spiegel,* 10. October: 166–69.

"Markus Lüngen. Portrait." 2005. *Die neuen Bücher 2005. Brigitte* Extra, 12 October: 32–34.

Martenstein, Harald. 2004. "Er liebt mich, er liebt mich nicht." *KulturSPIEGEL* 26 July. <http://www.spiegel.de/kultur/literatur/0,1518,309892,00.html>.

Matt, Beatrice von. 1998. *Frauen schreiben die Schweiz: Aus der Literaturgeschichte der Gegenwart.* Frauenfeld: Huber.

"Mehr Lust auf Bücher: Die Deutschen lesen wieder häufiger." 2004. *ZDF. de Unterhaltung und Kultur* 29 September. <http:www.zdf.de/ZDFde/inhalt/30/0,1872,2198206,00.html> .

Moritz, Rainer. 2005a. "Der Einfluss der Medien auf den deutschen Büchermarkt." *Fulbright German Studies Seminar.* Hamburg. 21 June.

———. 2005b. "Wanderhure und Almwiesenfrau. Unendlich viele Kreationen." *Börsenblatt Online,* 21 July. <http://www.boersenblatt.net/92987/template/b3_tpl_suche_detail/>.

Mues, Ingeborg. 1998. "Statt eines Vorworts: Von *Häutungen* bis zum *Superweib*: Bilanz einer Lektorin." In *Was Frauen bewegt und was sie bewegen: Sechsundzwanzig Originalessays,* ed. Ingeborg Mues. Frankfurt am Main: Fischer. 9–15.

"Neu! Die *Brigitte*-Buch-Edition, erlesen von Elke Heidenreich." 2005. *Brigitte,* 3 August: 13.

"Noch Fragen?" [no date] *Lesen!* <http://www.zdf.de/ZDFde/inhalt/0/0,1872,2043232,00.html>.

Praesent, Angela. 1997. "Bemerkungen zur Geschichte der im Rowohlt Taschenbuch erscheinenden Reihe *neue frau.*" In *Das Lektorat—eine Bestandsaufnahme: Beiträge zum Lektorat im literarischen Verlag,* ed. Ute Schneider. Wiesbaden: Harrassowitz. 41–51.

Schnitzler, Meike. 2005. "Erst gefeuert, dann gefeiert." *Brigitte*, 3 August: 76–77.

———. 2006. "Ein Jahr hat 26 Bücher." *Brigitte* 16 August. <http://www.brigitte.de/buchedition/jahr_26_buecher/index.html>

Seelbach, Tanja. 2006. "Betreff: Die Frau in der Gesellschaft." E-mail to Katya Skow. 17 October.

"Sein letztes Solo." 2002. *ZDFreich-ranickisolo* 3 December. <http://www.zdf.de/ZDFde/inhalt/24/0,1986,2025400,00.html>.

Soltau, Heide. 1984. *Trennungs-Spuren: Frauenliteratur der zwanziger Jahre*. Frankfurt am Main. Extrabuch.

"Stark, stark!" 2005. *Brigitte*, 2 February: 201.

Vetter, Bernhard. 2006a. "Das war nicht der Schluss." *Lesen!* 19 September. <http://www.zdf.de/ZDFde/inhalt/19/0,1872,3979763,00.html>.

———. 2006b. "Du musst sein wie das Gras." *Lesen!* 21 November. <http://www.zdf.de/ZDFde/inhalt/8/0,1872,4078440,00.html>.

Vogel, Regina-Maria. 2005. "Trends und Käufer." *Fulbright German Studies Seminar*. Leipzig. 17 June.

Vorspel, Luzia. 1990. *Was ist neu an der "neuen frau"? Gattungen, Formen, Themen, von Frauenliteratur der 70er und 80er Jahre am Beispiel der Rowohlt-Taschenbuchreihe "neue frau"*. Frankfurt am Main: Peter Lang.

"Wie haben die Zuschauer gewählt?" 2004. *Unsere Besten: Das große Lesen*. 1 October: Slide 5. <http://www.zdf.de/ZDFde/inhalt/26/0,1872,2198906,00.html>.

Wittmann, Angela. 2005a. "Die fünf *Brigitte*-Favoriten." *Brigitte*, 20 July: 58.

———. 2005b. "Du kannst nicht immer 18 sein." Rev. of Markus Lüngen, *18*. *Brigitte*, 28 September: 86.

———. 2005c. "Es lebe die Liebe." Rev. of Anna Gavalda, *Zusammen ist man weniger allein. Brigitte*, 2 February: 100.

———. 2005d. "Liebe in Häppchen." Rev. of Cecilia Ahern, *Für immer vielleicht. Brigitte*, 2 March 2005: 71.

———. 2005e. "Mit T.C. Boyle auf *Brigitte*-Lesetour." *Brigitte*, 2 March: 72.

⚜ 13

SOCIAL ALIENATION AND GENDERED SURVEILLANCE: JULIA FRANCK OBSERVES POST-*WENDE* SOCIETY

BERET NORMAN

Born in East Berlin in 1970, author Julia Franck has published four works, in which one can trace her critique of social alienation in post-*Wende* German society.[1] Franck's project employs unreliable first-person narrators who believe that their acts of gendered surveillance will give them access to symbolic and social capital, which these narrators lack, in the vacuum of meaningful relationships in which they find themselves in contemporary Germany. Examples of the desired symbolic capital include honor, prestige, and having a voice to which others listen, and the sought-after social capital consists of networks, reciprocal connections, and trust.[2] But this analysis also leads to Franck's more complex and subtle critique of post-*Wende* indifference to *Vergangenheitsbewältigung*, or coming to terms with the past, which one finds in two narrators' offhand, almost unremarked (but quite remarkable) references to Germany's past.

This essay seeks to connect Franck's recent novel, *Lagerfeuer* (Campfire, 2003) to her first three published works through the lens of gendered surveillance. Surveillance provides the narrators a means to fill up their otherwise empty modern-day lives, as well as a method to gauge their own social positions—i.e., by watching others, they also determine their own social standing. In *Lagerfeuer*, a sociopolitical novel set in 1978 in East and West Berlin, Franck provides pointed references to the use of surveillance in the context of the Cold War; here the ideologies of power—as well as the narrators' powerless positions—are clear.[3] But in her three earlier works that take place in present-day Germany, Franck still employs a type of residual Cold War surveillance by first-person narrators, but without the Cold War context and toward a different end; these narrators engage in surveillance of others in their struggle to negotiate their claims to and desires for symbolic and social capital in a contemporary landscape of social alienation. Surveillance also played a part in Franck's personal history: as a child in 1978 she left the German Democratic Republic (GDR) with her mother and siblings and lived in a West Berlin relocation camp—like that depicted in *Lagerfeuer*—for nine months (Franck 2003b).

The adjective "gendered" is added here because Franck employs women watching men and men watching women, resulting in unexpected shifts in power dynamics. Feminist critical discourse analyst Michelle M. Lazar describes gender as an "ideological structure that divides people into two classes, men and women, based on a hierarchical relation of domination and subordination, respectively" (2005, 7). My concern here with gendered surveillance addresses what Lazar refers to as the underlying dualism in the reinforcement of the existing gender structure (8), which the female narrators reproduce in the first three works. Although the three narrators, who observe men and men's routines, appear to topple the conventionally gendered structure of the woman as the viewed object of male desire (Mulvey 1975, 12–13), their sexual attraction to the (male) objects still suggests the traditional idea that women gain access to power through their relationships with men. Yet their attraction to their subjects remains secondary to the desire for knowledge and access to hierarchical (gendered) structures of power. These narrators expect to gain access to what R.W. Connell calls the patriarchal dividend—access to symbolic, social, political, and economic capital (1995, 82)—via observation, not necessarily via direct interactions. Power relations based on traditionally gendered social structures become clear and illuminate how these female narrators aim their observations not merely at a sexual goal but also at social currency.

Although her first works do not reference specific political or historical contexts, the surveillance by the narrators in all of Franck's texts replicates the ubiquity of constant observation that permeated the former GDR. It has been estimated that in the GDR every fiftieth person between the age of 18 and 80 worked in some capacity for the Ministry of State Security or Stasi (Falke 2004). By providing pointed references to the use of surveillance in the Cold War in *Lagerfeuer*, along with less overt yet constant instances of surveillance in her first three works, Franck points to the problem of privacy and power in contemporary society. In their passivity, these narrators exhibit what surveillance studies scholar David Lyon describes as a "compliance with surveillance systems ... as participation in a kind of social orchestration" (2001, 7). And as amateur secret agents, Franck's narrators remain detached and are drawn to deception. Although examples of deception connect the narrators, the theme of numbness establishes a critical fabric underlying *Lagerfeuer*. Social isolation starts with numbness—a self-centered lack of compassion, as in Franck's first novel *Der neue Koch* (The New Cook, 1997)—and leads to alienation in individuals and eventually in society, as in Franck's third novel, *Lagerfeuer.*

Sex and Surveillance

The four works under discussion implement two kinds of surveillance. The first three involve first-person female narrators who observe men in order to gain a type of social capital or, as Robert Putnam describes it, "social networks and the norms of reciprocity and trustworthiness that arise from them" (2000, 19). In Franck's *Der neue Koch*, a nameless thirty-year-old narrator has inherited her mother's hotel, for which she has hired a new cook. With little action in the plot development, this novel leads the reader through the narrator's myriad thoughts, most of which concentrate on her observations of the hotel guests and the cook, as well as her envy of the cook's popularity. Franck's second novel, *Liebediener* (Love Servant, 1999), again presents a female narrator's (Beyla's) observations of her immediate surroundings—an apartment house in Berlin—and two of its inhabitants: Charlotte, who dies at the novel's beginning, and Albert, who Beyla believes is involved in Charlotte's death. Franck's third publication, *Bauchlandung: Geschichten zum Anfassen* (Belly Flop: Stories to Touch, 2000), is a collection of eight short stories. Throughout these stories Franck employs only female narrators in a variety of domestic settings. In the story where surveillance plays the greatest role, "Für Sie und Für Ihn" (For Her and For Him), a female narrator stares at her male neighbor and then reports what she sees. Franck's fourth publication, the novel *Lagerfeuer*, introduces political reality. The four first-person narrators—three who are refugees in and one who works in a West Berlin relocation camp—negotiate their way within the ideological competition of the Cold War going on around them.

In these texts, surveillance often overlaps with voyeurism, in that several of Franck's narrators derive sexual pleasure from the viewing. Yet because it is not sexual desire, but rather the quest for power and information that animate these observations, the surveillance includes, but remains different from, voyeurism. However, Franck does weave in elements of voyeurism when, for example, sexual stimulation keeps the female narrator in "Für Sie und Für Ihn" watching as her male neighbor has sex with an unknown woman. But the unnamed narrator has been regularly watching him and knows his routine long before this unexpected sexual scene takes place. Only upon gaining this new information—this curious change in her neighbor's routine in the form of this sexual affair—does she report it to a third party, the bartender, who she hopes will lust after her. She watches her neighbor, but her excitement focuses on the bartender: "I can hardly wait to tell him [the bartender], what I've seen" (Franck 2000, 54).[4] The Freudian active form of scopophilia, with its sexual gratification derived from looking (Gay 1989, 251), thus plays a role in the narrative. Yet Katharina Döbler's summary of Franck's stories in this collection as "more protocol-like than erotic" (2001) is to the point. The mundane quality of the "surveillance" described here thus reflects the tedium of these narrators' constant observations, as well as their frequent speculations about the observed person's self-image as connected to his or her appearance and actions. Little else of note happens in the first three narrators' lives; they mention only briefly other events beyond those that concern their objects. Thus watching, eavesdropping, leaning out of windows, and waiting for their objects' routine activities become habitual.

The story "Für Sie und Für Ihn" provides the most obvious example of a system of both spying on one person and then reporting to someone else; it also presents a failed attempt to upend the gendered structure of viewing, because the narrator loses her access to symbolic capital after her story reveals more truth than mystery. This narrator's routine reflects the emptiness of contemporary society. The unnamed female narrator mentions nothing of her own routine, of friends, or of work, and she knows no one in the building in the Moabit section of Berlin in which she has lived for two years; she obsessively watches her male neighbor, knows his routine, and presumes he has low self-esteem based on his actions—specifically how fastidiously he grooms himself upon his return home, after which he does not leave his apartment (Franck 2000, 56). As if she were waiting for exactly such information about this isolated man, she uses that day's staggering deviation—her neighbor's erotic rendezvous with a woman in his apartment—as her opportunity to report the information to another person, the male bartender on duty that day in her neighborhood bar.

The act of reporting on the neighbor, the fruit of her routine spying, becomes her currency at the bar. It is through this exchange of information—her only source of power—that she receives an otherwise unobtainable intimacy (symbolic capital) with this bartender, even though she does not find him very attractive. Having succeeded in winning his attention, she points out that the pale neighbor and the woman—the two whom she has just been watching—are now in the bar. The bartender had already asked if he could join her to watch this couple; with his request, the narrator moves closer to a type of reciprocity from social capital. But then the bartender realizes that the woman is his ex-girl-friend. The story ends as the emasculated bartender (Fitzel 2000) turns his back on the narrator, tends to his bottles, and sinks below the bar where he "simply does not [want to] surface" (Franck 2000, 64). The narrator fails to gain her desired contact and loses any symbolic capital that the reporting of her surveillance appeared to give her; thus she remains detached from the social and emotional circumstances around her.

"Für Sie und Für Ihn" is set in a post-*Wende* context and depicts the still-emerging New Germany. Change is visible in the former West Berlin border region of the narrator's apartment house, Moabit, and the reader learns of the neighborhood's successful gentrification as the narrator expresses surprise at how busy her local bar is in this blue-collar area known mostly for its prison (Franck 2000, 53).[5] As the narrator waits to tell her salacious story to the bartender, her attention turns to the bottles on the wall; she thinks about alcoholic beverages made "for her and for him" with differing colors and tastes (61). Living in a context of ambiguity, near an infamous prison and in an anonymous dwelling, she wonders whether consumer items like a cocktail might lead to social capital or, at least, some companionship.

In *Liebediener*, the female narrator, Beyla, pursues symbolic and social capital after her neighbor's death propels Beyla's life out of her cellar apartment. More than the previous narrator, Beyla mentions fragments of her professional and personal life: for instance, a pregnant friend helps her move, and she recalls her childhood with three brothers and a negligent father. This narrator claims to recognize her neighbor, Charlotte, mainly by her shoes—seen through Beyla's cellar window—and late-night, drunken homecomings. Yet Charlotte is from the West, and Beyla disdainfully recalls Charlotte's pride in being "one of the first *Wessis* (Westerners)" who moved into this East Berlin neighborhood, and, on a "search for adventure," at first illegally occupied her apartment (Franck 1999, 24). The novel opens with Charlotte's sudden death after falling in front of a streetcar; the dead woman's aunt hands over all the belongings in Charlotte's third floor apartment, as well as the keys and lease, to Beyla; this sudden reversal of fortunes reflects the uncertainty of possession in post-*Wende* Berlin, when property changed hands quickly. This new apartment elevates Beyla, yet it becomes the location of the "battle for truth and control" (Meise 2005, 131), as it is here that Beyla's obsession with her new downstairs neighbor, Albert, begins.

Beyla, a clown by trade, now fills the aloofness of her life with her new view from above and with the man and his sounds from below. Her skillful detachment becomes apparent early on in the novel as we read her unemotional assessments of people and scenes. At Charlotte's funeral, for example, Beyla gathers outward details of the attendees and quickly determines each person's potential position in Charlotte's circle of friends, as if she were to later report on them. A subsequent, more problematic example of her emotional detachment comes as she drives by the former concentration camp Ravensbrück; this will be discussed in more detail below. Her recurring and impassive descriptions of Charlotte's death also affirm this aloofness; however, one detail—that Charlotte is wearing Beyla's borrowed red, high-heeled shoes at the time of her death—betrays her professed detachment from Charlotte (Franck 1999, 18). After recognizing Alfred as the possible driver of the car that caused Charlotte to jump in front of the streetcar, Beyla's focused surveillance of and attraction to her neighbor begins. She looks from her windows toward his, "To check, if I could see something of Albert" (72); she notices which lights are on and how they signify his presence and potential mood; she construes the meaning of his lengthy phone conversations, believing that his laughter on the phone indicates a pretense of happiness, and of his repetitive piano playing: "I heard [in his playing] the sadness, but also the determination that I had seen in his eyes at the funeral"(60). She notices his bicycle in the courtyard when he does not answer her knock (97), and she stands by his door and listens: "I admit that I eavesdropped at his door, at least twenty minutes" (104). She even leans over the sink drain to listen to him talking in his apartment below her (129).

But Beyla remains primarily concerned with her significance as the only witness to Charlotte's presumed accidental death and Albert's role in the accident. Although Beyla believes him guilty of leaving the scene of the accident, she creates excuses for his innocence: "it was not intentional. Coincidence. Just a coincidence" (57); "it wasn't his fault, not really" (97). Her self-interested favor to Albert seems to be that she wants to protect him from others knowing the truth of his role in a fatal accident. But this is oddly also her key to power: beyond the physical intimacy, she demands that he reveal himself to her—she wants to be "in possession of his thoughts and secrets" (179); she wants to know if he feels remorse about his role in Charlotte's death. She believes this will give her symbolic and social capital—as only the two of them would know of his guilt; she thus would gain trustworthiness from and reciprocity with him.

Throughout their eventually amorous relationship, Beyla's suspicions of Albert turn into an argument about truth, which reveals a surprise: Albert's mysterious profession, which causes his phone to ring at all hours of the day, is that of male prostitute. With this information, Beyla gains more of the knowledge she desires; but because his profession both repudiates her position in his life and limits his social capital, she fails in her attempt for power. Yet his profession is also an expression of the inexact and shifting post-*Wende* economy, which permits and even rewards disrepute. Abandoning her alleged goal of finding out if Albert knows right from wrong—i.e., if he was involved in Charlotte's death and feels remorse—she rejects him and his eventual assertion of love for her without compassion. The social detachment, which had been curbed by her surveillance of and relationship with Albert, returns. She continues her own profession of deception by choreographing Charlotte's death into part of her clown routine.

The female narrator in the novel *Der neue Koch* is similar to Beyla in her social detachment and her desire for dominance through knowledge. She is also similar to the narrator in "Für Sie und Für Ihn" in her observations, but she watches everyone in the hotel (not just the men), and her gendered observations focus both on the negative traits of other women—which show her ignoble need for superiority—and on the men whom she tries to manipulate.

The narrator in *Der neue Koch* is a seemingly reluctant hotel owner who relates details—not just of how the new male cook takes control of both the hotel and of the hotel guests' affections—but details of every guest who passes under her watchful eyes. This narrator has never strayed beyond the nearby school of hotel management from which she failed to graduate, and her fictional duties—her own invention of ongoing surveillance—tire her: "It is sometimes strenuous, to know a lot about each person, to think their thoughts" (Franck 2001, 67). She believes that she makes no judgments, nor has any feelings about the people or the events: "[the guests' actions] never interested me. Curiosity drove me, pure curiosity, not even mixed with benevolent sympathies" (124). Her lack of commiseration with her guests, emphasized throughout the story, makes her a poor business owner. Yet the underlying reason for her constant surveillance becomes clear through her descriptions of these guests: she needs to affirm her imagined superiority over others, in order to maintain what she believes is her symbolic and social capital. She does this through close observation and "reporting" what dull things the others say and do, or what distasteful or unhygienic traits the guests possess. For instance, Madame Piper is a favorite target; about this overweight older woman, for whom the narrator at times acts as a personal care attendant, she observes, "She can no longer close her legs when she sits, the flesh in between obstructs her" (5). And as Madame Piper applauds the cook, the narrator notes this woman's inanity: "I am not sure if [Madame Piper] understands her occasion for joviality. She leans back, stupidity trickles through her half-opened lips" (129).

The narrator's self-centered need to affirm her prestige and symbolic capital starts to crumble because of the cook. When she fails to get his sexual attention, she attempts to ignore her life's loneliness—made visual by her small, disorderly room with food molding in the corner. Yet she continues marking details of the cook's proprietary behavior. After he boldly asks to sleep with her (to which she agrees, yet he never visits her room), she prepares to assert the only advantage she has, her power as his boss: "Well, he'll see, I'll reduce his pay. . . . And if he can't learn to love me, then he'll fear me" (25). Thwarted in her plan to burn down the hotel, she also fails to leave for Havana, Cuba—the alleged homeland of her rival, the cook. Although he escorts her to the airport, she returns that evening to her one remaining position of power—that of watching him, with his false Caribbean identity, from her reception desk. The reader must speculate about the unspecified events that kept her from boarding the plane. Thus once again, isolation and failed social connections characterize this narrative.

But there is another commonality among these first three narrators: their intentional lying and deceit. After the narrator in *Der neue Koch* correctly accuses the cook of lying about his Cuban identity and then finds the others applauding him anyway, she reveals her own distinction in the art of deception, by admitting that the hotel should not belong to her: "I lie too, I think to myself, but better, so that no one notices. . . . Didn't I find and burn the note on which my mother wrote her will by hand? On which she wanted to make Berta [hotel employee] heiress of the hotel" (130). Beyla in *Liebediener* lies regularly: she lies about which circus employs her, "it was my favorite lie" (Franck 1999, 34), about certain matters of opinion, "of course I lied," she says describing an argument with Albert, "sometimes even about important things, but which were important, I always determined myself"(176), and about being a witness to Charlotte's death. In this latter instance she ignores any moral or legal significance by focusing on her own immediate physical needs: "Why I said that [that she hadn't seen the accident]? Laziness most likely—I lied often, I got used to it, mostly when it wasn't important and I wanted to avoid bothersome questions. I was probably thirsty" (12). And the narrator in "Für Sie und Für Ihn" deceives herself by stating that she is not actually spying, rather she just notices what any neighbor would notice, or so she says to the bartender: "I don't stand there and gawk with a spyglass. You pick up on things like the toast or the computer, you just notice, can't get around 'em" (Franck 2000, 57), and "Not that I'd intended to watch him, or that

I often watch my neighbor having sex, but with my pale neighbor the view was just so fetching"(62). Interestingly, it is through lies that each narrator does achieve some symbolic or social capital: the narrator in *Der neue Koch* lives a lie and thus claims ownership of the hotel; Beyla, under the guise of finding out if Albert feels remorse, has a relationship with him; and the narrator in "Für Sie und Für Ihn" claims false innocence and gains momentary symbolic capital with the bartender. Thus where surveillance fails to provide the sought-for social capital, the narrators compensate their post-*Wende* reality with dishonesty.

Lagerfeuer, the Conflagration

In her fourth publication, *Lagerfeuer*, Franck complicates the narrative strategy by using four first-person narrators and by introducing a different sociopolitical framework: the late 1970s. Yet similar to the narrators in the first three works, these narrators are also caught between shifting definitions of identity, of occupation, and of space. Three of them are refugees in the relocation camp: Nelly Senff, a young German-Jewish chemist with two children, whose interrogations in and subsequent departure from East Berlin open the novel; Hans Pischke, a GDR actor who was jailed in East Berlin and whose passage out of the GDR was purchased by the Federal Republic of Germany; and Krystyna Jabłonowska, a Polish cellist who gives up her career to bring her demented father and cancer-stricken brother to West Berlin in hopes of better medical treatment. The fourth narrator is John Bird, an African-American secret security agent who becomes enamored of Nelly during the interrogation. However only one of them, Hans Pischke, fits the pattern of Franck's previous three detached narrators—he observes others in order to fill his own life with activity.

Nelly's first-person narration relates Hans's social-misfit status within the camp. She calls him "the little man who is tracking me" (Franck 2003a, 176) and recalls other residents' comments about him as the "dwarf" (255) and "the little bug" (267). Tellingly, this latter description, "Wanze" (bug), has several layers of meaning, as it does in English: it is an insect, but in colloquial usage it can also mean a wiretap.[6] This description builds upon the residents' suspicion of Hans as an East German informant. As a man, he is already located closer to the gendered position of privilege or to Connell's patriarchal dividend (1995); but he fails to appropriate any of the (limited) social capital otherwise potentially close at hand, i.e., the job of subway driver that a social worker offers him would provide him some social networks and trustworthiness in West Berlin, his new community, but he rejects the position. Thus his failure to gain symbolic or social capital becomes more clear in his pronounced paranoia, suspicion, and attempted suicide.

Hans's suspicion rules his life. In his perpetual role as eavesdropper, he overhears others discussing signs in the camp from the 1950s: "One should not speak with roommates or with other residents. They could be spies. . . . Today these signs are gone. The signs had been removed and yet, even in their absence, the unsettling effect they created was greater than the security they provided" (Franck 2003a, 123). Thus upon leaving his room, he deposits a strand of hair in the door, and if he later finds it missing, he knows that someone opened the door while he was gone (85). Hans's first detailed impressions of Nelly convey his suspicion of her diminished social faculties and thus, through comparison, provide an elevation of his own. He relishes her weaknesses—embodied in her inappropriate clothing and her uneasy body language as they both wait in line for their ration of food on a rainy fall day: "The young woman . . . wore a light yellow summer dress with large flowers and obviously had not thought it would rain. . . . She bit her lower lip and came across as self-conscious, so I surmised that she could be from Russia or Poland and did not understand anything" (117). Since this first meeting, Hans follows Nelly's movements. His first attempt to transform the one-sided watching occurs during Nelly's narrative; he tosses a bottle with a message in it, as Nelly and her daughter walk by his window and tells Nelly to pick up the bottle. She thinks to herself, "This little man is stalking me. His appearance had become more prevalent and intrusive, as if his entire ambition were not to let me out of his sight for a minute" (176). She removes the scroll from the bottle, puts it in her pocket, but never reads it; Hans's communication remains unread and unheard. Little does Nelly know that the message in the bottle is blank—another marker of the emptiness in Hans and all around her.

A metaphorical reading of the title, *Lagerfeuer*, hints at an image of the flames as symbolic of the camp occupants' desires—for instance, desires to be approved to leave the camp and to assimilate into West Berlin. But in actuality there is a fire in the camp on the last pages. Hans's previously unmentioned teenage daughter, Doreen, has just arrived. After receiving her gift from the capitalist Dr. Rothe at the camp's Christmas festival, she trips over a cable and causes the Christmas tree to fall and eventually to catch fire. Panic ensues in the volunteers, but not among the refugees: the children scream "rather in joy than in panic" (301), and Nelly, who is Jewish, describes her own position among the observers: "the adults formed a circle around the fire and watched silently as the flames grew out of the sparks" (301). This is the residents' ironic campfire, made out of the traditional Christian *Tannenbaum* (fir tree), which terminates the feigned generosity of the Western capitalists. With chaos all around them, Hans stares aimlessly. Nelly's observation ends the novel: "Hans had folded his hands in front of his mouth, maybe he laughed, his dark eyes reflected the flames" (301). The meagerness of his reaction echoes the stagnation and emptiness of the narrators' post-*Wende* lives in Franck's first three works.

Connection to German Past

More than just Hans's surveillance filling his life, it is Franck's discussion of an indifference to the German past that connects *Lagerfeuer* to the previous works and enriches this novel. While Franck uses the narrator in *Liebediener*, Beyla, to show an explicit indifference in her comments about a concentration camp, and thus a numbness toward Germany's past, Nelly's Jewish presence in *Lagerfeuer* allows Franck to criticize latent anti-Semitism in the GDR and to present a gendered exposé of the GDR's Cold War suspicions.

It is in the connection to Germany's past that we find more of Franck's critique of the alienation of the social order, from the inside out, as Germany's twentieth-century history fades to the possibilities of the future. Franck's young narrators, especially Beyla in *Liebediener*, do not consider themselves part of a collective guilt for the Holocaust's atrocities. Instead, those in the younger generation focus on ways to gain symbolic and social capital. Beyla's brief mention of the Holocaust is self-absorbed; in a flashback she recalls a previous incidental visit to Ravensbrück, the concentration camp for women and children, as she and a girlfriend happened past the camp en route to the Baltic Sea. Beyla says they both felt numb after they had visited the Ravensbrück exhibit and had seen bones in the cellar (Franck 1999, 179). But in her subsequent reflection, Beyla does not contemplate the tragedy of those women's lives, or the conditions in the concentration camp, but rather reflects only on her current situation, the "unreality of her suspicions about Albert" as they contrasted with "the reality of the number of dead women and children." With this realization of her own fortunate situation, she feels better (179). Beyla admits her shame: "I was a bit embarrassed, I had misused Ravensbrück, in order to make the ridiculousness of my suspicions about Albert clear" (180–81); but her thoughts do not develop further, as she merely decides to have a more open mind about Albert.

Thus the reader recognizes a particularly unreliable narrator in Beyla, a judgment that is confirmed toward the end of *Liebediener* as she reveals more lies. At age twelve, Beyla's youngest brother, age fourteen, points to her as he talks to two social workers, "She had serious difficulties with Father, because she was a girl. He grinned, full of the double meaning" (230). Beyla's silence and lowered gaze appear to affirm the allegations of sexual abuse. "At the least, my youngest brother had lied. My silence was enough. More than betray him, I slandered him [her father]" (231–32). Beyla learned that lying—or in this case, not speaking up to refute a lie—was a way to be "heard" and to get what one wants; in this instance, to be placed into a children's home where she and her brother would not lack for school supplies. As an adult in *Liebediener*, Beyla continues to use lies throughout her *"Entdeckerzwang"*(198), her need to know "if [Albert] feels guilt" (193). But at the end of the novel, after leaving the relationship with Albert and even convincing herself that Albert may have committed suicide (she continues to eavesdrop and hears no noise in his apartment), Beyla remains taciturn but empty of serious contemplation. Franck uses Beyla to demonstrate alienation from the past: in the post-*Wende* era, individuals are self-absorbed and the tainted German past serves only to reveal how good things have become.

In contrast to Beyla, Nelly, who is a young mother and is Jewish, reflects on the past and must live with its negative consequences. The references to anti-Semitism in 1978 indicate Franck's critique of the lack of *Vergangenheitsbewältigung* in the GDR. Nelly must respond to the GDR guards' racist myopia, as she leaves East Berlin for West Berlin. She had lived in the GDR because her grandmother believed in communism and thus intentionally returned to the Russian sector, but at least one East German does not believe that Jews exist within the GDR borders. After one guard says that Nelly is a Jew, the second guard can only exclaim, "Gibt's doch gar nicht" (that can't be), and eventually adds, "You don't look Jewish" (Franck 2003a, 18–19). Nelly then speaks of her mother, at which time this guard interrupts; and the reader hears Nelly's (and Franck's) derisive reflection: "'Was she famous?' As soon as a German hears of a living Jew, he thinks, [the Jew] must be famous. This assigned celebrity appeared as the only possibility to escape one's own strategies of killing" (18). Later the two American secret security agents believe Nelly must have been approached to work for the Stasi. Nelly assures them she was, but as a Jew she had a type of "protection" from having to work with the Stasi: "as if it were understandable, that one did not want to work with you, if you were from a Jewish family" (68). Both of these instances display a latent anti-Semitism in those in power around Nelly, but also reveal detachment from the past, from any association with collective guilt.

Both Nelly and her grandmother also suffer physical consequences from the GDR's Cold War suspicions. During her interrogation upon leaving East Berlin, Nelly recalls the shocking strip search that her eighty-seven-year-old grandmother was subjected to. A survivor of the Holocaust, her grandmother was allowed to travel and leave the GDR, but that did not stop the GDR functionaries from searching her upon one of her many returns to East Berlin; they even removed her dental work, believing that secret Western materials were concealed there (30). Nelly's situation is worse, as she endures a gynecological exam. The exam presumably checks whether she is smuggling something out of the GDR, but she feels as if the "mechanic," as she calls the doctor, instead puts something into her: "they wanted to send me off as a Trojan horse" (31), just as her grandmother was seen as a possible Trojan horse when she came to the GDR. As she is strapped into the chair Nelly thinks: "That we were living during war, I hadn't really noticed up to now" (30). Excluded from combat, women remain targets in the gendered male power game of war, even a cold war (Talvi 2002).

Finally, one can add the theme of numbness to Franck's critique of the lack of *Vergangenheitsbewältigung* in Germany. Nelly informs her American interrogators: "Scars are often numb, didn't you know that?"(72). As John Bird listens to Nelly during her seven-hour interrogation, he touches the scar on his forehead: "The scar felt nothing, only my fingers felt it, as if it were a foreign body in the middle of my skin" (72). Later John refuses to tell Nelly—after they share an hour of physical intimacy in a hotel room—how he got that scar. (The reader knows it is from a covert military action.) Yet upon reentering his office, he describes the "pleasantly numbing feeling" (216) he has at work. John Bird embraces the system of suspicion that numbs his sense of trust, because he retains a level of responsibility, and thus symbolic capital, in his role within the power structure. He describes it thus: "Responsibility meant always being one step further and one thought ahead" (227). He finds symbolic capital within this numb contentment of his position defined by suspicion. This element of *Betäubung*, or numbness, plays into a more nuanced reading of Franck's works. And with Nelly Senff, in *Lagerfeuer*, Franck shows how the wound, the Holocaust, has turned into a scar. The pain of the German past remains as a scar in the middle of Germany's consciousness.

Julia Franck used the gendered surveillance practiced by the detached female narrators in her works before *Lagerfeuer* to depict the powerlessness and inactivity of people isolated in contemporary society—specifically women who, in observing men, both uphold gendered structures and hope to gain access to social capital, to the patriarchal dividend (Connell 1995), through their scrutiny. Their lives are shown to be insular, while also focused on watching outward events that do not happen directly to them, but become their experiences vicariously through intentional observation. Deception also appears as part of these narrators' lives; interestingly, in an interview about *Lagerfeuer,* Franck says, "What is the truth? What is a lie? My first novel [*Der neue Koch*] asks these questions, and that book also tells about an imprisonment. A different type" (2003b). This imprisonment within these narrators' routines of surveillance connects the works to each other within Franck's critique of social alienation.

One can connect *Lagerfeuer* to Franck's three earlier works through Hans's narrative of gendered surveillance, through all the narrators' alienation, and also through Beyla's (mis)use of the memory of the concentration camp. Anke Biendarra points out how Franck's narrators in the short story collection *Bauchlandung* all live in Berlin, and how the disjointed nature of the city affects their social alienation: "Franck . . . soberly narrate[s] the toll that not the city itself, but a metropolitan event society takes on human relations" (2004, 230). The "event society" is a particularly Western element in post-*Wende* Germany, and thus often alienating for former eastern Germans. As Franck's narrators bring to light the vacuum of meaningful relationships in contemporary society, they also reveal an emptiness brought about by the post-*Wende* situation. They confront western Germans with everyday situations from an eastern German standpoint, as Beyla in *Liebediener* views Charlotte's initial apartment squatting in the Prenzlauer Berg neighborhood as a West Berliner's careless adventure (Franck 1999, 24) and as Nelly discovers the humiliation her son Aleksej suffers as an "Ostpocke" (derogative term for an East German) in school (Franck 2003a, 169). And although *Lagerfeuer* is about Cold War demarcations in the late 1970s, Franck creates a parallel to the post-*Wende* situation in this novel that reflects Germany's ongoing social division: these narrators—especially the Polish narrator, Krystyna Jabłonowska, who gives up her music career in her unsuccessful search for medical treatment for her brother—confront both western and eastern Germans with the emotional, linguistic, and economic plight of contemporary refugees and asylum seekers in Germany. Such marginalized figures play a role in the post-*Wende* transformation of social order.

The multiplicity of voices and experiences in Franck's first four published works corresponds to Germany's social configuration at the beginning of the twenty-first century. Yet a quiet warning appears in the theme of indifference. Just as the passage about the Ravensbrück concentration camp in *Liebediener* can quickly be overlooked, these works question whether there has yet been a numbing of memories of the German past.

Notes

1. With her fifth novel, *Die Mittagsfrau* (The Noon Woman, 2007), which was published after this article was written, Franck won the esteemed Deutscher Buchpreis in 2007. The setting in *Die Mittagsfrau* is pre–and post–World War II and thus it precedes this article's post-*Wende* time period.

2. The discussion of symbolic and social capital is based on Bourdieu (1984, 14, 291) and Putnam (2000, 19).

3. Of the four first-person narrators in *Lagerfeuer*, only three are powerless. The fourth, John Bird, has a position of power, albeit a low level of power. A longer discussion follows below.

4. Unless otherwise indicated, all translations from the German are by the author.

5. It was in the Moabit prison that the former general secretary of the GDR's Socialist Unity Party, Erich Honecker, was held briefly under the Nazis in the 1930s and again in 1992 (McAdams 1996).

6. "Wanze" also appears in *Liebediener*, as Beyla considers wiretaps to eavesdrop better on Albert; she states such devices are wasted on enemies: one should eavesdrop on those one loves (Franck 1999, 171–72).

Works Cited

Biendarra, Anke. 2004. "Gen(d)eration Next: Prose by Julia Franck and Judith Hermann." *Studies in Twentieth and Twenty-First Century Literature*. 28.1: 211–39.

Bourdieu, Pierre. 1984. *Distinction: A Social Critique of the Judgment of Taste*. Trans. Richard Nice. Cambridge, MA: Harvard University Press.

Connell, R.W. 1995. *Masculinities*. Berkeley: University of California Press. Quoted in Lazar 2005, 7.

Döbler, Katharina. 2000. "Schleimhaut inklusive: Julia Franck will Hautkontakt." *Die Zeit*. <http://www.zeit.de/2000/01/Schleimhaut_inklusive>.

Falke, Michael. 2004. Spurensuche, e.V: Informationen zur Aufarbeitung der SED-Diktatur <http://www.stasiopfer.de/content/category/5/25/55/>.

Fitzel, Tomas. 2000. "Nähe als Utopie: Julia Francks erotischer Erzählband *Bauchlandung*." *Die Welt*, 22 July. <http://www.welt.de/data/2000/7/22/573033. html>.

Franck, Julia. 1999. *Liebediener*. 2nd ed. Cologne: DuMont.

———. 2000. "Für Sie und Für Ihn." In *Bauchlandung: Geschichten zum Anfassen*. 5th ed. Cologne: DuMont. 53–65.

———. 2001. *Der neue Koch*. Frankfurt am Main: Fischer Taschenbuchverlag.

———. 2003a. *Lagerfeuer.* 2nd ed. Cologne: DuMont.

———. 2003b. "Narben sind häufig taub." Interview by Antje Schmelcher. *Die Welt,* 29 August. <http://www.welt.de/print-welt/article256146/Narben_sind_haeufig_taub.html>.

———. 2007. *Die Mittagsfrau.* Frankfurt am Main: Fischer.

Freud, Sigmund. 1953. "Three Essays on Sexuality." In *The Standard Edition of the Complete Psychological Works of Sigmund Freud,* ed. James Strachey, trans. Anna Freud. Volume VII (1901–1905). London: Hogarth Press. 135–245.

Gay, Peter, ed. 1989. *The Freud Reader.* New York: WW Norton.

Hage, Volker. 1999. "Ganz schön abgedreht." *Der Spiegel,* 22 March: 244–46.

Lazar, Michelle M. 2005. "Politicizing Gender in Discourse: Feminist Critical Discourse Analysis as Political Perspective and Praxis." In *Feminist Critical Discourse Analysis: Gender, Power and Ideology in Discourse,* ed. Michelle M. Lazar. New York: Palgrave Macmillan. 1–28.

Lyon, David. 2001. *Surveillance Society: Monitoring Everyday Life.* Buckingham, UK: Open University Press.

McAdams, A. James. 1996. "The Honecker Trial: The East German Past and the German Future." *Review of Politics* 58.1: 53–80.

Meise, Helga. 2005. "Mythos Berlin. Orte und Nicht-Orte bei Julia Franck, Inka Parei und Judith Hermann." In *Fräuleinwunder literarisch: Literatur von Frauen zu Beginn des 21. Jahrhunderts,* ed. Christiane Caemmerer, Walter Delabar, and Helga Meise. Frankfurt am Main: Peter Lang. 125–50.

Mulvey, Laura. 1975. "Visual Pleasure and Narrative Cinema." *Screen* 16.3: 6–18.

Putnam, Robert D. 2000. *Bowling Alone: The Collapse and Revival of American Community.* New York: Simon and Schuster.

Talvi, Silja J.A. 2002. Review of *War and Gender: How Gender Shapes the War System and Vice Versa* by Joshua S. Goldstein. *Z Magazine* 15.7. July/August. <http://www.zmag.org/ZMag/articles/julaug02talvi2.html>.

SMALL STORIES

The Novels of Martina Hefter

KATHARINA GERSTENBERGER

When *Spiegel* critic Volker Hage (1999) created the term *literarisches Fräuleinwunder* (literary girl wonder), he did not propose a return of feminism or a renewed critical attention to gender. Rather, he suggested that young women writers, whose presumed artistic naïveté and uncomplicated attitude toward sex and eroticism Hage underscored in his essay, had succeeded in making German literature attractive again for readers in Germany and beyond. Hage's was an intervention in the debates about the status of contemporary German literature, much of which revolved around the repeatedly expressed demand for a "new readability" and an insistence on literature's obligation to entertain (Wittstock 1995, 7–35). The recent works of young women writers, according to him, meet this demand better than the creations of their male counterparts. To what degree this indeed applies to the individual work would need to be examined, but it seems clear that the *Fräuleinwunder*-phenomenon suits the purposes of those who want a literature that entertains and is part of a general trend toward authors who embody, quite literally, generational change.

Not surprisingly, Hage's coinage triggered a flurry of debate and scholarly work, most of which seem to agree that the term is belittling (Graves 2002, 196) as well as generalizing (Delabar 2005, 241) and does not do justice to writing by women at the beginning of the twenty-first century. Yet even critics who oppose the term tend to acknowledge the growing importance of marketing strategies for literature and the specific position of young women writers in this context, whose media aptness has contributed significantly to their success (Müller 2004, 19–40). Hage's article is a case in point when it turns the nexus of women's sexuality and writing, traditionally used to exclude women from literary creation and therefore a central aspect of feminist struggle, into a marketing device aimed at a contemporary audience. Hage's intervention might thus serve as an incentive to develop strategies for reading women's literature in and for the twenty-first century and to ask what role gender, including the author's, might play not just as a marketing strategy but as a critical category. As "engaged literature" lost much, though certainly not all of its currency after 1990, the focus on feminist literature and criticism diminished as well. Furthermore, the post-Wall context, with its debates about the changing status of literature and the shifting role of intellectuals, including writers, and the predominance of topics such as *Wende* or settings like Berlin, has a significant impact also on women writers of this period. In the literature of the 1990s and beyond, the centrality of feminist concerns can no longer be taken for granted, and issues of gender both in the literary texts and pertaining to the author's public persona need to be examined in a new light if we are to understand women's literature for and in the twenty-first century.

Two novels by Martina Hefter, *Junge Hunde* (Young Dogs, 2001) and *Zurück auf Los* (Back to the Beginning, 2005), serve as examples of contemporary German literature by a woman writer. In addition to these novels, Hefter has also published lyric poetry and short stories in literary magazines. Questions of gender and feminism continue to matter but are very much integrated into a concern with language and communication on the one hand, and history and the challenges of everyday life on the other. Martina Hefter is in many ways "representative" of contemporary writers and their careers: born in 1965, she belongs to the generation of German authors who began publishing about ten years after the fall of the Wall. By some accounts this makes her a member of the generation of '78.[1] Her biography is shaped by German unification. Born and raised in Bavaria, she moved to Leipzig in the mid-1990s to study at the Deutsches Literaturinstitut, a former East German academic institution that became the first in united Germany to offer courses in creative writing. Hefter still lives in Leipzig today. Her work is perhaps not widely known, but her publications are reviewed in major newspapers and she has been supported with literary scholarships, including the Hermann-Lenz Stipendium in 2005 and the Lessing-Förderpreis in the same year. The Hermann-Lenz Stipendium in particular, with Peter Handke on the selection committee, honors the preoccupation with language characteristic of Hefter's writing. Also in 2005, she participated in the Bachmann-competition in Klagenfurt. Her notable success notwithstanding, Hefter is less caught up in the *Literaturbetrieb* than some of her fellow writers, and her work does not easily fit into the classifications that emerged in the 1990s, including the *Fräuleinwunder*-phenomenon, with its calculated use of author photographs and its depiction of presumably taboo-free sexuality. As a result, perhaps, her works have so far not attracted the attention of scholars who are otherwise interested in the question of women's writing "after feminism" (Nagelschmidt 2006). Hefter's work is not included in any of the anthologies that engage critically with the term *Fräuleinwunder*-literature (Müller 2004; Caemmerer 2005; Bartel 2006; Nagelschmidt 2006a). The contributors to such volumes tend to insist on the importance of gender in the writings of authors associated with the label.[2] An inadvertent outcome of this focus is that writers like Hefter, whose critical reception and marketing apparently do not necessitate rescuing from the designation, have been overlooked. This also suggests that the attention lavished on the term *Fräuleinwunder* runs the risk of narrowing our understanding of twenty-first century women's literature.

Hefter's work does not easily fit into any of the categories that emerged in the 1990s. Regarding *Zurück auf Los*, her second novel, *taz* critic Gerrit Bartels (2005, 15) suggests that it should be considered "literature of transition" because it goes beyond earlier trends such as pop literature and reintroduces the seriousness absent from "fun literature." Indeed, the topics of the 1990s—most of all unification, the tensions between East and West Germans, and the search for new ways of narrating the past—resonate in Hefter's texts but have lost the urgency and newness with which they were presented in the literature of the previous decade. Sexuality and gender relationships likewise play a central role in Hefter's writing, but her approach is different both from the feminist texts of the 1970s and 1980s, with their aim to expose and challenge patriarchal arrangements, as well as the postfeminist writings of the 1990s, with their depictions of female sexuality as unrestrained yet often unfulfilling (Dückers 1999; Hermann 1998; Franck 1999). By the early twenty-first century, Hefter suggests, a normalization of sorts has taken place that may also be described as resignation. Its most salient feature is the return to an everyday life in which women as well as men search for an intimacy they know they will not find.

Love Stories: Lonely Lives in United Germany

Junge Hunde, Hefter's first novel, is set in Leipzig during the winter of 1997 and 1998 and tells the interconnected stories of three main characters. As in Judith Hermann's celebrated *Sommerhaus, später* (1998) (*summerhouse, later*, 2002) the protagonists are in their twenties, have few social attachments or obligations, and their daily pursuits are almost devoid of future aspirations. Less ostentatious than the Berlin of Judith

Hermann or Tanja Dückers, Hefter's Leipzig is a provincial town where people enjoy activities such as "winter barbecuing" (14) and take time to feed the ducks on a city pond. Construction is ubiquitous, but it does not carry the symbolism many Berlin novels of the 1990s attribute to the erection of new buildings. Unlike their counterparts in Berlin literature, Hefter's protagonists do not believe they are witnessing history when observing the reconstruction of the city, and they do not share the sense of newness and fresh beginnings so frequently expressed in Berlin novels. Having just moved to Leipzig from Berlin, one character says that she imagined the city to be like Berlin, "just without a subway" (30).[3] The difference between the metropole and the provinces, which is so important in much of 1990s literature, is reduced to its most basic feature, namely, size. *Junge Hunde* shares with Berlin literature an attention to geographic detail and includes references to street and place names. Unlike Berlin, where designations like Potsdamer Platz or Prenzlauer Berg carry specific connotations even among readers only superficially familiar with the city, in the case of Leipzig, the use of geographic references creates for the majority of readers the reality of an average yet identifiable city, with names like "Zschochersche Strasse" (57) evoking a local geography and a regional linguistic identity.

Published in 2001, *Junge Hunde* shifts the attention away from Berlin as a prime setting for postunification literature. Set in the late 1990s, it also moves beyond the East German perspective on the immediate postunification era we find in novels like Ingo Schulze's *Simple Storys* (1998). Instead, the novel describes a version of the "normalcy" that has been the focus of much post-Wall debate. Construction cranes (29) refer to the rebuilding of the city and references to prefabricated apartment blocks are reminders of East German architecture, but unification itself is an event of the past. Political and cultural rifts of the immediate postunification period no longer play a major role, but personal happiness, stability, or hopes for the future elude Hefter's protagonists, most of whom are students or failed students who go about their lives without much sense of purpose or direction. Helen is a twenty-six-year-old dancer, a native of Bavaria, who has just moved to Leipzig from Berlin to study choreography and dance pedagogy. She passes her school's entrance exam, but then loses interest in her career and does not attend classes. Vinz, a native of Chemnitz who abandoned his studies in physics, drives a cab. His friend Fruehling, a West German, drifts through life without any apparent occupation. Helen's roommate, a young man named Per Larsen, is training to become a dentist. Later in the novel we find out that he has left Leipzig for his native Bonn (126). Helen's neighbors, Ines and Bernd, have moved to different apartments several times over the course of the past years, never satisfied with the present situation, and are again looking to move for no particular reason, except for a "change" (29). "Moving is an addiction," says Ines (30). Motion, which plays a role not only for Ines but also defines the life of Vinz, the cab driver, and the dancer Helen, is stripped of its purposefulness and future dimensions, emphasizing the characters' confinement in the present.

At least one of the main characters—Helen, Vinz, and Fruehling—is present in each of the novel's fifteen short chapters. While Helen's sections are narrated in the first person and the past tense, the other chapters are narrated in the present tense from Vinz's perspective, but in the third person. This absence of a unified narrative perspective underscores the tenuous nature of the protagonists' relationships and draws the reader into their attempts to connect with one another. Information about the characters' history tends to be sparse and fragmented. The use of the past tense in Helen's sections indicates that the plot takes place in the past, but Helen's present circumstances and her narrative position remain unclear. Hefter describes a present that is neither rooted in the past nor propelled by anticipation of the future. Her characters' aimlessness, which pertains to East and West Germans alike, may be a result of the changes since unification, although none of them puts forth this interpretation. As the fall of the Wall becomes a distant memory, the image of a sun that Vinz had tattooed on his arm in 1989 is fading (97). When Fruehling surmises that Vinz got his tattoo in Berlin, his friend corrects him that he went to Nuremberg for his body art a few weeks after the fall of the Wall (98), once again underscoring the novel's emphasis on characters for whom Berlin is neither site nor symbol of unified Germany. Hefter's characters, who are not engaged in projects of personal growth or availing themselves of new economic opportunities, accept that their moves and movements do not lead anywhere. The novel's fragmentary narrative structure underscores this lack of linearity.

Junge Hunde is about the desire for relationships and the difficulty of connecting with others. At the beginning of the novel, Helen, having just arrived in Leipzig, gets into Vinz's cab and asks him to show her the city. Vinz, whose last love relationship ended five years ago (37), falls in love with her, without even knowing her name. They meet again by coincidence at a housewarming party. In one of the novel's most tender moments, they pet a couple of young dogs someone brought as gift for the new owners, their eyes not making contact as they caress the animals (89). In a similar scene somewhat later, Vinz removes a—perhaps imaginary—spider from Helen's head, barely touching her hair (115). Toward the end of the novel the two talk on the phone. While Vinz is standing at the noisy central train station in Leipzig, where construction continues even at Christmas, Helen is at her home in Bavaria, recounting a dream in which she and Vinz walk through Leipzig, transformed into the puppies from the party (126). The timelines never converge: In the final chapter, Vinz anticipates picking up Helen from the train station after her return from Bavaria (134), but Helen's recollections of this period in her life leave open whether her acquaintance with Vinz ever matured into a love relationship. If the young dogs are a stand-in for the protagonists, the animals embody a longing for carefreeness that can only be disappointed. Political involvement, from this perspective, must appear futile.

Literary depictions of sexuality can arouse the reader, challenge taboos, or protest social hierarchies. In contrast to these traditional functions of sex in literature, the encounters in *Junge Hunde* are casual and devoid of emotional attachments. Narrated in sparse language, the descriptions emphasize isolation as a disappointing, yet accepted, characteristic of contemporary society. Helen sleeps with her housemate Per Larsen after she hears him crying in his room. She perceives the sex act, to which she agrees out of pity, as a choreography whose existence precedes her and for which she takes no responsibility (80). After the encounter, Helen decides to move out of their shared apartment. Vinz has sex on the roof of a high-rise with a prostitute sent to him by his friend Arne, an East German who engages in small-time criminal activities after his career as a political economist was cut short by the end of the GDR. The experience leaves Vinz, who was reluctant in the first place, wondering if it should have happened at all, given that he is in love (61). After a gallery opening on the island of Rügen, Vinz observes how the owner first touches a young woman's pubic area and later has sex with her in the parking lot. Wishing he had not joined his friends on this trip, he fearfully imagines the "woman from the cab" running into men like the gallery owner (43). Gender difference, which is so central to the depiction of sexuality in the feminist texts of the 1970s and 1980s, plays a minor role in Hefter's novel. Either sex can be the active or the passive participant in the encounter; neither society nor internalized moral codes limit the protagonists' actions. Helen's sex with her roommate out of compassion, the parking lot scene as well as Vinz's rendezvous with a sex worker recall traditional gender arrangements, but more important is the dissociation of sex from intimacy for both men and women. Two of the three acts take place outside in wintry temperatures, underscoring the coldness of the encounters. Sex is neither constrained nor does it bind; instead, it brings to the fore the loss of the closeness for which the characters long.

Vinz's closest relationship is with Fruehling, a young man seven years his junior. Fruehling, to whose unhealthy complexion, poor eating habits, and unwillingness to get enough sleep the narrative refers repeatedly, dies in the end of hypothermia after a fall through the ice on a lake near Chemnitz. His symbolic name (Spring) and early death encapsulate the characters' disbelief in their own future. Fruehling appears only through the perspective of others, mainly Vinz and sometimes Helen. Very perceptive—"nothing escapes him" (102)—he is aware of Vinz's love for Helen and encourages Vinz to trust his feelings. Alone in his grief after Fruehling's death, Vinz finds it hard to reconcile the loss of his friend with his love for Helen (132).

The novel's final chapter is set in a laundromat in Leipzig, a day after Fruehling's death. Vinz, while waiting for his washing machine to finish, is engaged in conversation by a Spaniard who is visiting Eastern Germany. The man wants to know if Vinz is East or West German and proceeds to talk about his travels through the "new federal states" (130). His bronze-colored skin in marked contrast to Fruehling's pale complexion, the Spanish tourist is the only character in this novel who praises the beauties of East German cities like Dresden and Leipzig (132) and does not seem to mind the cold weather and the dirty snow that covers the streets of Leipzig (131). "The East is an old, venerable land!" (135) are the novel's last words, spoken by the Spaniard. Vinz, who refuses to answer the question concerning his own background, agrees with the Spaniard's assessment of Eastern Germany but does not himself experience the beauty evoked by the traveler. Attractions such as the Nikolaikirche and Thomaskirche, which play such an important role in Leipzig's recent as well as long-term history, are mentioned here for the first time, suggesting that they have no meaning for Vinz and his friends. While waiting for his laundry, Vinz notices that the Spaniard's machine finishes faster than his (133). Once again, the unsynchronized timelines underscore the difficulty of connecting with others.

Memory of the GDR plays a subtle yet recurring role in *Junge Hunde*. For the Bavarian-born Helen, East Germany means a foreign vocabulary. "Strange" place names like Eisenhüttenstadt or Karl-Marx-Stadt (51), which her teachers used in her West German classroom, become even stranger to her as she repeats the words over and over again until they lose all original meaning. She continues the childish practice to the present of the novel with "East products" like Zörbiger marmalade (52), making the everyday item both strange and familiar at the same time. When Per Larsen, the dentist from Bonn, suggests that the smell of burning coal in the air evokes Bitterfeld (50), the East German city infamous for its industrial pollution, Helen questions the appropriateness of the comparison and rejects it as a cliché. Sitting in Vinz's cab, Helen tells him that she sometimes pictures herself living in Leipzig in the 1980s, picking up her children from the "day care" or going to a meeting (114).[4] Everything would be the same, she imagines, except for different cars in the streets, no billboards, no rows of stores, and no dogs. Helen's fantasy about her life as a woman in the GDR, with children and social activities, is significantly different from her own realities as a young woman in the late 1990s with few attachments and responsibilities. Vinz, who grew up in the GDR, corrects her concerning the presence of dogs, arguing that there were just a few, and that he in fact had one as a child (114). In a chapter titled "The Ducks of the East," an old East German, who has been feeding the ducks for the past thirty years, insists that city ducks are the same in the East and the West in their reliance on humans for food. When Helen admits that she does not know very much about the East, he answers that this does not matter as long as she knows something about ducks (51) and their needs beyond political systems and historical caesurae. Hefter's text does not invoke nostalgia for the GDR. The characters' memories and fantasies, some of which emphasize difference while others stress universality, suggest that less than ten years after unification, the GDR has become available for a number of different memory projects. The assumptions about East Germany as a society with strong social and emotional ties, which both East and West German characters share, are most of all a statement about contemporary life.

Women's Stories: Female Lives in the Twentieth Century

Martina Hefter's most recent novel, *Zurück auf Los* (2005), creates a broader historical and cultural context but revisits some of the themes already present in her first work. The fragile nature of relationships is a topic here as well, this time solely from a female perspective. The setting is a small town in Bavaria, probably very similar to Helen's hometown in *Junge Hunde*. German unification is even further in the past and at this point is simply an event in Germany history rather than an ongoing process. The plot, even more sparse than that of *Junge Hunde*, conjures up stories of finding and losing love across three generations of women in one family, spanning the time from the Third Reich to the present. Fundamentally about the protagonists' private lives and seemingly trivial concerns and observations, the text explores the influence of large-scale political events and transformations on individual lives. The question of how such connections might work is central, but the

answers are deliberately tentative. Quite the opposite of a "master narrative," whose end scholars and critics have declared repeatedly since
the early 1990s (Jarausch and Geyer 2003, 33), *Zurück auf Los* questions
the possibility of grand explanations. The slim novel, which critics
praised for its artful language, responds to the narrative challenge of
the twentieth and the twenty-first centuries with "small" stories and an
aspiration to aesthetic mastery (Hess 2005).

Zurück auf Los is set in the present and takes place during one night.
Marlen, the narrator, is on duty at the reception desk in her mother's
hotel in Johannisbach in the Bavarian Alps. Working her shift, she
imagines how Raimund, her lover, will move out of their shared house
the next morning, get into his car, and leave her. She also anticipates
the arrival of her brother Paul and his girlfriend, until Paul calls and
informs her that he has missed the exit on the highway but hopes to be
there the next morning for breakfast. The night at the reception desk
is uneventful: A family with a young daughter checks in, and another
guest tells Marlen the story of her husband, who disappeared fifteen
years ago in Toronto, never to be heard of again. Marlen's friend Heike,
a young woman from Crimmitschau in Eastern Germany, works at the
hotel bar. At one point Marlen's mother stops by and talks with her
daughter about her own future plans.

The novel's title suggests a setback and new beginning: the expression "zurück auf los," of course, refers to board games like Ludo, in
which bad luck forces a player to start all over again. How a player
fares in the game depends to some degree on skill, but most of all the
return to the starting point is contingent on the throw of the dice and
thus beyond the player's control. The assumption that the individual's
fate is determined by circumstances and the actions of others is central
to this novel. Nothing happens in isolation, but the connections that
tie people and events to one another are neither one-directional nor
deliberate or causal, and they tend to defy the individual's grasp. An
old computer in the narrator's home with a tangle of cables symbolizes this thinking. Raimund, the lover who is about to leave Marlen,
had hooked it up for her when her laptop failed and, she knows, will
not take it with him, even though Marlen no longer has any use for it
either. The superfluous computer with its daunting cables is her point
of entry into reflections about connections and their complicated work-
ings. The now obsolete machine triggers memories of her relationship
with Raimund, or, more precisely, her inability to remember details.
Marlen is certain that setting up the computer with its "tangled mass
of cords and wires" (6) must have caused tensions between her and
Raimund—how could it not have—but is not sure that she can trust

her memory about this incident. Marlen's reflections about the now superfluous computer, itself a memory storage device, highlight the importance, the complexity, and the frailty of the networks with which the novel is so concerned. The title "Back to the Beginning" emphasizes circularity over linear progression.

The focus on networks and connections extends to questions of history and politics. Hefter interweaves the big narratives of the twentieth century, in particular the memory of the Nazi period and the aftermath of the fall of the Wall, with the everyday experiences and small, if not trivial occurrences in the lives of "normal" people. As Marlen contemplates her relationship with Raimund from its beginnings to its imminent end, she also thinks back on what she knows about her mother's and her grandmother's lives. The narrator's grandmother relocated from her native Mecklenburg to Bavaria after she fell in love with the nephew of a Bavarian hotel owner during a *"Kraft durch Freude"* (Strength through Joy) trip in 1937. The fact that Marlen's grandmother only went on the trip because of a cancellation (64) highlights the importance of coincidence; the basket of fresh strawberries that her future husband placed on her breakfast table every morning during their courtship (70) underscores the impact of small things on the course of people's lives across generations. Hefter's story confirms the historian Alon Confino's (2006, 222) argument about tourism as a "measure of normality" that shapes memory of the Third Reich for the postwar period. As important as the events themselves is their transformation into narrative: "The first threads form so quickly," the narrator comments on this often-told family story, "and, once begun, one can no longer escape the weaving pattern of sentences" (65). The narrator's mother, in turn, who was born and raised in the Alpine village of Johannisbach, plans to sell the hotel in Bavaria and to open a fish restaurant in Quasow, the small town in Mecklenburg's Lake District where her own mother was born. The return to Eastern Germany is, of course, possible only after the fall of the Wall. As with her mother, who at the time of her KdF trip was a shop clerk in Berlin who could only afford such a vacation with the support of the Nazi program that fostered tourism among lower-class Germans, the characters' movements and fantasies are determined by political circumstances.

The motivations for such moves are individual longings together with cultural assumptions and gendered experiences across generations. When Marlen cautions her mother, who was born in the late 1930s or early 1940s, that she might not like it in Quasow because none of her relatives live there anymore, her mother replies: "But our roots are there!" (90). Perhaps inspired by the US television series *Roots*, which aired on German television in 1978, she uses the English word "roots" to clarify her desire. "People fall ill when they do not acknowledge their roots. The soul does not find peace if one does not return to one's original home at least to die, that's what the Indians say" (90). The reference to Native Americans and African Americans invokes ideas of origin and a connectedness with land and home that contemporary Germans have presumably lost but, according to Marlen's mother, need to regain. The allusion to historical experiences of victimization and expulsion also references the recent turn in German culture toward the topic of Germans as victims.

One central theme in this novel is the loss of love relationships, told from the perspective of the women who are left behind. As Marlen anticipates Raimund's departure, she also thinks back on her mother's and grandmother's life stories. Her grandfather never returned from the war, leaving his wife to raise their daughter and run the hotel on her own. The "Versprechen auf Versorgung" (promise of material and emotional sustenance) (70) she expected when she married her husband never materialized, forcing her to rely on the resourceful independence of her youth. The narrator's father left the family when Marlen and her brother were children. As he was getting into his car to begin his "new profession" as the innkeeper of an Alpine hut, Marlen answered her brother's question "Where is he going?" with the counter question "You don't know that?"(75), implying that she herself could gain a degree of control over her father's movement by naming his destination and his travel connections if only she chose to do so. The women in Marlen's family are the ones who tell and pass on the stories of their male partners' disappearance. The circumstances change with historical conditions and, furthermore, have different effects on the narrator. Her grandfather's absence in her life influences the way Marlen looks at his photographs. "There is a hole in all pictures, I never got to know the grandfather," she comments (69). Without memories, a picture does not create a presence. The opposite is true in her father's case. Marlen recalls an incident where her father formed an impression in the snow with his whole body. The contours of his body are visible even after the snow melts, leaving behind a fine trace on the grass (75). While lasting, the imprint is also much smaller than expected.

Finding and losing love, leaving one's place of origin, and trying to make a home are the themes that run through all three life stories. The lack of stability is constant, although the actual experiences differ across generations. Marlen's grandmother, born in 1914, was not preoccupied with ideas of belonging and insists that she decided "on a whim . . . to change homes (67). When she embarked on her KdF trip, she had

already left her native village of Quasow for Berlin. Her relative financial independence and her ability to make quick decisions characterizes Marlen's grandmother as a modern woman who took advantage
of women's enhanced self-determination without a particular interest
in politics or an active commitment to feminism. Considering the city
of Berlin as her home rather than the village of Quasow, she had hoped
to return to Berlin but abandoned the plan after a visit to the destroyed
city in 1946 (68). Quasow to her was a place to which she would return
only to die and to be buried (69). After a lifetime in Johannisbach,
she no longer has a need for other places and wishes to die in her private room in the hotel (69). With her husband's death in the war at
an unknown location and the unfulfilled promise of "sustenance,"
the hotel, a transitional home that is a temporary accommodation to
its guests, befits the grandmother's life experience. For her daughter,
who is a respected businesswoman in her community, the hotel provides the financial means that she hopes will buy her peace of mind in
her ancestral village. The grandmother's departure from Quasow and
her daughter's planned return echo women's growing socioeconomic
independence as well as the geopolitical effects of twentieth-century
history on their lives.

Like her mother and grandmother before her, Marlen is left behind
in the home she sought to make with her lover, never having completed
the renovation of the old house they shared. Unlike her resourceful
grandmother, who nevertheless pinned her hopes for security on her
husband, and her enterprising mother, who seems to have managed
well without her husband, Marlen does not think of Raimund in terms
of his ability to support her financially. Instead, she reflects on the substance of their relationship and its basis in the stories and memories
they share. Still sitting behind her reception desk, Marlen anticipates
how Raimund will drive north on the A7 "toward the lowland" (124).
Alternatively, she envisions that he might ask her to get into the car
and ride with him. "I would not even know where to go" (126), she
imagines herself saying. Freer in her choices than her mother or grandmother, Marlen finds herself unable to realize any of them. In the end
she, too, contemplates going back to Quasow for a visit (127). Watching
a late-night television show about train connections in Mecklenburg,
Marlen hopes that Quasow will never be featured in such a program
(129). Any representation, she fears, would interfere with a process
of aging and regeneration that also connects the three generations of
women in her family.

If isolation and a lack of future perspectives are the central themes in
Junge Hunde, family networks and definitions of home across generations

and historical junctures is the focal point in *Zurück auf Los*. Heike, Marlen's friend from the eastern German town of Crimmitschau who works at the hotel bar, justifies her departure from eastern Germany with her changing relationship to her parents. Asked why she left home at the young age of eighteen, she explains: "'They [her parents] grew smaller, that's the diagnosis, that is all,' said Heike, 'there is nothing more to say about that, they grew smaller, and I left, period'" (52). Hefter's novel contextualizes the departure from the parents with the experience of being left behind by a parent. Perhaps in response to his father's departure, for Marlen's brother Paul, a professional photographer and the first in their village to journey through Europe on a seasonal train ticket, travel has become so integral to his life that he misses the exit for his hometown on the highway. He has exchanged the hotel in which he grew up for the hotels of the world. Within this larger framework of cross-generational comings and goings, Hefter also breaks with the convention of conceiving the departure from the parents as an act of breaking free, often after prolonged conflict. Heike realized that her relationship with her parents had reached the point at which she could simply go away. She keeps in touch with her family by sending gifts (50). For Heike, who was born during the GDR's last decade, World War II, Germany's subsequent division, and the postwar conflicts over the commemoration of these events play no role in how she relates to her family. By contrast, Marlen's memories of her family, in particular her grandmother's stories, are embedded in history, but she, too, is interested in the mechanisms through which memories are passed on and in the connections they create rather than in delimitation from the previous generations.

Ambiguity, nuance, and new interpretations of common concepts are central to *Zurück auf Los*. *Heimat*, for instance, is defined not through its traditional opposite, *Fremde*, the place where one is a stranger, but through the practices of travel and tourism through which one becomes a stranger deliberately and for a limited period of time. Hefter's novel traces this contemporary definition back to the grandmother's trip in 1937. Both the Bavarian Alps and the Mecklenburg Lake District are sites of tourism and, unlike "un-touristy areas" (91) such as North Rhine-Westphalia or Lower Saxony, not regions that can ever really be home. "Everyone just camps out in the upper floors of the pensions and hotels," Marlen observes (92). The hotel, in whose lobby the entire novel is imagined, embodies this complicated notion of home, which can only be approximated through the idea of travel and tourism. The hotel itself shares these dual qualities as temporary home for the guests and makeshift accommodation for the owners. Landscape, traditionally so central to the idea of *Heimat* that it gave rise to the theory that it shapes people in certain ways, here can only be appreciated by the tourists who have the time to do so and who enjoy mountains or lakes precisely because they live in areas without such geographical features. Networks, finally, can also lead to dead ends: In response to the guest's story about her husband who never returned from Toronto, Marlen looks up the city on the Internet. The first Web site she opens cautions that not all of the information it offers might be legible on screen, advising the visitor to pick up brochures and maps upon arrival (109). The beautiful landscapes that cannot be home and the Web site that fails to deliver on its promise of virtual travel point to their respective limits and underscore the importance of connections for the creation of meaning.

Conclusion

The novels of Martina Hefter are set in present-day surroundings and feature protagonists who come of age in united Germany, but they refrain from offering the ethnographic insights into the peculiar lives of post-Wall Germans that were proffered in much of 1990s literature. Hefter's works engage in a search for personal and historical connections, and memory of the GDR and the Third Reich are integral rather than extraordinary elements of this project. When this search fails, and it often does, it strips characters and narrative of a future dimension, as if to suggest that without such relationships the loss is not merely personal but also detrimental for Germany's culture. Hefter's writings defy the category of *Fräuleinwunder*-literature and its presumed return to uninhibited narration, featuring instead sparse plot lines and linguistic sophistication. Gender relationships are no longer conceived of in terms of victimization, and the female characters in particular can take their social and sexual independence for granted. All of this may well be the new normality of the twenty-first century. Its arrival is a welcome development but, as Hefter's work shows, the fading of the big stories into the fabric of everyday life also means a loss of direction and the need to tell the old stories in new versions. Women's literature has already begun to show the way.

Notes

1. The term was coined by the writer Matthias Politycki (1998) in distinction to the generation of 1968 and their sociopolitical agendas.

2. The writers Karen Duve, Tanja Dückers, Judith Hermann, Julia Franck, Elke Naters, Jenny Erpenbeck, Alexa Hennig von Lange, and Sybille Berg are most commonly associated with the term "Fräuleinwunder."
3. Unless otherwise noted, all translations by the author.
4. She authenticates her fantasy by using the East German term "Hort."

Works Cited

Bartel, Heike and Elizabeth Boa, eds. 2006. *Pushing at Boundaries*. Amsterdam, New York: Rodopi.

Bartels, Gerrit. 2005. "Ein Gefühl von Zukunft." *Tageszeitung*, 11 May: 15.

Caemmerer, Christiane, Walter Delabar, and Helga Meise, eds. 2005. *Fräuleinwunder literarisch: Literatur von Frauen zu Beginn des 21. Jahrhunderts*. Frankfurt am Main: Peter Lang.

Confino, Alon. 2006. *Germany as a Culture of Remembrance: Promises and Limits of Writing History*. Chapel Hill: University of North Carolina Press.

Delabar, Walter. 2005. "Reload, Remix, Repeat—Remember: Chronikalische Bemerkungen zum Wunder des Fräuleinwunders." In Caemmerer et al., eds. 231–49.

Dückers, Tanja. 1999. *Spielzone*. Berlin: Aufbau.

Franck, Julia. 1999. *Liebediener*. Cologne: DuMont.

Graves, Peter. 2002. "Karen Duve, Kathrin Schmidt, Judith Hermann: 'Ein literarisches Fräuleinwunder'?" *German Life and Letters* 55.2: 196–207.

Hage, Volker. 1999. "Ganz schön abgedreht." *Der Spiegel*, 22 March: 244–46.

Hefter, Martina. 2001. *Junge Hunde*. Berlin: Alexander Fest.

———. 2005. *Zurück auf Los*. Göttingen: Wallstein.

Hermann, Judith. 1998. *Sommerhaus, später*. Frankfurt am Main: Fischer.

Hess, Silvia. 2005. "Kleines Schmuckstück." *Die Zeit*, 5 November.

Jarausch, Konrad H., and Michael Geyer. 2003. *Shattered Past: Reconstructing German History*. Princeton, NJ: Princeton University Press.

Müller, Heidelinde. 2004. *Das "literarische Fräuleinwunder": Inspektion eines Phänomens der deutschen Gegenwartsliteratur in Einzelfallstudien*. Frankfurt am Main: Peter Lang.

Nagelschmidt, Ilse. 2006. "Was kommt nach dem Feminismus? Junge Autorinnen leben mit anderen Botschaften." In Nagelschmidt et al., eds., 2006. 7–11.

Nagelschmidt, Ilse, Lea Müller-Dannhausen, and Sandy Feldbacher, eds. 2006. *Zwischen Inszenierung und Botschaft: Zur Literatur deutschsprachiger Autorinnen ab Ende des 20. Jahrhunderts*. Berlin: Frank und Timme.

Politycki, Matthias. 1998. *Die Farbe der Vokale: Von der Literatur, den 78ern und dem Gequake satter Frösche*. Munich: Luchterhand.

Schulze, Ingo. 1998. *Simple Storys*. Berlin: Berlin Verlag.

Wittstock, Uwe. 1995. *Leselust: wie unterhaltsam ist die neue deutsche Literatur?* Munich: Luchterhand.

THE YOUNG AUTHOR AS PUBLIC INTELLECTUAL
The Case of Juli Zeh

PATRICIA HERMINGHOUSE

In a tart commentary on the long-overdue award of the Georg-Büchner Prize in German literature to poet Friederike Mayröcker in 2001, literary critic Iris Radisch attributed the striking underrepresentation of women receiving this honor to their invisibility in the public sphere. Which women writers, she asked, would publish something as controversial as "Bocksgesang";[1] debate with Ignatz Bubis, head of the Central Council of Jews in Germany;[2] travel to the Balkans;[3] or speak out on other contended topics such as Rwanda, the crisis at Volkswagen, or in vitro fertilization? Indeed it is usually the male senior citizens of the German literary world who regularly register opinions on politically charged topics in the media, whereas younger writers, especially women, have not enjoyed such presence in the public sphere.

A notable exception to this pattern has been Juli Zeh, with dozens of opinion pieces in recent years in such politically disparate newspapers and magazines as *Die Zeit, Die Welt, Brigitte, Stern, taz,* and *Der Spiegel.* Her commentaries encompass a range of topics, such as the 2005 German election campaign (Zeh 2005a), her own generation's attitudes towards consumption and politics (Zeh 2002a), and alternative, cooperative communicative models evolving in the cybersphere, such as Wikipedia and Linux open-source development (Zeh 2006b). Her remarks in a recent forum on the summer 2006 "literary scandals" involving Günter Grass's late admission of his youthful membership in the Waffen-SS and Peter Handke's travel to the funeral of Slobodan Milošević were praised in most press reports in terms such as "analytically brilliant" and "refreshingly ideologically independent" (Kilb 2006; März 2006).[4] Of concern here is the nexus between Zeh's stunning success as a novelist and her emergence as an arbiter of public opinion. How do her literary depictions of the degraded underside of contemporary life relate to the position she has come to occupy as a "public intellectual"? And how did she manage to escape the trivializing label *literarisches Fräuleinwunder* (literary girl wonder), which Volker Hage had introduced in 1999 to characterize a generation of popularly successful women writers, distinguished—in his view—by their good looks and their tendency to write uninhibitedly about private anguish and failed relationships?

To begin with the last question: Zeh's two novels to date, *Adler und Engel* (2001; *Eagles and Angels*, 2003) and *Spieltrieb* (Game/Play Instinct, 2004a) take on, respectively, the big topics of international drug dealing and asocial behavior in a German school. Central to both are the main characters' experiences as pupils deposited in a boarding school by parents for whom they had become a problem or an inconvenience. Dysfunctional personal and love relationships are also narrated, not for their own sake as in the pop literature to which Hage referred, but rather to carry a socially critical story line. Furthermore, much of the buzz about the *Fräuleinwunder* had subsided by the time of Zeh's literary debut with *Adler und Engel* in 2001.

By the time that novel appeared, Zeh had already established formidable intellectual credentials, having earned her first law degree with honors for the top *Staatsexamen* in Sachsen, served a 1999 internship at the United Nations in New York, and, in 2000, completed a program of East European studies at the Jagellionian University in Krakow. She subsequently earned a master's degree (LL.M.Eur) in European law, producing a thesis on the rights of applicant states to the European Union (2002b). In that same year, *Die Stille ist ein Geräusch* (Silence is a Sound) appeared, a narrative based on her travels in Bosnia-Herzegovina that explores the extent to which the Bosnian areas of the former Yugoslavia have overcome the effects of ethnic struggle in that region (2002d). In almost picaresque fashion, the narrator sets out with a backpack and her faithful dog in August 2001 to see how the reality of postwar Bosnia compares with what meager, clichéd journalistic reporting reaches Western Europe. Before completing her second *Staatsexamen* in 2003, Zeh furthered her credentials in international law by working for several months in the German embassy in Zagreb and in the Office of the High Representative in Sarajevo charged with the implementation of the Dayton peace accords (in 2003).

Since then, two more novels, *Spieltrieb* (2004a) and *Schilf* (2007) have appeared, in addition to three more nonfiction books, including *Alles auf dem Rasen: Kein Roman* (Doing It on the Grass: Not a Novel, 2006a), which anthologizes thirty of the many essays she has produced since 1999. Her first drama, *Corpus Delicti*, with a story line that employs elements of science fiction and witchcraft to satirize society's obsession with personal health and body control, premiered at the Ruhr Triennale festival in September 2007. Between her two law degrees, Zeh also furthered her literary career by earning a diploma at the Deutsches Literaturinstitut Leipzig in 2000, where she recently held an appointment as guest lecturer.

These achievements of the last half-dozen years comprise the credentials that have accorded Juli Zeh access to a wide range of public media. In her thought-provoking commentaries on issues of the day, she is, of course, also heir to the particularly strong postwar German habit of expecting cultural figures to address moral and political aspects of whatever controversies constitute the headlines of the moment. It is in this sense that Zeh has joined the class of "public intellectuals"—cultural producers and scholars who by dint of their achievement have access to an audience beyond their own sphere of accomplishment when seeking to influence public opinion on complex cultural, social, and political issues. Regarding her political views, Zeh indicates being most concerned about issues of justice, having thus far used her legal training primarily in pro bono work against what she calls "democratic colonialism" in the Balkans, against Ugandan war criminals, and against Telekom (2004b). As ambassador of the German animal protection foundation Stiftung Vier Pfoten, she recently lived—at her own expense—as artist-in-residence at a Bulgarian refuge for dancing bears (*Tanzbären*), working on her next publication.

Zeh has consciously shaped her public image as a serious writer who is ready to offer well-thought-out opinions on a wide range of topics. Regretting that in an age of individualism, most writers have simply relegated politics to the realm of the private, Zeh expresses dissatisfaction with the current inclination to look only to specialists and commissions when opinions are sought (2004b). In a recent interview (Tittel 2005), she stated that, in addition to her literary projects and teaching obligations at the Deutsches Literaturinstitut Leipzig, she had written some thirty essays and given at least twice as many interviews, often by telephone, in 2005 alone. Claiming that it is much harder for the reading public to dub a fully qualified lawyer a "Fräuleinwunder," she points out, "I don't just spend my life in the literature business [*Literaturbetrieb*]. I'm also traveling around to embassies and universities and giving lectures. People should know I must be reckoned with."[5] In a recent debate in a series commemorating Emile Zola's intervention in the Dreyfus affair, she affirmed her own belief that society needs intellectuals to take public positions on matters of general concern, adding, "it would be dangerous to just leave the important topics up to others" (Stenzel 2006).

Whether, given her current level of activity, Zeh will ever find time or opportunity to pursue her pet project of drafting a new, more democratic system of constitutional law (*Staatsrecht*) for Germany remains to be seen. It is a project she admits to working on only casually, knowing that such an undertaking is a touchy matter, but also believing that more democratic ways could be found to increase individual participation in political decision making rather than leaving everything up to the political parties (Tittel 2005). In an interview with Ingo Niermann, she suggests, for example, that in filing their tax returns, citizens could be allowed to designate what branches of government they want some portion of their taxes to support. Just as radically, she imagines a ballot system where one does not make choices according to party platforms, but rather chooses among the options each party offers in response to a range of particular issues, such as the amount, if any, of a tax increase (Niermann 2006). She concludes the conversation by asserting that "money" is just a substitute for social and emotional successes that can be had in other ways: "Stated more simply, respectful and courteous behavior in everyday encounters makes a person confident, content, and happy with a kind of intensity and permanence that cannot be attained in the realms of economic success and consumption." The generation that populates her novels demonstrates the consequences of the lack of this experience.

World without Values: The Novels

The fact that *Adler und Engel* appeared when Zeh was only twenty-seven years old accounts for much of the initial attention accorded to her and her novel, which has now been translated into twenty-eight languages and brought her almost a dozen literary prizes. Depicting unsparingly the world of drug addiction, international trafficking, and deadly conspiracies, the story is dictated in fits and starts into a digital recorder by Max, a thirty-year-old lawyer who once enjoyed a brilliant career in a Viennese international law firm. There, he worked closely with the UN, trying to shape a treaty that might end the bloody ethnic conflicts in the former Yugoslavia. But when Max discovers that his law firm is more involved with the international drug trade than with the peace process, he is relegated to Leipzig. Zeh's device of having the novel related by such a character serves an almost parodistic function, playing upon many details of her own biography[6] while simultaneously distancing herself from its manifestations in the novel. In order to be able to tell the gruesome story, Max incessantly snorts lines of cocaine. Especially difficult are his attempts to narrate the mental torment and suicide of Jessie, the waif-like woman he has loved since their boarding-school days together, although he had lost track of her in the intervening twelve years. When Jessie, who since her school days had been dealing cocaine for her drug kingpin father, shows up in Vienna, Max learns details of her involvement in the sordid world of cross-border drug trafficking in Eastern Europe. In trying to break free of the cartel, she is in danger of being killed by her father's gang. Attempting to protect her, Max himself becomes implicated in the death of her boyfriend Shershah, son of an Iranian diplomat and his former boarding school roommate, who is also involved in this vicious business.

The story Max relates is framed by his relationship to Clara, a late-night radio talk show moderator, whom he has called to unburden himself of the fact that Jessie has killed herself with a bullet to the head while talking on the phone with him. Clara coaxes him into recording the story for her own use in a psychology dissertation and persuades him to return to Vienna with her as he reconstructs the story. In the course of the days he spends there with her in an abandoned and decrepit hideout, there are hints that her professor may have other reasons for wanting whatever information she can elicit from Max about the world of organized drug crime. Realistic details of brutalities perpetrated by the paramilitary "Tigers" of the Serbian mobster Arkan (assassinated in 2000 by partisans of Milošević) in order to protect the drug cartel or images of Jörg Haider smirking at passers-by from campaign posters plastered around Vienna add to the nightmarish quality of the novel, as does a visit that Max and Clara pay to an "artist who encases human corpses in translucent plastic.[7] Zeh was able to bring much of her own international experience and legal expertise to this horrific depiction, but also her own highly developed sense of language and literary ambition. Without preaching, she has constructed a novel that shocks the reader into recognizing the link between the legal corruption and international crime so chillingly depicted here and the moral void and absence of binding values[8] that enable it.

Spieltrieb takes an equally disturbing look at the world of adolescents in a private Bonn *Gymnasium* and boarding school. As in *Adler und Engel*, Zeh keeps the reader keenly aware of the contemporary context, with pointed allusions to the Erfurt school massacre of 2002, the events of 9/11, the Madrid train bombings, and the war in Iraq. The school, with its Nietzschean motto "Thinking means overcoming [*überschreiten*]" (19), bears the name of Ernst Bloch, but is referred to by one of the protagonists as a "reprocessing center [*Wiederaufbereitungsanlage*] for lost souls" (122) since many of the pupils come from broken families or have been expelled from other schools. This is the case with the protagonists, fourteen-year-old Ada and the cosmopolitan eighteen-year-old Alev El Qamar ("half Egyptian, one-quarter French, raised in Germany, Austria, Iraq, the United States, and Bosnia-Herzegovina,") (122), both unnervingly intelligent and arrogant, the ultimate outsiders in this universe. Looking down on their less precocious classmates, these self-identified "great-grandchildren of the nihilist generation" often seek to demonstrate their sophistication with superficial spoutings of Nietzschean hyperbole. As one of them explains, the nihilists at least believed that there was something that they could NOT believe in; these two assert that there is not even anything (no-thing) that they could have the luxury of not believing in (309f.).

Absent any commitment to normative values in the moral void they inhabit, Ada and Alev are drawn to game theory as a model for human behavior, a tool for maximizing outcomes in strategic situations. Their version of the classical prisoner's dilemma[9] is played out in a perfidious experiment devised by Alev, in which Ada engages their idealistic, but somewhat naïve, Polish-born teacher Smutek in sex games every Friday after school. Alev photographs the encounters, secreting them on the school's Web site and using them to blackmail the teacher into further compromising behavior, for which he is all too willing because of his growing attraction to Ada. The trysts continue from week to week, conforming to economist Robert Axelrod's demonstration that outcomes in a game situation, such as the prisoner's dilemma, are optimized—and predictable—when both parties in a situation such as this behave pragmatically by cooperating with rather than betraying one another. Indeed the plot was hatched after, at Alev's urging, Ada reads *The Evolution of Cooperation*, Axelrod's 1984 book that popularized game theory in the social and natural sciences.

How well Ada has absorbed the theory becomes clear in her remarks to the judge in the courtroom where Smutek is on trial for having brutalized Alev when the latter announced the end of their Friday "games." Explaining to the judge that Alev wanted to prove that the game provides the optimal way of achieving happiness today, she asks, "Do you know what remains, if a person loses all concept of values? . . . *Spieltrieb* remains" (547). With this mention of *Spieltrieb,* she refers less to Freud's behavioral theory of the play instinct in children[10] than to Alev's interpretation of the "Spieltrieb" that underlay the experiment with Smutek: "The game [*Spiel*] is the epitome of democracy and the only way of being available to us today. It takes the place of religion; it dominates the stock exchange, the courts, and journalism; and it is what keeps us intellectually alive since the death of God" (260). In this worldview, the coldly pragmatic, self-interested logic of game theory substitutes for a system of social and moral values to which these protagonists cannot relate. Indeed Ada's courtroom testimony on behalf of Smutek and Alev relies on the principles of game theory when she argues that because they refuse to testify against one another, they are behaving honorably and sensibly (552).

Only retrospectively does the reader realize the extent to which the opening chapter has offered us the key to the ethical concerns of the entire novel. Here the judge known as "die kalte Sophie" (Sophie the Cold), the omniscient narrator of the entire story, reflects on the implications of the trial just concluded.[11] With Alev sentenced to six months of probation for his perverse blackmail scheme and Ada and Smutek driving off toward the sunset in Bosnia-Herzegovina, she asks herself—and us: What if the Bible, the constitution (*Grundgesetz*), the law itself were of no more significance than the rules for a parlor game? If politics, love, economics were only about competition? If "the good" meant merely maximized efficiency with minimized risk, "the bad" nothing more than a suboptimal result? "If it's all just a game, we're done for. If not, then for sure" (7–8).

As serious as the issues at the heart of this novel are, Zeh weaves numerous playful elements into the narrative. Smutek, for example, in an attempt to familiarize himself with contemporary German literature, picks up a novel that resembles some of the pulp fiction popularized in the *Fräuleinwunder* phenomenon (423–26). Its title, *Fliegende Bauten* (Portable Structures), however, is identical with that of an essay published by Zeh herself, which reflects on her own peripatetic lifestyle and the need it engenders for domesticating strange places by following certain fixed routines. The definition of the term *fliegende Bauten* that Smutek looks up in a dictionary (425) is word-for-word the one that Zeh cites in her essay (2003b, 100). In yet another gesture even more reminiscent of Thomas Mann's ironic practice of self-quotation, Smutek, waiting for Ada to awaken on the morning after the trial, again picks up his copy of *Fliegende Bauten*, mentally replacing the name of the main character with that of Ada and entering into a meditation on the importance (or nonimportance) of place. Remarking that "the blue sky . . . has turned into the colorful lid of a box of games," he concludes, thus emphasizing the very words the judge had used at the beginning of the novel, "If it's all just a game, we're done for. If not, then for sure" (559).

More subtly in another passage, Zeh grants the protagonists of *Adler und Engel* a little reprise in *Spieltrieb*, where a party becomes the occasion of Ada and Alev's fleeting encounter with a young woman named

Jessie, who is apparently selling drugs to the guests, and her companion, a man with the dark wavy hair that distinguished Shershah in the earlier novel (391).

Much more elaborate is the web of allusions to Robert Musil. Like *Die Verwirrungen des Zöglings Törleß* (*Confusions of Young Törless*), Musil's 1906 story of adolescent cruelties in a boarding school, *Spieltrieb* offers a disturbing depiction of this milieu, which Zeh, like Musil, appears to know from experience. But the connection becomes more complex in the narrative strand that traces the hapless Smutek's attempts to read Musil's enormous fragmentary novel *Der Mann ohne Eigenschaften* (*The Man without Qualities*, 1952) with his advanced class. When called upon to read the paper she wrote for the course assignment, a retelling of one chapter of the novel, one pupil presents her version of Musil's first chapter, describing a 1913 accident, in which a truck hit a Viennese pedestrian (1952, 10–11). While recounting the course of the incident and even maintaining Musil's style, the girl in Zeh's novel updates her narration with contemporary details: mentioning a streetside clothing collection container, having passers-by attempt cardiopulmonary resuscitation, and substituting a flashing blue light and siren for the whistle of the 1913 ambulance (440–41). To this sly hint of her affinity to Musil,[12] to whose precise language, intriguing chapter headings, and rambling narrative her own novels bear a striking resemblance, Zeh has also added an example of her own penchant for bizarre animal metaphors. The truck that caused the accident, now resting with one wheel on the curb near a lamppost, is described by the schoolgirl as resembling a dog, with its hind leg lifted, "while a dark cloud of pedestrians gathered like flies around its muzzle in order to look at what lay, motionless and shapeless, on the pavement before it" (441).[13] Although such metaphors, sprinkled throughout both novels, have annoyed some critics, none of them seems to have recognized the way in which Zeh employs them ad absurdum in a sort of playful self-parody (see Maus 2001; "Verkokste Roadshow" 2001; "Im Literatur-Leistungskurs" 2004; Hückstädt 2004). The jarring effect of these often comic/grotesque formulations serves an ironic function by breaking the spell of the narrative and refocusing the attention of the reader on the author who has thus insinuated herself into the text. As the reader becomes aware of the immanence of the author in the text, an opening is created for more conscious reflection on the deeper implications of the text.

Such recognition of an author at work in her text is, however, something quite different from what Zeh, in a spirited essay entitled "Zur Hölle mit der Authentizität!" (The Hell with Authenticity!), termed the "voyeurism" of readers who approach her novels with a mindset formed by television "reality shows, docu-soaps, and 'Big Brother' formats" (2006e, 59). Zeh stresses the Aristotelian notion of mimesis, which differentiates between reality and its interpretation in artistic representation. She explains that the lived experience of the writer functions as a "quarry" from which she extracts materials (people, events, ideas, thoughts) that can be shaped into literature by means of metaphors, motifs, and symbols. Asserting that the *Dogma des Echtheitsbegehrens*" (doctrine of the desire for genuineness) is just as limiting as self-censorship, she reminds her fellow writers: "We have the language, we have the idea, we have the privilege of not having to make any truth claims—*mon Dieu, stay fictional*—and the hell with authenticity!" (2006e, 60) (italics of French and English in the original).

Aesthetics and Politics: "Relevant Realism"

In 2005 an essay that reads like a turn away from the pop literature trend of the preceding decade appeared in *Die Zeit* (Dean et al. 2005). Entitled "Was soll der Roman?" (Expectations of the Novel) it was written collectively by novelists Martin R. Dean, Thomas Hettche, Matthias Politycki, and Michael Schindhelm. Rejecting the trend of so-called fun literature (*Spaßliteratur*), they call for "relevant realism," for books that move us deeply, even against our will: "We believe that the novel today has a social function. It must take up the cause of forgotten or taboo issues of the day and offer a valid representation of problem areas, whether local or global." The challenge, they claim, is not to bridge reality and fiction, but to conjoin morality with aesthetics. "Story-telling," they assert,

> is the moralist's way of disguising his message, practiced with the attitude of someone who is not only indulging in the pleasure of inventing stories but also carrying out the duty of writing as a member of one's own generation. . . . Maybe we, old Left liberals that we are, have to finally get used to the idea that our thinking must reflect conservative values in order to overcome the cultural cannibalism all around us. (Dean et al. 2005)

Among the respondents to this position paper, Zeh took issue primarily with the authors' vagueness about what constitutes the political relevance and morality they were advocating as well as with their uninflected use of "we" in an age of individualism, where people are no longer willing to line up behind a common ideology. Dubious that the aesthetic is always allied with the "moral," she argues that it is insufficient merely to be an "aesthete" if one wants to produce a moral effect: "Political or moral effectiveness requires a fundamental decision about that which one wants to bring to pass or, at the very least, about that which one wants to prevent. Such a decision . . . is a good beginning—but it is only a very, very small step, and if there is no follow-up, it's worth nothing" (Zeh 2005b). While supporting the call for something more substantial than the "*Larifari-Pop-und-Befindlichkeitsliteratur*" (trashy pop and navel-gazing literature) (2005b) that followed her generation's rejection of the moralizing stance of older writers, such as Günter Grass and Martin Walser, she indicates that to be effective, the concept must be much more precise and carefully thought out. In a speech she gave upon receiving the Ernst-Toller Prize in 2004, she attempted to explain her own firm belief that

> literature per se has a social and, in the broadest sense of the word, political function. People have a natural need to know what other people—as represented by the writer and his characters—are thinking and feeling. For this reason alone, in the realm of politics, literature cannot be replaced or repressed by journalism, and it cannot just hide behind its lack of expertise or specialization. Rather [literature] bears the responsibility to close the gaps that are exposed through journalism's attempt to present a supposedly "objective"—and therefore distorted—picture of the world. . . . I want to give readers ideas, not opinions, and to give them access to a nonjournalistic, but nonetheless political view of the world. (2004b, 218–19)

For an example of the "relevant realism" towards which Zeh and her fellow writers were grasping, one could do worse than to look to her novels, offering as they do a diagnosis of her own generation that employs a precise, often jarringly poetic language while unflinchingly depicting examples of contemporary degradation and depravity. In other words, one might say that the values she seeks to advance in the public sphere are inscribed *ex negativo* in her literary productions.

"Common Sense and a Decent Heart": The Essays

Zeh's many published opinion pieces often center on issues such as politics in the Balkans and Eastern Europe, law and the European Union, her views as a writer, and—perhaps most provocatively—the individual and society, where her independent-minded stance comes to the fore.

Central to her notion of personal freedom is a rejection of the fixation on buying, getting, and having that she sees all around her, which she termed *"Das Gregor-Prinzip"* in a witty essay in *Der Spiegel* (2002a). The "Gregor" type that she mocks is a business student whose chief goal is to have "a gold credit card with his name on it and a Porsche 911 with a blond woman passenger . . . a materialist person in a materialist world, with no enthusiasm, no ideas or values . . . broadly disinterested in things that have no clear monetary value" (184). In contrast to Gregor, Zeh cites her circle of friends, who have a much more pragmatic and idealistic attitude towards money, willing to work when they need it and happy to share it when they don't, preferring community and communication over competition and consumption (186).

In an age of individualism, Zeh recognizes that the force of tradition in social structures such as the family can no longer be counted on to provide safety and security. But the answer, she insists, is not to return to a repressive social system. Rather, she argues:

> If we don't want people feeling lonely and unhappy and not having children because they don't know in what kind of dependable situation they can raise these children; if we don't want people constantly screaming for "the state" and expecting it to compensate the perceived loss of security with its completely overextended social support system, then we have to compensate for the lack of social constraints with our own efforts. . . . People need one another, always. Individualism is not at all identical with egocentrism; up to now, however, it [individualism] has been lacking a solid foundation of values. (Niermann 2006)

Zeh was particularly prolific in offering commentary during the 2005 German election year. Acknowledging that many writers in her circle of acquaintance are committed to political abstinence, Zeh attributes this to the fact that hers is a generation of loners, who refuse to identify with groups or collective actions. In her Ernst-Toller Prize acceptance speech, she points out, however, that there is a difference between an aversion to politics (*Politikverdrossenheit*) and an aversion to political parties (*Parteiverdrossenheit*) and reminds us that in a democracy where the majority—itself a group of sorts—rules, one can be political without belonging to a political party (2004b).

Although she joined Günter Grass in supporting the SPD in 2005, Zeh is adamantly not a party member and, indeed, her views cannot be mapped unambiguously along party lines. When asked about her political orientation, she defined it as "left" insofar as it is a position "that does not reduce human relationships to economic exchange between people, that considers 'culture' important, that assumes the right of access to basic social support systems, and that believes that freedom of thought and action is the supreme human value" (2005e). In her view, a writer is privileged in being able to develop positions on particular political topics and, occasionally, to make them public, combining the roles of political thinker and author, yet maintaining her existence as a loner: "In order to be political, one doesn't need a [political] party and one certainly doesn't need any officially recognized expertise. Rather one needs just two things: common sense and a decent heart (*ein Herz im Leib*)" (Zeh 2004b).

In her provocative response to the "Heuschreckendebatte" triggered in April 2005 by SPD chief Franz Müntefering's references to contemporary global capitalists as "locusts" (*Heuschrecken*), published in *Der Spiegel,* Zeh (2005a) appears to stake out positions that, at first glance, might seem more closely identified with FDP liberalism. Harshly critical of the obsessively economic orientation of Germany's contemporary political parties, Zeh argues against the naïve belief that government can end unemployment by regulating executive salaries, prohibiting outsourcing and job cuts, and limiting imports, private equity investments, and hedge funds. Instead, she repositions the terms of the debate from "left" vs. "right" to the abiding tension between (social) security and (personal) freedom. Zeh is clearly committed to the idea of the "social contract," but prefers to assign responsibility for it to the individual rather than to the state, contending that it is possible to reconcile the right of self-determination with the social ideals of equal opportunity and responsibility for one's own actions in relation to the larger community.

She elaborated on her conviction that individual freedom is compatible with the goal of a decent society in a letter she published on the election Web site of the Heinrich Böll Stiftung:

> Individualism is a good thing. But that doesn't mean just rejecting any sense of responsibility per se. A society in which neither employers nor workers, neither child nor parents, neither husband nor wife are ready to assume responsibility for one another and their life together cannot function. Because the state is (da capo, da capo) not omnipotent. If you're looking for omnipotence, try praying. (2005c)

Writing in *Die Zeit* after the election, Zeh expressed disappointment that the focus of all parties on economic issues, such as unemployment and growing the economy, obscured attention to equally important questions. The functioning of the economic system, she pointed out, is determined not just by the level of value-added taxes and labor over-head. It also depends on human factors, such as what people actually buy, "when, how, and how much they want to work, and how they want to spend their leisure time. . . . [The economy] is closely tied to the situation of families, the state of education, and even to the foreign policy of the country." By suggesting that fixing the economy will take care of all problems, politicians raise expectations that lead not only to disappointment and excessive dependence on the state, but possibly to political instability. The avoidance of urgent issues, such as foreign policy, national security, and atomic energy—areas where she believes public debate could lead to cooperative solutions—could have, she warns, grave consequences for the future of the country (2005d).

During the run-up to the election, Zeh staked out her position on the candidacy of Angela Merkel, the first woman to seek the German chancellorship, with a piece in the popular women's magazine *Brigitte* (2006d). With sharp, satirical wit, she sets up a mock interview with JuLi, a *"Jung-Literatin"* (young female writer), to express her opposition to Merkel, charging her with political opportunism, chumming with George W. Bush, and mouthing Germans' self-pitying complaints instead of advancing constructive ideas. If someone must run as a woman rather than as a politician with a program, JuLi concedes, it might as well be Merkel because she is "even tougher, even more conservative, and even more opportunistic" than her male colleagues. Pointing out that a number of Muslim countries already have female heads of state, Zeh makes her final point: "If Germany needs Merkel [*das Merkel*] to overcome its backwardness, then all I can say is that every country gets the stateswomen [*Staatsmänninnen*] it deserves" (35). She also claims that the time for talk about discrimination against women is past: "I'm really grateful to Alice [Schwarzer, PH] and her sisters for what they did, so to speak, prenatally for me. But that does not oblige me to fight on empty battlefields." What the country does need, she states, is less discourse of discrimination and more concrete action, such as improved childcare, flexible working hours, and changes in the pension system. Failing to solve these problems will mean that Germany will also not be able to save its pension system or resolve the problems of unemployment; furthermore, without more women in positions of leadership, it will continue to lose out in international comparisons of know-how and competence (32–33).

As her comments on the Merkel candidacy suggest, Juli Zeh might be described as a "postfeminist," if by that term one means someone for whom the struggle against "the patriarchy" is no longer at the center of her political interest. For her, like many young women making their literary debut in the twenty-first century, most of the issues addressed by the feminists of their mothers' generation in the 1970s and 1980s have lost their urgency. The freedom and opportunities that have been won for her and her generation enable Zeh to intervene in the public sphere with notable ease and self-confidence. While she does not call attention to her gender in addressing social and political issues, neither in her prose fiction nor in the essays, gender obviously does play a role in how her texts are perceived by commentators and critics: as the work of an exceptional young woman writer—but, fortunately, not a *"Fräuleinwunder"*!

Notes

1. Refers to Botho Strauß's controversial 1993 essay, "Anschwellender Bocksgesang" (Swelling Lamentation), which attributed the diminished vitality of German culture to proliferating left liberal values.

2. Refers to the debate that ensued after Martin Walser's acceptance speech upon receiving the Friedenspreis des Deutschen Buchhandels, in which he complained that Auschwitz was being used as a "moral club" against Germany (1998).

3. Refers to ongoing controversies in connection with Peter Handke's defense of Serbia and of Slobodan Milošević, beginning with *Eine winterliche Reise zu den Flüssen Donau, Save, Morawa und Drina oder Gerechtigkeit für Serbien* (1996).

4. See also Zeh's published comment on the Grass affair in *Stern* (2006d).

5. Unless otherwise indicated, all translations from German sources are my own.

6. Max even claims to have won a certificate for the best degree in his law school class (2003a, 125).

7. This figure, who refers to work he has done for the James Bond film *Goldfinger*, bears an uncanny resemblance to Gunther von Hagens, whose "plastinations" have been seen worldwide in "Body Worlds" museum exhibitions and very recently in the 2006 James Bond film *Casino Royale*.

8. Among the values she finds missing when individualism is replaced with egocentrism are the triad respect, courtesy, and kindness (Niermann 2006).

9. The prisoner's dilemma refers to a hypothetical situation in which a pair of criminal suspects are offered a deal: if, for example, one testifies against the other, he will go free and his accomplice will serve ten years. If neither testifies against the other, both will serve six months; if each testifies against the other, both will serve two years. Rational choice would seem to dictate that each pursue his own self-interest by testifying against the other, but since neither of them knows how the other will behave, the optimal outcome for the pair—a total of one year in prison for both of them rather than a total of four years for

282 | Patricia Herminghouse

the two or ten years for one—occurs when both behave cooperatively by refusing to betray one another.

10. This is not to deny some applicability of the behaviorial notion of *Spieltrieb*, which holds that in normal development, play provides children the opportunity to learn by trial and error until the onset of puberty. The novel also alludes briefly to this meaning of the term.

11. While one might be tempted to conflate the views of this judge/narrator with those of the author herself, Zeh traces her preference for the more challenging task of writing from the perspective of an omniscient narrator to Robert Musil's *Mann ohne Eigenschaften*, rejecting as too limited ("Froschperspektive," worm's-eye view) the first-person narrative preferred by many young writers today (Zeh 2002c).

12. Zeh continues her allusions to *Der Mann ohne Eigenschaften* in her new detective novel *Schilf* (2007), which appeared too late to be considered here (see Porombka 2007).

13. A few other examples: "The obese [fettleibig] old [school] building with its two wings cowered on the asphalt like a sleeping albatross that had been paralyzed by fear before taking flight" (54). "Time relaxed [entspannte sich], spread out, formed piles of minutes, stretches of seconds, puddles of hours, then tensed up like a jellyfish that has been poked by a finger as Rocket . . . began to sing" (80). "Her thoughts constantly descended on Alev, as if they were just waiting to find something they could circle around, like flies swarming over fresh excrement, eager to land, to nibble, to fight, and then to take off again" (134).

Works Cited

Axelrod, Robert. 1984. *The Evolution of Cooperation.* New York: Basic Books.

Dean, Martin R., Thomas Hettche, Matthias Politycki, and Michael Schindhelm. 2005. "Was soll der Roman?" *Die Zeit*, 23 June: 49.

Hage, Volker. 1999. "Ganz schön abgedreht." *Der Spiegel*, 22 March: 244–46.

Handke, Peter. 1996. *Eine winterliche Reise zu den Flüssen Donau, Save, Morawa und Drina oder Gerechtigkeit für Serbien.* Frankfurt am Main: Suhrkamp.

Hückstädt, Hauke. 2004. "Frau Cogito im Internet." *Frankfurter Rundschau*, 6 October. <http://www/frankfurter-rundschau.de/_inc/_globals/print.php ?sid=c>.

"Im Literatur-Leistungskurs: Mädchen ohne Eigenschaften." 2004. *Frankfurter Allgemeine Zeitung*, 24 December: 44.

Kilb, Andreas. 2006. "Lob und Tadel des Verschweigens." *Frankfurter Allgemeine Zeitung*, 25 August: 44.

März, Ursula. 2006. "Der Fall H. als weites Feld." *Frankfurter Rundschau*, 25 August.

Maus, Stephan. 2001. "Im Rahmen des Lehrplans: Juli Zehs staatlich geprüftes Roman-Debüt *Adler und Engel.*" *Frankfurter Rundschau*, 8 September 2001. <http://www.stephanmaus.de/rezension-juli-zeh.htm>.

Musil, Robert. 1952. *Der Mann ohne Eigenschaften*, ed. Adolf Frisé. Hamburg: Rowohlt.

———. 1906. "Die Verwirrungen des Zöglings Törleß." *Prosa, Dramen, Späte Briefe*, ed. Adolf Frisé. Hamburg: Rowohlt, 1957.

Niermann, Ingo. 2006. "Demokratie ohne Parteien" [Interview with Juli Zeh]. *Welt am Sonntag*, 18 June: 56.

Porombka, Wiebke. 2007. "Sprachaufmotzerin." *Die Tageszeitung*, 8 September: vi.

Radisch, Iris. 2001. "8 gegen 58: Der Georg-Büchner Preis für Männer." *Die Zeit*, 10 May: 45.

Stenzel, Ulrich. 2006. "'J'accuse': Der Publizist Régis Debray und die Autorin Juli Zeh eröffnen eine neue Veranstaltungsreihe im Literaturhaus." *Stuttgarter Nachrichten*, 12 July 15.

Strauß, Botho. 1993. "Anschwellender Bocksgesang." *Der Spiegel*, 8 February: 202–7.

Tittel, Cornelius. 2005. "Nur keine falsche Bescheidenheit." *Welt am Sonntag*, 20 November: 65.

"Verkokste Roadshow." 2001. *Frankfurter Allgemeine Zeitung*, 9 October: L21.

Walser, Martin. 1998. "Erfahrung beim Verfassen einer Sonntagsrede." <www.dhm.de/lemo/html/dokuments/WegeInDieGegenwart_redeWalser-ZumFrieden>.

Zeh, Juli. 2001. *Adler und Engel*. Frankfurt am Main: Schöffling.

———. 2002a. "Das Gregor-Prinzip." *Der Spiegel*, 4 November: 184–86. [Slightly edited version as "Das Prinzip Gregor" In *Alles auf dem Rasen*. 11–20].

———. 2002b. *"Recht auf Beitritt?" Ansprüche von Kandidatenstaaten gegen die Europäische Union.* Schriften des Europa-Instituts der Universität des Saarlandes, Rechtswissenschaft Vol. 41. Baden-Baden: Nomos Verlagsgesellschaft.

———. 2002c. "Sag nicht ER zu mir." In *Alles auf dem Rasen*. 220–34. [Originally in *Akzente* 4 (2002)].

———. 2002d. *Die Stille ist ein Geräusch: Eine Fahrt durch Bosnien*. Frankfurt am Main: Schöffling.

———. 2003a. *Eagles and Angels*, trans. Christine Slenczka. London: Granta.

———. 2003b. "Fliegende Bauten." In *Alles auf dem Rasen*. 95–102. [Originally in *Magazin der Süddeutschen Zeitung*, 23 February 2003].

———. 2004a. *Spieltrieb*. Frankfurt am Main: Schöffling.

———. 2004b. "Wir trauen uns nicht." [Ernst-Toller Prize Speech] *Die Zeit*, 4 March: 53. [Edited version as "Auf den Barrikaden oder hinterm Berg?" In *Alles auf dem Rasen*. 214–19].

———. 2005a. "Euer Sündenbock-Spiel nervt." *Der Spiegel*, 23 May: 142–44. [Also as "Der Kreis der Quadratur" in *Alles auf dem Rasen*. 21–28].

———. 2005b. "Gesellschaftliche Relevanz braucht eine politische Richtung." *Die Zeit*, 23 June: 50.

————. 2005c. "Liebe Parteien!" <http://www.wahltagebuch.de/juli-zeh/index.html>.

————. 2005d. "Viele Farben, keine Wahl." *Die Zeit*, 22 September: 49. [Also as "Deutschland wählt den Superstaat" In *Alles auf dem Rasen*. 37–47].

————. 2005e. "Was ist links, Juli Zeh?" *die tageszeitung*, 10 September: 4.

————. 2006a. *Alles auf dem Rasen: Kein Roman*. Frankfurt am Main: Schöffling.

————. 2006b. "Es werde Linux." *Die Zeit*, 30 March: 39.

————. 2006c. "In der Hysteriemaschine." *Stern*, 17 August: 46.

————. 2006d. "Sind wir Kanzlerin?" In *Alles auf dem Rasen*. 29–36. [Originally as "Wir werden Kanzlerin! Werden wir Kanzlerin?" *Brigitte* 14 (2005)].

————. 2006e. "Zur Hölle mit der Authentizität!" *Die Zeit*, 21 September: 59–60.

————. 2007. *Schilf*. Frankfurt am Main: Schöffling.

CONTRIBUTORS

Donovan Anderson is assistant professor of German at Grand Valley State University near Grand Rapids, Michigan. He has written on salon culture in early nineteenth-century Germany and on the early history of *Germanistik*. His research focuses on literary reception and on disciplinary history. He is currently working on a book that examines the development of the academic study of German literature within the context of local city culture in various university towns.

Laurel Cohen-Pfister is assistant professor at Gettysburg College, where she teaches German language, literature, and cultural studies. Her research interests encompass twentieth- and twenty-first century German literature and culture. She has published articles on GDR literature, contemporary German cultural memory, and the literary representation of war. She is co-editor of the volume *Victims and Perpetrators 1933–1945: (Re)Presenting the Past in Post-Unification Culture* (2006).

Birgit Dahlke (PhD 1994, Habilitation 2003) teaches literature at the Humboldt-Universität Berlin. Her areas of interest include East German literature, in particular poetry, and gender studies. Her most recent publications are *Jünglinge der Moderne: Jugendkult und Männlichkeit in der Literatur um 1900* (2006) and *Papierboot: Autorinnen aus der DDR – inoffiziell publiziert* (1997). She has co-edited volumes on Kerstin Hensel (2002), *LiteraturGesellschaft* (2000), and *Zersammelt: Die inoffizielle Literaturszene der DDR nach 1990* (2001). She has held a number of visiting positions, most recently at the University of Nottingham.

Katharina Gerstenberger (PhD, Cornell University) is associate professor of German at the University of Cincinnati. She is the author of *Truth to Tell: German Women's Autobiographies and Turn-of-the-Century Culture* (2000) and *Writing the New Berlin: The German Capital in Post-Wall Literature* (2008). Her recent publications include articles on the Austrian writer Ilse Aichinger, the German-Turkish writer Zafer Şenocak, and contemporary Berlin literature. Her work has appeared in *Monatshefte*, *Women in German Yearbook*, and *German Quarterly*, and in several anthologies, including *Recasting German Identity* (2002) and *German Literature in the Age of Globalization* (2004). She is co-editor of *Women in German Yearbook*.

Rachel J. Halverson (PhD, University of Texas at Austin) is associate professor of German at Washington State University, where she teaches in the Department of Foreign Languages and Cultures and in the Honors College. She has published on works by Jurek Becker, Thomas Brussig, Günter de Bruyn, Hanna Johansen, Judith Kuckart, and Siegfried Lenz. Currently, she is working on a book-length manuscript on autobiographies by East German authors published following the *Wende*.

Patricia Herminghouse is Karl F. and Bertha A. Fuchs Professor emerita of German Studies at the University of Rochester. She has written on nineteenth- and twentieth-century German literature, the social contexts of women's writing, the history of German Studies, and the culture of German émigrés in nineteenth-century America. Founding member of Women in German and past president of the German Studies Association (2003–04), she has edited or co-edited volumes on contemporary women writers, GDR literature, German feminism, gender and national identity, as well as the *Women in German Yearbook*, 1995–2002.

Julia Karolle-Berg received her AB in German and Political Science from the University of Michigan at Ann Arbor, and her MA and PhD in German from the University of Wisconsin–Madison. She is an assistant professor of German at John Carroll University near Cleveland, Ohio. Research focuses include twentieth- and twenty-first-century German literature and culture, narrative theory, detective novels, linguistic approaches to literature, and Holocaust literature.

Sean M. McIntyre is currently a research assistant with the Forum on Contemporary Europe at the Freeman Spogli Institute for International Studies at Stanford University. He is a former post-doctoral teaching fellow in the first-year humanities program at Stanford University, where he also taught German and Portuguese Language as a lecturer. His research interests include late Enlightenment, Classical, and Romantic period German literature and thought, philosophical aesthetics, the sociology of literature, and European cinema. He is currently at work on a manuscript titled "Aesthetic Liberalism" that examines the tradition of ironic German literature from Goethe to Thomas Mann from the perspective of the liberal philosophical tradition that began with the Scottish Enlightenment.

Erika M. Nelson is assistant professor at Union College, where she teaches German language, literature, and culture courses. Her doctoral research, completed at the University of Texas at Austin, focused on issues of identity construction and sound in Rainer Maria Rilke's Orphic poetry and was published as a book entitled *Reading Rilke's Orphic Identity* (2005). Her current research explores twentieth- and twenty-first-century transnational poets and their work, modern German spa culture and sound, as well as modern renditions of mythic figures in film and literature.

Beret Norman is assistant professor of German at Boise State University, where she teaches literature, culture, and language courses. She received her PhD at the University of Massachusetts–Amherst, where she completed her dissertation entitled "Bricolage As Resistance: The Lyrical, Visual, And Performance Art of Gabriele Stötzer." Her current research focuses on writers and artists who were socialized in the GDR and includes an interest in the new field of surveillance studies.

Sydney Norton is curatorial assistant in the department of modern and contempory art at the Saint Louis Art Museum, where she researches pre-1945 European painting and sculpture. She received her doctorate in German literature and cultural studies from the University of Minnesota, Minneapolis, and her master's degree in German literature from the University of Massachusetts, Amherst. Her publications include articles on contemporary art, the performing and visual arts from the Weimar Republic, German and Swiss artist colonies, and the history of the literary salon. In St. Louis her arts features and reviews have appeared in the *St. Louis Post-Dispatch, Sauce Magazine,* and the *West End Word.*

John Pizer is professor of German and Comparative Literature at Louisiana State University. His research and teaching are primarily in the area of German literature and thought from the eighteenth century to the present day. His most recent books are: *Toward a Theory of Radical Origin: Essays on Modern German Thought* (1995), *Ego-Alter Ego: Double and/as Other in the Age of German Poetic Realism* (1998), and *The Idea of World Literature: History and Pedagogical Practice* (2006).

Gary Schmidt is assistant professor of German at the University of West Georgia in Carrollton. His published research on sexuality in twentieth-century German literature includes two books, *Koeppen-Andersch-Böll: Homosexualität und Faschismus in der deutschen Nachkriegsliteratur* (2001) and *The Nazi Abduction of Ganymede: Representations of Male Homosexuality in Postwar German Literature* (2003), as well as articles on biographical interpretations of Thomas Mann's novella *Death in Venice*, Joachim Helfer's semibiographical novel *Cohn & König*, and Wolfgang Becker's film *Good Bye Lenin!*

Patricia Anne Simpson is associate professor of German and German Coordinator at Montana State University, Bozeman. Her book, *The Erotics of War in German Romanticism*, appeared with Bucknell University Press (2006). She co-edited *The Enlightened Eye: Goethe and Visual Culture* (2007). Simpson has also published articles and chapters on a range of topics including popular music and masculinity, retro-nationalism in the GDR, and the reception of Brechtian dramaturgy in contemporary fiction. She is working on a new book, "Cultures of Violence in the New German Street," about the representation of violence in music, film, and literature in the Federal Republic.

Katya Skow is associate professor of German at The Citadel, where she teaches literature, culture, and language. She earned a PhD in German from the University of Illinois at Urbana-Champaign with a dissertation on *Die sieben weisen Meister*. A medievalist, she has expanded her interests to include contemporary fiction, specifically the image of the past in popular fiction. Until recently, she has published mainly on medieval and early modern topics, including Heinrich von Morungen, *Die sieben weisen Meister*, and Feyerabendt's *Buch der Liebe*. Her participation in the 2005 Fulbright Berlin Seminar has led to new directions in her research.

Aine Zimmerman has been translating academic texts, poetry, and technical documents for the past twelve years. Recently, she translated selected poems by the German writer Claudia A. Becker, as well as poems included in *The Bittersweet Land: An Anthology of Recent German-American Poetry*. She earned a PhD in German Studies from the University of Cincinnati and is currently a Visiting Assistant Professor at Hunter College.

INDEX